WORDCOM ORDER CODE

RECyxxx	Read a card.
PNCyxxx	Punch a card.
RTtyxxx	Read tape.
WTtyxxx	Write tape.
RWt___	Rewind a tape.
SISyxxx	Set index y.
INCynnn	Increase index y.
CISyxxx	Compare index y.
CMPyxxx	Compare accumulator and location xxx.
JINyxxx	Jump, if accumulator negative.
JOV xxx	Jump, on overflow condition.
CAAyxxx	Clear accumulator and add.
STAyxxx	Store accumulator.
CAMyxxx	Clear and add into M-Q.
STMyxxx	Store M-Q.
ADDyxxx	Add.
SUByxxx	Subtract.
MLTyxxx	Multiply.
DIVyxxx	Divide.
HLT xxx	Unconditional halt.
SHL nn	Shift left.
SHR nn	Shift right.
EXOyxxx	Extract characters.
JMPyxxx	Unconditional jump.

FIELDCOM ORDER CODE

RC	Read a card.	SB xxxx ±n xxxx ±n	Subtract.
PC	Punch a card.	ML xxxx ±n xxxx ±n	Multiply.
Rt xxxx	Read tape t.	CM xxxx xxxx	Compare.
Wt xxxx	Write tape t.	JS xxxx C	Jump if switch is on:
Mt	Mark tape.	E	C, last card; E, equals;
Tt	Rewind tape.	F	F, field mistake;
PT	Print.	H	H, high (A > B);
RD xxxx	Read disk.	L	L, low (A < B);
WD xxxx	Write disk.	N	N, negative;
SD xxxx	Seek disk.	R	R, last tape record;
CS xxxx xxxx	Clear storage.	U	U, unconditional
FM xxxx	Fieldmark.	HL xxxx	Halt.
CP xxxx ±n xxxx ±n	Copy contents.	NP xxxx xxxx	No operation.
CE xxxx ±n xxxx ±n	Copy and edit.	AL xxxx ±111 . . . 1	Assign literal to
ZR xxxx	Zero contents.		address A.
BM xxxx	Blockmark.	AA xxxx ssss	Assign A address
AD xxxx ±n xxxx ±n	Add.		to symbolic.

BUSINESS DATA PROCESSING & PROGRAMMING

ROBERT H. GREGORY
&
RICHARD L. VAN HORN

BUSINESS
DATA PROCESSING
&
PROGRAMMING

WADSWORTH PUBLISHING COMPANY, INC.
BELMONT, CALIFORNIA

PREFACE

Business Data Processing and Programming is a compact, introductory book on data processors and their programming for business use. It focuses on equipment, systems design, and programming. It covers data representation and organization into records and files, equipment components, systems analysis, systems design and implementation, editing, accuracy and auditing, file processing, and programming for business data processing.

Hardware components—control, arithmetic, storage, and input-output—are discussed to cover the basic features of electronic data-processing equipment. The myriad systems offered by manufacturers are not discussed as such, because yesterday's X038 is today's Y038.1 and tomorrow's Z038.14. All models are basically similar and new equipment may differ only in having a faster operating cycle, more storage, or faster tapes. While such changes are important to the user, they are not to a person just entering the field. Thus, rather than discuss the design features of the most-recently-announced equipment, the objective here is to deal with fundamentals worth knowing both today and tomorrow.

The treatment of systems analysis and design in Chapters 5 and

6 includes two new features: information flow analysis and decision tables. Unlike traditional systems-analysis work aimed at a single application, information flow analysis analyzes the flow of data concerning an *event* from its origin, through files, to output. This *event-chain* approach opens up the opportunity to use processors for analyzing the *actual flow* of data in an existing system and the *planned flow* in a proposed system. Thus it is both a systems-analysis *and* a systems-design technique at the data-flow level.

Decision tables are used to relate conditions and actions in a tabular form for the various rules that are applicable. Decision tables facilitate careful statement of conditions and actions, aid in developing correct and complete program logic, point up ambiguities and inconsistencies, and serve as a documentation device. Tables are a promising alternative to detailed flow charting in both the design and programming-coding phases of systems development.

This book treats programming in both problem-oriented and machine-oriented languages. COBOL-1, a simplified version of COBOL-61 (Common Business Oriented Language, 1961 edition), is covered first to bring out the fundamentals of processing business files. COBOL-1 is presented with the intricacies and options of COBOL-61 stripped away. It is more important, we think, to develop the concepts and drive home the fundamental points than it is to give encyclopedic but hasty sketches of the numerous features of programming. The coverage of COBOL-1, though short and disarmingly simple, introduces many features of problem-oriented languages. COBOL-1 is a real programming language, compatible with COBOL-61. Instructions for compiling and running COBOL-1 programs on one processor serve as a guide for compiling and running programs on other processors. COBOL-1 programs can be run on any processor for which the manufacturer has prepared a COBOL-61 compiler.

Programming in machine-oriented language, covered in Chapter 8, is discussed in terms of a fixed-word-length processor, WORDCOM, which is representative of this widely used class of machines. FIELDCOM, a "field" or variable-word-length machine, is also covered briefly to show the features of this class of machines. COBOL-1, WORDCOM, and FIELDCOM programming are covered at the introductory level to offer the reader some choice of where he wants to start. The sequence used here, and the one we recommend, is to study COBOL-1 first in order to learn programming fundamentals with the fewest embellishments. Then the reader is ready, we think, to go to the machine-oriented languages of WORDCOM and FIELDCOM.

Business Data Processing and Programming is designed as a one-semester text for a basic course. Corresponding to each chapter are numerous questions and problems, carefully designed to emphasize the important points and to develop the student's facility in applying them. Ranging from simple to complex, these problems offer variety and potential enrichment for higher-level or more intensive courses.

This book is also oriented toward the person in business who is getting his first serious exposure to business data processing. Systems analysts, designers, and programmers who want to put data processing into proper perspective should find it most useful.

We wish to express our appreciation to several of our friends and associates who provided valuable help. Solomon Pollack made numerous detailed comments on the manuscript and suggestions on the use of decision tables. O. T. Gatto supplied information on AUTOSATE. Arthur Carlson, Richard W. Conway, James Gibbons, Elmer F. Judge, and Robert Schlosser read the manuscript and offered many useful observations. Edward Chappelear provided us with a variety of technical material, and Willard Harriss prepared illustrations. Mary Cole coordinated typing of the manuscript and handled a multitude of production details.

Robert H. Gregory
Richard L. Van Horn

CONTENTS

ix

BUSINESS
DATA PROCESSING
&
PROGRAMMING

CHAPTER 1

INTRODUCTION TO BUSINESS DATA PROCESSING

Substantial changes in business activity during recent years have encouraged the creation of new data-processing systems. Conversely, changes in data-processing equipment and methods are suggesting new methods of doing business. Electronic data processing, operations research, and other new scientific and engineering developments are fast becoming a part of common business practice. And it is probable that data-processing and management-control methods will change more rapidly during the next decade than they have in recent years.

This progress will not make manual data processing and conventional control techniques completely obsolete, but it will make knowledge of automatic data processing invaluable for business managers, data-processing personnel, and systems and procedures analysts. All people who rely on facts for performing or managing business operations—people who need facts for answering questions and making reports—have a vital interest in the origination and processing of data.

WHY PROCESS DATA?

Data about business events are gathered, stored, processed, and reported for various reasons. Some of the more important reasons are to keep detailed *facts* about individual transactions; to produce routine *operating documents,* such as paychecks and purchase orders; to summarize masses of facts into useful, *informative reports,* such as reports on sales in given areas and on costs of production; and to make *analyses* of business problems, such as finding locations for factories and warehouses that will give minimum transportation costs.

Data Availability

Facts are the raw material of data processing. Initially, the collection of facts may be restricted to the minimum immediately required; but supplemental facts are often obtained at first in order to anticipate probable or possible demands for them in the future.

Often the solution of a problem has to be postponed until necessary facts are obtained. An efficient scheme for obtaining facts depends on balancing the *cost* of having them available—either too many or too few—against the *benefits* of having the necessary facts when they are wanted. The point is that it is usually impossible to obtain just the right set of facts about events "today." One must choose between trying to search out and reconstruct facts about yesterday, or waiting for tomorrow and gathering facts about events as they occur.

Document Production

The preparation of readable documents is an important phase of data processing. Documents are still a common means of communication among companies, and they are widely used within companies that have manual data-processing systems.

Where data collection is done by people and the output from processing goes to people, it is usually taken for granted that readable documents are required. This need is reduced, or even eliminated, when equipment is used for gathering and processing data. The output of machines at one stage—whether punched tape, cards, magnetic tape, or machine-readable printed characters—can be used as input at the next stage of processing, in either the same or a different company. The use of readable documents is sometimes restricted to small-volume operations where mechanization at the next stage is not feasible. Readable documents that are distributed to a wide audience—bills to customers and reports to managers—will continue to be used for many years.

Management Information

An important reason for developing elaborate data-processing schemes is to supply the management organization with the critical facts needed to control operations. The word *data* might be used to cover *all* the facts obtained; the term *information* is useful for denoting the *particular* facts management wants to know.

Although information derives from raw data, information has certain qualities that can serve as a guide in processing data. A manager in a company is interested in getting facts about operations he is responsible for. He wants these facts to be accurate, timely, and related to problems he can solve by his decisions. Furthermore, he is more interested in learning about unpredictable than about predictable developments. He has no need to be told repeatedly something he already knows. In short, the information given him should be accurate, have an element of newness or novelty about it, focus on a selected area, and deal with the unexpected.

Some examples will help distinguish *data* from *information*. Newspapers are bought for information. Someone who feels that a particular issue has little news to offer, either because so little is happening or because too many other editions are published, will not buy it. To stimulate their sluggish circulation, newspapers often try to create an air of bright novelty around the humdrum, or revive interest in old mysteries; the Loch Ness monster, for instance, is said to be a summertime phenomenon that obligingly reappears for the benefit of Scottish newspapers. Likewise, reports to management about unexpected or undesirable events, such as the costs of production jobs exceeding their standard, select and emphasize items to increase the reader's attention. The costs of jobs not exceeding standard may be included in reports for completeness or omitted for brevity, according to the reader's immediate interests or his needs for later reference to the whole picture.

The difference between a mass of facts and a few critical facts is illustrated by the plight of a businessman who furnished 1350 pounds of records to a tax collector. He was brought to court by the collector, who wanted five additional books, weighing only 10 or 20 pounds, that he considered critical. Every day businessmen are given pounds of reports when they want only a few critical facts. Managers do not really care about source reports, documents, and data, however useful they may be elsewhere in the organization.

The nature of information can be described, but it is difficult to measure information itself as a quantity. Whether a new system will produce better information than the old system did is difficult to determine, and will be even after the new system is introduced. Information production and the related areas of management control, including automatic decision-making, are challenging and profitable areas of study.

HOW DATA ARE PROCESSED

The basic functions of processing data are well established. Managers and operating personnel in business, government, and other enterprises have long been accustomed to processing data to obtain facts about operations and information for their control.

The basic operations in processing data are (1) to originate data, (2) to manipulate, according to some plan, the new data and files prepared in an earlier cycle, and (3) to report results.

Origination of Data

The origination of data in a form suitable for processing includes three necessary stages—collection, conversion, and verification.

Data Collection. Data collection captures facts when they are available; they may be processed later, when needed. For example, the time an employee starts or stops work on a particular job may be recorded in *writing* by a timekeeper, *stamped* in numerals by a time clock, or *punched* into a card. A storekeeper identifies and counts any material received in the stockroom in order to write a receiving report. Requisitions for material, on the other hand, specify desired quantities and serve as the original records of issuance. Employees of utility companies record customer meter readings by marking cards that are later run through equipment that "senses" the marks and punches them.

Data collection often starts with the *manual operation* of keyboards that punch cards or paper tape, or that record data on magnetic tape. Several devices recently developed for business use are capable of automatically collecting data in *machine-processable* form, though one class of these devices yields data in a machine-processable form that people cannot read. Examples of devices producing machine-readable media are point-of-sale recorders, transaction recorders, and time clocks that punch tape or cards. Another class of automatic data-collection devices produces numerals and letters on paper or cards in a form readable by both machines and people. Character-reading machines "read" the characters and convert them to a form suitable for automatic processing.

Other important techniques for data collection are pre-preparation of constant data, by-product preparation as a part of other operations, and duplication from card, plastic, or metal plates. A simple time clock records the basic facts for a transaction; a more complex clock might record all the facts—worker, time, job involved, and units produced—and thereby deserve the name "automatic transaction recorder."

New input data may be only a small part of the total data handled at each cycle. The inventory file, for example, is used repeatedly to introduce necessary changes for receipts, issues, and price changes, and to introduce and delete items. Data already in files are much easier to handle than new data, because master cards or tapes may be selectively duplicated for use as input data. The date, batch number or transaction serial number, and fixed data can be supplied automatically during the data-collection operation.

Data Conversion. Data collected on the medium—paper, cards, or tape—that is most efficient at the first stage must often be converted to a different medium for further use. Some companies, for example, use audio tape recorders to record inventory counts. Until automatic voice-to-digital converters become practicable, conversion by people is required for further processing. People are able to work with oral, handwritten, or typed data, but equipment usually requires that data be recorded in a carefully prescribed form. Data from oral recordings or handwritten documents may be manually punched into cards or tape or written on magnetic tape for input to automatic processors. In many cases, punched cards or tape are prepared manually and the data are then converted automatically to magnetic tape for input.

Machines are used now to read typed, printed, and handprinted characters and to convert them to a form suitable for machine processing. Enough research has been done to indicate the feasibility of automatically converting the spoken word into a form suitable for further processing.

The form in which data are originally captured, and the manner in which data are converted, depend on several things: the volume of data involved, the number of points of origination, the permissible financial investment at each point of origination, transmission requirements, conversion costs, and the most efficient form for use in subsequent stages. Large volumes of data originating at a few points warrant big investments in elaborate collection and conversion facilities.

Data Verification.   Data are verified to obtain a desired degree of accuracy. The standard "a desired degree" does not imply perfection. Some inaccuracies—a slight misspelling of a name, for example—may be trivial, but other inaccuracies, such as crediting the wrong customer for a collection on account, can cause trouble unless they are corrected soon after they occur and before much processing is done. Verification includes checking data to determine whether they are in the approved format, convey the correct meaning to the reader, and will lead to the appropriate action.

The simplest type of *format* verification is to ensure that each data field contains the correct kinds of characters: numeric, alphabetic, or both. An alphabetic character in a numerical statement of amount—say, "$1,2A3.46" on a check—violates the rules of format, and it defies further processing because an alphabetic quantity cannot be handled arithmetically. Such an error in format must be corrected before processing.

A broader problem in format verification concerns the completeness of data input. Each business event requires these elements of data to describe it: (1) identification of parties to the transaction (one being the firm itself), (2) description by name and number of what is involved, (3) quantity involved, (4) the time of the transaction, and (5) the unit price or dollar amount, if money is involved. A receiving report, for example, must have the first four elements in order to be complete; it can be easily examined for correct format without referring to anything else.

More difficult problems of data verification arise from failures to originate documents for *all transactions* or to receive all of them for processing. Mechanical recorders, document numbering, and careful control over valuable items are used to assure complete reporting and correct handling.

The *meaning* of some data in terms of reasonableness serves to verify it. It is possible for an employee to work 80 hours in a week, but it is unreasonable to assume unquestioningly that he did, even with a two-shift operation. Detection of a possible error need not stop the checking process. After the questionable data are flagged or noted for verification before further processing, the checking activity may be continued.

Some data that pass the format and meaning tests may require some verification *action* before processing. For example, a check may be received, signed

John C. Smith

—legible, but unaccompanied by any other identification. If there are several customers named John C. Smith, the only way to credit the check to the correct one is to take action to identify him. The clues are the signature itself (if a signature file is kept), account number and balance, amount of payment, and address. Without identification, it is not possible to credit the correct Smith—but he will take action when he receives his next statement.

To summarize, there are several ways to verify data before further processing, and the method chosen will depend on how easily the deficiency can be detected and corrected.

Processing of Data

The principal operations in processing data are rearranging input data and processing files.

Rearranging Input Data. Rearrangement involves classifying data by type and ordering them into sequence without changing their content by computation. There are many reasons why data are rearranged. Two or more kinds of transactions may originate together, but then require separate handling. Payroll, inventory, and sales data, for example, may be intermixed on arrival at the processing center. They are usually classified or sorted by type before processing, since procedures and files are designed to cope with only one class of transactions at a time. The task of sorting transactions into classes is made easier by arranging to have only one or a limited number of types of transactions originate together. This procedure also facilitates better control over who can originate certain kinds of transactions—that is, who can issue material, authorize payment of bills, or inquire into the contents of restricted files. This kind of arrangement for separate origination of each class of data is preferable to unscrambling mixtures of several classes.

A second way of rearranging data is to use each *type* of transaction to produce several outputs. Depending on the kind of output desired and the file arrangement, the transactions are arranged in different sequences for efficient processing. Consider the steps in processing customers' orders. Orders are the basis for sales analysis, customer accounting, inventory and production control, and salesmen's compensation. Data on sales might be summarized by geographic area or by product class, without sorting data into any sequence. If efficient magnetic-tape processing methods require that the customer or inventory file be kept in a certain order, transactions must be sorted into that sequence before updating a particular file. Still another sorting may be required before the transactions can be processed against a file organized in a different sequence. Two sets of sorted data already in the same sequence may be merged to obtain one over-all sequence. For example, inventory transactions for the first four days in a week can be sorted into sequence according to stock identification number, and transactions for the fifth day can be sorted separately. Merging the two sequences into one reduces the workload after the end of the week and permits processing against an ordered file.

In addition to the problem of arranging transactions in the same sequence as the file before processing them, there is the related problem of keeping the file itself in a specified sequence and eliminating inactive records. Maintaining a file of customers' accounts, for instance, may involve inserting records for new customers in alphabetic or customer-number sequence and deleting inactive records. Files kept on magnetic tape are often arranged in alphabetic or numerical sequence and are most efficiently processed in the same sequence.

Random-access equipment is designed to handle transactions without regard for file or transaction sequence. A file may contain records arranged in one sequence but the transactions may occur in a different, perhaps a *random sequence*. They may be processed together satisfactorily, if facilities are available for random-sequence processing. With these facilities, changes introduced into the file—and perhaps the file itself—need not be in any particular sequence; consequently, neither the file nor the transactions need be rearranged.

A third kind of rearrangement occurs when the elements of data in an item are in one sequence but are wanted in a different sequence. Data may be rearranged within an item during input conversion, processing, or output editing.

File Processing.   "File processing" is restricted here to those operations not included in data origination, rearrangement, and output. It thus involves the following kinds of operations: updating files for inventory receipts and issues; computing gross and net pay; making decisions based on quantitative criteria, such as allowing a customer further credit if the amount and age of his balance are within credit limits; estimating sales based on predictions of market behavior, advertising expenditure, and economic forecasts; converting sales estimates into material requirements, labor estimates, and production schedules; summarizing numerous individual transactions into a few numbers; recognizing and dealing with exceptional cases; and looking up table values, such as prices or discounts applicable for various quantities.

In addition, the following processing operations are used to ensure accurate results: (1) verifying data by comparison with facts already in files, (2) controlling input data to guard against losing a valid transaction or introducing a spurious one, (3) checking arithmetical accuracy by repeating operations or by performing them in parallel through separate channels, as when two book-keepers in a bank post the same depositor's account on separate machines to reduce the risk of inaccurate results, and (4) determining that prescribed procedures are actually used. When such precautions are required to facilitate processing, they are incorporated in the main stream of processing. Other precautionary measures are used primarily to keep interested parties, such as managers and auditors, informed of the degree of accuracy. Such measures are used in addition to the main stream of processing rather than included in it.

Some operations are often considered nonproductive because they merely facilitate the performance of other operations directly related to the desired output. This classification corresponds to the indirect-direct labor classification in factory operations. Actually, all essential operations are productive because work done at one stage facilitates work at another. Consider, for instance, the damage that failure to verify input data could wreak at a later stage. An issue of materials charged against an incorrect number might later cause the creation of a new account with a negative balance, be sent to the wrong account, be set aside for investigation, or halt processing until the mistake is corrected. Verifying identification numbers against a master list at an early stage of processing may improve over-all efficiency. Keeping file maintenance—insertion and deletion of records in the file—separate from file processing— updating records in the file—may have some advantages for control purposes over trying to do both at once.

Output

Output preparation follows the origination and manipulation of data. Since processed results are seldom in precisely the form desired, it is often necessary to select what is wanted and present it in acceptable form. Job manufacturing costs are examples of *historical reports* about what has happened. A manufacturing schedule is a *forecast* of what is supposed to happen. A bill sent to a customer is an example of an *action document*. The content, frequency, and format of output are determined jointly by the people who use the output and those who prepare it.

Methods of output preparation depend on the way that demands occur—either scheduled or at random—the length of time available for meeting the demands, and the ability to forecast what will be demanded. Some examples will show how these factors bear on output preparation and, incidentally, will show that output requirements help determine the processing methods. There will be adequate time to prepare an *annual report* of fixed assets within one *month* after the end of the year if the assets are classified by number of years owned (less than one year, one to five years, and so forth). If the data about fixed assets are available and activity is low during the year, there will be ample opportunity to plan procedures, and the permissible one-month delay in reporting will allow fairly smooth scheduling of work.

Output preparation is more difficult, however, if the number of transactions is high and the reporting interval and permissible delay in processing are short. Buyers (merchandise managers) in a department store might want *weekly reports* of receipts, sales, and inventory for each item by the following Monday afternoon. This demand will put heavy loads on the system, but the work of output preparation will be several times greater if buyers want *daily reports* at 10 a.m. every day. Entirely different file-processing methods might be required, however, if buyers want *up-to-the-minute reports* on the sales activity or inventory of any one item. Furnishing quick answers to questions about current status involves continual updating of files and complex interrogation equipment.

Outputs not anticipated in advance may pose extremely difficult problems. Novel output requirements may require new methods of preparing output and new processing techniques to get the desired results. Still worse, *unexpected output* requirements may demand the use of data that are not readily available, if at all. Or the data available may be in a raw form that cannot be processed economically. In such a case, samples can be taken from the data and studied to determine whether they answer the questions, whether a complete analysis of the data is needed, or whether new data must be collected. An equally perplexing situation may arise when there is an immediate need for data which, although collected once, have since been discarded. In some cases, it may be possible to reconstruct data, but in others it is necessary to start afresh. For example, suppose an oil company were to ask, "Do service stations on the right-hand side of a street leading out from the center of town sell more gasoline than those on the left?" The answer may demand, for the first time, that data on station location be used in conjunction with sales data already available. Another question, "Do left-handed employees sell more than right-handed ones?" may not be answerable at all, either because data are not available or because the turnover of employees makes it impossible to reconstruct the data. It is impossible to answer this disarmingly simple question until enough time elapses to permit the gathering of new data. Often, it is not possible to reconstruct even partially complete statistics, so unanticipated questions about the past cannot be answered. Reflection often shows, as in the case of the effect of left- and right-handed employees on gasoline sales, that the question is trivial and doesn't deserve an answer. The ability to distinguish between valid and worthless questions and take appropriate action is an important part of data processing.

The most *open-ended output* requirement, and the most difficult if not impossible requirement to deal with, springs from the question, "Look, we have these kinds of facts on file; what useful reports can we get out of them?" Exploiting unstructured facts is a task for researchers, rather than data-processing personnel. This situation, which is the bane of data processing, can be avoided by advance planning.

In summary, data processing involves (1) collecting data for new transactions; (2) manipulating new inputs and data already in files according to prescribed plans; and (3) producing output documents, reports, and instructions for various purposes.

PROCESSING FACILITIES

In order to reduce the *how* of processing data from general to concrete terms, we must consider the facilities that are used. These facilities must be able to receive input data, manipulate them according to some plan, and produce output. For processing, they must be able to control operations to follow the prescribed plan, hold data and processing instructions, and perform arithmetical and logical operations. Many kinds of facilities are used to process data; in the broadest sense, they range from people working without benefit of equipment to equipment operating with little aid from people.

People

The human being is the earliest form of data processor. A person receives input data chiefly by seeing or hearing them, and stores them in his brain, which also serves as an operating and control unit. His outputs are oral or written reports and various physical actions.

The human mind can *perform,* or at least *control* the performance of, many different operations: starting work, getting instructions and data; adding, subtracting, multiplying, and dividing; remembering results; performing the operations on a different set of data each round; comparing two items; modifying instructions to follow a path that depends on the outcome of a comparison; putting out results rearranged and edited as required; and, of course, stopping when the process is completed.

The ability to select the subsequent processing path dependent on the outcome at any stage is invaluable for modifying operations as they are performed. For example, suppose that a person calculating gross-to-net pay, is told to stop making voluntary deductions if net pay falls below a certain amount—say, $15.00. He would unconsciously apply this rule if gross pay appeared large enough to cover all possible deductions. He would exercise more care, and apply deductions one at a time, if net pay approached this criterion. He would skip any remaining deductions for that employee, but would, of course, return to the original procedure in calculating the next employee's net pay.

The human mind is an adaptable but often unreliable processor. It is slow in performing arithmetical operations and erratic in applying logical rules. Where judgment is required, however, people are well-nigh indispensable because some operations of data processing and decision-making are inseparable. Even with elaborate data-processing systems people are needed to make decisions at some stages because of the extreme difficulty of planning to handle every eventuality. In short, a person unaided by other facilities is an efficient processor for small, relatively simple situations and is a vital element of every data-processing system.

Records

Records were the earliest aid developed to help process data. Consisting first of pictures and marks, writing now relies on "alphabets" of letters and numerals. Business alphabets consist of ten numerals, twenty-six letters, and other symbols, which allow the compact storage of huge quantities of facts. The alphabets are often represented as A through Z; 0 through 9; #, ., &, /, $; and, perhaps, a through z. Characters are also represented by punched holes in cards or paper tape and by positive and negative charges in magnetizable material. The familiar shape of A, B, C, and so on, is sacrificed in favor of other schemes that are more efficient for processing purposes, although often they are not readily usable by people.

Viewed in the broadest sense, records tremendously increase the size and reliability of data storage, which otherwise would be restricted to what people can remember. Schemes for representing characters in written form also provide a simple way to transmit data. People remain responsible for data input, control, and output, unless aided by other processing facilities.

Special-Purpose Office Equipment

Calculating machines perform simple arithmetical operations quickly and accurately and some print results on paper. Since people are slow and oftentimes inaccurate at arithmetical operations, the invention and improvement of calculating devices to add, subtract, multiply, and divide was an important step forward.

With the invention of the typewriter, writing speeds—about ten words a minute—were increased to sixty or more words a minute. More important, the typewriter improved legibility and enabled the preparation of multiple copies with carbon paper and duplicating devices.

The functions of the calculator and the typewriter were combined to create bookkeeping and accounting machines. These machines allow an operator to perform at the same time such multiple operations as preparing statements, ledgers, and journals. Electrically powered office machines for punching and reading paper tape are widely used to reduce data to a form that can be processed mechanically; they often do this as a by-product of other operations.

Punched Card Equipment

The basic operations of punched-card equipment are punching, sorting, calculating, and printing. Early punched-card machines required manual effort in punching data in cards, handling cards individually during the sorting operation, and counting the sorted cards. Since 1890 machines have become more nearly automatic, requiring less manual effort to originate data, sort cards, make calculations, and copy results from tabulators. People handle cards in bulk, and start, feed, tend, and stop machines. With people handling cards between stages, present-day punched-card machines and electronic calculators can receive punched input data, perform about a dozen different arithmetical and logical operations at the rate of 15,000 a minute, and produce printed reports or punched cards for further processing.

Electronic Data Processors

The most recent development in data-processing facilities is the electronic data processor. The unique feature of an electronic processor, also called an "internally stored program computer," is the fact that it stores operating instructions in the same way and in the same place as the data to be processed. Instructions read into storage direct the processor to perform specified operations in a desired sequence. Furthermore, like data, these instructions can be manipulated or changed. The capacity to *change instructions* while operations are in progress increases the applicability of instructions to a wider, although not unlimited, variety of situations that arise in processing.

Electronic digital processors execute a *variety of instructions*, both arithmetical and logical, ranging in number from about a dozen to two hundred. Speed of execution ranges from a few hundred to several hundred thousand or even millions of operations per second. High speed is an important feature of these computers. One company, for example, that spent 3 man-months calculating the critical shaft-speed for a steam generator found they could solve the same problem in 40 hours with punched-card machines, in 1 hour on an early-model electronic computer, in 15 minutes on a second version, in 15 seconds on a later version, and in about 3 seconds on a still newer model. With this last model, the ratio of computer to manual time needed to solve the problem was about 1:500,000.

Electronic Data-Processing Systems

An electronic data-processing system performs standard data-handling operations with a minimum of manual help. Thus, it greatly increases the ratio of equipment to labor used in processing data.

An electronic data-processing system consists of the following:

1. An electronic data processor (the central processing unit)
2. Associated peripheral equipment, such as data preparation, input, and output devices
3. Procedures that tell what data are needed and when, where they are obtained, and how they are used
4. Instruction routines for the processor to follow
5. Personnel to operate and maintain equipment, analyze and set up procedures, prepare instructions, provide input data, utilize reports, review results, and supervise the entire operation

The alphabet used in business for data, files, and reports is alphanumerical; that is, it includes both alphabetical and numeric characters. Large volumes of data about transactions are processed in conjunction with files to update the records in files and produce documents and reports. Records in files are analyzed to find relationships and searched to answer simple inquiries.

Business data processing involves repetitive cycles and tight time schedules for producing results that are intimately related to company operations. Scientific and engineering computation, on the other hand, generally deals with small volumes of data that may be drawn from the business file, from facts about current operations, or the engineering department. These data are processed intensively to answer specific questions, to prepare tables, or to control processes. However, the distinction between business and engineering computations is not radical, and today's electronic data-processing systems are often used for both purposes.

IMPLICATIONS FOR MANAGEMENT

The introduction of electronic data-processing systems into business has many implications for management. Reductions in manpower, space for processing and storage of data, and costs per unit of data processed may result. On the other hand, if the workload increases greatly, total costs may increase. The total workload often does increase when unit costs are reduced, because it is then practicable to collect and process data that were previously ignored.

Another advantage lies in the production of more *accurate and timely information*. Often the processing delay—the time between the occurrence of events and the availability of reports—can be greatly reduced. A shorter delay in processing may make more frequent reporting practicable. In some cases, the use of more equipment may actually increase the delay in getting certain results, even though the average delay is shortened for all output as a whole. An analogous situation occurs in manufacturing. The mass production of many units may take a longer time to set in motion than it would take to complete a few units or a special model by hand. Decreased manual handling of data increases accuracy by eliminating certain types of mistakes. Two major areas where mistakes occur—preparation of input data and interpretation of reports—require special attention for improvement.

Present and future developments in data processing will impinge on four fields of management: (1) decision-making, (2) human relations and supervision, (3) planning and operations, and (4) organization growth.

Decision-making will become more efficient because a manager will spend less time making routine decisions than he does now. Today, many problems go to top management because the simple facts that lead to specific answers are not available. In the future, decisions will follow a course based more on facts and less on intuition, although judgment will still be required. When sufficient facts are available and explicit decision rules are developed, more advanced systems will be programmed to make many decisions that managers now make. Of course, managers will continue to use their judgment and broad experience to make decisions when facts are missing or objectives are not explicit. Improvements in data processing will enable them to make better decisions by having more useful facts available, but managers will continue to deal with uncertainties that persist.

Human relations in business will change because equipment will do more of the work people now do. Improved processing methods will enable a manager to get more work from the same number of people because they are aided by more equipment. But an increased demand for more facts may require a larger over-all effort. Now, a manager frequently needs subordinates to collect and screen out control-information and to implement decisions. In the future, a data processor can do much of this work of data selection, thus allowing a manager to concentrate on the best plan of action. Improved information and control schemes will eliminate many routine problems that are now brought to a manager's attention. People will still have to direct, review, and maintain the operations of the most automatic systems now considered feasible. The main result of progress will be increased output per person. Thus, new ideas about the span of control and the training ground for future managers will become necessary.

Planning and operating a business will be different because an organization can respond faster to changed conditions. An entirely new program may be put into operation in a few minutes merely by giving the data processor a new set of objectives. Occasionally, a company connects the data system directly to the factory to control its operations, and it appears likely that this practice will spread. Management will take more preventive control action rather than having to rely upon after-the-fact corrective action.

Organization growth will be faster, if growth has been hindered by a lack of information for controlling operations and planning the future. Although larger equipment requires a higher investment in equipment and procedures, it can process more data at a lower cost per unit handled. A company may gain some competitive advantage by obtaining the largest-size equipment practicable for it.

To design a new data-processing system takes a long time and a huge amount of effort. Business management must learn to deal with developing data-processing and control systems that will become operational two or more years in the future. Whether an automatic system is desirable, and how it can be applied most advantageously, are questions that should be answered in advance by carefully planned and conducted studies. Systems studies involve selecting the objectives for the system, cataloguing all major data-processing areas, determining whether automatic techniques have merit, and investigating possible systems that appear to have merit. Following a systems study that leads to a positive recommendation, management will face problems of obtaining and installing equipment, training people, designing and testing the system required to go with the equipment selected, running old and new systems in parallel, cutting over from the old to a new system, and evaluating results from the new system to revise it as required.

A resourceful, carefully planned approach to a new system can yield large benefits—and a serious mistake, either from the wrong action or from inaction, can exact a severe cost. Electronic systems are not the answer to all data-processing problems, but they can prove highly effective when correctly designed and implemented.

SUMMARY

Important changes are occurring in the methods of business management and operation, and the widespread use of data-processing systems has accelerated the rate of change.

Data are gathered, stored, and processed in order to keep *facts* about transactions, produce operating *documents,* prepare informative *reports,* and make *analyses* of problem areas. The objective is to balance the quantity of data-processing work against the pay-off expected from the facts, documents, reports, and analyses produced.

Data and *information* have subtle but important differences. The term "data" represents collected raw facts. "Information" denotes the output after processing—sorting, organizing, file up-dating, and calculation. The information content of such output is measured in terms of accuracy, newness, degree of relevance to a selected area, and whether it deals with the unexpected. The distinction between data and information is important in systems-design, for there is a strong tendency to give too much attention to data collection and processing. It is in fact more important to concentrate on the information content of output to keep it at a high level.

This distinction is comparable to the difference of viewpoint between television station engineers and the people responsible for program content. Both station engineers and data-processing specialists concentrate on technical processes, with little concern for content, which they regard as someone else's responsibility. It is no wonder that business reports are often as barren a "wasteland" as television is accused of being.

The origination of data for processing involves collecting data as and when events occur and by whatever means will work efficiently. Origination in a form suitable for machine processing can simplify or eliminate subsequent conversion operations, but some conversion operations are usually necessary because different pieces of equipment with various operating speeds are used at each stage.

Data are verified to ensure that format is *correct,* that all the data elements appear to be *complete,* and that the meaning is *reasonable.* Initial origination and processing stages can include some verification steps. Complete verification often requires reference to files to obtain additional facts and answer questions that arise.

The processing of data includes the operations of rearranging input data and updating files for addition of new records and changes for records already in files. Initial data about transactions are classified by type and, if the files are kept in sequence, sorted into the same sequence for efficient processing. Transactions processed against several files may have to be re-sorted into the corresponding sequence before processing against each file.

The foregoing comments apply to files kept in a certain sequence, as magnetic-tape files usually are. Files maintained on random-access storage equipment, such as disks or large drums, need not be organized in any particular sequence. A stock item number, for example, or some variation of it, can serve as the "address" of a record, and any record in the file can be obtained about as quickly as any other. Therefore transactions need not be sorted into sequence before updating the file.

File processing consists of updating files for inventory transactions, calculating gross and net pay, making decisions based on numeric criteria, and calculating sales projections.

Output is taken from the facts on file and involves selecting, aggregating, editing, and rearranging in order to present results in a suitable form. Reports can be historical, forecast, or action documents. The frequency of report preparation—day, week, month, year, or when required—and the length of time available to prepare a report after the close of a period have important bearing on the design of the output subsystem if it is to operate as an efficient part of the whole data-processing system. Unexpected requests for reports pose great problems for a data system because of the need to try to anticipate them and have at least the basic facts available for preparing such reports. The problem is accentuated if the reports must be up-to-the-minute when released.

Broadly considered, processing facilities include people, records, special-purpose office equipment, punched-card equipment, and electronic data processors.

An electronic data-processing system consists of a central processing unit, associated peripheral equipment for input and output, a staff of operating personnel, procedures for them to follow, and instruction routines for the processor.

For alert and progressive managers, electronic data-processing systems have important implications. Management will get more accurate and timely information. Decision-making will improve because managers will spend less time on fact-gathering and more time on using the available information. Human relations, business planning and operations, and business growth are likely to change greatly as data-processing systems gain wider acceptance.

CHAPTER 2

DATA FOR MACHINE PROCESSING

The ability to obtain and store data for later use is invaluable to technical and cultural progress. The efficient storage and use of data depend on the combination of symbols, media, writer, and reader.

Symbols used to represent data are the numerals 0 through 9, the alphabet from A through Z, notes on a musical scale, and many others. Some alphabets are represented by symbols that, although useful for their intended purposes, are either difficult or impossible for people to read: dots and dashes for telegraphic transmission, holes in player piano rolls, punched cards and paper tape, and magnetized spots on a suitable surface.

Many *media* have been used for recording data: clay, stone, wax, sticks, papyrus, paper, cardboard, photographic plates, metal, and plastic. Two examples of plastic media are identification charge-plates with embossed characters, and magnetic tapes (plastic coated with iron oxide) for sound recorders and data processors.

The *writer* for recording data is an instrument and an operating or controlling element, although the two appear inseparable at first glance. Writing instruments have included the brush, pencil, knife, hammer and chisel, seal, movable type, typewriter, punch, and magnetic recorder. The operating or controlling element is commonly a person, either working alone or with the aid of electrical or mechanical power.

The *reader* for data can be a person, a punched-card or punched-tape reader, or a magnetic-tape reader. The reader may even be factory equipment; weaving machines, for example, read cards or tape with instructions for weaving a pattern in cloth or lace, and some milling machines are controlled by data stored on punched or magnetic tape.

MACHINE-PROCESSABLE DATA

Methods for recording business data in machine-processable form have been in use for about seventy years. Knowledge of the principles and methods involved in representing data in machine-processable form is vital to a study of automatic data processing. Some widely used methods of representing data are punched holes in cards and tape, marks in specified locations, specially shaped printed characters, and magnetic marks in a magnetizable material.

Punched Cards

Holes punched in cards are a basic way to store data for mechanized processing. Herman Hollerith invented the punched card and some rudimentary electric processing equipment while working at the U. S. Bureau of the Census in 1886. The punched cards he developed for census enumeration had space for punching 240 holes, each hole representing the presence or absence of a single fact in "yes-no" form.

This limit of 240 holes of course restricted the data content of a card. The content was increased by using smaller holes and punching more of them in a card, by adopting a numerical value (0 through 9) for the holes at each of ten positions in a column, and by using two or more columns together to represent larger numbers. In this way, three columns containing a total of 30 positions could provide for any number between 000 and 999, while 1000 positions would be required if each position were used to represent one fact.

Figure 2-1 shows numerals in 80- and 90-column cards. The standard 80-column card has *ten punching positions* (0 through 9) in each vertical column; only one hole is punched for each numeral to be represented. Each set of data punched in a card is assigned a group of columns called a *field*. Compare the punched with the printed numerals in the number "1734529." Although this number has seven digits, a field of twelve horizontally arranged spaces are allotted to it on the card. The first five spaces are punched with zeros so that the corresponding numbers on all cards are right-justified—that is, aligned on the right-hand digit. Filling out a field of spaces with leading zeros—zeros preceding the desired number—also helps in detecting skipped or double-punched columns, because each column is supposed to have one and only one punch for a numeral.

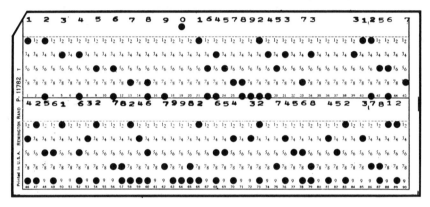

FIGURE 2-1. *Punched cards with numeric data.*

The data on a 90-column card are arranged in *two banks* of 45 columns each. The rows in each bank have a single or dual value: $0, 1_2, 3_4, 5_6, 7_8, 9$, although 0 and 9 are not marked. Zero and odd-value digits are punched by a single hole representing 0, 1, 3, 5, 7, or 9. Even-value digits are represented by punching both the appropriate dual value hole marked 2, 4, 6, or 8 (which are the same positions used for 1, 3, 5, or 7) and the 9 hole.

Another important development in punched-card data storage was the coding of letters and special symbols by two or three holes in the same column to increase the capacity for alphabetic data. Multiple punches consist of a *zone punch* to indicate the portion of the alphabet and a *numerical punch* to indicate a particular letter within that portion. Figure 2-2 shows cards with two kinds of codes for alphanumerical symbols.

Punched cards are important because data stored on them can be processed electro-mechanically. To do so, people must follow in-

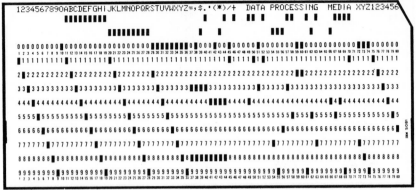

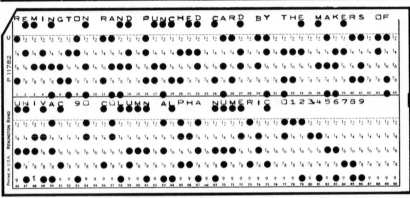

FIGURE 2-2. *Punched cards with alphanumerical codes.*

structions for handling cards and insert suitable programs in the form of wired plugboards into the machine. A punched card is processed by being passed over a sensing device (electric brushes, feeler pins, or photoelectric cells) that reads the holes. Simple calculations and *sorting* (arranging according to kind, class, or numerical sequence), *collating* or *merging* (combining two individually sorted decks of cards into one sequence) are done at speeds of 100 to 2000 cards per minute.

Punched cards are widely used for business data collection and processing. Examples of business uses are time cards, personnel records, inventory control records, and cost accounts. A punched card, perhaps of reduced size, can be attached to an item to identify it while in inventory. When the item is used or sold, the card can be detached and processed either directly or after conversion to a card better suited to machine handling. Punched cards are also used for documents that pass between companies and people, such as checks, bills, airplane and toll-road tickets, and purchase orders.

Punched Tape

A common type of punched paper tape has ten columns or frames per inch and can store an alphanumerical character in each frame. Paper tape stores data more compactly than do punched cards, since it is narrower (about $^{11}\!/_{16}$ inches wide) and thinner. One basic format for paper tape allows holes for each character to be punched in only five positions or channels. Consequently, the schemes used to represent characters on punched cards will not work directly. If all possible combinations of holes and no holes in each of the five channels are used, a total of 32 different codes are possible ($2^5 = 32$). These 32 combinations, however, are inadequate to handle the required 10 numerals, 26 letters, and several punctuation symbols. To overcome this problem, two combinations are used for shifting between the figures and letters mode. These modes correspond to the upper and lower case key on a typewriter, which permits dual use of each position. In this way, 60 alphanumerical and special characters are practicable—the 64 possible characters, less the figure and letter mode, shift characters that are the same in both modes: $64 - 2 \times 2 = 60$. (See Figure 2-3.) Actually, only

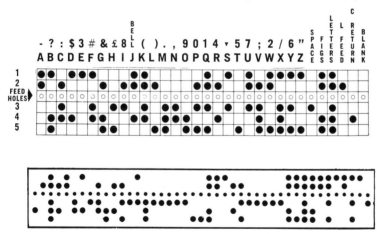

FIGURE 2-3. *Punched tape and five-channel code.*

52 characters are obtained because several more codes are used to control machine operations.

Wider tape will hold still more channels, of course, and thus further increases the number of possible characters. The characters possible with six-channel tape are basically the same as with five-channel, except that they include both upper and lower case letters.

Seven-channel code is the same as a six-channel code with a checking channel to help detect mistakes in transmission.

Recent work on what is called *integrated data processing* has aimed at developing a system of completely mechanized handling from the original collection of data to the preparation of final documents and reports. An important facet of some integrated systems is the use of punched tape as a common language for communication among the many kinds of office equipment, ranging from cash registers to punched-card equipment, which punch or read the five-channel code. Five-channel code is not restricted to tape; it can be punched along the edges of ordinary or continuous-form cards used for filing, or even on standard-size cards that are punched in the usual fashion. Although commonly made of paper for single or infrequent use, tape may be laminated from paper and Mylar or paper and metal to withstand repeated runs.

Limitations of Punched-Hole Equipment

Although punched-card equipment is an important advance over manual methods, it has some serious drawbacks. The *mechanical problems* of punching, reading, and card-handling limit operating speeds. Since the plugboards in which wires are inserted to select and sequence operations hold only a small number of *fixed instructions*—for example, "multiply hours worked by wage rate to get gross pay"; or "subtract withholding and payroll taxes from gross pay to get net pay"—processing flexibility is limited for each pass of the cards. Simple arithmetical calculations can be readily handled, but extensive, complex calculations can be made only inefficiently if at all.

The *data density* of cards—the number of characters that can be recorded per square inch or other measure of area or volume—is low because of the hole size required, the alphanumerical codes used, the thickness of cards, and the fixed-field-length requirement. The fixed-field requirement means that the number of columns assigned to a field must cover the longest item that may occur—for example, if stock on hand may reach 10,000 units, then a field five positions long must be provided on every card even though, for most items, only a few hundred units are on hand. More data can be typed or printed on a card (up to 25 lines) than can be punched into the same card. Punched-tape strips are more compact than cards but are clumsy to handle and file. The difficulty of altering data punched in cards or tape is a desirable feature when they must be retained as evidence, but it restricts them to a one-time use. Paper or plastic file-cards, on the other hand, may be used repeatedly.

Cards are bulky to send by mail, and transmission over a telegraph line is limited to a few cards a minute with one receiving-sending unit, although card transmission over telephone lines is much faster.

The *serial nature* of punched tape—one character follows another in a word although the holes for a character are in parallel across the tape as a *frame*—and its indefinite length speed up reading and perhaps calculating and tabulating, but it makes sorting more difficult because it is not feasible to cut a tape into short lengths and physically manipulate them to sort data into sequence. Despite these deficiencies, the acceptance of punched-card and tape processing equipment has been widespread, and has stimulated the development of more efficient means of storing data for machine processing.

Magnetic Recording

Magnetic recording of digital data corresponds to audio recording methods, except that signals are recorded separately instead of continuously. More care is also required, for the loss of even a few digits may be worse than losing part of a voice recording.

Magnetic spots, which represent data, are recorded in an iron oxide coating on a plastic, aluminum, or even cardboard backing. The iron-oxide-coated material is used in the form of drums, disks, cards, or reels of tape. Magnetic recording media are shown in Figure 2-4.

The operations in magnetic recording are (1) erasing of prior contents, (2) recording the desired data, and (3) reading whenever wanted. Two heads—one for erasing unwanted contents and another for recording and reading—are close to but usually not in contact with the iron-oxide surface. The magnetic spots can be erased and the material reused almost indefinitely.

Characters are often written on tape ½ or ¾ inches wide at densities ranging from 100 to 1500 characters per inch. The 80 alphanumerical characters that can be punched in a card can be recorded on 0.053 to 0.8 inches of tape. Recording density on drums is usually lower—not more than 100 characters an inch on each track around the drum, in eight or so tracks per inch along the drum in the direction parallel to the axis. Tapes are moved past the read-write heads at speeds ranging from 75 to 200 inches a second, and drums rotate at speeds between 1,000 and 20,000 revolutions a minute. The read-write process is controlled electrically and is extremely fast, being done while the tape or drum is in motion. Tape-reading or writing speeds range from 5,000 to more than 100,000 alphanumerical characters a second.

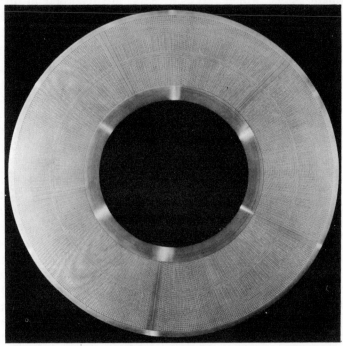

FIGURE 2-4. *Magnetic tape and disk (with data bits along tracks).*

Magnetic cores are small doughnuts of magnetizable material strung on stationary wires and are not moved. Electricity is sent through the wires to write or read the magnetic state of any desired core. Data can be written into or read out of magnetic cores in a few millionths of a second and, in newer equipment, in a fraction of a millionth.

Data Representation

At various stages in a data-processing system, many different methods can be used for representing data: handwriting; hand-printing; punched holes; the positions of wheels, gears, and levers, as in a desk calculator; electric pulses; and magnetic states. The proper choice depends on whether people, machines, or both will use the data. Ordinarily, several methods are used and conversion is required among them, since, if a single method were used throughout, efficiency would drop.

Just as many different frequencies, shapes, and amplitudes of audio signals are used to record music on a magnetic tape, many different sizes and shapes of holes, spots, or electric pulses can represent alphanumerical data. Although few components would be needed to handle digital data represented in this way, they would be very complex. Thus, another approach is to have simpler components and use many of them. Automatic processing equipment is designed with many components that can exist in either one of two states. The two states may be represented in various ways: by a punched hole or no hole; by a magnetic spot with either north-south or south-north polarity; by a relay open or closed; by an electric pulse or no pulse; or by a dot or dash. The "yes-no," "on-off," or "0-1" scheme is popular because it is easier to design equipment that can be put in one of two states and make it stay there—equipment with two *stable* states—than it is to provide for many stable states. A light switch is a simple example of a two-state, "on-off" device. Combinations of the two symbols 0 and 1, called "binary digits" or "bits," are used in a variety of ingenious schemes to represent numerals, letters, and other symbols.

NUMBER SYSTEMS

The various number systems in use are treated here only in enough detail to show the relationship between schemes that people like to use and those preferred by computer designers.

People like the decimal number system because it seems "natural"; they learned to count on their fingers, and often still do. Many other number bases are widely used; however, we tend to think of them merely as counting schemes. Examples are 12 for a dozen, 16 for ounces in a pound, 3 for feet in a yard, and 5280 for feet in a mile. Nondecimal fractions are also used; for example, ⅛ for security prices and 1/16 for fractions of an inch. People even find the British monetary system of mixed radices comprehensible (4 farthings to a penny, 12 pennies to a shilling, 20 shillings to a pound, and decimal thereafter), although far more complex than a single-radix scheme.

The *base or radix* of a number system need only be greater than 1, and is usually but not always an integer. The radix in the decimal system is 10; in counting by the dozen it is 12, and for counting by pairs it is 2. The number of marks in a number system is equal to the radix used. The decimal system has ten marks or digits—0 through 9. The binary system has two digits, 0 and 1. The octal system has eight symbols, 0 through 7.

Decimal System

When counting goes beyond one position in the decimal system, the digit in the next position to the left is increased by 1 and counting is resumed at 0. Counting beyond 9 seems easy because of constant practice; it seems "natural" that 10 and 11 should follow 9, or that 1000 should follow 999. In brief, all large numbers make use of the same digits, 0 to 9.

By way of contrast, consider that in using roman numerals—I, V, X, L, C, D, M, $\overline{X}$, $\overline{C}$, and $\overline{M}$— the value of a number depends on the characters used and their sequence (if they are different), but not on their individual positions. For example, III is 3, IV is 4, VI is 6, both XC and LXXXX are 90, and $\overline{M}$MCLXVI is 1,001,166. In this system, representations of large numbers are difficult to create and to understand.

The concept of positional value is fundamental to simple, straightforward number systems. Whenever a digit is written, it has an individual value that is independent of the digits to its left or right. But—and this point is important in modern number systems—the over-all value of a digit is the product of its individual value and its *position value*—the number base raised to the power of the digit position occupied.

In a decimal number, digits have individual values of 0 through 9 and position values that are multiples of 10, the number base of the decimal system. The first digit to the left of the decimal point is multiplied by 10^0, which is equal to 1, so that the first digit is counted at face value. The second or tens digit is multiplied by 10^1, which is 10. The hundreds digit is multiplied by 10^2 or 100, and so on.

Digits to the right of the decimal point are divided by 10^1, 10^2, 10^3 (or multiplied by 10^{-1}, 10^{-2}, 10^{-3}), corresponding to each digit position to the right of the decimal point.

The complete number is *the sum of each digit multiplied by its positional value*. For example, the digits 4, 9, 7, 6, 5, written as the number 497.65, have positional values as follows:

Position Value	$\begin{cases} 10^2 \\ 100 \end{cases}$	$\begin{matrix} 10^1 \\ 10 \end{matrix}$	$\begin{matrix} 10^0 \\ 1 \end{matrix}$	.	$\begin{matrix} 10^{-1} \\ \frac{1}{10} \end{matrix}$	$\begin{matrix} 10^{-2} \\ \frac{1}{100} \end{matrix}$
Digits	4	9	7	.	6	5
Products	\multicolumn{6}{}{$(4 \times 100) + (9 \times 10) + (7 \times 1) + (6 \times \frac{1}{10}) + (5 \times \frac{1}{100})$}
Number	\multicolumn{6}{}{497.65}

Powers of 10 are used to find positional values because there are 10 symbols. The largest digit is 9, but it is possible to represent 10 by assigning a positional value to the smallest nonzero digit, 1, and attaching 0.

Long familiarity has led people to think that the decimal system is objectively "natural." It is easy for us to forget how difficult it once was to learn the sums and products of two decimal digits. The decimal addition and multiplication tables are difficult to learn because the table for single-digit numbers has a hundred entries.

Binary System

The fact that it is easiest to design and build equipment with two stable states, that might be thought of as "yes-no," "on-off," or "0-1," makes the binary system desirable. The 0 and 1 are the only two binary digits and are often referred to as "bits."

The bits in a *binary number* have position values of 2^0, 2^1, to 2^n, which are equal to 1, 2, 4, and so on. This is similar to the scheme of 10^0, 10^1, 10^2, etc., for decimal digit positions.

Position values in binary are as follows, to the left and right of the binary point:

2^5	2^4	2^3	2^2	2^1	2^0	.	2^{-1}	2^{-2}	2^{-3}
32	16	8	4	2	1	.	$\frac{1}{2}$	$\frac{1}{4}$	$\frac{1}{8}$

Counting in decimal and binary shows the positional values and the similarities in advancing to the next position each time:

Decimal	Binary
0	0
1	1
2	10
3	11
4	100
5	101
6	110
7	111
8	1000
9	1001
1.0	1010
11	1011
12	1100
50	110010
100	1100100
512	1000000000

To the right of the binary point, each bit is divided by 2, 4, 8, and so on. Examples of fractions in one number system also show how some numbers may be difficult to express in the other:

Decimal	Binary
0.5	0.1
0.25	0.01
0.125	0.001
0.375	0.011
0.33333 . . .	0.01010101 . . .

Codes Based on Binary

Users and designers of data-processing equipment have different viewpoints about the ideal number system to use. Business users generally prefer a decimal number system because input and output data are typically decimal. Computer designers, on the other hand, prefer a binary system because it is easier to design and build equipment with components expected to maintain two stable states rather than ten. There are two ways to compromise this conflict. One way is to retain decimal numbers for input and output, and design the machine to operate with pure binary numbers. However, this use of two number systems requires converting input from decimal to binary and output back to decimal. Because people find manual conversion so burdensome, the processor is designed to handle it. Converting a *decimal number* to a *binary number* may be done during a card-reading cycle, or after data are read in from magnetic tape. Since most modern machines handle the conversion, it is of little concern to the supplier of input which mode the machine is operating in.

Another way to reconcile the decimal-binary conflict is to represent each *decimal digit* in a code of four binary digits and avoid the task of converting the number as a whole into binary. The conversion of each *decimal numeral* into *binary-coded decimal* is simpler than that from decimal numbers to binary numbers, but this advantage is gained at the cost of longer numbers, since more digits are required. The decimal number 403, for example, might be written as 0100 0000 0011 in binary-coded decimal. Manipulating binary-coded decimal numbers also entails either more circuitry or slower processing.

Decimal	Binary	Binary-Coded decimal	
		8421	Excess 3
0	0	0000	0011
1	1	0001	0100
2	10	0010	0101
3	11	0011	0110
4	100	0100	0111
5	101	0101	1000
6	110	0110	1001
7	111	0111	1010
8	1000	1000	1011
9	1001	1001	1100

TABLE 2-1. *Numerical coding systems.*

Values for 0 to 9 are shown in Table 2-1 for several code schemes including two versions of binary-coded decimal. The 8421 version uses a straightforward binary representation with leading zeros to fill out a four-digit field. The "Excess 3" code scheme is similar to the binary, but the binary value of a decimal 3, which is 0011, is added to each numeral in binary to facilitate arithmetical operations—for example, the decimal complement of an Excess 3 digit can be obtained simply by changing each 0 to 1 and each 1 to 0.

Many other codes exist, some of which are used for processors. Business applications involve a higher ratio of input-output operations to computations than do engineering and mathematical applications; therefore, equipment intended for business applications may be designed with a machine code, such as binary-coded decimal, that is easily converted from (or to) a code that can be used by other machines and people.

ALPHANUMERICAL SYSTEM

Alphabetic characters are more difficult to represent than numerals since they are more varied—26 letters and a dozen or so special characters, instead of merely ten numerals. Furthermore, alphabetic characters are not convertible into binary numbers by the usual scheme of division. The name "John Jones" cannot be represented in binary in any easy way.

Six-Bit Code

The binary-coded decimal scheme in which four bits can represent 16 characters can be extended to six bits to represent 64 characters, since six bits yield 2^6 or 64 possible combinations. Using six bits for each character makes it possible to represent the alphabet A to Z in upper-case characters, the numerals 0 to 9, and 28 other characters in what might be called a *binary-coded alphanumerical* scheme.

Examples of special symbols, numerals (in Excess 3 code), and letters in binary-coded alphanumerical are as follows:

(	00 0010
)	00 0011
/	01 0010
0	01 0011
1	01 0100
7	01 1010
C	10 0010
D	10 0011
S	11 0010
T	11 0011

Notice that (, /, C, and S have the same four right-hand bits but differ in the two left-hand bits called "zone" bits. In some ways this is comparable to the two top-row or zone punches—X and Y— that are used with punches for 0 to 9 to represent alphabetical characters in a standard 80-column punched card. The four right-hand bits, which yield 16 combinations, are used with two left-hand bits yielding four combinations for a total of 64. This range of characters serves for many purposes but does not provide for both lower-case (uncapitalized) and upper-case characters. An important and easily overlooked point is that the combination of bits "10 0010" does not mean "C" to a computer, but is merely assigned that value by people using the equipment. The bits 10 0010 can just as easily stand for any letter in any alphabet that does not use more than 64 characters. For readability by people, the desired letter is placed on keyboards used for preparing input and on printers for output.

Parity-Bit

An extra binary digit, called the *parity-bit,* is often attached to each character solely to detect whether the equipment is malfunctioning by dropping or gaining a bit. If the equipment designer chooses to use an *odd-parity-bit* rule, an odd number of bits is used to represent each character. The gain or loss of one bit results in an even number of bits and violates the odd-bit rule. In the illustration below, the character "B" is represented as 100001, with an odd parity-bit attached in the parity channel to give 1 100001. The loss of one bit leaves two bits or the gain of one bit gives four, and both of these violate the odd-parity-bit rule.

Channel		Character				
Name	Number	)	*	8	B	X
Parity-bit channel	7	0	0	1	1	0
Zone channels	6	0	0	0	1	1
	5	0	0	1	0	1
	4	0	1	1	0	0
Numerical channels	3	1	1	0	0	1
	2	0	0	1	0	1
	1	0	1	1	1	1
Number of bits		1	3	5	3	5

Some equipment is designed with the even-parity-bit rule—which is to add a bit, if required—to make the number of bits in a character even, giving essentially the same result as the odd-bit rule.

There are other ways of detecting the complete loss of a character, such as counting the number of characters each time they are handled, or using a parity-bit for each channel along a tape. The lengthwise, or *longitudinal parity-bit* scheme is useful for detecting the loss of a bit in a channel. In conjunction with the vertical parity-bit, the longitudinal bit can be used to detect and correct an equipment malfunction of one bit. The message "213786 42 390 JOHN

DOE" (with < and > for "start message" and "end message," respectively, and • for "item separator") might be recorded on tape with a parity-bit for each character in Channel 7 and for each channel in the position marked "p" as follows:

```
              < 2 1 3 7 8 6 • 4 2 • 3 9 0 • JOHN • DOE > p
Channel
   7       0 0 1 0 0 1 0 1 1 0 1 0 0 0 1 0 1 1 1 1 0 1 1 0 1
   6       1 0 0 0 0 0 0 1 0 0 1 0 0 0 1 1 1 1 1 1 1 1 1 1 0
   5       1 1 1 1 1 1 1 1 1 1 1 1 1 1 0 0 0 0 1 0 0 0 1 0
   4       1 0 0 0 1 1 1 1 0 0 1 0 1 0 1 1 1 0 1 1 0 1 0 1 1
   3       1 1 1 1 0 0 0 1 1 1 1 1 1 0 1 0 1 1 1 1 0 1 1 1 1 ←
   2       1 0 0 1 1 1 0 0 1 0 0 1 0 1 0 0 1 1 0 0 1 1 0 0 0
   1       0 1 0 0 0 1 1 0 1 1 0 0 0 1 0 1 0 1 1 0 1 0 0 1 0
                     ↑
```

If a bit were lost so that the first 3, for example, was recorded as 0010010 with only two bits, the odd-parity-bit rule would be violated in both the column and the row marked with arrows. With only one bit lost (or gained), correction could be made by complementing whatever exists at the intersection of lines drawn from the two arrows. The complementing of 0 to 1 or 1 to 0 would correct the malfunction of the recording equipment. More elaborate parity-bit schemes, especially longitudinal ones, are used to detect and correct more severe malfunctions. A six-bit code with parity-bit is commonly used to detect the loss of bits in alphanumerical codes on magnetic tape. When data are transferred into some processors, the parity-bit scheme is omitted because the risk of losing a bit during processing is far less than during tape-reading or writing.

Sorting Sequence

Figure 2-5 shows an example of a six-bit code with parity-bit at the left of the character. This code is arranged in the collating or *sorting sequence,* which means that data in this code could be arranged in numerical and alphabetic sequence. The five messages, < 4357 • DOE, JOHN >, < 2476 • ROE, RICHARD >, < 1289 • BAKER, CHARLEY >, < 2476 • ROE, JOHN >, and < 7365 • BAKER, ABLE >, could be sorted into two difference sequences by using either the whole message or only the second item (and following items, if desired) as a key to identify the message.

The sequence using the *whole message* as the sorting *key* would be correct numerically.

Channel No. columns are numbered 7 6 5 4 3 2 1, with bit values P*, 2^5, 2^4, 2^3, 2^2, 2^1, 2^0.

CHARACTER DESCRIPTION	SYMBOL	7 (P*)	6 (2^5)	5 (2^4)	4 (2^3)	3 (2^2)	2 (2^1)	1 (2^0)	OCTAL EQUIVALENT
Blank		1	0	0	0	0	0	0	00
Space	—	0	0	0	0	0	0	1	01
Cross	‡	0	0	0	0	0	1	0	02
Open Parenthesis	(	1	0	0	0	0	1	1	03
Close Parenthesis	)	0	0	0	0	1	0	0	04
Quotes	"	1	0	0	0	1	0	1	05
Colon	:	1	0	0	0	1	1	0	06
Dollars	$	0	0	0	0	1	1	1	07
Percent	%	0	0	0	1	0	0	0	10
Semicolon	;	1	0	0	1	0	0	1	11
Ampersand	&	1	0	0	1	0	1	0	12
Apostrophe	'	0	0	0	1	0	1	1	13
Minus	⊖	1	0	0	1	1	0	0	14
Asterisk	*	0	0	0	1	1	0	1	15
Period	.	0	0	0	1	1	1	0	16
Carriage Shift (CS)		1	0	0	1	1	1	1	17
Page Change (PC)		0	0	1	0	0	0	0	20
Line Shift (LS)		1	0	1	0	0	0	1	21
Slant	/	1	0	1	0	0	1	0	22
Zero (Numeric)	0	0	0	1	0	0	1	1	23
One	1.	1	0	1	0	1	0	0	24
Two	2	0	0	1	0	1	0	1	25
Three	3	0	0	1	0	1	1	0	26
Four	4	1	0	1	0	1	1	1	27
Five	5	1	0	1	1	0	0	0	30
Six	6	0	0	1	1	0	0	1	31
Seven	7	0	0	1	1	0	1	0	32
Eight	8	1	0	1	1	0	1	1	33
Nine	9	0	0	1	1	1	0	0	34
Comma	,	1	0	1	1	1	0	1	35
Number	#	1	0	1	1	1	1	0	36
Carriage Normal		0	0	1	1	1	1	1	37
A	A	0	1	0	0	0	0	0	40
B	B	1	1	0	0	0	0	1	41
C	C	1	1	0	0	0	1	0	42
D	D	0	1	0	0	0	1	1	43
E	E	1	1	0	0	1	0	0	44
F	F	0	1	0	0	1	0	1	45
G	G	0	1	0	0	1	1	0	46
H	H	1	1	0	0	1	1	1	47
I	I	1	1	0	1	0	0	0	50
J	J	0	1	0	1	0	0	1	51
K	K	0	1	0	1	0	1	0	52
L	L	1	1	0	1	0	1	1	53
M	M	0	1	0	1	1	0	0	54
N	N	1	1	0	1	1	0	1	55
O	O	1	1	0	1	1	1	0	56
P	P	0	1	0	1	1	1	1	57
Q	Q	1	1	1	0	0	0	0	60
R	R	0	1	1	0	0	0	1	61
S	S	0	1	1	0	0	1	0	62
T	T	1	1	1	0	0	1	1	63
U	U	0	1	1	0	1	0	0	64
V	V	1	1	1	0	1	0	1	65
W	W	1	1	1	0	1	1	0	66
X	X	0	1	1	0	1	1	1	67
Y	Y	0	1	1	1	0	0	0	70
Z	Z	1	1	1	1	0	0	1	71
End File (EF)		1	1	1	1	0	1	0	72
End Data (ED)		0	1	1	1	0	1	1	73
Item Separator (ISS)	●	1	1	1	1	1	0	0	74
End Message (EM)	>	0	1	1	1	1	0	1	75
Start Message (SM)	<	0	1	1	1	1	1	0	76
		1	1	1	1	1	1	1	77†

* The parity bit (P) is shown as it appears on magnetic tape (odd parity); on paper tape, parity is even.

† 77 with odd parity (1111111) is a legitimate octal number on magnetic tape. On paper tape, 77 is a legitimate octal number only when there is no punch in the seventh (P) channel (even parity). The Paper Tape Reader ignores a row in which all seven channels are punched, interpreting this as a corrective measure.

FIGURE 2-5. *The RCA 501 code, with odd parity-bit.*

1289	BAKER, CHARLEY
2476	ROE, JOHN
2476	ROE, RICHARD
4357	DOE, JOHN
7365	BAKER, ABLE

The sequence using the *second item* as the sorting *key* would be correct alphabetically.

7365	BAKER, ABLE
1289	BAKER, CHARLEY
4357	DOE, JOHN
2476	ROE, JOHN
2476	ROE, RICHARD

Each of these sequences is in ascending order according to the key used and the values in the collation table. When keys contain both alphabetic and numerical characters, the resulting sorted sequence depends on whether numerals precede letters (as is true for the code shown above) or vice versa.

Multi-Mode Codes

A dilemma arises from the fact that four bits are enough for a numerical code whereas six are required for an alphanumeric code that has more than 32 characters but not more than 64. If a four-bit code is used for representing numerals, then one alphabetic character might be represented by a two-digit number—a *two-for-one* scheme. For example, "A" might first be assigned the decimal number 32 and then coded as 0011 0010 in binary-coded decimal. The two-for-one scheme is efficient for numerals—each one is represented by four bits. But it is inefficient for alphabetic characters because each one is represented by eight bits, whereas six bits are enough to represent 64 different characters. The two-for-one scheme is acceptable when the volume of alphabetic data is small and the equipment prints letters as letters and not as two decimal digits that people must convert into letters when they read output. In this case, as in all multi-mode codes, the bits can be used to represent a character in either one mode or another, but obviously the same bits cannot be used in two modes at the same time. The programmer must keep track of which mode is being used.

The *three-for-two* scheme is more compact for representing both alphabetic and numeric data than the two-for-one scheme. Three numerals require twelve bits which can, alternatively, be used to represent alphabetic characters. This condensation is possible because numeric characters do not need the fifth and sixth bits—called "zone" bits—that are required for representing alphabetic characters. Thus, three numerals or two alphabetic characters can be represented by the twelve bits ordinarily thought of as being adequate for two alphabetic characters. The four zone bits of two alphabetic characters can be used along with the eight other bits to represent three numerals. The scheme of representing either three numerals or two alphabetic characters with twelve bits is useful for compact storage on tape. Numerals can, if desired, be returned to the usual six-bit form for internal storage and processing. Alphabetic characters are represented by six bits on tape and also in internal storage for processing.

The multi-mode scheme is carried further in some equipment so that 24 bits treated as a word may be used as eight octal, six decimal, or four alphanumerical characters. These modes are alternatives to using the 24 bits as one binary number. Examples of these different uses are shown in the following illustration. One or more parity-bits may be used with the 24 data bits. Longer words of 36 and 48 bits, which also are multiples of 3, 4, and 6, are also used in similar fashion by some processors.

Twenty-four individual bits **Binary**	101001110100101101100100
Eight groups of three bits **Octal numbers**	5 1 6 4 5 5 4 4
Six groups of four bits **Binary-coded decimal** **(Excess 3)**	7 4 1 8 3 1
Four groups of six bits **Alphanumerical**	J U N E
One group of twenty-four bits **Decimal**	10963812

Multi-mode codes have important practical considerations. The fact that data can be packed more densely at some stages of processing permits higher tape capacity and reading speeds. But it becomes necessary for the programmer to keep track of the mode being used and deal with it appropriately.

The selection of an efficient data code depends on whether alphabetic or numerical data are involved and on the amount of processing to be done each time the data are handled. If numbers predominate in the data, a numerical code—either pure binary or binary-coded decimal—offers more compact storage than does an alphanumerical code, although at the cost of clumsy methods for handling letters.

Conversely, alphabetic data can be handled directly by alphanumerical codes, but they are not efficient for handling numerals because six bits are used for a numeral, whereas four would be enough in binary-coded decimal and about three and a third in pure binary. Processors handle binary numbers more efficiently, but a conversion is required to decimal or alphabetic form for people to use. Frequent conversion between alphanumerical and binary offsets some of the benefits derived from more efficient internal processing. Newer machines, however, are designed to handle data in binary, octal, decimal, or alphabetic modes. In order to process the data in the same code in which it was encoded—say, binary out of several possible codes—it is necessary to specify to the processor the mode selected.

ORGANIZATION OF DATA

Data-processing equipment senses, stores, and manipulates a wide variety of characters. Individual characters must be grouped together in a way that is practical for use by people and machines.

The organization of data can be illustrated by the Jameson Knitting Company's scheme for keeping track of customers' orders (see Figure 2-6). An order record is prepared on paper for each order received from a customer; it identifies the customer, lists the

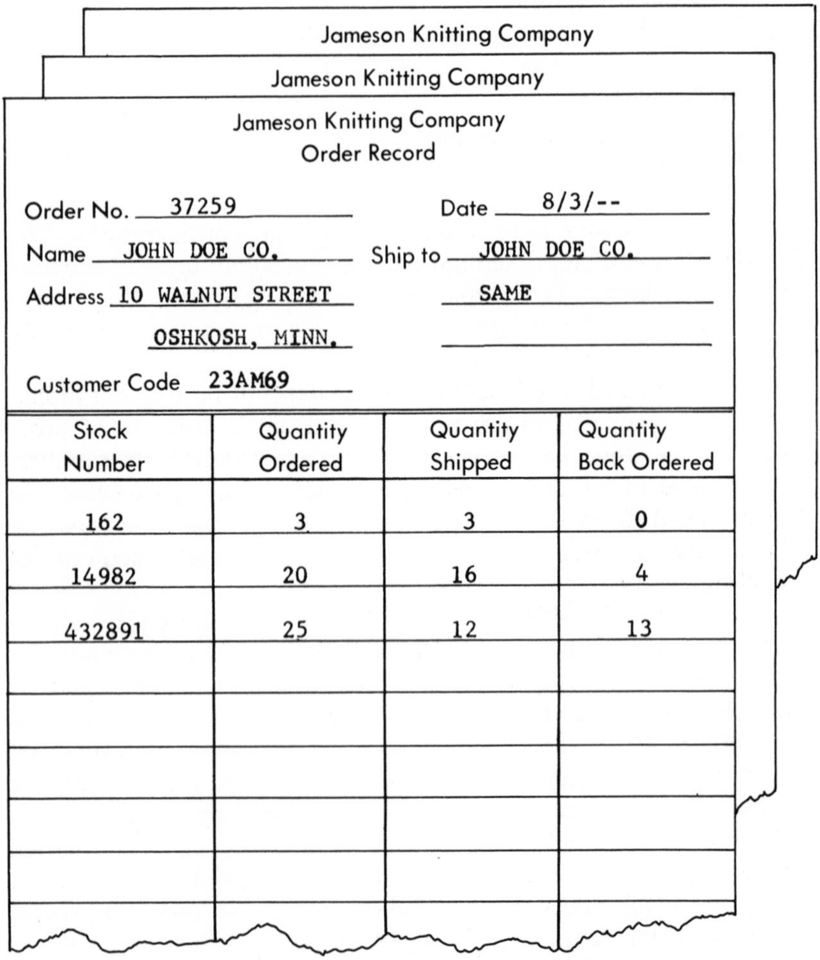

Jameson Knitting Company

Jameson Knitting Company

Jameson Knitting Company
Order Record

Order No. ___37259___   Date ___8/3/--___

Name ___JOHN DOE CO.___ Ship to ___JOHN DOE CO.___

Address _10 WALNUT STREET_   ___SAME___

        OSHKOSH, MINN.

Customer Code ___23AM69___

Stock Number	Quantity Ordered	Quantity Shipped	Quantity Back Ordered
162	3	3	0
14982	20	16	4
432891	25	12	13

FIGURE 2-6. *Customer order record, paper.*

items ordered, and posts the quantity shipped or back-ordered. Each numeral, letter, punctuation mark, or symbol is a *character*. Characters are grouped into *data elements* to specify a particular order number, date, alphabetic name, street address, stock number, and quantity. Data elements are grouped into *records*.

Examples of records in this case are the customer's order and the shipping department's report of the quantity of each stock number shipped or back-ordered. These records comprise the back-order *file*. The organization of data on paper, from the smallest to the largest unit, is thus: character, data element, record, and file. The concept of organizing data into a structure running from element to file is an important one for business data processing.

Another aspect of data organization is the quantity of storage assigned to a character, data element, record, or file. Data elements and records are of primary interest here.

Selectable-Length Data Elements

A customer order file kept on paper records illustrates the use of selectable-length data elements. The maximum number of characters needed for any element is anticipated and provided for in printing the form. The length provided for each element can be fixed individually, so that a long space can be provided for customer name. Customer name is an example of externally-originated data—data whose format is selected by someone outside the organization that must process it. Customer name may take 30 or 40 characters, although it can be limited in size and excess characters merely cut off or dropped. Stock numbers, on the other hand, can be established as desired and restricted to a few digits, although 10 or 20 digits are often used for unique identifications in large inventory systems. Since space on paper records is inexpensive, field lengths can be set generously to handle the longest element likely to occur. And, of course, people are clever enough to modify the length of an item merely by writing in the margin.

Punched cards pose a more difficult problem for fixing item length. Since the total number of columns available in a card is usually 80 or 90, their use must be economized to prevent some records from carrying over to several cards. Once a field—the number of columns—is assigned to a data element, the maximum length is selected for punched-card processing. If the longest *stock number* is 20 characters, then a field of 20 columns is assigned for use with both long and short numbers. For example, the numbers

387-A4295725-9291 and B7070 are punched into a 20-column field as 000387-A4295725-9291 and 000000000000000B7070. The *quantities of items,* on the other hand, might range from 1 to 9999 and thus require only four columns. An entirely different number of columns might be used for customer *name and address* in the cards.

In short, the term "selectable" means that the number of characters allotted to a data element in a record is open or free until a certain number is assigned. Thereafter, the number of characters for that element is fixed, so that shorter elements are filled out and longer elements cannot be fitted into the space assigned.

Variable-Length Elements

If the facilities used for processing data can deal about equally well with long and short data elements—that is, elements of *variable length*—one need only identify the element and use the number of characters necessary. Blank paper, without any designation of length, is a simple example of a variable-length element record. On blank paper a record might contain explicit identification and elements in sequence without regard to format or spacing.

> Order No. 37259 Date 8/3/—Name John Doe Co. Ship to John Doe Co. Address 10 Walnut St. Same Oshkosh, Minn. Same Customer code 23AM69 Stock number Quantity ordered Quantity shipped Quantity back-ordered 162 3 3 0 14982 20 16 4 432891 25 12 13

The order record written in variable-length elements occupies less space on blank paper than does the selectable-length record on the printed form shown earlier. It takes more skill to associate headings—stock number, quantity ordered, shipped, and back-ordered—with the related elements in the line-by-line scheme shown here. The loss of one item, furthermore, might cause the others to be misinterpreted.

The elements can be organized in more logical ways. Related data may be grouped together and then described as a particular element or set of elements that is repeated a specified number of times. A file of 10,000 customer orders, for example, is fully explained by a single description of the format to be used. The name of each element need not be listed explicitly but can be implied from the sequence in which it appears. The order for John Doe can be compressed if • is an element or item separator, < indicates start of record, and > indicates end of record.

< 37259 • 8/3/— • John Doe Co. • John Doe Co. • 10
Walnut St. • Same • Oshkosh, Minn. • Same • 23AM69
• 162 • 3 • 3 • 0 • 14982 • 20 • 16 • 4 • 432891
• 25 • 12 • 13 >

The item following the second item separator should be the
customer's name; hence if the date is omitted, two separators are
included for counting purposes: < 37259 • • John Doe Co. •
. . . .When records are organized in this manner, a repetitive pattern develops—stock number, quantity ordered, shipped, and back-
ordered—so that the tenth, fourteenth, or eighteenth item is always
the stock number. Computers designed to handle variable-length
items can store and process data recorded in this fashion on magnetic tape (see Figure 2-7). They are called "variable-length field"

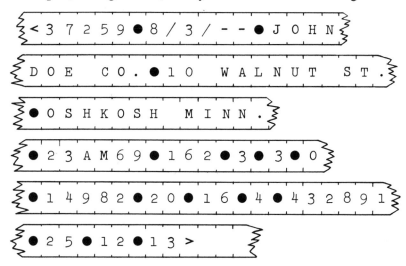

FIGURE 2-7. *Schematic for content of customer order record, magnetic tape,
variable-length field.*

or "character" machines since it is possible to use any number of
characters desired.

Fixed Word and Block

Word is often defined as a fixed number of characters or character locations that are treated as a unit. Word length is fixed by the
computer designer and incorporated in the circuitry. Common word
lengths are 10 or 12 alphanumerical characters and 24, 36, or 48
bits. Every computer word must contain the specified number of

characters or bits. Excess positions in *computer words,* occurring because the data elements are shorter, can be filled with zeros or spaces. Figure 2-8 shows the layout for a customer order on mag-

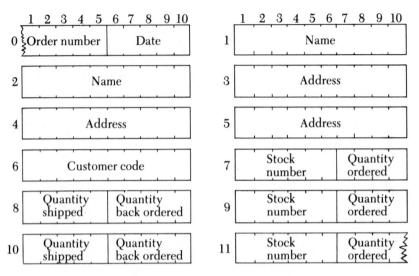

FIGURE 2-8. *Schematic for customer order record, magnetic tape, fixed word length, twelve words.*

netic tape with fixed word length. Longer items occurring in the data can be handled by using two or more computer words together to represent one item.

Fixed-word equipment uses extra storage space for shorter data elements because it fills out the word with spaces. If two or more short items of data are *packed* into one word, extra steps are required to separate or unpack them for individual processing. An opposite situation arises when an item is longer than a computer word so that two words are used to store an item. Both words must be treated together when making comparisons during sorting or when performing arithmetical operations.

Block means a fixed number of characters or words treated as a unit on magnetic tape and in computer storage. Data on magnetic tape can be read only while the tape is moving at speeds of about 100 inches a second. Inter-block gaps—blank spaces of about one-half inch on tape—are required for starting and stopping tape movement. If the tape-packing *density* is 200 characters an inch, ten characters in a word occupy one-twentieth of an inch of tape. Tapes written with individual words would have ten times as much start-stop space as data space. In order to conserve space on tape, data are handled as fixed-length blocks of characters; a block, for example, may contain 720 characters arranged in 60 words of 12 characters each. A computer designed to handle variable-length elements may handle blocks as short as several characters and without an upper limit for long records. In the conversion of data from punched cards to tape, the block length may be limited to the 80 characters in a card. Short blocks may be consolidated into longer blocks during the first processing run in order to reduce tape length and read-write time in subsequent passes. In such cases, the data are said to be "blocked" and the length of magnetic tape used for recording the data is reduced. Additional handling may be required to unblock the records and process them individually.

Because people and machines each work best with data in different formats, problems arise of placing two or more data words into one processor word and two or more data records into one block on tape, and subsequently separating them for processing.

SUMMARY

Many methods are used to represent, store, and process data. The efficient storage and use of data depend on the symbols, media, writer, and reader. Any particular combination selected from the available possibilities imposes restrictions on data-processing techniques, since all members must operate compatibly.

Punched cards and punched paper tape are widely used for storing business data. Both cards and tape involve the mechanical operations of punching holes in paper. The width, length, and thickness of cards and tape influence the code used, data density, and processing methods. As originally developed, the codes were mostly limited to numerals, but more recently they have been extended to include alphabetical characters.

Magnetic recording media are similar to cards and paper tape in some respects, but have two highly desirable features: they require fewer mechanical operations, and they can be reused for other data.

Number systems owe much to the historical context in which they originated and developed. Various number systems—decimal, duodecimal (base 12), hexadecimal (base 16), octal, and binary—are widely used today, although people seem to favor the decimal system. Computer designers prefer the binary system of data representation, because two-state devices are easier to build and operate than multi-state devices. As a result, conversion from one system to another often is required; this conversion is usually performed by the processor.

Four-bit codes, with sixteen possible combinations, are often used for numerals. Six-bit codes are used to represent numerals, letters, and special characters, but are, of course, limited to a total of 64 characters ($2^6 = 64$). Alphanumerical codes usually provide an additional parity-bit for detecting the gain or loss of a bit that would change a desired character to an illegal character. A total of seven bits—six bits for the character plus a parity-bit—will represent 128 characters ($2^7 = 128$); but only half the possible characters are considered legal. The adoption of an odd parity-bit scheme makes illegal all characters that have an even number of bits. The loss resulting from ruling out half the possible characters, when one bit is designated as a parity-bit, is considered a fair price to pay for the increased ability to detect errors. The general idea of parity-bits need not be limited to one bit for a character (*vertical parity*). Additional parity-bits may be used along the channel for several characters (*horizontal parity*). Both vertical and horizontal parity are sometimes used to increase the ability to detect and also correct errors in data recorded on tape.

Multi-mode schemes are used to represent different mixes of characters in a format that is basically binary. The eight bits designated for two numerals can be used for one letter—a two-for-one scheme—or the twelve bits designated for three numerals can be used for two letters—a three-for-two scheme. Some processors are designed to treat the bits of a word in any one of several ways at the programmer's option—binary, octal, decimal, or alphanumerical —to maximize the density of data storage for the particular kind of data involved.

Data are organized into four levels for processing:
1. *Character:* numeral, letter, punctuation, or other symbol.
2. *Data element:* characters grouped to specify a particular unit of information—order number, date, customer's name and address.
3. *Record:* one or more data elements related in some meaningful way—same transaction, same physical object, same customer, etc. Records can consist of several levels of data elements. For example, the data element "customer's address" can be further classified into "street," "city," and "state," as separate data elements.
4. *File:* a collection of related records.

There are several schemes for organizing data elements for processing, based on the fact that the length of the elements may vary greatly. Under the "selectable-length" scheme any length may be chosen for an element—say, the stock number—but, once chosen, all stock numbers must be given the same length at the expense of filling out short numbers with zeros. Selecting a long record to handle the longest stock number may entail additional processing for all records.

The "variable-length" scheme allows any item to be any length, without restraint. The end of each item is identified by an item indicator (which may be combined with its last character or the first character of the following item) or an item separator used between every two items. Under this scheme, an item is identified not by its location but by its sequential relationship to other items. To keep the item-count correct, this plan requires identification of any items omitted.

The "fixed-word-and-block" scheme specifies the number of characters that are treated as a word, and the number of words handled as a block. The word and block length are designed into the equipment by the manufacturer, and the user must adhere to his specifications.

CHAPTER 3

PROCESSING EQUIPMENT—BASIC PROCESSOR AND STORAGE

A data-processing system consists of a number of individual components, each of which has its own tasks. Efficient processing requires units to prepare data in machine language, read the data into the processor, store the data, perform arithmetical or logical operations, accept data from the processor, present results in usable form, and control the entire operation.

MAJOR COMPONENTS

Figure 3-1 is a schematic diagram of the major components of a data-processing system. *Data preparation devices* include card punches, character readers, and by-product paper-tape punches. They convert data in written or verbal form into machine media— generally magnetic tape or punched cards. Special *communication devices* bring data to the processing system over telephone and telegraph lines from remote locations—different rooms, buildings, cities, or even countries. Sometimes data preparation or communication devices transmit data directly to high-speed storage, but generally

51

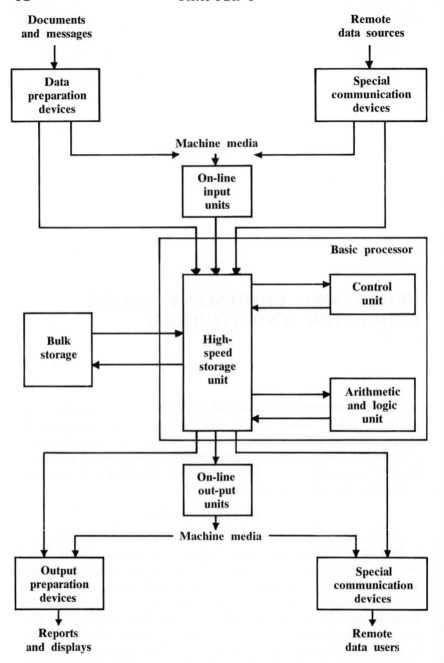

FIGURE 3-1. *Schematic of major components of a data-processing system.*

they produce machine-processable media as an intermediate step. *On-line input units*—commonly magnetic-tape or punched-card readers—are directly connected to the processor in order to read data from the machine media into the processor.

The *basic processor* consists of a control unit, an arithmetic and logic unit, and a high-speed storage unit. The *control unit* is comparable to a telephone switchboard, for it sets switches to direct the flow of data through the system and to initiate the desired arithmetical or logical operations. The *arithmetic and logic unit* might be viewed as a combination of a desk calculator and a dependable, extremely fast clerk. This unit performs addition, subtraction, multiplication and division. By comparing data items, it decides whether Jones precedes or follows Brown in alphabetical sequence, or whether the quantity of a particular inventory item is above or below its reorder point. The *high-speed storage unit*—usually magnetic cores or a magnetic drum—receives data from input units, supplies data and instructions to the control and arithmetic units during processing, and furnishes results to the output unit. The high-speed storage unit contains thousands of individual locations that can store either data or instructions at any time.

Since high-speed storage is costly, and therefore limited in size, many processors have *on-line bulk storage* as an option to supplement the high-speed storage. All the contents of the bulk storage unit, which may contain both data and instructions, are available directly to the processor, but at a slower speed than data in high-speed storage. Bulk storage units—magnetic disk files and large drums—will hold millions of characters of data or instructions.

Processor *output functions* and equipment are similar to those used for input in many respects. Results of processing are often written out of high-speed storage onto magnetic tape, although the data may go directly to a printer, a card punch, or a communication device.

Modern data-processing systems are highly *modular*. Various input, output, and bulk storage devices can be attached to most basic processors and even to small-scale ones. The basic processor itself is generally available with two to four different sizes of high-speed storage plus many special options to increase processing speed and to simplify programming. The careful and informed user often can find, or assemble, a system closely tailored to his needs. If his workload grows or declines, he can modify, within limits, his processor to fit.

The remainder of this chapter discusses the equipment and operation of the basic processor and bulk storage. Input, communications, and output are covered in Chapter 4.

CONTROL AND OPERATIONS

The control and operation functions are at the heart of an electronic data processor; they are responsible for on-line data handling throughout the processing system. The *control function* includes the circuitry that selects each instruction in the proper sequence, interprets each instruction, and causes all other parts of the processor to carry out the actions specified in an instruction. The various operations—addition, subtraction, comparisons, rearrangement—are carried out by circuitry in the *arithmetic and logic function*. Briefly, the steps in over-all control and operations for read-in, process, and write-out are as follows. Under guidance of the control unit, the input units read data for transfer into specified locations of the high-speed storage unit. To process data, the control unit obtains an instruction from high-speed storage and interprets it. The control unit then sets up arithmetic and logic circuitry as specified by the instructions, gets data from high-speed storage, executes the specified operation on the data, and returns the result to high-speed storage. Later, the control unit interprets the output instructions to send results to an output unit.

Instruction Routines

The control unit causes other components to carry out the necessary operations. A list of coded instructions, called an *instruction routine* or *program routine,* tells the control unit what to do and what sequence to follow. The instructions might say "ADD X TO Y," "WRITE PAY-RECORD ON TAPE UNIT 3," or "STOP." Each instruction tells the control unit what operation to perform, which data to use, and where to place the results.

Instruction routines are supplied to data processors in several ways. The method used by *internally-stored program* processors is to read instructions into high-speed storage just as if they were data and then execute the instructions while they are in internal storage. Another method is to design the routine into the equipment to perform a special purpose. A third method is to set up the routine in a wiring board as an externally-stored program.

Internally-Stored Programs.   A processor with the capability for an internally-stored program reads instruction routines and data from input units and places them in high-speed storage (or perhaps bulk storage). The routines are then ready for execution by the control unit and can be used to operate on the data. Instructions and data look alike to the processor and can be placed anywhere desired in storage. The programmer must plan to have the processor *execute* instructions and *operate* on data. It is, furthermore, useful to operate on instructions to modify them; but it is not meaningful to try to execute data.

The important point here is that reading in another program enables the processor to do different things to a different kind of data. The read-in operation takes seconds or only minutes depending on the length of the program and whether it is stored on magnetic tape, punched cards, or paper tape. Typical programs range from several hundred to many thousands of individual instructions.

The amount of work accomplished by each instruction in a program depends on the *instruction format* of the processor. Each instruction for a *single-address* processor consists of two parts: an *operation code*—ADD, SUBTRACT, READ, WRITE, or other verb—and the *address* of data in storage or the identification number of a device, such as a tape unit.

The instruction "ADD 200" has a *single address* and means, "Add the contents of high-speed storage location 200 to the contents of a special area where sums are formed." A *two-address* processor is designed for instructions that contain an operation code plus two addresses. "SUBTRACT 200, 300" might mean, "Subtract the contents of location 200 from the contents of location 300." Some processors are designed with a *three-address* format. "MULTIPLY 100, 200, 300" might mean, "Multiply the contents of location 100 by the contents of location 200 and store the product in location 300." Many variations of instruction format exist, but each consists of an operation code plus one or more addresses or special designators. Note the important point that the *references to storage* locations 100, 200, and 300 above are just that. Each reference *does not* say anything at all about what a storage location contains. The programmer must arrange, either by read-in or by prior processing, to have the desired *operand*—the data item to be worked on—in the correct storage location when an instruction involving the contents of that location is executed. This idea is basically a familiar one: desk calculators and adding machines will add whatever is set up in the keyboard when the add key is depressed. The add key is, in effect, an instruction to add the *contents* of the keyboard to the contents of the machine's accumulator. Of course, the number has to be set up in the keyboard, but that operation is a separate action.

Processors that use internally-stored programs have three highly desirable features. Most important is the ability to change programs easily and quickly merely by reading in another program from magnetic tape or punched cards. The second is the ability to select the next instruction on the basis of the results of processing up to that point. The instruction "IF ACCOUNT BALANCE IS NEGATIVE GO TO INSTRUCTION 37, OTHERWISE GO TO INSTRUCTION 85" allows the processor to select the appropriate next instruction—37 or 85—depending on whether "ACCOUNT BALANCE" is negative or positive when tested by this "IF" instruction. Finally, the control and operations functions can process or operate on instructions as well as on data. The processor can modify instructions to change the address part, operation part, or both, as required to cope with conditions encountered in the data during processing. Chapters 7 and 8 discuss the address format of instructions and these features.

Special-Purpose Equipment. Special-purpose equipment with instruction routines designed into its circuits and wires can prove efficient for a single important application, such as inventory control or demand analysis. Special-purpose equipment is sometimes used for operations requiring many remote input-output stations. But special-purpose equipment has high research and development costs per unit since few systems are made from a particular design. The inherent inflexibility of special-purpose equipment exposes it to the risk of being discarded whenever the application changes for any reason; and most applications tend to change frequently.

Externally-Stored Programs. Several models of small processors have instruction routines stored in a wiring board or plug board. Wires or pins are manually put into a board, which is later inserted in the machine. The wires or pins call up operations in their proper sequence. Each application requires the use of a separate, individually prepared control board for the processor. Wired instruction routines can make some decisions and choose different processing paths, but the wires or pins, being physically inserted by hand, are not alterable while the machine is running. Wired instruction-board equipment is more flexible than special-purpose equipment, but it is less readily adaptable to new applications than internally-stored program equipment. Instruction boards are powerful enough for most problems handled by small computers, but they are unwieldy for a lengthy routine because a different board is needed for each major phase of processing.

Arithmetic, Logic, and Control Unit

The arithmetic, logic, and control units for internally-stored program processors contain registers, decoders, and counters. A *register* is a special-purpose storage location that may be as large as a few hundred characters. It is designed as part of high-speed storage or as a separate device inside the basic processor. An *instruction register* holds the program instruction that the processor is currently executing. An *address register* holds the address of the operand specified by the instruction. In simple terms, an *operand* is the content of a storage location that is to be operated on or that results from an operation. Examples of operands are inventory quantity and unit cost, which can be multiplied together to get inventory value. A *decoder* translates the operation code part of an instruction by setting up the appropriate arithmetic and logic circuits for its performance.

Instruction Counter. The instruction counter stores the address of the next instruction to be executed. If instructions in storage are being executed in sequence, the number in the counter is increased by one in each cycle. To change the sequence or go to a different part of the program, the counter is reset to zero or to any desired instruction by a "jump" instruction (also called "transfer," "branch," or "go to" instruction).

Accumulator. Circuits and devices in the arithmetic and logic function vary widely with equipment, but they are essentially similar from the user's viewpoint. An *accumulator* is a register to form sums and other arithmetic results for single-address equipment that handles one operand at a time.

The accumulator is as long as a processor word with provision for a plus or minus sign and an overflow bit to indicate the sum is too big to store.

For performing addition, the control unit instructs the equipment:
1. Copy the first number or operand from a storage location into the accumulator

2. Get the second number from a storage location and add to (or subtract a negative number from) the number in the accumulator
3. Continue to add (or subtract) other numbers or copy the accumulator content into a storage location

Note that the accumulator is necessary for single-address equipment. Since the processor handles only one number at a time, it needs a special location to "accumulate" the numbers it is working on.

A two-address or three-address processor brings up both operands simultaneously and adds them in an adder capable of forming the sum of two or more quantities instead of in an accumulator. Addition and subtraction of seven-digit operands (seven digits are used as a specific word size for discussion here and in Chapter 8) can be handled by an eight-digit accumulator. Seven digits are for the answer and the eighth digit is for *overflow* (a single bit would serve for overflow) to indicate when an answer outgrows the seven-digit space.

M-Q Register. The M-Q register (short for multiplier-quotient register) is used in multiplication and division. Multiplication of two seven-digit numbers may give a fourteen-digit product. The accumulator holds the first or high-order seven digits of the product, and the M-Q register (think of it as a right-hand extension of the accumulator) holds the right-hand seven digits.

All fourteen digits of the product in the accumulator and M-Q register are available and can be stored, if the degree of *precision*— the number of digits in the answer—warrants. Otherwise, the significant seven digits can be saved and the effect of rounding carried over from the discarded digits to the right-most digit in the accumulator. If any number of significant digits other than the seven in the accumulator or the M-Q register are to be saved, some shifting operations—movement to left or right of the digits in the product— will be required for positioning the desired digits in either the accumulator or the M-Q register before storing them. In division operations, the quotient ends up in the M-Q register and the remainder is in the accumulator.

Chapter 8 describes how arithmetic operations are carried on from the programmer's viewpoint. It is sufficient for our purposes to say that arithmetic operations are performed *quickly and accurately* at a rate from a few thousand to a million or more per second, with only one mistake in hundreds of thousands or millions of operations.

The foregoing comments about the location of the results of arithmetic operations refer to actual machine operations. When a programmer uses a higher-level language, say, COBOL (described in Chapter 7), he can use SUM, REMAINDER, PRODUCT, QUOTIENT, or some other convenient name to refer to the result of each of the arithmetic operations. A special program called a "compiler" is used to translate these names to the machine equivalent of accumulator and M-Q register before the program is executed. In this way, the programmer is not concerned with the precise arrangement and location of arithmetic results, although he may be able to improve processor performance if he understands the operating details.

Control Unit.   Somewhat simplified, the control unit of a typical processor operates in the following way to execute an instruction.

1. The control unit *reads* the instruction contained in the particular storage location indicated by the *instruction counter.*
2. The control unit *decodes* the pulses in the instruction received from storage. Each sequence of pulses causes the control unit to *carry out* a specific operation, such as compare, add, or store operands. Pulses also indicate the location of the operands involved in the operation.
3. The control unit reads either the next instruction in sequence or goes to one at another place, as directed by the instruction counter.

Instructions and data in processor storage are distinguished solely by the routing of pulses from internal storage. Pulses routed to the control unit are interpreted as instructions; those routed to the arithmetic unit are treated as data.

Operating Cycle

The operating cycle for a single-address processor is shown schematically in Figure 3-2. Assume that computations are in process and one operating cycle is observed just after an instruction is put into the instruction register. The instruction register contains an instruction, such as "ADD 268," copied from location 062. The instruction "ADD 268" means, "Add the contents of storage location 268 to the contents of the accumulator." The operating cycle, for present purposes, consists of seven steps repeated as many times as are required to execute a program The numbers in the steps below correspond to those on Figure 3-2 showing data flow and control lines.

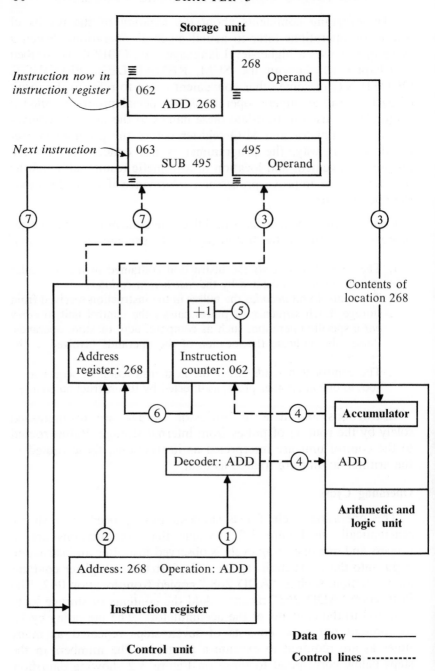

FIGURE 3-2. *Operation of control unit in a single-address processor.*

1. Transfer the operation part of the instruction, ADD, from the instruction register to the decoder.
2. Transfer the address part of the instruction, 268, from the instruction register to the address register.
3. Copy into the arithmetic unit the operand (which may be either data or an instruction) contained in storage location 268.
4. Execute the required operation, ADD, in the arithmetic unit, and notify the control unit that the operation is complete.
5. Increase the number 062 in the instruction counter by 1 to 063, to indicate the address of the next instruction.
6. Transfer the number 063 from the instruction counter to the address register.
7. Get the instruction located at address 063, "SUB 495," and put it into the instruction register.

This simplified operating cycle is repeated in the sequence given unless the program instructs the processor to halt operations or some condition arises during program execution that forces it to halt. Examples of conditions forcing a halt are a nonexistent instruction or address encountered in the program and a sum that overflows accumulator or storage capacity.

Control Console

The operator and the machine communicate with each other through the machine console. Man-machine communication is necessary for several reasons. An operator places the first program instruction in the instruction register or sets its location in the instruction counter to start processing operations. The internally-stored program then takes over and controls operations.

The control console is used for detecting some program mistakes —a process often called "debugging." The console, along with test equipment, is useful for locating machine malfunctions. The console has neon lights or other means of displaying the contents of desired storage locations or registers. An operator can set switches to stop operations in order to read the content of a storage location, observe an instruction, or examine the arithmetic unit after each instruction. A console usually shows why a machine stops—defective input, a mistake in the program, an overflow condition, or the end of the program.

Debugging. An operator or the programmer might trace a mistake by repeating the program step by step while he watches the console, but experienced users rule out *console debugging.* Console tracing of a routine is inefficient because machine speed is limited to the individual's reaction time. Special debugging programs—traces and post-mortems—are more efficient. While the program is running, a *trace* routine will obtain, for each instruction executed, the contents of the instruction counter, instruction register, accumulator, M-Q register, various cycle counters (to indicate the number of times a particular program segment has been executed), and other selected storage locations. This information on how the program operated while it was running can be printed for the programmer to study at a later time.

Post-Mortems. A post-mortem routine causes the processor to record selected information about the contents of registers *after* a mistake causes the program to stop running. The programmer uses print-outs from the trace and post-mortem to locate mistakes without tying up the processor.

The console may be used to enter small quantities of data when the processor is stopped or to interrogate a file record stored on a drum or disk. The record desired is indicated on the console keyboard, the processor locates it in storage and sends it to the console typewriter for type-out.

The console may also be used in checking equipment operation to locate specific malfunctions when something is wrong. Some processors have a separate maintenance console since the problems and level of detail in checking equipment are different from those handled by the operator's console.

INSTRUCTION REPERTOIRE

Each data processor is designed to execute a repertoire of machine operations, instructions, or commands. The programmer uses combinations of these operations to process data in a desired fashion. Actually, a few basic operations—subtract, shift a number to left or right, store, read, write, and go to another point in the program if the result is negative—are sufficient to do extensive processing. This is true in much the same way that a pocketknife can be used to make anything out of wood—assuming that the whittler has enough wood and patience. However, several of these basic instructions would be needed for each step of a problem and their use would be slow and inefficient in both programming and machine operation. Therefore, manufacturers design a much larger repertoire of operations into each processor. Typically ranging from thirty to more than a hundred operations, it offers programming convenience and faster operating speeds. The instruction repertoire includes arithmetic, logic, and input-output control operations.

Arithmetic Operations

Commands to accomplish addition, subtraction, and multiplication of numbers are commonplace in most modern processors, but a command to perform division may be available only as a special option at extra cost. For economy of machine design the manufacturer may omit the divide command but provide a *subroutine*—a set of instructions—for division. A subroutine obtains the same result but uses more machine time than direct division. If the division operation is infrequently used in business data processing, then separate circuitry for it may be an unnecessary expense. This example typifies the design problem facing the equipment manufacturer and user: "How to balance the convenience and speed of another machine command against the cost of providing it?" Arithmetic operations as a group are only a small fraction—say, one-fifth to one-third—of the processor operations performed in business data processing.

Program Modification.   Arithmetic operations are performed equally well on data and on instructions. The programmer may wish to send an instruction to the arithmetic unit while the program is running in order to treat it as data and modify it. For example, the programmer's written instruction "ADD 485" could mean, "Add the *contents* of storage location *485* to the *contents* of the accumulator." This instruction is read into the processor as part of the instruction routine, and converted by the processor into the number 010 485 for internal storage and execution. The "010" means ADD to the processor, although "ADD" is more easily understood by people. The instruction "010 485" can be altered by placing it in the accumulator and adding to it the contents of a storage location that contains "000 001" to get "010 486." When this modified instruction is returned to storage and executed in a later cycle, it specifies the *contents* of location 486 for use in the next addition operation. The ability to operate on and change an instruction during processing is the most important feature of internally-stored program processors. Address modification, which in this example is done in a simple machine language, is handled more adroitly from the programmer's viewpoint by the programming languages described in Chapters 7 and 8.

Decisions. The arithmetic capability of processors is also used to make *simple decisions* or choices between alternatives. When *numbers* are involved, a decision is merely an extension of addition or subtraction operations. The arithmetic unit distinguishes between positive and negative numbers. Depending on whether the remainder obtained by subtracting one number from another is positive or negative, the appropriate sequence of instructions is selected next. For example, a 5 per cent discount may be allowed on sales of $50.00 and over. To check for a discount, the $50.00 is first converted to 5000 pennies by eliminating the "$" and "." from the data before read-in. Processors will perform arithmetic operations on all-numeric operands, but not on operands that contain symbols such as "$" and ".". It is then possible to determine whether the amount of sale is 5000 pennies or more merely by subtracting 4999 pennies from the sales price and examining the remainder. If the remainder is positive, program control is sent to the subroutine for calculating discount. No discount is allowed, of course, if the remainder is zero or negative, so the program execution continues without going to the discount subroutine.

Logical Operations

Logical operations differ from arithmetic operations in several ways. First, logical operations can deal with any or all of the characters available to the processor—numerals, letters, punctuation, and special symbols. The business user does not want to do arithmetic on letters, punctuation, and frequently not on numbers. He wants to sequence, compare, or rearrange these data items. Second, logical operations treat data as a fixed set of symbols; there are no carries to or borrows from another position as is the case for arithmetic operations. Logical operations are important in business data processing.

Comparison. The comparison operation is useful for examining the individual character positions of two fields. A data item containing letters usually cannot be subtracted from another item to find which is smaller or, more correctly, which comes first in the collating sequence. Most processors "hang up" when attempting to operate arithmetically on operands containing letters, for letter codes do not fit the rules for addition and subtraction operations.

Data items consisting of *letters, numerals,* or *both* can be compared in order to find which one is earlier or later in the *alphanumeric* sequence of the collation table. The binary value for B is higher than for A, that for C higher than for B, and Z has the highest binary value of the letters. Numerals may come before or after letters depending upon the particular processor. *Logical comparison* of the name entries "Jones, John" and "Brown, John" shows that "Jones, John" has a higher collation table value. In a sorting run using names, "Jones" will be placed after "Brown" to develop an alphabetic sequence. The essence of alphabetic sorting is comparison of keys so as to arrange records in the collation table sequence of letter values. One type of comparison instruction has three possible results—"less than," "equal to," and "greater than"—and the proper use is made of each outcome to branch— jump or send program control—to three places (or perhaps two if primary interest is in the greater case and the other two—say, less than and equal to—are treated alike) in the program to continue processing.

Numeric values—for example, stock numbers and invoice numbers—are also used as keys to sort items into numeric sequence. Comparison is preferable to subtraction for numbers (even though subtraction could be used) to find whether one item is smaller or larger than another. The comparison operation leaves the two numbers unchanged; subtraction, on the other hand, may change one number to a remainder.

Editing. Editing by use of an extraction command is another logical operation provided by some processors. To "extract" means to remove from a set all the items that meet some criterion. Extraction is used to edit one or more selected characters either out of or into a word in the following way. An extractor consisting of 0's and 1's is placed in a storage register. The accumulator holds the data to be edited. Another storage location contains the editing symbols—such as decimal points, commas, and dollar signs—to be combined with desired characters in the accumulator to give the edited result. When the edit or extract command is executed, the extractor word guides the combining of the accumulator and the editing characters. Assume the following content in the processor:

Extractor	1000100
Accumulator	0684029
Storage location 379	$ - - - . - -

Execution of an *extract odd-character* order, written here for simplicity as EXO 379, will replace the characters in the accumulator with characters from location 379 that have *positions* corresponding to the odd-value characters in the extractor. The content of the accumulator after executing the EXO 379 order is as follows, with nothing else changed:

Accumulator $684.29

The extract order or variations of it can be used for editing— inserting the dollar sign, commas, and decimal point and for replacing leading zeros with asterisks (***)—in money amounts before printing checks to pay employees or vendors. Other schemes for output editing are discussed in Chapter 7.

Shifting. The *shift instruction* is another logical operation. Shifting involves moving a word to the right or left within the accumulator and M-Q register. That is, simultaneously all characters in a word are moved one or more positions to the right or left. An important use of shifting is to align data items containing letters before comparing them or to align data items containing numerals before adding them. Continued shifting in one direction causes characters to drop off at that end of a word; and zeros occupy spaces arising at the other end.

Many variations of the basic logical operations are possible. Each manufacturer supplies the set that he believes will be most useful to the user. The programmer then puts together combinations of these basic operations to do his particular jobs.

Input and Output Control

A user needs adequate capabilities for getting data in and results out of a processor; therefore, input and output operations are usually well represented in machine instruction repertoires. A processor with magnetic tape has commands to read data from tape into storage, write data from storage onto tape, back-space the tape, rewind it, and, perhaps search the tape. It also has commands to read punched cards, or other form of data input from devices attached to the system. In addition to writing on tape, commands are available to write data out on printers and display data on console or remote typewriters and even on television tubes. Control features include the ability to specify format in printing: single or double space, skip any desired number of lines, and start new pages when desired.

Data Channels.   A basic processor is designed to perform only one of three operations at any one time: read, compute, or write. Performing only one operation at a time makes total processing time equal the sum of the individual times spent for reading, computing, and writing. By designing the system to handle three (or perhaps only two) of these operations at one time—called "concurrent" or "overlapped" operations—total processing time is reduced. It may be shortened to the longest one of the three operation times instead of being the sum of the three. There are several design schemes for getting overlapped operations between the central processor and input and output operations.

Large processors have *data channels* for input and output control. A data channel, which is almost a small processor by itself, compensates for the differences between processing speed and input and output speeds. When programming for a data-channel machine, the programmer merely writes an instruction—for example, "Read a punched card." When the processor encounters this instruction, it sets up the circuits to read the card and then continues other operations. While the card-reading unit is reading one card at the restricted speeds of card handling and reading, the processor can independently perform many thousands of other operations.

Trapping.   After the card-reading operation is finished, the data channel *traps* or *interrupts* the main program, and transfers control to a special location simply by resetting the instruction counter. At this special location, the programmer has placed all the instructions he wants executed each time that a card-reading operation is finished.

With data-channel operation, an input or output unit that finishes its assigned task interrupts the main program and, in essence, asks for further instructions. By operating in this fashion a large processor can, at one time, be reading data from one unit, writing on another, and doing an arithmetic or logic operation. As might be expected, data channels are expensive. Small processors with slower internal speeds have less need for concurrent operations and generally are designed without channels.

HIGH-SPEED STORAGE

Fast and efficient processing of large volumes of data depends on the availability of adequate high-speed storage. In large processors, the arithmetic, logic, and control circuitry can perform a few hundred thousand or perhaps a million or more operations per second. Utilization of this capability requires that data and instructions be obtained and put away at corresponding speeds. Indeed, the development of more powerful processors is closely linked to the availability of larger and faster high-speed storage. Early processors had a few hundred to several thousand words of high-speed storage, with any word typically available for processing in several *milliseconds* (thousandths of a second). Today's large processors offer perhaps a hundred thousand words, and each word is available in a few *microseconds* (millionths of a second). Tomorrow's processors will probably have larger storage with access times measured in *nanoseconds* (billionths of a second).

Storage-Unit Characteristics

Proper evaluation and selection of high-speed storage is critical if one is to obtain balanced performance from a processor. However, selecting the most suitable storage unit on the basis of its characteristics and application requirements is a complex task. Even the informed user has difficulty in precisely stating his requirements. If one knows nothing of the jargon, diverse measures, and various attributes of storage, he might as well resort to flipping a coin. More rationally, data storage can be analyzed and evaluated by the way that data are represented, method used to get and put away data, time required to obtain data, capacity of the storage unit, and permanency of storage.

Data Representation. Most units use some version of a *binary* scheme, as described in Chapter 2, to represent data in storage. Processors that handle numbers only may use four bits for one decimal digit. Many alphanumeric computers designed primarily for business applications use six bits for each letter, numeral, or other symbol. Some processors are designed to combine the eight bits that would be used for two numerals and store one letter—a "two-for-one" scheme. Others store two six-bit symbols for letters in the twelve bits that could represent three numerals—a "three-for-two" scheme. Some newer processors have dual or multiple modes: they represent numbers in pure binary, but use groups of six bits for alphabetic data. In this way, a binary word represents a number without wasting any bits, and represents alphabetical characters as efficiently as a machine with the six-bit, alphanumeric mode. Arithmetic and logic operations on binary data tend to be fast and efficient, but binary processors often must convert numbers from decimal to binary when they are first handled. After the numbers are converted, the binary form may be retained throughout all processing until the final stage, when a conversion from binary to alphanumeric mode and printing is necessary for people to read the output.

Addressing Schemes.   A storage unit may be designed so that numerals and letters can be stored at identifiable locations; this scheme is called *addressable storage.* When a data item is wanted, it is obtained from its known location. With *nonaddressable storage,* storage locations are not specified, and some type of scanning or searching through a file is required to locate a data-item.

An address is assigned to each location in addressable storage units. The programmer must organize data in storage to obtain data when wanted. A programmer can use as *absolute addresses* the numbers that identify locations in storage.

However, most manufacturers supply schemes that use the processor to assist the programmer in keeping track of the storage locations he assigns to data and program instructions. By these techniques, the programmer can use *data-names,* such as "CUSTOMER NAME" and "CUSTOMER ADDRESS," in his program to refer to the name and address data items in each record in the customer file. He also can use *procedure-names,* such as "CALCULATE NET-PAY" or "UPDATE INVENTORY," to refer to the sections in his program designed to perform these operations. The programmer must, of course, describe his identification scheme to the processor by means of a *data description* section in his program so that the processor can correctly associate the assigned names with storage locations. By following a specially written program, called an "assembler" or "compiler," depending on how it works, the processor can associate such names with specific addresses in storage. A programmer can refer to an item in storage by some identifying name when writing his program even though he does not know where it will be when the program is executed. He need not worry about the exact location of data or even program routines in storage so long as they actually will be there when wanted and he knows what name to call each one in his program.

The number of characters referred to by an address within a program is different for word and character machines. For a fixed-word machine, one address refers to a *word* of, say, 8, 10, or 12 characters as designed by the manufacturer. Processors designed to handle each character individually use an address to refer to one *character,* and any character can be addressed, if desired. Either the first or last character in a group being handled as a data-item or field is usually addressed, depending on the equipment design; and the other end of the field is indicated by a special field or item mark.

Mode of Operation. "Mode of operation" refers to the way that bits, characters, and words are moved. In the *serial* mode, the bits, characters, or words of data are moved one after another in time sequence. In the *parallel* mode, two or more bits are read simultaneously. Generally, some combination of the two modes is used. On magnetic tape the bits in a character are usually read in parallel, and characters that make up a word are read serially—parallel by bits and serial by character. If storage and arithmetic unit modes are different, data go through a buffer for modification as required. The problem of serial versus parallel operations, like most other problems, is resolved in terms of economics. The question is whether the increased speed achieved at a particular stage by using more equipment for parallel instead of serial operations is worth the cost.

Capacity. The capacity of a storage device is expressed as the number of bits, decimal digits, alphanumeric characters, or words it can store at one time. Each of these units of measure is used under varying conditions, so that conversion from the various units to one standard is helpful for comparison. The cost of storage is closely related to the number of bits, so that bits are one possible standard. If most of the data handled are numeric, the capacity might be measured in numeric digits. If much of the data is alphanumeric, the capacity for alphanumeric symbols is relevant.

Effective capacity for storage organized as *fixed-length* words is often less than the stated capacity because short data items may waste some of the space allotted to each storage word. *Packing* two or more short data items into one word will save space; but packing and unpacking operations may increase processing time. Long data items may occupy more than one storage word. The loss of storage is small in a word machine if storage is used mainly to hold program instructions, most of which are designed just to fit in one word. But some processors are designed with a variable-length instruction format that uses fewer characters for short, simple instructions.

A *variable-field* processor, on the other hand, uses minimum space to store each data element, but it raises questions about how to keep track of where each element is. In addition, the special symbol that indicates the end of each field may occupy part of available storage. Similar comments apply to short data records because they may waste storage space on tape: either they are filled out to longer blocks or there are too many inter-record gaps, if stored individually in variable-length fields. *Blocking* data records together into longer blocks, depending on design and operation of the processor and tape units, can economize space, operating time, or both.

Access Time.   Another major characteristic of storage is its *access time*—the length of time between a call for data from storage and completion of the delivery. Some processors with magnetic core storage have access times of less than a microsecond, though most are in the range of 1 to 20 microseconds. These high speeds are obtained because data in core storage are electronically addressable and no mechanical movement, which is much slower than electronic switching, is involved.

In magnetic drum and disk storage units, another addressing method is used: the data move serially past read-write heads until the desired address or item is found. *Average access* time for data on drums ranges from 2 to 50 milliseconds. Average access for data in disk storage runs from 10 milliseconds to several seconds.

A third method for getting access to an item involves scanning the data because there is no specified address. The data on magnetic and paper tape, for example, are scanned until a desired item is found; however, this method is seldom used by high-speed storage devices.

Minimum access time is the length of the time required to get data from the storage location that is most readily available. *Maximum access* time applies to the least readily-available storage location. For magnetic core storage the minimum and maximum are the same. In most others—drums, disk, tapes—these times are substantially different. Both the average access time and the range from minimum to maximum have an important effect on over-all processing time. Transfer rates—the speed at which individual characters are handled after the first one is accessed—also bear on storage speed and its effect on processor control of storage and operating speeds.

Most magnetic and electronic storage devices are erasable and nonvolatile. *Erasable* means that previously stored data can be removed and replaced by new data. *Nonvolatile* means that stored data remain intact when electrical power is stopped; but the lack of this feature need not be critical. Either lost data can be reconstructed by reprocessing original data, or intermediate results can be stored as a precaution. Interestingly, some processors designed for military purposes are required to have volatile storage for security reasons. The contents of storage, and even the storage unit itself, can be destroyed whenever advisable.

High-Speed Storage Devices

Typically, high-speed storage facilities form an integral part of the basic processor circuitry, although the storage unit may be physically separated from the processor. The storage device holds the program that is being used and the data involved in processing. The data are read directly from storage to the arithmetic, logic, and control units for processing.

High-speed storage is organized into thousands of individual *locations*—at the level of character, word, or field—that can store data or instructions. Each location has a *unique address* so that it can be located by its number or by a simple description—as we would locate a house by its address: "1627 Ann Arbor Avenue." The access time for high-speed storage is short, but capacity is limited by economic considerations. Core storage to hold one bit may cost about half a dollar, whereas drums are less expensive though slower. Magnetic cores and magnetic drums are the most commonly used high-speed storage devices.

Magnetic Core. A magnetic core is a doughnut-shaped ring of iron the size of a match-head capable of retaining either one of two magnetic states. Magnetic cores are placed where *write* wires cross to form a grid. Electric current passed through selected "X" and "Y" wires goes through each core and changes the magnetic state of the core at the junction of the two wires. The state of other cores along each one of the two wires remains unchanged. A current passed in one direction through the wires magnetizes the core; a current sent in the opposite direction along the wires reverses the core's magnetic state. One state represents a 1, the other a 0.

Reading is done by writing a 0 in the core and watching what happens. In addition to write wires, *read* wires pass through every core and detect if its magnetic state changes when a 0 is written. If the core already contains a 0, nothing happens. If it is in the 1 state, a change occurs which is detected by the read wire. The magnetic state of the core is, in effect, "read" from the induced current caused by writing. For a core in the 1 state, this reading technique is destructive; its prior state must be regenerated by an appropriate write signal. Newer designs of magnetic cores have nondestructive readout, therefore no rewrite is required, and they can operate at higher speeds.

Each magnetic core holds one bit. Cores are arranged in planes (Figure 3-3) that may have, say, 32, 64, or some other number

FIGURE 3-3. *Magnetic core storage plane and assembly.*

of cores in each direction for a total of 1024 or 4096. Many core planes—say, 37 or 48, depending on the number of bits for data and parity treated as a word by the designer—make up a storage unit. The bits that make up a word are often placed in the same X and Y position on each plane and read in parallel. Thus a word of 37 bits may be stored in the cores located in row 9 and column 53 of every one of the 37 planes. The 37 cores may be used to store a variety of data—a 36-bit binary number and sign, or 6 six-bit alphabetical characters, or 9 four-bit decimal numerals and sign.

The basic storage capacity of 1024, 4096, or 8192 words in a single set of core planes may be increased by using several storage units for one processor. Modular construction of storage units allows the user to order and "plug in" one or more units to meet his storage requirements.

Magnetic-core access time is in the range of a fraction of a microsecond to 200 microseconds and is the fastest and most common high-speed storage device in general use. It is both erasable and nonvolatile. Magnetic cores are individually inexpensive, but the associated electronic circuits make them much more expensive than a magnetic drum for each bit of storage capacity.

Magnetic Drum.   A drum is a metal cylinder coated with magnetic material. Read-write heads are mounted in the drum housing and the drum rotates past them. Circular recording tracks, or *bands* are thus formed around the drum by the heads, which are located close together so that there are several bands to the inch (Figure 3-4). Each band around the drum can be thought of as being divided into many small areas, each of which can store a bit. A magnetized area represents a 1; an area magnetized in the opposite direction, or perhaps left unmagnetized, represents a 0. A read-write head is usually located at one point for a band on the drum so that all data written on the band come into reading position once each revolution. A bit is written into or read from a particular unit area on a track as it rotates under the read-write head; and access time to data stored on a drum depends on rotational speed and the location of desired data. The maximum access time of a full revolution arises when data that are wanted have just passed the track reading head. The minimum access is for data just coming into reading position when wanted. The average access time is equal to one-half of a drum revolution, plus some time to set up the reading circuit.

There are several ways to reduce average access time. One is

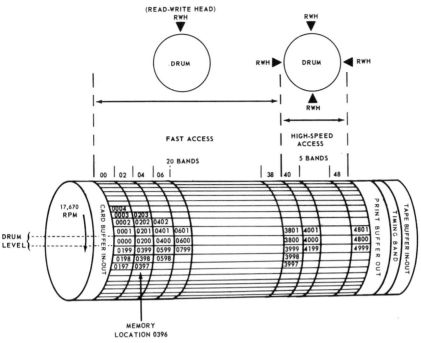

FIGURE 3-4. *Magnetic drum, schematic.*

to space program instructions and data around the drum so that the content of each desired location becomes available just as it is needed.

Another is to place separate writing and reading heads at short intervals around one band. In such cases, a writing head records data on the drum, and a fraction of a revolution later, when the data move under the reading head, they are read and returned to the prior writing head. This combination of a writing head, a short space on the drum, and a reading head connected back to the writing head makes a *revolver loop*. All data in the loop are read continuously as the drum revolves and can be sent off for processing, if desired. Some drums have several revolver loops to shorten the access time for data on a few tracks to a small fraction of the maximum access time.

Magnetic drums in use today vary greatly in capacity and operating speeds. Drums used as high-speed storage range from 4 to 12 inches in diameter and rotate at speeds of 3,000 to 17,000 revolutions a minute to give average access times of 2 to 10 milliseconds. Capacities range from 10,000 to 60,000 numeric characters. It costs less to store a bit on a magnetic drum than on other devices used for internal storage; the data are erasable and nonvolatile.

Magnetic drums are sometimes utilized for high-speed storage in small or medium-sized processors, but slow access rules them out for primary storage in large processors. The use of slow-access drums to provide secondary storage—*bulk storage*—for processors will be discussed later.

Some large processors use a *combination* of devices for high-speed storage. For example, a machine with 4000 words of magnetic-drum storage may in addition have 100 words of magnetic-core storage. Data and instructions are moved from drum to core at the start of a series of operations. The cores are used to hold intermediate results and instructions during processing. When processing is complete, the results are returned to the drum.

A relatively small amount of *very fast storage* substantially increases processing speeds under other conditions. Machines with 4-microsecond-access magnetic cores as the main high-speed storage unit may have a hundred or so words of either ultra high-speed core or thin film storage with access times of a few hundred nanoseconds. *Thin film storage* consists of a glass or ceramic plate with small dots of magnetic material that operate in about the same way as magnetic core storage.

As mentioned earlier, the *registers*—accumulator, address registers, instruction counter, and others—in the arithmetic, logic, and control units are actually special types of storage devices. Sometimes these registers are reserved locations in the main high-speed storage unit; for example, word 1000 might be the accumulator, 1001 the M-Q register, and so forth. In other machines, special devices with fast access are used for registers. Registers in the main storage unit are generally cheaper, but slower than special devices.

BULK STORAGE

Two or more levels of storage are used in every data processor to achieve an efficient balance between access, cost, and capacity. Quick-access storage costs more per unit than slow-access storage. Most processors have limited amounts of fast-access storage and large amounts of slow-access bulk storage as an option. Bulk storage facilities are not an integral part of the basic processor, but they often are directly connected to the processor and controlled by it. The processor reads from bulk storage into high-speed storage before processing.

Some bulk storage is called *random access*. Carefully defined, random access means that access time to the next desired storage location is independent of the previously-accessed location. Among commonly-used storage devices, only magnetic core actually meets this criterion. But the name "random access" is widely used to mean large storage with relatively low access time. Some form of random access is imperative for on-line data flow. For this purpose, random access storage may be used to hold large master files while processing transactions that occur in random sequence.

Addressable Bulk Storage

Bulk storage units may be designed as addressable or nonaddressable. The most widely-used addressable bulk storage devices are magnetic disks and magnetic drums.

Magnetic Disk File.   A magnetic disk file is a stack of metal disks with magnetic material on both sides which are mounted on a rotating shaft. An access arm with read-write heads, under program control, writes on or reads from a selected data track on either side of the disk. A typical disk file is shown in Figure 3-5.

One disk storage unit is designed to operate with 250 concentric

FIGURE 3-5. *Magnetic disk file (with multiple arms).*

tracks on a disk side, and each track holds a maximum of 2800 six-bit characters. A maximum of 40 disks (80 sides) in a unit holds 56 million characters. Five units can be attached to one processor to provide 280 million characters of storage. Each disk surface has its own read-write head and all the heads move in and out together like teeth on a comb to any one of the 250 track locations. At each head setting, one track on each side of the 40 disks can be read or written, so one revolution of the disks provides access to a maximum of 112,000 characters. If no head movement is required, average access time is 17 milliseconds (one-half of a disk revolution). Moving the heads between tracks requires from 50 to 180 milliseconds, depending on the distance moved.

Several other varieties of disk files are available. Some models have only one arm to hold the read-write heads at any particular setting, so that only two tracks on one disk or two adjacent disks are available. Access to other tracks and disks is obtained by moving the arm in or out and up or down. As one might expect, access time is large and averages 0.5 seconds. Another disk file has an arm containing six read-write heads for each disk surface. This arrangement permits operations with six tracks on both sides of all disks without any arm movement and yields short access times to a large block of data. A jukebox file arrangement moves the appropriate disk to the reading head, searches out the correct track and reads it. Although average access time is several seconds, this device provides a large amount of addressable storage at low cost. A slightly different type of file features removable disks. When the user is finished with one file, he can remove it and replace it with another in less than one minute.

Bulk Drums. Bulk storage drums also supplement the high-speed storage unit of many processors. One application uses file storage drums arranged in pairs that hold six million characters, and a total of ten pairs holding 60 million characters can be connected to the processor. Instead of the usual plan of one read-write head for each data track, one set of read-write heads is moved back or forth for use with all tracks on the drum. This scheme reduces the amount of equipment at the expense of mechanical movement and slower operating speeds.

Strips and Cards. In several devices, strips of magnetic material are used to provide addressable bulk storage. A *tape-bin* storage unit consists of strips of magnetic tape arranged so that a read-write device can move directly to a desired strip. The reading head then scans that strip to find a record. Access is faster than for an ordinary reel of tape but is slow compared to modern disk files. A *magnetic card file* contains a set of cards comparable to punched cards but with a magnetic coating. The desired card is selected from the "deck" by electro-mechanical indexing and passed under a set of read-write heads. Each unit of one version of this file contains 256 cards holding 21,700 alphanumeric characters each for a total of over 5.5 million; and 16 units will operate with one processor. The entire set of 256 cards may be manually removed and replaced with another set in less than a minute. This capability allows the user to process many files with only one read-write mechanism.

Several manufacturers have built or proposed addressable bulk storage files that use *photographic media* instead of magnetic. The storage density—number of characters stored per square inch—of photographic material is ten or more times greater than magnetic media but is nonerasable. To date, photographic storage units are used in special applications only.

Nonaddressable Bulk Storage

The majority of business data is held in nonaddressable bulk storage—either punched cards, punched paper tape, or magnetic tape. These media hold large amounts of data at low cost and in forms suitable for machine processing, but with high average access time. To select random data, the storage media is put into a suitable handling unit and each piece of data examined in sequence until the desired data are found. Nonaddressable bulk-storage, however, is seldom if ever used as a random access device.

The role of nonaddressable bulk storage is to hold data that are used either as one large block—say, a processor program—or a sequence of groups—a file containing a record for each customer arranged by customer number. In the large-block case, the object is quick transfer of the *entire block* from bulk storage to high-speed storage. In the sequence case, the object is quick transfer of the *next group* of data from bulk storage to high-speed storage. When used sequentially, the time required to find data in a particular storage location—access time—is not relevant. The important feature of nonaddressable bulk-storage is the *transfer rate* or read-write or read-punch speed.

Most medium- or large-scale processors and many small ones use *magnetic tape* as the main nonaddressable bulk storage. Magnetic tape is usually from ½ to 1½ inches wide and, ordinarily, a tape unit is designed to handle reels holding 1500 to 3600 feet of tape.

Data are recorded in blocks ranging from one to a few thousand characters. Each block may consist of one or more data records for customers, employees, or stock items. Recording density commonly ranges from 100 to about 800 characters per inch, although some newer tape recording is at densities of 1500 characters per inch. A 2400-foot reel of half-inch tape can store about 3 to 16 million characters, but the effective storage capacity is less than the apparent maximum because of inter-block gaps. An *inter-block gap* of ¾ to about 2 inches of tape is left blank between successive blocks of data to permit the tape unit to start or stop and not lose any data by failure to read correctly. Also, the pause afforded this way enables the processor to handle the data—make calculations, update files, and write out results—that were read in from the previous block. Inter-block gaps may occupy a large fraction of the tape if short records are written on tape. For example, when data on cards are converted to tape as 80-character records, inter-block gaps exceed record lengths and occupy much more than half the tape. After read-in, several short records can be blocked to record them on tape as a larger block to improve tape utilization and increase effective read-write speeds. A 2400-foot tape with 200 characters per inch holds as many data as 25,000 eighty-column cards.

Maximum *data-transfer rates* depend on tape speed and data density; and rates of several thousand to several hundred thousand characters per second are common. Tape-movement speed is generally about 75 to 125 inches per second. Stop and start times between records reduce the effective transfer rates. Some tape-oriented processors will read or write a few hundred thousand characters per second from one tape and may simultaneously read or write on two or even more tapes. Reading a 2400-foot tape at maximum speed may take about four and one-half minutes, and rewinding ranges from one to three minutes. This time must be counted when calculating processing time, because rewinding and dismounting tapes (unless the manufacturer provides for demounting unwound tapes and later rewinding them) takes another minute or more and may impede processing. Many tape-changes are done with little interruption of processing by using an alternate tape transport. The next tape is mounted before it is needed so that only a "tape-swap" is made under program control to the next reel of tape when the end of a reel is reached.

Effective reading speed is increased in some systems by reading tape while moving in either the *forward* or *backward* direction. For example, in sorting data stored on tape by means of the merging scheme to consolidate two or more sequences (as described in Chapter 9), output tapes from one pass can be read backwards on the next pass. In this way, the merging operation is continued without delay for tape rewinding, which is required for machines that read tape moving in one direction only. Many business data processors have about ten to twenty tape read-write units, and some can handle several dozen. Tapes are mounted for processing as required and returned to the tape library for storage after processing or for reuse after the data are no longer wanted.

Magnetic tape is durable under ordinary operating conditions, for tapes can be read satisfactorily several thousand times. Data on a worn tape can be transferred to a new tape but, of course, should be transferred while still readable. Maximum tape performance involves some precautions in handling: temperature and humidity variations cause magnetic oxide surfaces to crack, dust on tape may cause a reading head to miss a signal, and manual handling of tape leaves oil and moisture that catches dust and impairs reading. Extremely high-density tapes—1500 characters per inch—are packaged in "cartridges" to avoid exposure to handling and dust. Metal tape resists temperature variations and extreme heat better than plastic tape. Exposure to strong magnetic fields that can erase all the data on tape, although rare, requires precautions.

Tape unit operations are controlled by the processor program, which orders a read-in of data when more records are needed for processing. The processor may also provide for automatic backspacing and rereading of a tape for data that do not pass the parity test. If a malfunction is caused by dust or some other transient reason, then a second or third reading will probably be satisfactory. Repeated failure to read warrants engineering service for the processor or a new tape. While the rereading feature is designed as automatic for some processors, it must be programmed for others.

SELECTION OF STORAGE EQUIPMENT

The types and quantities of storage required for a business data processor depend on the nature of applications. Some applications require high-speed storage alone; others rely heavily on bulk storage. Some factors affecting storage requirements are outlined below.

The *type* of processing performed varies greatly. Problems involving extensive calculations can effectively utilize large high-speed storage. Lengthy instructions and many numbers are involved in calculations. If storage capacity is exceeded, instructions and data must be segmented for handling in several runs.

Business applications usually involve *limited* computations on *huge* files that are affected by numerous transactions, but the activity rate for master-file records may be low. Transaction and master-file data nearly always exceed high-speed storage capacity. One plan is to read in one or more transactions and master-file records, update these records, write them out, and repeat the cycle. Some applications often have long instruction programs that exceed the high-speed storage capacity available at any reasonable price. In such cases, some scheme for *segmenting* instructions, transactions, and files is imperative for efficient processing.

The *time limit* between the occurrence of an event and the need for information about that event affects the selection of storage equipment. Reliance on nonaddressable bulk storage may be suitable, if the permissible elapsed time limits are not stringent. Transactions accumulated over a period of time can be sorted and processed in batches against a master file maintained on magnetic tape. External storage and batch-processing may be economical for huge master files. On the other hand, tight time schedules may require that files be available for frequent updating. The idealistic arrangement for tight processing and reporting schedules is to have all files available for processing at all times. If transactions must be handled immediately, the master file is usually kept in addressable bulk storage for *on-line processing*—data origination devices are directly connected to the processor for handling transactions as they occur. Core, disk, drum, magnetic cards, or tape strips are used for quick processing of transactions in random sequence.

Fast-access storage costs much more per unit than slow-access storage; hence, system design involving huge amounts of high-speed storage should be examined with care. Equipment and operating cost involved in meeting extremely short time limits may exceed the value of the information obtained.

Information requirements are reflected in the frequency and nature of reports prepared and references made to files. The nature of information required affects the selection of storage methods. A need for scheduled, formal reports may be met efficiently from files kept in external storage, if time limits permit. Scheduled processing at reasonable time intervals may be an efficient plan for updating huge files. Part of a file—one fifth or one twentieth—may be updated each day to complete the cycle over a period of a week or month. Current reports covering a part of the file can be prepared when that part is updated. If reports are needed immediately after events occur, quick-access storage is required. Examples of unscheduled reports are references to the file and *interrogations*—questions requiring quick answers. A need to know the quantity of stock on hand involves a file interrogation. Frequent interrogation of files demands storage devices suited to the need. Quick answers require quick-access storage. An event may trigger the need for information even though the event is part of the stream of regular transactions. A withdrawal below inventory reorder point is determined during inventory processing and, for example, triggers a replenishment order.

Interrogation of current files poses critical problems. Many solutions have been proposed, and special equipment has been designed to cope with file-inquiry problems. The point is often overlooked, but interrogation of relatively inactive files becomes more difficult as the volume of the files grows. External storage appears to be mandatory for historical files because of their huge volumes. Infrequent reference and loose time limits may make external storage useful for many purposes. In fact, the unit cost of high-speed storage precludes its use for mass storage. The reusability of storage has an interesting feature that makes it valuable for historical reference purposes. Some items in a record are useful for only a short period of time. Consider how the usefulness of data declines over a period of time. Data about individual receipts and issues of inventory may be vital for the current and past quarter. Monthly data pertaining to the third and fourth quarters in the past may be adequate. Quarterly summaries may suffice after one year and annual totals after three years, so that file volume can be reduced by condensing unwanted data. In summarizing data, some details will be lost unless they are available elsewhere. Condensing records on a reusable storage medium and discarding the parts no longer wanted corresponds to the transfer of paper or card records to inactive storage. But—and this is the important point—paper records must either be put into inactive storage as whole documents or destroyed, whereas records on magnetic tape can be *selectively condensed* in order to discard only those characters or words that are no longer wanted. Reusable storage that is released by condensing or discarding unwanted records can, of course, be used for other purposes.

Data *volume* is an important factor in selecting efficient storage methods. Huge volumes restrict system design to some method with low unit cost in order to keep total costs in bounds. Wider choices of methods exist for moderate volumes of data. Business applications involve large volumes of data and varied processing methods so that the use of two or more storage methods is likely to be more efficient than the use of a single method.

SUMMARY

Processor instruction routines are furnished by internal circuits or wires for some special-purpose equipment. External wiring or plugboards give other equipment limited flexibility. General-purpose equipment operates with programs that are read in like data and stored internally during execution. Quick read-in of programs makes the equipment highly versatile.

Internally-stored program equipment is designed with a particular instruction format. A *single-address* instruction specifies an operation and one operand. A *two-address* instruction specifies one operation and either two operands or one operand and the location of the next instruction. Each instruction format is best suited to certain applications.

The arithmetic unit has registers for storing words while they are being used. The *accumulator register* is long enough to hold a sum, overflow bit, and sign; it forms sums, remainders and other arithmetical results. The *M-Q register* holds the multiplier when the multiplication starts, but after multiplication, the left-hand digits of the product reside in the accumulator and the right-hand digits in the M-Q.

A control unit usually contains an instruction register, address register, and instruction counter. These elements hold the instruction being executed and the addresses of the operands and next instruction to execute. The control unit also sets up circuits for executing the instruction.

An operator communicates with the processor via the control console, which is used to start operations, monitor processing, read some data in and out of storage, detect certain kinds of mistakes, and keep a "log" of operations, including changes in instructions and insertion of data in a running program.

Instruction repertoires range from a few dozen to more than a hundred commands for various processors. A large repertoire affords the good programmer just the right instruction for many situations, but may prove overwhelming to the beginner.

The arithmetic unit performs the arithmetical operations of addition, subtraction, multiplication, and division. Variations of these operations give increased flexibility. The control unit executes instructions in the proper sequence by interpreting each instruction and applying proper signals to the arithmetic unit and other parts in keeping with an instruction.

Logical operations, which are a special kind of arithmetical operation, include comparison, extraction, and shifting.

Input facilities are used to bring in data; output facilities give results to users. High-speed input and output are obtained by fast magnetic-tape units and high-speed card transports. Data channels permit simultaneous operations of the processor and input-output units. Trapping mode operation enables the in-out device to interrupt the processor when the device is ready to give or accept data and simplifies the programmer's task of testing whether a device is ready to operate.

Important features of storage units are capacity, access time, and erasability. *Capacity* is the quantity of data that a storage unit holds. *Access time* is the length of time between a call for data from storage and completion of delivery. The *transfer rate* for delivery of successive characters (after the first is delivered) is another facet of storage speed. *Erasability* means that previously stored data can be replaced by new data.

Storage is classified here as high-speed storage and bulk storage that may be either addressable or nonaddressable. High-speed storage of magnetic cores is common (and some processors have a small quantity of ultra high-speed storage of magnetic cores, thin films, or other devices) for holding active data and program instructions. Addressable bulk storage "backs up" the high-speed storage with larger capacity but at slower access speeds. Examples are magnetic disk files, bulk drums, tape strips, and magnetic cards. Nonaddressable bulk storage on magnetic tapes or cards is not connected to the processor, but holds most of the business data that are kept in processable form.

Three levels of storage are used with most business processors to get an efficient balance between the volume of storage and unit cost of storage. But the equipment manufacturer decides what kinds of high-speed and addressable bulk storage units he will offer and thereby limits the user's choice.

Factors involved in selecting storage methods are the types of processing and their time limits, information requirements, interrogation demands, and volume of data. Time limits—the elapsed time between an event and required reports—are important. Short time limits and on-line interrogation demand quick-access storage units. If report preparation can be scheduled, files may be kept in nonaddressable bulk storage. References and interrogations that must be handled immediately after being triggered by events require file maintenance in addressable bulk storage to give quick replies.

CHAPTER 4

PROCESSING EQUIPMENT—
INPUT AND OUTPUT

Business data-processing systems handle a large volume of data that can originate in various forms and in widely separated locations. Although relatively simple, individual arithmetical operations are performed, the over-all processing may be complex, and the results of it put to a number of different uses. Input devices must originate data about events and move the data quickly to utilize the full capabilities of high-speed processing; expensive processors should not wait for data in the "pipeline." Output devices must handle results rapidly to keep up with the speed of the processor and furnish output in desired forms to meet the requirements of different users. Widely scattered operations rely heavily on communication networks for data input and output. Suitable input, output, and communications are costly but essential parts of an efficient system.

INPUT PREPARATION

Before considering the input devices available and how they are used, it is useful to look briefly at the activities involved in getting data into a form suitable for read-in to a processor.

Activities in Input Chain

The chain of activities leading up to the input of data to a processor is as follows:

1. Events occur and are detected or observed
2. The observed events are translated into symbols
3. Symbols are recorded as data
4. Data are converted into processable form
5. Processable data are transmitted to the processor

A simple example of this chain of events is illustrated by the steps in keeping track of the attendance time of workers—when they come and when they go. The arrival or departure of each worker from the plant is an *event*. A timekeeper *observes* each worker to identify him, decide whether he is coming or going, and note the time from a clock. He *translates* these observations into *symbols* that represent the worker's name or badge number, direction "in" or "out," and the clock time. The timekeeper *records* the symbols as *data* on a suitable form, which might be blank paper or a ruled form with appropriate spaces. Even in the simplest case, a form prepared in advance is likely to have some data already filled in, such as the employee's name and badge number. The data for each employee's daily attendance can be keypunched into cards as a suitably *processable form*. Messengers or ordinary mail can *transmit* the data to the point where the processor is located. The data about attendance time of workers are then ready for input to a processor. A card reader can read the cards directly into the processor for use with other records, say, job-time tickets, to reconcile the two reports of time from different sources and calculate costs and payroll.

This example merely illustrates the steps in the chain leading up to making data available for processing. There are more elaborate schemes for performing or combining operations in the chain. For example, a time clock that prints "time in" and "time out" for each employee and machine-stamps his time card, which is prepared before the start of the week, combines the occurrence and detection of an *event* with its translation into *symbols*. If the time clock is designed to punch the card instead of merely print it, then the event and symbols are originated in a *data form suitable for processing*. The data content of the cards can be transmitted by wire to a central location and repunched into cards. The cards may be used for input to the processor either directly or after conversion to some higher-speed media such as magnetic tape.

Input Preparation Devices

This section deals with the kinds of input equipment available and their use in each step of the input chain.

The usual procedure for getting input data ready for a processor is to convert the symbols concerning events into a suitable machine-processable medium—punched card, paper tape, or magnetic tape. Manual keyboard operators convert typed or written copy to a desired medium. Manual conversion is slow, and the error ratio is high enough that verification by duplicate operations, calculations, or editorial checking is used to detect mistakes and increase accuracy. The manual work in key-punching can be reduced and accuracy increased by pre-punching or otherwise mass-producing the elements that are common to many records. When possible, data output from one stage is retained in machine-processable form to simplify input operations at a later stage. Character-recognition devices optically or magnetically "read" typed or printed documents to prepare suitable media for processing. Data punched in cards are often converted to magnetic tape for faster read-in to a processor.

Input preparation devices are used for recording and converting data. The devices are called "off-line devices" because they are not connected to the processor when the data are first prepared. At a later stage, and after transmission, the data are introduced into the processor.

Paper-Tape Punches.   Simple devices of this type merely punch paper tape; more elaborate ones also produce readable copy, duplicate other tapes, or control the content and format of the copy. Special electric typewriters, for example, will convert source data to punched paper tape. Manual keyboard operation thus produces paper tape and readable page "hard copy" at the same time. Some electric typewriters also type hard copy from punched paper tape or punch a second tape, or both, as desired.

Office machines are available that can punch paper tape as a by-product of preparing regular printed output. Many kinds of office equipment, including adding machines, calculators, and posting machines, produce five-channel paper tape and some produce six-, seven-, or eight-channel tape. Several of these devices are shown in Figure 4-1. Some office machines can also punch cards as a by-product of ordinary operations.

In preparing a sales order, for example, a suitable office machine also punches paper tape or cards containing either the same data or

FIGURE 4-1. *Tape-punching office equipment.*

only a selected part of the data. The by-product tape or cards eliminate the duplicate work that would be involved in later punching the data. The sales order, which can be produced in multiple copies for ordinary purposes, is useful for checking accuracy since the hard copy and punched media must agree. The degree of accuracy achieved depends on the skill and care used in original preparation and verification plus the skill of subsequent users in detecting mistakes. The tape or cards can be used for input to other machines or to a data processor.

Card Punches.   Punched cards are a common medium for originating data in machine-processable form. When an operator strikes a key on a card punch (Figure 4-2), it punches a hole or

FIGURE 4-2. *Card keypunch.*

holes in a column to represent one character. A printing-punch prints each character along the top of a card above the corresponding punched column when a card is first prepared. Or a machine called an "interpreter" later reads the punches and prints the characters for selected columns.

The original data and punched cards may be given to a second operator for complete or partial verification. Numeric data may be verified but alphabetical data skipped, since sometimes a lower margin of accuracy is tolerable for letters than for numerals.

Manual keypunching work, which is done at about half the speed of typewriting, can be reduced by machine duplication of master copies of constant or repetitive data. Some data are in machine-processable form when first generated because they originate from card-punching time clocks or transaction recorders. Marking a card in specified locations with a special lead pencil enables a mark-sensing machine to punch the marked data. Several other schemes involving only a small amount of equipment are available for originating punched cards: portable hand punches, a stylus and punched platen for guiding the punching of characters in one or more of 40 columns in cards that are pre-perforated in all twelve positions, portable devices that punch a fixed set of repetitive data in certain columns and have a keyboard to set up and punch a small number of additional columns, and ink marks for optical reading and punching. After the cards are punched, ordinary card equipment can be used for processing.

Magnetic-Tape Writers. A manually operated keyboard machine will record data on magnetic tape directly from source data and produce a typed copy for record and checking purposes. The typed copy is an important aid to the operator because he cannot read magnetic tape as he can punched cards and paper tape.

The typical verification schemes of scanning hard copy or of preparing a second record on magnetic tape and comparing the two recordings can be used with magnetic-tape writing systems. A mistake can be erased from magnetic tape and the correct character substituted.

Prior Preparation

The input equipment and methods described above usually start with data on typed, handprinted, or handwritten documents that are not machine-processable. That is to say, the event that occurred was translated into symbols, and the symbols were recorded as data. The next step—manual character-by-character conversion of data on documents to a form suitable for processing—is expensive and fraught with mistakes.

The *prior preparation* of input data means that output from one stage is used directly as data input at the next stage of processing. This concept of data origination essentially eliminates two activities—translating events into symbols and recording symbols as data. Thus, the task of converting data into processable form is made much easier. It is necessary only to observe that the event occurred and the data are then ready for processing, although an automatic conversion step may be required.

The most interesting and challenging examples of prior preparation of data arise when numerous people originate data for processing. These people may be warehouse stockkeepers, customers, or agents. A common example of prior preparation of input data is the punched-card bill prepared and sent to a utility customer for him to return with his payment. When he does, a cashier gets the money and customer's bill card to identify the collection event. The collected bill card is then used as data input for crediting the customer's account, so that manual conversion of input data is eliminated. Bills printed with the correctly-shaped characters on paper are also being used in a similar way. Of course, a character reader, instead of a card reader, is used when the printed stub is received with the collection from a customer. Commercial checking-account numbers are printed in machine-processable characters on checks before they are issued to depositors. Pre-numbering facilitates sorting when checks reach the bank for payment. Preparation of data at one stage—say, bill issuance—can minimize manual conversion at the next stage—for example, account collection and posting.

Tag Readers.   Inventory control is facilitated by mass-producing punched cards or other machine media at the time inventory items are obtained. Special devices print and punch or otherwise prepare tags with the item name, size, manufacturer, and other desired facts. Tags may be designed for direct input to processors, otherwise machine conversion puts the data in the proper form.

A section of an inventory tag may be detached and placed in a transaction recorder at the point of transaction—sale to a customer, issuance to manufacturing department, or whatever. The recorder automatically reads the tag and produces a continuous punched tape or other specified media, which also includes the variable data that the operator manually enters on a keyboard. Whenever desired—hourly or daily—the data on tape can be converted to punched cards or fed directly into a processor for inventory, sales, and customer accounting. Direct wire-transfer of data from transaction recorders to a processor is useful for updating account balances fast enough to permit interrogating them about current inventory status.

Factory Data Collection. The important data required to keep tabs on factory operations may be who operated the machine, which machine was used, and what was produced—the item and quantity. Data collection devices (Figure 4-3) located in each production center in a factory may collect data about factory operations in the following way. Machine-readable identification cards or tags are prepared once for each machine operator and each machine and as required for each new production order. When starting a job, the operator inserts the three cards—man, machine, and job—into the reading device in his production center. The data are read and transmitted via wires or cable to a central unit that records the data about the operator, machine, and job, and also the starting time of the job, which is supplied by a wired-in clock. When an operator finishes the job, he repeats the input cycle for the three cards and then enters the quantity produced via a keyboard on the reading device. After the central "compiler" receives these data and also notes the stopping time, the essential data are available for calculating and summarizing what items were produced, how many units, on which machine, and who ran it. With little modification, records from a factory data-collection system may go directly into the next stage of data processing.

Character Readers. Another data-input system reads characters printed on ordinary paper documents. Character-recognition devices convert visually readable characters into machine-processable form. There are several versions, but they can be classified into two broad types: magnetic-ink and carbon-ink readers.

The most widely used *magnetic-ink character reader* was designed for use by commercial banks, although the concept has broader implications. Before issuing checks to a depositor, a bank prints its identification number and his account number on each check. The characters are printed with ink that contains iron-oxide in a visually readable type font consisting of the digits 0 through 9, four letters, and some special symbols to indicate data fields. After a customer writes a check, the first bank handling it is supposed to imprint the amount of the check in a similar way. Then the inks can be read magnetically by machines as well as visually by people. The identification numbers—bank and customer—are used to sort the check to the required degree of fineness (Federal Reserve or correspondent bank, bank on which written, and finally customer's account) by high-speed check sorters. The amount coded on the check is used for bookkeeping at each stage of transfer between

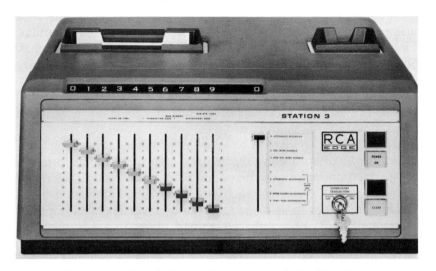

FIGURE 4-3. *Factory data collectors.*

banks and also within a bank for each depositor's accounts. The magnetic-ink character scheme has several interesting features. First, the character can be read by *both* people and machines. Second, readability and accuracy of machine handling remain high even though the characters are overprinted with endorsements. Third, and probably most important, it is the first significant application of machine-processable documents to gain acceptance throughout a large industry.

Optical character readers work with documents printed or typed in ordinary carbon inks by typewriters, high-speed output printers, or special imprinters. Machines for reading characters imprinted from credit cards convert each customer's number from a man-machine readable form to punched cards or to magnetic tape for efficient machine processing. Accuracy of reading (or complete rejection) of each document is assured by a self-checking feature in the design of each character so that it differs from every other character in at least two of the horizontal and vertical bars that compose it.

When a retail gasoline station, for instance, makes a sale, the customer's name and account number are imprinted from his plastic plate to an unpunched card. The gasoline station is also identified by use of a similar plate. The product and quantity involved and dollar amount of sale can be recorded manually or the dollar amount can be imprinted from dial digits set by hand before imprinting. The station turns in the imprinted and written cards to the tank-wagon driver as payment for more gasoline. The driver delivers the cards to a central location where a reading unit reads the customer's number (and amount of sale, if printed in the machine-readable dial digits; otherwise a keypunch operator reads and punches the written amount) and punches the data into the same card. Optical equipment scans each numeral, and a logical network decodes the scan pattern into a character. These cards containing basic data—customer's number and amount of sale—are then used for billing customers and in any other ways desired.

Considered from the viewpoint of the utility cashier's department, character reading for utility bills is, as pointed out earlier, one step in advance preparation of data. The billing department need use only a suitable type font on its high-speed printer when printing bills to make them machine-readable when customers return the bills with payment in full. The bill stubs are put through a character reader to get the required data—customer number and dollar amount—for updating the customer's account in the files.

The concept of character recognition for near-ordinary type fonts printed with carbon inks has much wider application than the foregoing examples of prior preparation—tag readers, factory data collection, and magnetic-ink reading. It is useful for business documents of many types that can be standardized enough for machine handling and reading. Along these lines, it is interesting to note that the post office department has done experimental work with character readers for reading and coarse-sorting letter mail addressed in any reasonably standard type font—typewriter, high-speed printer, and duplicating plates.

Another use is the conversion of ordinary typed data to machine-readable form. For example, customer names and addresses for magazine subscription file-processing may be typed and then put through a character reader to convert to cards or magnetic tape for processor input. Typewriters are more economical—considering both equipment and labor for the output obtained—to operate and are more accurate than keypunch machines.

Input Converters

Automatic converters transfer data from one medium to another. The methods of recording (punched hole or magnetic spot) and of number-system representation (decimal, binary, binary-coded decimal, and five or more channel codes) are ordinarily changed during conversion. Efficient converters increase the compatibility and flexibility of different types of equipment, so that each unit of equipment can be selected on its own merits, with less regard for whether all use the same medium and data code. Current high-speed processors operate best from data on magnetic tape because of its high read-in rate; however, many accept data in other forms.

When electronic processors were first used for business applications, special converters were designed as separate units to convert data from one medium to another, such as from punched cards to magnetic tape, paper tape to magnetic tape, and magnetic tape to the others. On the output side, special control units were designed to work with a magnetic-tape unit and a high-speed printer or a card punch. Now small- and medium-scale processors are frequently used to handle the work formerly done by these special converters. The philosophy is that such a processor, acting as a satellite to a large processor, can handle all the conversion operations required throughout the system, perform extensive editing, and do some processing on its own if it still has idle capacity. Examples of processing considered suitable for a satellite processor are editing input data for completeness and format, maintaining disk files (updating, sorting, and answering inquiries), and editing and arranging the large processor's output for printing.

DATA TRANSMISSION

The transmission of data to the processor is the last stage of input prior to data read-in. In some cases—factory data collection, remote keyboard, or special set inquiry—transmission is an inherent part of the recording and conversion operations. However, communication arises as a separate facet when the transmission stage is not integrally related to data origination.

Communication Channels

Data are often transmitted from one location to another over some form of electrical or electronic circuit—wires, cable or microwave. The Bell System, Western Union, or other communication firms supply most of these communication circuits. With appropriate conversion equipment, the regular telephone and telegraph networks may be used as needed at standard prices. For example, the manager of a branch office might send data to a main office simply by dialing the telephone number of the main office and transmitting the data via an appropriate device after the main office answers the call.

Many different types of service are available. The occasional user may find it cheapest to use the dial telephone system and pay the price for a regular telephone call either local or long-distance. For transmitting a large volume of data, leasing a private telephone or telegraph circuit may be most economical. Charges depend upon the number of miles of leased circuits and the time of day and night that the circuits are used. The wide area service of the communication companies—for a fixed monthly fee a user has unlimited calling privileges in a prescribed area which may encompass the entire United States—is available for data as well as voice use.

Telegraph, Telephone, and Microwave Services. Circuits are classified mainly by their capacity—the rate at which they will transmit data. Teletype is low capacity, telephone is intermediate capacity, and microwave or a service called Telpak is high capacity. Actually, microwave, telephone, and telegraph circuits are closely related. A single high-capacity microwave circuit might be used as several Telpak channels, several hundred telephone channels, several thousand teletype channels or some combination.

Regular commercial *telegraph* service is used to transmit limited amounts of data sent to a telegraph office. If volume is sufficient, a telegraph grade circuit between offices or firms may be leased for exclusive use. Teletypewriter Exchange Service or TWX Service provides dialed connections between any two points on the TWX network. Manually and paper-tape operated typewriters and punched-card devices are often connected to teletype circuits. The maximum rate of data transmission over a telegraph grade circuit is ten characters a second.

Standard voice or *telephone* grade channels will transmit data at rates up to several hundred characters per second depending on the type of service. For example, circuits leased for exclusive use by one customer may have a maximum rate of 300 characters per second while circuits in the dial network may have a maximum rate of 250 characters per second for local service and 150 characters per second for long distance service. Telpak service is available on a leased circuit basis in several grades at data rates up to 60,000 characters per second. Transmission techniques for all circuits are improving and maximum rates are expected to increase.

Some companies have set up private *microwave* systems which are capable of extremely high-speed transmission rates of millions of bits per second. However, since relay stations must be within ten to twenty miles of each other, numerous stations make installation expensive enough to limit widespread private use of such systems.

Errors. Errors reduce the useful capacity of a circuit. If, for example, a circuit will handle 336 bits per second, then it can transmit six-bit characters with no error checking at a rate of 56 characters per second. Communication circuits, however, introduce "noise" similar to static on a radio, and this noise may change one character to another. If undetected changes are not acceptable, a seventh parity bit can be added to each character, but capacity is reduced to 48 characters per second. Furthermore, each time a parity check fails, the character must be retransmitted so that capacity is less than 48 valid characters per second. The valid characters, however, may well have more value to the receiver than a larger number of unchecked characters. Higher accuracy will result from two parity bits per character or special parity characters and words. Early teletype transmission provided no automatic error checking and was not satisfactory for some users. At present, leased lines are more error-free than the dial networks.

Modulation Equipment. Modulation units, often called Data-Phones, are required to translate data into an electrical form suitable for transmission. This equipment replaces the ordinary telephone with a device that connects to an input reader. When dial service is used, the modulator contains the dialing mechanism and may even contain a telephone for voice communication before or after the data are transmitted. Modulation equipment is available for use with punch-card, paper-tape, and magnetic-tape units, or for direct transmission between processors.

Transmitting Devices

Transmitting and receiving devices can handle all common machine-processable media. Since transmission circuits require data in a different form than most basic processors, each major data-processing equipment manufacturer has a special line of input and output equipment designed for use with standard modulators. However, some special modulators are built for direct hook-up to standard input-output equipment. In one way or another, compatibility between the input-output equipment and the circuit must be provided.

The data transmission rate is more often limited by the *grade of circuit* than by the characteristics of the transmitter. For this reason, maximum rates are often the same for various models of equipment produced by different manufacturers.

Paper Tape. Five-channel tape is standard for use with telegraph equipment. Tape data can be transmitted directly over telegraph wires. The Teletypewriter accepts and automatically transmits five-channel tape pre-punched for higher-speed read-in and produces a typed copy of data transmitted, if desired. The keyboard can be operated manually for direct, although slow, transmission. Receiving equipment prints messages or re-perforates them into paper tape at speeds of six to ten characters per second. Similar devices that operate over telephone grade circuits are capable of transmitting at rates up to 100 characters per second.

A device called Teledata transmits, receives, and checks data coded in five-, six-, or eight-channel punched-paper tape. As data in punched-paper tape are sent through the reader, they are simultaneously re-perforated and checked on the punch of the Teledata unit located at a distant point. For five-channel tape, parity checking is by words or groups of characters between space codes. Six- and eight-channel tape permit single and double parity checking.

Transmission speeds are six to ten codes per second depending on the commercial telegraph channel grade used—60, 75, or 100 words per minute.

Punched Cards.   Data on punched cards can be transmitted and received directly over telegraph or telephone circuits by many units. A widely used device called a Transceiver transmits three to five punched cards per minute over telegraph circuits and eleven cards per minute over telephone circuits. One telephone circuit can handle four units at the same time so that 44 fully punched cards can be transmitted per minute, and the card-rate output is increased if fewer columns are punched. Self-checking features assure the degree of accuracy in transmission necessary for accounting and computing.

The Kinecard Converter used in conjunction with a card read-punch unit transmits and reproduces data in standard punched cards at the rate of 100 cards per minute over a telephone circuit. Malfunctions in data assembly and transmission are detected by odd- and even-parity checks on each card; defective cards are isolated by offset stacking. Other card units read and transmit up to several hundred cards per minute.

Magnetic Tape.   Several devices are available for transmitting data recorded on magnetic tape. They read data from magnetic tape, transmit the data over telephone wires, and record on magnetic tape at the destination. The transmission speed over commercial telephone channels is from 150 to 300 characters per second.

While tape-reading rates are only a few inches per second for transmission over wire circuits, forward and reverse tape speeds for editing and rewinding tape are very fast in some equipment. Automatic error checking and correcting features are obtained by character and channel parity-bits. Dual parity-bits (channel parity is introduced just before transmission if not already on tape) add enough redundancy to reproduce data at an undetected error rate as low as one error in 10,000 bits. A record containing a parity error, which usually is caused by interference on the voice circuits, is automatically retransmitted when a transmission error is detected. After three unsuccessful attempts, the machine halts to allow the operator to decide what to do.

Microwave and Telpak facilities transmit data from magnetic tape at much higher rates than those achieved over voice grade telephone lines. Effective transmission rate in an early microwave system was about 8000 characters per second. The magnetic-tape unit involved had a capability of 15,000 characters per second, but operating speed was reduced because of delays in moving data from a receiving buffer into the recording tape. Microwave and Telpak channels are capable of transmitting data from magnetic tape at rates over 60,000 characters per second.

Processor-to-Processor. High-speed transmission techniques and special control units permit direct communication between the internal storage of two processors. Since processors can make data available at storage access speeds—many thousands to hundreds of thousands of characters per second—the limiting factor is the transmission circuit capacity that is economical to install and use. With processor-to-processor communication, any input device attached to the processor can be used indirectly as a transmitter and any output device as a receiver. Figure 4-4 shows a schematic diagram of a processor-to-processor hook-up.

INPUT READERS

Input readers are connected to a processor for direct read-in. Selection of a reader depends on data volumes, equipment speeds, and the permissible processing time. Magnetic-tape read-write units are used for large-volume data input, whereas punched-card or punched paper-tape readers are widely used for smaller volumes. Keyboard devices are used to read in limited amounts of data, program corrections, and file interrogations. The processor console switches may be used to read in some data or fragments of a program and especially the initial steps required to start program read-in.

Magnetic-Tape Units

Several features of magnetic tape for data storage were discussed in Chapter 3; others deserve discussion here. Magnetic-tape units, also called "tape handlers" and "tape transports," are used to read in huge volumes of data for processing.

A typical tape unit (Figure 4-5) moves tape past the read-write heads at speeds of 75 to 125 inches per second, depending on the tape unit specifications. A speed of 100 inches per second for tape written at a density of 400 characters per inch produces a data transfer rate of 40,000 characters per second, apart from inter-block gaps. Actually, different magnetic tape units have transfer rates ranging from 5000 to 100,000 characters per second and more. Some tape units operate with tapes in both low- and medium-density modes. The tapes written on them can be used with higher-

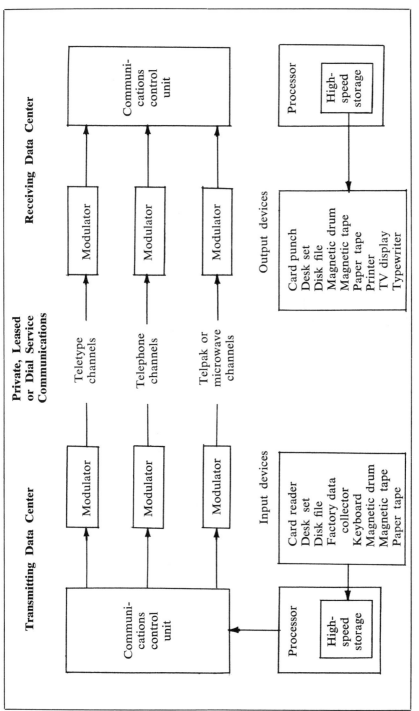

FIGURE 4-4. *Schematic of processor-to-processor communication.*

 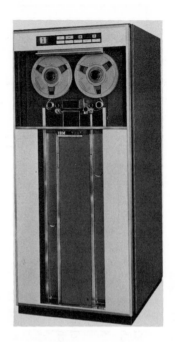

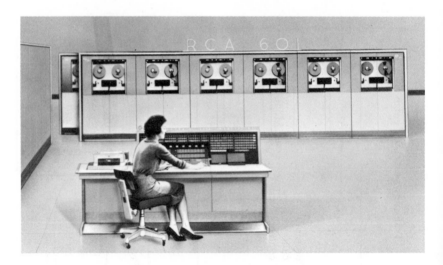

FIGURE 4-5. *Typical magnetic-tape units.*

capacity tape units on larger processors that operate in medium- and high-density modes. Thus the medium-density mode is common between tape units operating with the two sizes of processors.

Steady high-speed movement of tape past the reading heads— there is one head for each data and parity channel on tape—generates a magnetic field for each bit recorded on the tape. Reading consists of sensing the magnetic field. Such high rates of data transfer would fill processor storage in a second or less; therefore, tape units operate intermittently to read in (or write out) data as required by processing.

Some tape units are designed to read or to write tape while moving in the forward direction only; other units can write in one direction and search tape moving in either direction. A few, however, have been designed to read and write in both directions. Two-direction capability speeds up some operations such as tape sorting, which requires many passes of the same tapes, as described in Chapter 9.

Many tape units have a high-speed rewind that takes a minute or so (compared with four to eight minutes to read or write during ordinary processing) to cut the time lost before the next tape reel can be mounted. Business data processors usually have enough tape units so that the next tape is merely mounted on another unit in order to continue processing while the used tape is being rewound. But some tapes are designed for demounting after reading or writing and later rewinding on a simple device. Many processors have two or more data channels for simultaneous operation of two or more tape units that are appropriately connected through the data channels.

Magnetic tapes are reusable because each tape unit is equipped with erase heads in addition to the read-write heads. The erase heads remove by electrical action any old data on the tape just before new data are recorded. Of course, precautions are required to avoid premature discard of data by erasing and writing over data that are still wanted.

Punched-Card and Tape Readers

On-line punched-card readers are used with many business processors. The processor can control the card reader and start and stop reading operations as required. Editing is done under program control to check for double punches, blank columns, and field consistency—no alphabetical characters in a numeric field and vice versa. Contents of columns can be omitted, altered, or rearranged for transfer into storage. Card readers usually verify operational accuracy by reading each card twice and comparing for identity, or by reading once and making a hole-count for each column for comparison with a second hole-count made at a read-check station. Conversion between the punched-card code and the code used in the processor is handled by read-in equipment, ordinarily with no loss in processor speed. Paper-tape readers are frequently used with small data processors and sometimes with large ones. Paper-tape readers may be useful for reading in data transmitted over wire circuits and punched into tape when received. Readers handle five-through eight-channel code under control of the processor.

Limited editing operations may be performed during read-in. Paper-tape readers can stop tape movement between any two adjacent characters, so that any one character can be read into the computer for examination and tape movement stopped, if required, before the next character comes into reading position. Thus, no special inter-block gap is required because the space between any two characters serves as a start-stop gap.

Keyboards and Multiplexed Input

A console keyboard may be used to enter data directly into processor storage. Keyboards are used for program testing, program alteration, and file interrogation. Console keyboards are seldom used for volume input because people type too slowly and are prone to error. It is desirable to perform the detailed steps of program testing and alteration away from the processor to save machine time and reduce mistakes.

Keyboard input, however, may be desirable even though limited by manual operating speeds. Simple interrogation can be made via a console or similar keyboard to all files under processor control that can be searched to give a rapid reply. This restricts such inquiry to files in magnetic-core storage, drums, disks, and, perhaps, magnetic-card records and short-tape files. Interrogation keyboards can be located on or near the processor console, or even in remote locations if suitable communication links are provided. For example, one medium-scale processor using disk files will accept inquiries transmitted via teletype, obtain an answer from the disk file, and send a reply to the inquirer without manual assistance.

Special-purpose input units called *desk sets* are designed for speed and accuracy in applications that require frequent access to large files, such as airline reservations or savings bank accounting. Each agent's desk set for airline reservations (Figure 4-6) accepts

FIGURE 4-6. *Airline agent set.*

data from metal or plastic plates indicating flight number and times, and from a keyboard punched for date, class of service, and type of transaction—inquiry, reserve, sell, or cancel. Lights on the agent's set indicate the processor's reply to the agent's action and he can follow through as directed.

A large number of desk sets connected to the processor at one time—multiplexed input—effectively increases speed. Data from each keyboard are accepted in turn by multiplexing but priority may be given to some keyboards to accept their input ahead of others. A processor can handle a large number of keyboard inputs in this manner without excessive waiting time. A program-interrupt feature in some processors permits a read-in unit filled with data to take the initiative and interrupt the program just long enough to start the transfer of data to main storage. Processing of other data then continues during the read-in of new data to the buffer.

Buffer Storage

A processor can ordinarily accept and record data in storage faster than input units can supply data. *Buffer storage* is used to compensate for this difference in operating speeds. A buffer may be a small intermediate storage unit between and connected to the input unit and processor storage. In other cases, part of the main storage is used for buffering, alongside program and data storage.

Either the processor directs the input unit to read data into buffer storage, or the reader does so on its own initiative. The processor continues with other operations until the buffer loading operation is completed and then transfers data from buffer storage into main internal storage. This transfer can occur at high speed regardless of the speed at which the buffer was filled. Of course, buffering does not increase the speed of data read-in above the rated capacity of a card or tape unit, but it does minimize processor delay during data read-in and thereby speeds up processing.

Some processors continue processing throughout the whole read-in cycle. Concurrent operations of this type are called "read-while-process" or "processing overlap" and neither the processor nor the read-in unit is delayed by waiting for the other. Other processors can read in data from two or more devices at once. Concurrent operations of this type require the use of two or more data channels so that each active input device has access to the processor through a channel. There are various schemes for connecting input and output devices to data channels. Simple schemes divide devices into groups and connect each group to one line only. More elaborate schemes offer more flexibility by connecting all devices to all channels and switching to any device desired.

Although read-while-process increases the efficiency of data-processing operations, data input is still limited to the rated speed of read-in units. When data are wanted faster than they are read in, data-processing operations are said to be "read-in limited"; they are called "processor limited" when the processing cycle is longer than the read-in cycle. The processing and read-in cycles are rarely exactly the same length, but the two can be brought into closer balance by shifting part of the processing load from one run to another or by making other changes in operating routines. For example, data editing and checking might be done in the last pass of the sorting run instead of the first pass of the file-processing run to shift the balance of work, if file processing is processor-limited.

OUTPUT DEVICES

Processed results may go directly to an on-line output device, if output is needed quickly. Ordinarily, results are recorded in machine-processable form for off-line printing, since, if there is a great deal of output, slow on-line printers can hinder the processor.

On-Line Output

On-line devices convert processor output directly to magnetic tape, punched cards, paper tape, printed reports, or visual displays in television-like tubes. Magnetic tape is frequently used for large volume output, whereas typewriters and special desk sets are adequate for answers to a limited number of file interrogations.

A *magnetic-tape unit,* as described earlier for data read-in, is also used interchangeably for data write-out. A magnetic-tape unit is efficient for write-out because it accepts data much faster than a punched-card or tape device. Some processors do not buffer input or output to magnetic tape, so that processing stops during data read-in or write-out. Processors of higher capability provide for concurrent operations of read-in, process, and write-out, although some are designed for only two concurrent operations—read-process, read-write, or process-write. The comments made in this and the preceding chapter concerning magnetic tape—high density, rapid data-transfer, read-reverse, back-space, accuracy, and reusability— also apply here. In fact, reusability and the similarities of the reading and writing operations, which the same magnetic-tape unit performs, are the chief features that make magnetic tape suitable for both input and output.

Card punches are often connected to and controlled by the processor for on-line output. Buffering units take up the speed differences between processor output and card-punching rates. Results are first read from processor working storage to buffer storage; the processor then directs the card punch to take data from buffer storage, and it does so if the prior punching cycle is complete. During the punching cycle, other operations continue. Some processors are designed so that the card punch retains the initiative to interrupt the processor and call for output when ready. This processor-interrupt feature simplifies the program because it need not keep interrogating the card punch to determine whether it is ready to accept more output.

To verify the accuracy of punching, a processor may retain for one punch cycle either the data or a column-by-column hole count of what is supposed to be punched in a card. The punch punches a card and moves it to the punch-check station for check reading. Either the card's data content or the columnar hole-count is compared with the data retained by the processor. If a discrepancy is found, the faulty card can be rejected, the operator alerted, and operations halted.

Some processors have directly connected *paper-tape punches.* Once in operation, a punch produces one particular code, but most can be converted readily to punch any code ranging from five to eight channels. Some punches perform limited editing during read-out at punching speeds ranging from 20 to 500 or more characters per second.

Airline reservation-agents' sets and bank-tellers' machines, described earlier as input readers, are also *direct display* devices operating as on-line output. An agent's set will indicate to him by means of lights the seat availability on selected flights. The information a bank teller needs about account balances, restricted deposits, and other special conditions may be displayed or printed. Printing is useful to give the depositor a record of the transaction.

Large processors may have a cathode-ray output device similar to a television tube to receive and display data either directly from the processor or from magnetic tape. The desired data—alphanumerics, graphs, and line drawings—are displayed in suitable form for viewing, photographing, or perhaps printing. With a direct scope display, it is possible for the processor to show the solution while it is being calculated. On-line scopes might be useful for quick display of information wanted by managers.

Output Converters

Many processors have output facilities for only one or two media so that converters are used to transfer the data to other media. A wide choice of output methods from the processor may be available, although some of these are not necessarily efficient in practice. One efficient scheme is to use magnetic tape for fast write-out from the processor and then convert off-line from tape to other media while the processor continues operations. Conversion may be done by a limited-purpose converter or by a satellite processor which, as described earlier, can handle this and other kinds of conversions.

Some applications require both printing and punching on the same card. Elaborate processing schemes are sometimes used to print cards on continuous forms only, burst them apart, punch desired data in the cards, and finally (since punches are less reliable than printers) verify that the corresponding data are printed and punched on the same card. The traditional approach has been to punch the cards and then "interpret" them to print whatever is punched. A newer approach is to print first and then use a character reader to read the printed data on a card and activate a card punch. For data already punched and printed, a character reader and punched-card reader may be used jointly to verify identity of the two kinds of data. Or mistakes in punching or printing can be detected by reading the printed characters and comparing summaries of them with control totals prepared in the prior stage of processing. Some equipment has been designed solely for the purpose of printing and punching into each card the data—customer, name and address, account number, and amount of bill—required for utility billing. The printed-punched card returned by the customer with payment can be used for direct input to the accounting process—an example of prior preparation of data, as discussed earlier, but slightly · different from the character-reader scheme.

Mechanical Printers

Page printers work from most forms of data media: magnetic tape, punched cards, and paper tape. Fast printers connected on-line to the processor save an intermediate step, but at the risk of delaying operations.

The traditional method of printing business documents, or any other, is well-known. It consists of holding the paper against a platen, placing an ink-bearing ribbon over the paper, and striking the ribbon with a metal type-slug embossed with the shape of the desired character. Variations of this plan are used to obtain high printing speeds, as described below.

Single-Character. A single-character device, such as an electric typewriter, types one character at a time and can produce five lines of 120 characters in a minute. Typing speeds of 600 characters per minute may be fast enough for a punched-card or punched paper-tape system with low-volume output. An electric typewriter is often used on-line with the processor for inquiries and replies, for typing out a log of machine operations, and for giving instructions to the machine operator. Some processors have a "locked-in" log and a program control routine that requires console type-outs before the operator alters internal data and their addresses by using the console.

Line-at-a-Time. A medium-speed line-printer uses either type bars or type wheels to print a whole line of characters at one time. Each printing position has a complete set of alphanumeric and special symbols on movable type bars. Each bar is raised until the desired symbol is in printing position and hammers strike the type-bars to print in all positions at one time. A type-bar printer produces up to 90 lines of 100 characters each in a minute.

A type-wheel printer has a wheel, instead of a type bar, at each printing position with numeric and alphabetical type faces arranged around the rim of each wheel. To print, each print wheel is rotated until its desired character turns into position. The print wheels move forward to strike the paper and produce a printed line at speeds of 150 lines of 120 characters each per minute.

One type of high-speed printer consists of a continuously rotating cylinder with raised characters arranged in bands around the rim of the cylinder. Every character to be used—and there are usually 50 to 60 in the "alphabet"—is located in each band to provide one printing position. A fast-acting hammer opposite each band of characters strikes the paper against the desired character at the correct time while the paper is momentarily stopped at each print line. Printing speeds of 1000 lines per minute of 160 alphabetical characters each, or 2000 lines of numerical characters, are obtained.

Another version of a high-speed printer uses five sets of characters attached to a chain that moves continuously in a horizontal path. A hammer at each of the printing positions across a line strikes the paper when the desired character reaches that position to print 600 lines of alphanumerical characters per minute. Much higher speeds for numerics only are obtained by substituting an all-numeric chain for the alphanumeric chain.

An interesting problem in trying to achieve high-speed printing is the fact that many business documents—checks and invoices are good examples—have more blank space than printed lines of data. A high-speed blank-paper skip feature that may operate at, say, 33 inches per second for skips up to eight lines and 75 inches per second for longer skips increases the effective handling rate for printing business documents. The combination of high-speed print and higher-speed blank-paper skip gives very high throughput rates for documents.

SELECTION OF INPUT-OUTPUT EQUIPMENT

Many characteristics of the business environment—the type of processing, time schedules, geographical location of operating units, report requirements, and the degree of accuracy required for output—influence the types and combinations of input-output equipment suitable for efficient operations. Some of the more important considerations in the development of an efficient input-output system deserve discussion here.

Business systems operate in *various environments* to cover many activities and functions. Data may originate in numerous forms at few or many points. Punched cards may be best suited for collecting data at one point, while paper tape is best for another. In a factory, transaction recorders are useful to capture original data, while special input-output sets are useful for airline agents and savings-bank tellers since they need to interrogate files and initiate transactions. Stock brokers use a simpler inquiry-reply device merely to obtain price quotations. Specialized equipment may be efficient for handling large volumes of repetitive data that originate on one medium and that can be brought to one point for mass-processing.

The *type of processing* required influences the selection of input-output equipment. Serial, periodic processing is efficient for files maintained on magnetic tape. Random-sequence processing is preferable when file-update cannot be scheduled, quick updating is wanted, and rapid reply to interrogations is needed.

Preliminary processing outside the processor is often justified, and design of the input system should exploit this possibility. Sorting a large number of records into sequence may be done more economically using punched cards than magnetic tape. The cards can be sorted and then read into the processor either directly or after conversion to magnetic tape. This is not to say that data already on tape should be converted to cards for sorting and then returned to the processor for further processing. Some factors other than economy of sorting are important. Sorting records with a data processor is often quicker than with punched-card equipment. The experience of some users has shown that processor sorting is both more accurate and less expensive than punched-card sorting and especially so for large numbers of records. The number of transactions to be processed and the need to sort them into sequence affects the point at which data are converted from card to tape. Disk storage with multiple access arms, which permits use of the "cylinder" concept of high-speed reading and writing (the corresponding tracks on all disks are handled before the heads are re-positioned), offers new opportunities for fast sorting of large volumes of data.

Time schedules may be loose enough that off-line input and output are adequate. On the other hand, current information may be so critical for successful management decisions and for automatic control of operations that on-line input and output are imperative. Automatic control reaches its highest present form when the processor is tied directly to manufacturing control devices. Automatic input and output devices are imperative for computer control of physical processes. When the data-information system and plant operations are considered as an integrated whole, the timeliness of information can be evaluated in terms of improved operating efficiency.

The *geographical location* of company operations, decision-making, and data-processing activities affects the choice of communication facilities. Widespread operations and centralized data processing require a large communication network for the mass flow of data. Network installation and operating costs, in addition to technical factors, help determine how much geographic centralization is feasible. If time schedules permit, mail may work as well as an elaborate wire-transmission system. High rates of data transmission can be achieved by messenger, air mail, or surface mail.

Requirements for reports vary greatly: the volume needed ranges from small to large, the number of copies may be few or many, and the content and format may be strictly repetitive or wholly unpredictable. Although ordinary printed reports and documents are suitable for external and internal use in many cases, the careful planning of document preparation, based on the idea of prior preparation, may facilitate the next stage of data input. The volume, format, and method of preparing reports and documents determine what type of output devices are required and how much capacity they must have.

It is generally thought that business reports should achieve an extremely high *degree of accuracy* or even perfectly accurate output, with absolutely no discrepancy between the results actually obtained and the perfect results that might be obtained. It is true that the degree of accuracy can be increased by providing enough capacity within the system to handle both the message and the mistakes that arise—erroneous characters, dropped digits, lost messages, transpositions, and, most important, misunderstandings that occur about system logic and operating procedures. If a system has sufficient extra capacity designed into it and such capacity is efficiently used, it is possible to detect and even to correct substantially all mistakes in data origination, transmission, processing, and output. Increased capacity for accurate data processing can be obtained by using more sophisticated codes, more elaborate equipment, and better communication channels. In the final analysis, the question of what degree of accuracy is warranted must be answered by balancing the cost of achieving the higher degree of accuracy against the cost of using inaccurate results. Inaccurate results are seldom fatal in business: gross mistakes usually are soon caught and small ones rarely change important decisions; it is the intermediate-size mistakes in output that cause the most trouble in business management. These comments are not intended to condone mistakes, but simply to put them in correct perspective.

The problems involved in achieving a high degree of accuracy in communications deserve some elaboration here. Various methods are used to try to assure that the message received is identical to the one transmitted. The idea of some redundancy—character and channel parity-bits or check sums—may range as high as 50 per cent or more by duplicate transmission of messages containing parity-bits.

Two general points are worth considering. The first is that every scheme for improving the accuracy of data transmission increases costs, because more capacity—better equipment and lines, elaborate codes, and higher-skilled personnel—is required to accommodate the inherent "noise" while still transmitting the message. A second point is that there is never complete assurance that the message received is identical to the message as it originated. There are only varying degrees of probability that the input and output messages are identical. In other words, perfectly accurate transmission might, and probably would, cost an infinite amount of money. The optimum degree of accuracy to achieve in data transmission is reached at the point where the costs incurred in raising the level of accuracy increase faster than the benefits derived from having the higher degree of accuracy in reports; that is to say, the net benefit reaches a peak.

SUMMARY

The input and output subsystem consists of devices and media for getting data into and usable results out of a processor; it is a critical element of a successful data-processing system. The chain of activities leading up to processor input are (1) occurrence and detection of events, (2) translation of events into symbols, (3) recording symbols as data, (4) converting data into processable form, and (5) transmitting data to the processor for read-in. All of these activities exist for any particular situation, but some of them may be obscured because they are combined with others in the single operation of translate and record, or even translate, record, and convert.

Input preparation usually starts off-line from the processor because it is a relatively slow process. Devices used for converting data into processable form are paper-tape punches, by-product tape punches, keypunches, typewriters with connected card punches, and magnetic-tape writers. Various schemes of sight reading and duplicate operations with comparisons are used for verifying that the original record of symbols is correctly converted into processable form.

Prior preparation of data—the performance of work at one stage to facilitate input operations at a much later time and different place —can both improve operating results and reduce costs. Important examples of prior preparation are customer charge-plates with embossed characters for imprinting sales tickets for optical machine reading; commercial checks imprinted with magnetic-ink numbers for customer and bank before issuance; and factory data collection systems to capture data about man, machine, and job from cards or plates and the number of pieces produced from keyboards on recorders located throughout the factory.

Input-data conversion is commonly required to bridge the gap in format and speeds between the medium best suited for data origination and for processor read-in. Originally, special-purpose converters were used, but now small to medium scale data processors are used as satellites to large processors to handle data conversion and to perform editing and sorting operations.

A wide variety of data-transmission techniques is available: telephone and telegraph, TWX, Telemeter, private wire, and microwave. Common data media used for data transmission are punched tape and punched card. Magnetic-tape data transmission is used by some companies and there is promise that high-speed transmission and even direct processor-to-processor transmission may be used.

Input readers connected directly to the processor range from manual keyboards operating at a speed of a few characters per second to magnetic-tape units as fast as a few hundred thousand characters per second. Magnetic tape has the desirable features of high-density storage, rapid data transfer, read-reverse, back-space, reliability, and reusability.

A most interesting development in input readers is the use of desk sets designed for people to make file interrogations, read in transactions, and receive immediate replies from the processor. Special sets that accept previously-prepared plates or cards for fixed data and also have keyboards for introducing variable data are commonly used in some industries. These sets may be connected to the processor by special lines or operate over the switched teletype network on a per-call basis. Since file interrogation interrupts the processor's operations, a processor with overlapped operations—read, process, and write at the same time—is desirable for handling frequent interrogations and transactions from numerous desk sets. Processor features used to handle communications from desk sets on a demand basis, yet still maintain high speed for other processing operations, are buffer storage, multiplexed input-output, and processor-interrupt with priority.

The most common high-speed output medium is magnetic, tape, since it has the same desirable features for writing that it does for reading. Card and tape punches may operate on-line but are likely to be run off-line from magnetic tape written by the processor. Direct display from a processor is used for desk sets via lights and printed listings. More elaborate direct displays of data—both digital and graphical—are made with cathode-ray tubes for viewing or photographing.

Processors are also connected directly to the factory to give instructions to operate automatic control devices. Processor output goes to operating control devices and people need not work in the control loop although they must prepare programs and monitor results. Automatic digital control was developed in the 1950's for metal-working equipment and for such process industries as oil refining and chemicals, but its use is quickly spreading to other industries.

High-speed printers that print 500 to 1000 full lines of alphanumeric characters per minute and two or three times as many numeric-only characters are now commonplace. High-speed blank-paper skip features give fantastic rates of business document throughput, since these documents usually contain more blank space than printed lines. Ingenious techniques are used to print and punch one document for a utility bill or a dividend check.

Important factors of the business environment affecting the selection of input-output equipment are the types of processing, time schedules, geographical locations of operating and data-processing departments, document and report requirements, and accuracy wanted in the output.

CHAPTER 5

SYSTEMS ANALYSIS AND
APPROACHES TO DESIGN

This chapter and the next one deal with systems primarily from the viewpoint of the objectives set for them and the environment in which they operate. Most of the discussion is independent of equipment, although equipment must be considered during the implementation phase. This chapter covers *systems analysis*—fact finding and critical examination of the facts—and *approaches to systems design*—deciding what general plan will be followed in design. Together they are the search and initial creative phases: what the present system does, what the proposed system should do, and what schemes can be devised to achieve the desired objectives. Creativity is the first phase of systems synthesis.

Systems design is the development of a plan or scheme for processing data based on the facts learned in the analysis stage and within the framework developed in the approaches-to-design phase. In addition to building on the analytical phases, systems design requires all the designer's ingenuity in devising new and improved systems. The designer must synthesize or put together the parts to devise an operating system. This is an entirely different job from that of the analyst, who analyzes—literally takes apart—the process he is investigating in order to understand it.

The *implementation* stage builds on the analysis and design phases by devising procedures, selecting and installing equipment, obtaining and training people to support a system, and putting the equipment and system into operation.

Although systems analysis, selection of design approaches, design, and implementation are discussed one at a time for simplicity, they are closely related and each one affects the others. When a new system or revision of an existing one is begun, each phase may be handled in sequence. But a question about one phase—say, systems design—often requires more systems analysis, or rethinking of the design approach, so that all three are soon carried on together. In later stages, the process becomes iterative and it may be necessary to cycle through the four phases of analysis, design approaches, design, and implementation several times in order to build an efficient system that is based on a thorough analysis of requirements and is well designed to use the most suitable equipment and techniques.

SYSTEMS ANALYSIS

Systems analysis involves collecting, organizing, and evaluating facts about a system and the environment in which it operates. This requires determining the demands for outputs—the data and information requirements of an organization for both operating and management purposes—the sources of data, and the processing methods and files that serve as a link between input and output.

Environmental features of interest in systems analysis are the business activity and the management pattern, since these bear on the kinds and volumes of information wanted for operating and control purposes. The nature and organization of the business also affect the types and quantities of data that are needed to produce the desired information. The number and variety of origination, processing, and use points determines the communication pattern, organization and location of files, processing procedures, and the techniques and equipment used at each stage.

Objectives of Systems Analysis

As used here, the word "analysis" is restricted to fact-finding and to examining systems to learn how they work; such analysis is applicable to existing or proposed systems. The act of synthesizing a system by devising, copying, or inventing is a design function, and is covered later. But, and this is the important point here, as soon as a proposed system is designed, it can be analyzed to estimate how well it is likely to work if put into practice. More elaborate testing in the form of simulation of a proposed system is possible, and may be extremely valuable.

The objective of systems analysis, then, is to learn enough about a system—equipment, personnel, operating conditions, and demands on it—to establish the foundation for designing and implementing a better system, if it is feasible to do so. A data-information system is *better,* if it increases the net over-all output of the organization after considering the cost of systems design as part of the total costs.

Closely related to the objectives of systems analysis are the questions "Why analyze?" and "How much analysis is worthwhile?" Analysis is usually the first step in either partial or complete redesign and implementation of a new system. Analysis may be triggered by dissatisfaction with those operating results of the business which can be attributed to the output of the present system. Important causes of dissatisfaction are late, insufficient, or inaccurate information, an excessive burden on operating personnel to collect data, or excessive system operating costs. Such dissatisfaction may occur following poor design or inadequate installation of the existing system. Or, because of new products, different management organization, additional manufacturing plants or marketing outlets, and increased competition, operating conditions may change, thus requiring revision of the data-processing system in order to regain its original or hoped-for level of adequacy.

Analysis may be worthwhile because of potential improvements arising from technical developments in equipment, advances in the state of the systems art, or increased capabilities of people. Analysis following improvements in one or more of these factors can lead to the design of either a superior system at the same cost or a system equal to, but more economical than, the one in use.

Some analysis of a system is warranted in any situation except the steady-state case. In the steady-state or static case, the system is considered to be performing satisfactorily, operating conditions within the business are not changing, and technical changes in data-processing equipment are at a standstill. This combination of circumstances, as one might expect, seldom occurs.

How much analysis is worthwhile? More analytical work is worth doing, if it is likely to lead to design and implementation of a new system with a total value exceeding all the costs involved. The expected value of an improvement depends on the combined probability of making the improvement and the amount of such improvement. Small improvements are almost certainly achieved from any analysis and design work, although substantial improvements are made infrequently. This pattern is typical, for important gains are uncommon in any field.

On the other hand, the costs of systems analysis are likely to continue at a steady pace and somewhat independently of the expected value of improvements. There is a continuing risk that the expected value of systems improvement will drop below the best estimate of costs still to be incurred to implement the improvement. If so, the project should be abandoned, since, according to best available estimates, continuing will lead to a net loss. Note that the criterion for continuing or stopping analysis and design work is not how much has been spent to date, but how much will be spent to completion. Past costs are "sunk," and only future outlays count in making the decision to continue or to stop.

The feeling is widespread that initial estimates of system improvements are optimistic and that estimates of costs of analysis, design, and implementation are conservative. If so, only those projects that have a large pay-off when initial estimates are made should be pursued seriously.

Analysis of Processing Procedures

Processing procedures are the common thread running between input data, facts in files, and output reports. Raw data originate on documents or other suitable media as events occur—business transactions with outsiders, transfers between departments, and operations within a department. Event data are processed against files to update existing records and to introduce new records into files. System output ranges from brief answers in reply to specific questions, through listings of raw data with little or no processing, to highly condensed summaries and periodic analyses of files.

Since data-information systems are large and complex, a systems analyst can remember only a small part of the details at one time. But an analyst must do more than obtain and remember facts about the existing system. In order to understand and appraise the system in broad terms, he must organize the facts, or get them organized with the aid of others and, perhaps, data-processing equipment. An understanding and appraisal of the existing system, coupled with some clear thinking, are necessary for selecting a design approach and designing a new data-flow system.

Steps in Analysis. There are five steps the systems analyst must perform in analyzing a typical data-information-processing system that is operated by people and uses readable documents.

First, *obtain facts* by interviewing people and observing activities about the events—their type, volume, and timing—that lead to the origination of documents, maintenance of files, issuance of reports, processing steps done at each work station, and flow of documents between stations. Both physical action and clerical events lead to the creation of more documents or initiation of more action.

Second, *collect sample copies* of filled-in documents, file papers, and reports with facts on activity—smallest, average, and largest number—during each period and the number of lines and characters of data per line to indicate the volume of activity.

Third, *study processing operations* to learn the how and why of every document that each person receives or issues, what processing steps he performs, the nature of files he keeps or uses, and the contents of any reports he prepares.

Fourth, *organize the facts* obtained into flow charts, flow lists or other suitable form to trace the path of data from origin, through each stage of communication and processing, into files, and out of files to reports. Systematic methods for organizing facts make them easier to deal with and help disclose gaps and mistakes in the analyst's data gathering and comprehension.

Fifth, *interview each user* of documents and reports to learn what information he uses in his work and what he thinks he needs. The systems analyst should determine what criteria management originally set up for the present system and is likely to establish for a proposed or merely prospective system. Management and operating-personnel demands for outputs influence the systems analysis work in determining how well the present system does or can meet such demands. These demands also influence selection of an approach to systems design and the design work, as described later.

With this catalogue of facts organized in a systematic fashion, it is possible to discover system weak points. These include failure to report data origination, duplicate origination, breaks in the flow because documents issued by the originator are either not received or not properly handled by the recipient, redundancy in file content, and delays in handling and transmitting data or taking the action called for by the output.

Documentation. Documentation is the first step in analyzing a data-processing system. It consists of detailed fact-finding about information flows: data inputs, processing actions, outputs, control points, quantities, file identification, frequencies of transfer, and special time requirements. Analysts interview people, gather specimen forms, and analyze activities. A standardized form, such as the Message Specification Sheet in Figure 5-1, can be used to collect uniform and complete facts about each form prepared in the organization.

In one approach to the fact-gathering stage, attention is focused on the *event* that creates the document and the *station*—a person, group of persons, or area where similar data originate. Tracing the series of events related to one document results in an *event chain,* as described below. Neither the data system as a whole nor individual applications are considered at this stage because it is difficult to assign each operation to an application. Boundaries between applications are ambiguous because events are interrelated and people often don't know how the papers they create fit into the broader picture—for example, one copy of a form prepared by production clerks goes to payroll and another copy goes to inventory control. Although many other approaches to analysis are used, the event and station one, which has several unusual features, will be pursued here.

The analyst interviews people and identifies them by the station to which they are assigned—say, the maintenance department, order-processing department, or a shop in the factory. The division by station seems arbitrary, but it has an advantage in that it follows the organization pattern and identifies the nodes—the points at which data-handling events occur—in the data-flow network.

Data Collection Sheet. Special data collection forms—document, message, file, and report specification sheet—are filled out during interviews at each station. The analyst also obtains copies or facsimilies of completed documents and reports, and descriptions of files during each interview. Data-flow in and out, as well as data retained at the station, are noted on the data collection sheet. Local documents and verbal messages are also covered in order to study the complete information-communication network.

The analyst assigned to a station—and several analysts can work in parallel at different stations—obtains the following facts for each document: official forms control number, name of form, station where interviewing is done, identity—its role at the station, such as input, file-output, or similar combinations, event that causes the form to be prepared, sequences within files, physical form, originat-

CARD CODE (1)	FORM NO. (2-8)		FORM TITLE (9-24)
I	**LØC** alpha	**F220** numeric	R E Q S T A D D L S K I L L

STATION (25-28)		IDENTITY (29)		
MANPOWER activity name	*1 3 0 0* code	Output	O	1 A
		File/Output	FO	2 B
		Report	R	3 C
		Input	I	4 D
EVENT or SEQUENCE (30-49)		Input/Output	IO	5 E
		Input File	IF	6 F
		In/File/Out	IX	(7) G
code R E V I E W R E Q U E S T ⧸ A N S W R		File	F	8 H

PHYSICAL FORM (50) all codes except 8			FILES - code 8		SOURCE (51-54)	
Document (manual)	DM	1	Drawer	1	**PLANNING** activity name	*8 1 0 0* code
Document (typed)	DT	(2)	Folder	2		
Document (process)	DP	3	Chart	3		
Punch Card	PC	4	Status	4	PROCESSING ACTION (55-56)	
Telephone Call	TC	5	Sheet	5	Section A: actions affecting forms	
Teletype Message	TM	6	Ledger	6	Section B: actions resulting in other actions	
Radio Message	RM	7	Kardex Cards	7		
Verbal Message	VM	8	3 x 5 Cards	8		
Paper Tape	PT	9	Tag	9		
Magnetic Tape	MT	0				

Section A

10	Operate	20	Sign	
11	update	30	Transport	
12	extract	40	Delay	
13	pull	50	Store	
14	post	60	Inspect	
(15)	prepare			
16	compare with			
17	reference	FORM NO. (57-63)		
18	complete			
19	tag	**LØC**	**F210**	

Section B

70	Notify	76	Inspect
71	Brief	77	Correct
72	Request		
73	Dispatch	STATION NO. (57-63)	
74	Scramble		
75	Return		

FREQUENCY (64)		SPECIAL TIME REQ'MTS (65-66)	
Hourly	H		
Daily	D	None	(blank)
Weekly	W	Immediate	IM
Semi-monthly	S	Hour	
Bi-weekly	B	Day	—
Monthly	M	Month	+
Quarterly	(Q)		
Semi-annually	E	VOLUME (67-70)	
Annually	A		
As Required	R	—	

DISPOSITION (71-75)		DISPOSITION (76-80)	
STATION NO. (71-74)		STATION NO. (76-79)	
DESTROY	**9999**		
Hand carry	1	Hand carry	1
Telephone	2	Telephone	2
Verbal	3	Verbal	3
Radio	4	Radio	4
Regular Mail	5	Regular Mail	5
Airmail	6	Airmail	6
Teletype	7	Teletype	7

FIGURE 5-1. *Message specification sheet.*

ing stations for documents being processed at a station, processing action, frequency of preparation, special processing-time requirements, volume, and disposition.

Completion of the data collection sheet yields enough information about data-flows to perform the systems analysis steps described below and closes the fact-finding phase.

Editing. An analyst or editor reviews the data collection sheets for completeness and correctness to facilitate coding and also keypunching, if machine processing is used to supplement manual analysis, and flow charting, as described later. He obtains codes for station source and disposition from a master listing, which he must prepare if unavailable. He assigns numbers to unnumbered local forms and files, and reviews and abbreviates descriptions. Editing and completing the data collection sheets is an important task for the editor when reviewing the work of all analysts. Many analysts can work in parallel to gather data quickly since the subsequent editing stage helps make their individual work uniform.

Conclusions from Analysis

The most important conclusion obtainable from the analytical scheme described here is a comprehensive, quantified understanding of data-flows throughout an organizational area. This involves examining the characteristics of different stations, their relationships with each other, and location of major files in the network.

Station Characteristics and Relationships. Station characteristics include a description of files and the type, frequency, volume, and special requirements of data processed at the station. These facts indicate whether a station is an origination, control, storage, or satellite point in the system. This knowledge is useful for deciding where to place input, terminal, processor, display, and storage equipment. Volumes for each station compared to total volume determine the relative importance of different stations.

Station relationships point out potential areas for integration or centralized processing. Local systems are preferable for stations that send or receive few documents from other stations. However, stations having large volumes of communications with each other might be efficiently integrated into a comprehensive system.

Major *file analysis* shows the need for different storage media—magnetic tape, random access, automatic display—and the redundancies in files. Redundancies arise when similar or identical data appear in two or more files. Analyses are made of document activity, document flow, and files to serve as a foundation for designing system improvements.

Network Load Analysis. The data obtained on the original message specification sheets are used to prepare a load analysis of the data-flow network. The data are sorted by station, identity, form number, and card code to develop volumes of documents for each station by identity codes, frequency of processing, and special time requirements. Calculating the workload percentages by data type is useful, along with total volumes, for comparing the activity of stations.

The *station* load analysis in Figure 5-2 lists all documents, forms, and reports processed at a work station grouped by identity code, frequency of processing, and special requirements. The volume of documents is listed by frequency of processing and converted to a monthly basis to facilitate comparison among work stations. Percentages can be calculated for each frequency. The immediate processing case deserves special consideration because it imposes extra loads on the system.

From an analysis of the volume associated with each identity code—output, file-output, report, input, input-file, etc.—the analyst can determine whether a station is primarily a terminal area, a control point, or a storage area. These conclusions can also be translated into needs for input-output, display, storage, or main-frame processing capability. Quantities and percentages about frequency and special time requirements suggest the need for random access, remote inquiry, or other processing capability.

The *network load summary* report (illustrated in Figure 5-3) shows activity volumes by identity and frequency for the total data-flow network and each station. Percentages are useful to indicate the importance of each category at a station, each station in relation to the total functional area workload, and each station in relation to the whole organization's workload.

Document Activity Analysis. An analyst uses the document activity report to see the document flow between different data processing systems, functional areas, and stations at various locations.

The document activity analysis is based on the same data used for the network data load analysis. Documents are identified by stations and compared by sources and dispositions to determine functional activity. The document activity report identifies documents processed at a particular station and a separate listing can be prepared for documents created and used by the same station.

NETWORK DATA LOAD DETAIL REPORT

STATION CCDE 4000	STATION NAME	COST ACCTG

ID FREQ	SPEC TIME REQ	DOCUMENT, FORM, NO.	TITLE	REPORT PRESCRIBING DIRECTIVE	VOLUME FREQ	MONTHLY	H	ID VOL	PERCENTS OF TOTAL MONTHLY VOLUME H	D	W	SM	BW	M	Q	SA	A	AR	SPEC TIME IM
2	M	LOC 108	DM OP COST REPT		01	1.	1												
2	M	LOCF012 OCR	DM LBR HOURS		01	1.	1												
2	M	LOCF014 OCR	DPEH ANALYS		01	1.	1												
2	M	LOCF130 OCR	BUD VAR SCHD		01	1.	1												
2	M	LOCF140 OCR	DM GEN EXP		01	1.	1												
2	M	LOCF150	OP COST REPT/BR		05	5.	1												
2	M	LOCF160 OCR	DM SUMM		01	1.	1												
2	M	LOCF170 OCR	SHOPS DIV		01	1.	1												
2	M	LOCF175	OP COST REPT/WC		34	34.	1												
2	M	LOCF232 OCR	SHOP GEN EXP		01	1.	1												
2	M	LOCF234 OCR	MATL VAR		01	1.	1												
			TOTAL			48.		1.86											
6	B	LOC 130	ACT PAYRCLL LIST		34	74.	1												
6		LOC 107	EARNED HR ANAL		01	1.	1												
6	C	LOC 131	ACT EXPENDTR LST		25	525.	1												
6	E	LOCA240	WORK REQUEST		10M	1667.	1												
6		LOCE100	END ITEM COST RP		-0	0.	1												
6	E	LOCE190	MTCE COST SUM/MO		-0	0.	1												
6	M	LOCE191	MTCE COST SUM/SA		29	29.2	2												
6		LOCE250	MATL IN MTCE		34	147.	2												
6		LOCE300	MATL VAR ANALY		34	34.	1												
6		LOCE440	STD + ACT LABOR		01	1.	1												
6		LOCF012 OCR	DM LBR HOURS		01	1.	1												
6		LOCF014 OCR	DPEH ANALYS		12	3.	1												
6	G	LOCF075	MO DIST/APRV BUD		01	1.	1												
6		LOCF130 OCR	BUD VAR SCHD		01	1.	1												
6		LOCF140 OCR	DM GEN EXP		01	1.	1												
6		LOCF150	OP COST REPT/BR		05	5.	1												
6		LOCF160 OCR	DM SUMM		01	1.	1												
6		LOCF170 OCR	SHOPS DIV		01	1.	1												
6		LOCF175	OP COST REPT/WC		34	34.	1												
6		LOCF232 OCR	SHOP GEN EXP		01	1.	1												
6		LOCF234 OCR	MATL VAR		01	1.	1												
			TOTAL			2528.		98.14											
F	Q	LOCE260	MATL STD COST LS		-0	0.	2												
			TOTAL			0.		0.											
		GENERAL FREQUENCY																	
		TOTALS FOR THIS STATION				2576.			0.	20.4	5.7	0.	2.9	6.2	0.1	64.7	0.	0.	0.

FIGURE 5-2. *Network data load detail report.*

128

NETWORK DATA LOAD SUMMARY REPORT

STATION CODE	STATION NAME		IDENTIFIER										
8100	PLANNING		O	FO	R	I	IO	IF	IX	SA	A	AR	GEN
		PCT	7.48	0.01	0.	0.67	0.20	3.97	87.66	0.	0.	0.	0.
		VOL	22260.	30.	0.	2000.	600.	11819.	260754.	0.	0.	0.	0.
						FREQUENCY							
			H	D	M	SM	BW	M	Q	SA	A	AR	GEN
		PCT	0.	98.27	0.05	0.	0.	0.	1.68	0.	0.	0.	0.
		VOL	0.	292320.	147.	0.	0.	0.	4995.	0.	0.	0.	0.

TOTAL STATION VOLUME 297462.
PERCENT STATION TO FUNCTIONAL AREA 96.60
PERCENT FUNCTIONAL AREA TO BASE 1.67

STATION CODE	STATION NAME		IDENTIFIER										
8110	CLERICAL		O	FO	R	I	IO	IF	IX	SA	A	AR	GEN
		PCT	0.	16.27	0.	0.	0.	67.47	16.27	0.	0.	0.	0.
		VOL	0.	1701.	0.	0.	0.	7056.	1701.	0.	0.	0.	0.
						FREQUENCY							
			H	D	M	SM	BW	M	Q	SA	A	AR	GEN
		PCT	0.	100.00	0.	0.	0.	0.	0.	0.	0.	0.	0.
		VOL	0.	10458.	0.	0.	0.	0.	0.	0.	0.	0.	0.

TOTAL STATION VOLUME 10458.
PERCENT STATION TO FUNCTIONAL AREA 3.40
PERCENT FUNCTIONAL AREA TO BASE 1.67

STATION CODE	STATION NAME		IDENTIFIER										
8200	SCHEDULING		O	FO	R	I	IO	IF	IX	SA	A	AR	GEN
		PCT	0.	0.32	0.	6.79	0.	92.82	0.06	0.	0.	0.65	0.
		VOL	0.	1000.	0.	21000.	0.	287001.	188.	0.	0.	2000.	0.
						FREQUENCY							
			H	D	M	SM	BW	M	Q	SA	A	AR	GEN
		PCT	0.	97.99	0.08	0.	0.	0.01	1.27	0.	0.	0.	0.
		VOL	0.	302967.	255.	0.	0.	29.	3938.	0.	0.	0.	0.

TOTAL STATION VOLUME 309189.
PERCENT STATION TO FUNCTIONAL AREA 62.74
PERCENT FUNCTIONAL AREA TO BASE 2.67

FIGURE 5-3. Network data load summary report.

129

The analyst obtains clues about the degree of potential integration within and between functional activities from the document activity report. (See Figure 5-4.) Independent stations are highlighted because they have little or no transfer of documents to or from other stations. Furthermore, the importance of various functions and their relationship with geographically separate segments of the company are indicated. These facts guide the analyst toward a sound decision about centralized or decentralized processing. Closely interrelated data-processing activities at numerous stations suggest a strong case for centralized processing, and vice versa.

Flow-Listing Analysis. The event-oriented approach to flow-list analysis emphasizes the fact that an *event* creates a document or action at a particular station and focuses analysis on the chain of related events. Event chains are studied rather than the flow of documents for individual applications, which is the customary approach. Flow lists showing all links in each event chain are easier to prepare, analyze, and modify than charts, and can be prepared by a data processor, as will be described later. Flow lists can, of course, be used to prepare flow charts, if a more graphic display seems useful.

It is important to have a complete chain of documents corresponding to the whole series of events from initiation to completion of some action. As an example, the chain of events related to the major failure of a machine in the factory might run as follows. The operator tells his supervisor of the failure; the supervisor diagnoses the trouble and calls the head of the machine repair section. He dispatches specialists to repair the machine and they may call back for parts and other workers. Upon completion of repairs, the repair specialists advise their heads and the departmental supervisor and return the machine to its production status. In the interests of speed, most of these communications are by voice or telephone; the documents for work orders, labor, time, and material used by the repair crew follow later. The interviewing analyst prepares a message specification sheet for each event, whether verbal or written, in the chain of data flow. An attempt to prepare a flow chart or a flow list will disclose any breaks that may exist in an event chain.

The event-type flow list in Figure 5-5 shows a particular event and its sequence in the chain of events listed by station and document identified with it. Message specification sheets are also identified with each event. The processing actions taken as a result of receiving a document at a particular station are identified on the flow list

STATION: 2000 DATA SERV

NO	TITLE	F	VOL	TYPE 1 STATIONS – INTERACTIONS FROM	TO	TYPE 2 STATIONS – INTERACTIONS FROM	TO	TYPE 3 OFF BASE
		D	1000	2000 2000	0	0 8400	0 9999	0 0
		D	026M	2000 2000 2000	0 2000	0	0	0 0
LOCC050	REQUISITION	R			1 2000 2000 2000	1 8200 8200 8500	0 2	0 0
		D		2000 2000 2000	0	0 8400	0 9300	0 0
		M	108M		0	0	0 8200	0 0
LOCC060	ROUTED ITM CARD	Q	1000	2000 2000	0 2000 2000 2000	1 8220 8210	0 8300	0 0
		D			0	0	0 8210	0 0
		M	015M		0	0	0 8210	0 0
LOCC070	SCH SKILL DECRSE	D			0	0 5000	0 5000	0 0
LOCC090	UNASSGN CUNT CD	D	0031		0	0 8110	0	0 0
LOCC080	STD ADJUSTMT CD	Q	7000	2000	0 2000	0 7000	0	0 0
		Q	011M	2000 2000 2000	2	0	0 9999 8100 7000	0 0
		Q	018M	2000	0	0	0 8110	0 0
LOCC090	UNASSGN CONT CD	D	0081		0	0 8110	0 8110	0 0
LOCD010	CONTROL NO CD	D	0081		0	0	0 8110	0 0
		M			0	0	0 8110	0 0
LOCD020	CONT NO CROSS RF	D	0081		0	0	0 8110	0 0
LOCD050	STK LIST CHG REF	W	0125		0	0	0 8200 8100 5000	1 0
LOCE010	ACTUAL LABR UTIL	D	0034		0	0	0 5000 8200	0 0
LOCE020	MATL COST TRANS	D	0100		0	0	0 4020	0 0
LOCE030	SKILL ANALYSIS	Q	0029		0	0	0 5000 8500	0 0

FIGURE 5-4. Document activity report.

131

FIGURE 5-5. Event-type flow list.

SEQUENCE NUMBER	EVENT	STATION	DOCUMENT NUMBER	ID	FM	F	SPEC TIME	VOL	PROCESSING O T D S I O	ACTION VERB	DOC/STAT	DISPOSITION HOW	DISPOSITION STATION	SEQUENCE NUMBER
0.	RECORD CURRENT WKLDS	DATA SERV	FILT080	IU	MT	E		0183	X	PREPAR	FIL 60		DATA SERV	4 1000000
100000.	APLY NEW FAC TO WKLD	DATA SERV	FIL 60	IF	MT	E			X	COMPUT	FIL 61		DATA SERV	4 200000
200000.	DET SPAC REQ BY WKLD	DATA SERV	FIL 60	IF	MT	E			X	COMPAR	FIL 61		DATA SERV	4 300000
300000.	AFTER APPLY FACTORS	DATA SERV	FIL 60	IX	MT	E			X	PREPAR	FILT180		DATA SERV	4 400000
310000.	SUMMARIZ TO DCSN COD	DATA SERV	FILT180	IF	MT	E			X	COMPAR	FILT150		DATA SERV	4 320000
320000.	SEMI-ANNUAL PROCESSG	DATA SERV	FILT180	F	PC	E							DATA SERV	4 330000
330000.	AFTER SUMMARIZATION	DATA SERV	FILT180	IF	MT	E			X	UPDATE	FILT180		DATA SERV	4 340000
340000.	PREPARE REPORT	DATA SERV	FILT180	IF	MT	E			X	PREPAR	LOCE110		AFLC HQS	4 350000
341000.	DISTRIBUTION	DATA SERV	LOCE110	O	DP	E						HNDCY	INDUST ENG	4 342000
												TRANS	AFLC HQS	4 343000
342000.	DETERMIN NEW WKLDS	INDUST ENG	LOCE110	IF	DP	E			X	COMPAR	LOCE180		INDUST ENG	4 344000
344000.	DETERMIN CHANGE REQD	INDUST ENG	LOCE110	IF	DP	E			X	COMPAR	FIL 55		INDUST ENG	4 345000
345000.	AFTER E180/55 COMPAR	INDUST ENG	LOCA020	IX	DP	E			X	PREPAR	LOCA020		INDUST ENG	4 345200
345100.	FORWARD FOR PROCESSG	INDUST ENG	LOCA020	O	DM	E						HNDCY	DATA SERV	4 345300
345200.	KEY PUNCH	DATA SERV	LOCB020	IO	PC	E			X	PREPAR	LOCB020		DESTROY	4 345220
345210.	RECORD BUILD MEASURE	DATA SERV	FIL 61	IF	MT	E			X	PREPAR	FIL 61		DATA SERV	4 345212
345211.	NEW SPACE/MAN RATES	DATA SERV	FIL 61	IF	MT	E			X	COMPUT	FIL 60		DATA SERV	4 345213
345212.	MATCH SPACE/WKLD REQ	DATA SERV	FIL 61	IX	MT	E			X	COMPAR	FIL 60		DATA SERV	4 345214
345213.	AFTER COMP SP/MN RAT	DATA SERV	FIL 61	IX	MT	E			X	UPDATE	FIL 61		DATA SERV	4 345215
345214.	SEMI-ANNUAL PROCESSG	DATA SERV	FIL 61	F	PC	E			X				DATA SERV	4 347000
346000.	AFTER E180/55 COMPAR	INDUST ENG	LOCE110	IX	DP	E			X	PREPAR	LOCA030		INDUST ENG	4 346300
346100.	FORWARD FOR PROCESSG	INDUST ENG	LOCA030	O	DM	E						HNDCY	DATA SERV	4 346300
346200.	KEY PUNCH	DATA SERV	LOCA030	IO	PC	E			X	PREPAR	LOCB030		DESTROY	4 346220
346210.	RECORD BLD/WKLD IDTY	DATA SERV	LOCE110	IF	MT	E			X	UPDATE	FIL 60		DATA SERV	4 348000
347000.	AFTER E180/55 COMPAR	INDUST ENG	LOCE110	IX	DP	E			X	PREPAR	LOCA050		INDUST ENG	4 347200
347100.	FORWARD FOR PROCESSG	INDUST ENG	LOCA050	O	DM	E						HNDCY	DATA SERV	4 347300
347210.	RECORD CURRENT UTILZ	DATA SERV	LOCB050	IF	PC	E			X	PREPAR	LOCB050		DESTROY	4 347220
348000.	AFTER E180/55 COMPAR	INDUST ENG	LOCE110	IX	MT	E			X	UPDATE	FIL 61		DATA SERV	4 349000
348100.	FORWARD FOR PROCESSG	INDUST ENG	LOCA060	O	DM	E							INDUST ENG	4 348200
348210.	RECORD FUTURE UTIL/N	DATA SERV	LOCA060	IF	DM	E			X	PREPAR	LOCA060	HNDCY	DATA SERV	4 348300
349000.	AFTER E180/55 COMPAR	DATA SERV	LOCB060	IF	PC	E			X	PREPAR	LOCB060		DESTROY	4 348220
349100.	FORWARD FOR PROCESSG	INDUST ENG	LOCE110	IX	DP	E			X	UPDATE	FIL 61		DATA SERV	4 350000
349210.	KEY PUNCH	DATA SERV	LOCA170	O	DM	E					PREPAR		INDUST ENG	4 349200
349200.	RECORD SPAC ALLOC	DATA SERV	LOCA170	IF	PC	E			X	PREPAR	LOCA170	HNDCY	DATA SERV	4 349300
349210.	REFERENCE + ANALYSIS	AFLC HQS	LOCB170	IF	DM	E			X	PREPAR	LOCB170		DATA SERV	4 349220
343000.	PREPAR BLDG DRAWINGS	INDUST ENG	LOCE110	IF	DP	E			X	UPDATE	FIL 61		DATA SERV	4 351000
350000.	AFTER LOC55 COMPARE	INDUST ENG	LOCE110	IF	DP	E			X	STORE	FIL 65		INDUST ENG	4 353000
352000.	DISTRIBUTION	AFLC HQS	LOCE110	IX	DP	E			X	COMPAR	LOC 55		AFLC HQS	4 352200
352100.	REFERENCE + ANALYSIS	INDUST ENG	LOC 56	IF	DP	E			X	PREPAR	LOC 56	AMAIL	AFLC HQS	4 352300
352200.	PREPAR COMMAND REGIS	AFLC HQS	LOC 56	IF	MT	E						AMAIL	AFLC HQS	4 360000
351000.	SEMI-ANNUAL PROCESSG	AFLC HQS	FILT180	F	PC	E			X	STORE	FIL 64		AFLC HQS	4 352000
400000.	SEMI ANNUAL PROCESSG	DATA SERV	FIL 60	F	PC	E			X	PREPAR	FIL 63		DATA SERV	4 500000

END OF THIS CHAIN

132

as affecting the document alone or as also initiating some physical operations.

Producing a flow list consists primarily of tracing the flow of documents throughout an organization and linking them to the events and documents that created them. Any incomplete event chains require further investigation to cure the fault: event chains may be incomplete because the functional area is still to be investigated, the interviewer's analysis was not complete and accurate, or there are actually gaps and inconsistencies in the data system being studied by reason of documents having been prepared but not issued, or received but not utilized.

From the flow list of event chains, the analyst obtains an over-all view of how the organization contributes and reacts to events. The document activity and relationships within each event chain are clearly depicted as an aid in redesigning data flow. Producing flow lists from data collection sheets and tracing them through to their logical conclusions force complete documentation and point up deficient areas resulting from incomplete interviewing and the possibility that either stations do not realize what documents they receive, or they fail to use them properly. Event chains that remain incomplete after further study point up a need to improve the present system either by discontinuing delivery of the document to that station or by advising the station of the existence of such information at no cost.

File Analysis. Facts collected for each file include details about data elements, activity volume by frequency of processing and activity type, and other characteristics. File analysis determines file characteristics, locates file redundancies or similarities, and compiles a list of documents and data elements in the files.

The data about inputs and files are analyzed to identify file redundancies in two ways. First, the forms that affect a file are identified with it; this is a *forms-to-file* approach. Second, files are examined to determine which ones are based on data taken from the same documents; this is a *file-from-forms* approach.

If one form is used in the preparation of two or more files, there is some duplication in file content. However, close examination of format, arrangement of items, time periods covered, and degree of detail is required to determine the actual degree of redundancy in the files and whether it should be eliminated.

A broad-gauge approach isolates obvious redundancies in files, so that people can study the most promising cases. First, a list is made

of all the forms and documents used with each file. The lists are
then arranged in the numerical sequence of the identification numbers for all documents going into that particular file; for example,
file A: forms 180, 213, 550, and 672.

Out of a given number of files, three selected files, A, C, and F,
each based on certain forms and documents, may be listed as follows:

File	Forms and document numbers going into each file
File A	180, 213, 550, 672
File C	109, 267, 435, 863
File F	109, 213, 267

Next, the form and document source numbers can be compared
for two files at a time to determine the degree of repetition or uniqueness of file content. The comparison can be made visually for a small
number of files. For a large number of files, a data processor can be
used to compare the document numbers and make the redundancy
search. Comparing the contents of files A and C indicates no documents in common. Comparing the contents of files A and F indicates one common document—213. Comparison of C and F indicates that two documents—numbers 109 and 267—are common
to both.

By analyzing all files and their source documents, it is possible
to determine redundant files that may be merged with little or no
loss of information. In the example above, file F could be dropped
if one more document—213—were used in keeping file C, for it
would be based on documents 109, 213, 267, 435, and 863. File A,
on the other hand, is based on only one form—213; which is in
either file C or F. Viewed differently, files A and C together contain
the same documents as file F. If files A and C are suitably arranged
so that the file F content—degree of detail, format, time period, and
user convenience—is available in them, file F can be dropped with
no loss of information.

Redundancy in files can occur in another way. Assume that
several files contain mostly dissimilar data from many different types
of documents, but that they also contain a small amount of the same
data from a limited number of other documents. Each time data in
the common part of each file changes, all the users must update their
files. In such a case, it may be worthwhile to design a new file for this

common element alone in order to increase user convenience. The actual problem of redundancy in files is much bigger and more intricate than these simple illustrations indicate. They merely give an inkling of the nature of the problem. An equally big redundancy problem exists for reports.

A file analysis report can be prepared to identify all the data elements throughout the whole organization and prepare an alphabetic list by name. It also identifies files by the station location and the particular data elements contained. The analyst can learn several things about data storage from file analysis as described here. Calculation of activity in and out of a file provides a check on the correctness of statistics gathered during interviews. Developing file-activity volume by frequency period for processing gives the analyst some idea of the static or dynamic nature of the files and therefore the type of storage media best suited for the files—magnetic tape, random access, punched cards, or microfilm.

File analysis for data elements, similarities, and redundancies serves as a guide to file reorganization. No hard conclusion is possible about each factor because other features of the operating organization—say, the need to have files nearby for ready reference in the sales department—may warrant keeping a file that is nearly a duplicate of one kept by inventory control. But it may be possible, through technical changes, to offer the several users a superior storage and reference technique even though files are centralized.

Automated Analysis. The analysis of processing procedures described above is similar in many ways to what people commonly do with paper and pencil alone in traditional office systems and analysis work. But it also has the interesting feature that data processors can do much of the routine work after systems analysts obtain the initial facts. One approach to using data processors for organizing the facts obtained about the flow of documents was developed at The RAND Corporation and has been named AUTOSATE (Automated Data Systems Analysis Technique). The introduction of an electronic processor for completely organizing and analyzing the facts collected about the flow of data in a system has three important features. First, input collection is simplified and standardized so that nonanalysts can be trained to collect facts. Second, most of the routine work that analysts do to organize and understand—checking, tracing, reconciling, verifying and flow-charting—can be turned over to the processor. Freeing people from these chores enables them to do more rigorous and thorough analysis. Third, analysts can devote their attention to higher-level analysis and creative design work. Schemes, whether manual or automatic, for analyzing data flows are applicable to proposed as well as existing systems. They can, therefore, be used during the design stage to test the feasibility of a system and discover weak points before the system is introduced. Such searching analysis during the design stage can lead to better systems design.

APPROACHES TO SYSTEMS DESIGN

Systems design is the creative act of devising or inventing a partially or completely new scheme for processing data. Design work, which follows systems analysis, should attempt to cope with more than just the problems discovered during the analysis phase. Systems designers should pay special attention to demands by management and operating personnel for information outputs from the system. These demands are important and even controlling objectives of systems design.

It might seem that both analysis and design work could be done by analysts because they have the best insight into problems and are best armed to solve them. Although this may be so, analysis and design have an important difference. One involves fact-finding, whereas the other depends on creativity, imagination, and an awareness of what might be done. The important point here is that systems analysis is only a base, and not the sole foundation for creative systems-design work.

The degree of freedom offered systems designers in any particular situation ranges from nearly none to almost carte blanche to design whatever seems useful for the organization. The approaches to systems design that are of interest here range from merely simplifying the present system, through mechanization, to developing either a new data system or a completely new management-information system. Each of these approaches to systems design and the conditions for which it is suitable will be considered.

Simplification

The systems designer may merely simplify the existing system. The techniques long used by systems and procedures analysts are suitable for this job, which may include designing forms that are easier to prepare and use, eliminating useless data, planning for more efficient flows of data, consolidating files, and devising improvements in the existing processing techniques. Simplification might be considered the *economy approach* to systems design. It requires a relatively small amount of manpower, time, capital, and technical skill.

The simplification approach is often appropriate, but its implications should be recognized. Its adoption implies that analysis shows the system is basically satisfactory in that it produces or, with minor changes, will produce the kinds of operating and management information wanted throughout the business. This approach may be adequate when inefficiencies exist that can be eliminated by simplifying or eliminating operations, documents, files, and reports that have only limited value. When, however, an important opportunity for technical improvement exists, then a broader approach is desirable.

Mechanization

The mechanization approach to systems design has an important feature in common with the simplification approach: the inputs, data flows, files, and outputs are considered essentially fixed. New equipment and processing procedures are then introduced to get a more efficient combination of hardware and people. This might be considered the *efficiency approach*. The existing structure of the data-processing system is, to the extent possible, merely retained while new equipment is introduced. Systems redesign is minimized, although some changes are required merely to utilize equipment or to take advantage of its best features.

The introduction of more equipment may be warranted merely because such equipment becomes available or because the nature of the business changes enough to deserve more elaborate techniques. Since some important technical changes are involved in the mechanization approach, advance planning is necessary to develop an efficient combination of equipment, people, and procedures. Advance planning extends to the preparation of detail specifications for the system designed around new equipment; the appraisal of system data loads, information requirements, and equipment capability in order to match them; and planning and debugging to make the equipment operate efficiently. Of course, mechanization requires installation of new equipment and displacement of some existing methods.

Example of Mechanization. An interesting example of an increase in the degree of mechanization with other system changes limited is that provided by one version of an integrated data-processing approach. This version of integrated data-processing started in the early 1950's by joint action of several industrial companies and many office machine and processing equipment manufacturers.

The concept of integrated data-processing discussed here was developed to cope with the inefficiencies of fragmentary processing. In fragmentary processing, the over-all task is divided into small parts for people and limited-purpose equipment to handle. The high degree of specialization needed to handle large, complex applications leads to excessive duplication for individual operations at each work station. Duplication reflected in merely recopying constant or repetitive data—for example, names, addresses and item descriptions—is an important cause of inefficiency resulting in high clerical costs and errors.

Each department in an organization wants documents and reports that may vary only slightly in content, but these small differences often require preparation of entirely new copies. Mechanization for repeating constant or common data at each stage of document processing is an important element of integrated data processing. Integrated data processing uses basically standard office machines— typewriters, calculators, cash registers, adding machines, and bookkeeping machines—that are modified to produce and to operate from some low-speed media such as punched paper tape or edge-punched cards. Repetitive data are punched in tape or cards when first originated or as soon thereafter as feasible. Tapes are stored and run through the machines to repeat the repetitive data when preparing new documents. New data are introduced at each stage through the machine keyboards. Selected portions of the old and new data are repunched into tape by the read-punch office machines in any department handling the transaction. Tapes are filed and later used when required.

Data in punched paper tape are transmittable over wire circuits. But some organizations mail punched tape overnight to save money yet suffer little delay in processing. Others convert punched cards to tape for mailing to avoid the cost of mailing cards or of wire-sending either the card or tape data. Rapid communication by one means or another is important for efficient processing in a geographically-scattered organization.

The fundamental point is that mechanization reduces the manual element in duplicating repetitive data. Operations are similar, in many respects, to those in a manual system except that five-channel tape or a similar media ties them together and increases the degree of mechanization. Of course, planning and personnel training are required to set up an integrated system, but the amount of preparatory work is limited, since procedures continue basically unchanged even though mechanized.

Data System Redesign

If the systems designer has fairly broad freedom to select an approach to design, he may devise a new data system. Management procedures, as reflected in the data-processing outputs, may be firmly established, but the processing procedures and data inputs may be modifiable. If so, the most that a systems designer can hope to do is develop a new data system consisting of new input and processing techniques that will improve operations yet produce essentially the same outputs as before. The designer can simplify inputs—for example, adopt a scheme of single point origination of data—consolidate files, and change processing. This greater freedom compared to the simplification and mechanization approaches may lead to designing a system to supply more data faster and cheaper than before.

After a new data system is designed, and to some extent during the design phase, it is useful to apply the analysis techniques described earlier to study the origination and flow of data, file redundancies, and preparation of outputs. Analysis helps ensure that the system will supply the outputs that management and operating personnel demand as necessary. In developing a new data system with the degree of freedom considered here, changes are not contemplated in the outputs wanted by management or in the way that management makes decisions. Such changes require a broader degree of freedom, which will be covered later.

Example of Data System Redesign. File processing is a typical area for data system redesign. Fragmentary processing implies multiple runs of the master files. Transactions are classified by type in a logical order for processing and then sorted into sequence corresponding to the file, if records are maintained in an orderly sequence. Logical ordering by transaction type—receipts ahead of issues—is required for correctly processing files regardless of storage technique. But sequencing within each type of transaction is not required for files in random-access storage.

In the more extreme case, all files for a business might be kept in one consolidated master file. Such consolidation minimizes duplication of file contents that ordinarily occurs throughout an organization. Any transaction, assuming an appropriate instruction program and capable processing facilities, can be processed against the files whenever desired. If access to files is quick enough, transactions can be handled on-line without any delay.

For a more realistic approach, the *functionally integrated* or *consolidated* approach means that the segments in a fragmentary system are combined into larger but not completely comprehensive units. Some degree of consolidation is warranted if various parts of the operating organization are closely related and if input, processing, files, and output have some usage in common. Consolidated processing requires larger-scale facilities than fragmentary processing, but eliminates the duplicate parts of files so that total file requirements are reduced. Any type of transaction can be handled in any logical sequence, since all files are available for processing. A master program calls up the appropriate operating program for completely processing each transaction encountered. Both kinds of instruction routines—the master and operating—are likely to be large and complex, and exceptional situations usually involve elaborate programming.

Functional integration goes much further than mechanized duplication because it cuts across departmental boundaries for the purpose of consolidating data processing as such. Inventory files containing quantity and dollar values illustrate the features of separate and consolidated files. Two groups of clerks—accounting and stock control—keep and maintain separate files in a manual system. Each group wants sole control over records for convenience and to fulfill its responsibility. However, electronic processors can handle equally well the dollar value and quantity transactions against both files. The two kinds of transactions and files are so closely related that one consolidated file for joint processing may be most efficient.

Functional integration may require fundamental changes in the organizational structure to achieve the most efficient combination of new equipment, procedures, and people. This *may* result in merging departments and making far-reaching procedural changes. Developing and installing a system to integrate functions is likely to involve large-scale equipment, personnel orientation and training, and intensive planning. Consolidated files permit more efficient processing because transactions can be entered in one or a few runs of the central file, whereas separate files require individual processing.

Management System Design

When the system designer has essentially complete freedom, the optimal approach may be to overhaul the present management information system or develop a new one. This means that the decision rules used by management and the information required to implement them are open for examination and possible change, but the power to make changes in the decision rules remains with management.

This broad-gauge approach to designing a management-decision system places the data-processing system in proper perspective as one of the factors of production for the whole organization. Each factor of production—factory worker, equipment, and material—has certain costs associated with it and makes some contribution to the organization's operations. Information about operations and the decision rules used to control operations also have their costs and benefits. Costs arise, first, in developing and testing a data-information-decision-making system, and second, in operating it to produce information and make decisions.

Measurement of the cost of information involves uncertainties because some data-processing operations are obligatory—for example, data gathering, processing and reporting for tax purposes. Some data are necessary for operating purposes almost independently of management considerations. Only a few circumstances require data gathering and manipulation solely for management and these may be primarily for operations-research type studies to answer such questions as, "What will happen if we make certain changes to operate this way instead of that?" Sometimes the study of available data will answer these questions, but in many cases new data must be gathered. Gathering new data is likely to increase costs for systems planning and design, for the operating department involved, and also for the data-processing department. Sometimes answers to specific questions are derived by intensive analysis of existing data.

The benefits that accrue from information and decisions are reduced costs or increased revenues throughout an organization. Some aspects of information output that are valuable for operating purposes are the degree of detail and arrangement of reports, frequency of reporting, time period covered, time limits permitted for issuing routine reports and answering special questions, completeness, the degree of focus on important problems, ease of use by management, accuracy, and precision. The benefits obtainable from having more information depend on the improvement achieved in operating results. Measurement, therefore, involves the same difficulties as measuring the results obtained for many of the support services in an organization or the overhead factors of production. The net value of having more or better information is equal to the increase in benefits minus the increased costs of supplying it.

Example of Management System Design.   The steps taken by a large organization to overhaul its inventory control and resupply policies illustrate the design of a substantially new data-information system. Before redesign, each sales-office warehouse kept books for stock on hand, managed its own stock position, and placed orders for its optimal resupply quantity when the balance reached the reorder point. Customer orders were cleared centrally for credit since many customers were located throughout wide regions and ordered from several sales offices. The warehouse nearest the customer filled the order, but the home office issued invoices and collected accounts receivable.

There were many possibilities for system redesign in this organization, but the one of most interest here is inventory control and resupply action. Problems were presented by the fact that each warehouse tried to manage its own inventory and guard against running out of stock. These precautions resulted in increased costs from carrying excessive inventories. Safety levels were higher than necessary and resupply action was earlier, more frequent, or for larger amounts than was required to maintain the company-wide optimum inventory. Economic order quantities and reorder points were recomputed for each warehouse each six months on a scheduled basis without regard for the stock level at that time and when reorders were placed. Such a system might be characterized as a *pull* system, for each warehouse kept its records, managed its inventory, and took its own resupply action to get its inventory.

Management was not satisfied with the scheme in use because customers' orders were not filled promptly, as reflected in the back-order and cancellation rate; inventory policies were sub-optimized at the warehouse level instead of optimized company-wide, and data-processing output seemed unsatisfactory and costs excessive. Furthermore, the prospects for improving the system seemed small, unless a radically new approach for data processing and management control was adopted.

One approach proposed for dealing with the problems described here is to centralize inventory management and switch from a pull to a push scheme for resupply action. *Push* means that action will be initiated centrally to send stock to each warehouse—literally to push it out of the factories to the warehouses. Adoption of the push approach to warehouse stockage implies important changes in the data-processing and management system. This plan involves centralizing inventory recordkeeping and discontinuing local records. Since orders are checked centrally for credit approval, information on customer demand is available when orders are first handled. Data for actual issues can be obtained as a by-product of invoicing. Factory shipments to warehouses will serve, with appropriate adjustments for time-delay, nonreceipts, and mistakes, as warehouse receipts. Thus adequate data are available centrally to keep stock records and manage inventory. Centralized calculation of reorder points and quantities permits optimum planning on a company-wide basis instead of sub-optimizing at the local level. Each time the balance at any warehouse drops to the reorder point, the position for all warehouses and the factory can be reappraised to determine the desired total stock throughout the company and the best allocation between warehouses and factories, including transfer between warehouses, if appropriate.

The important implications of the push system of inventory control are centralized recordkeeping and company-wide stock management. Recordkeeping and inventory control at sales offices can be virtually eliminated, thus allowing concentration on selling, warehousing, and order-filling. Local management may believe their authority reduced, since they are likely to consider inventory management inseparable from recordkeeping. However, the ability of local management to forecast and plan sales can and should be used as an input to central planning of stock levels and resupply action. The company gains in several ways from centralized control. Better information about customers' demands are available for inventory management, since original order data can be analyzed at the earliest point. Company management is not forced to rely on warehouse resupply action, which is, at best, a delayed and erratic indicator of customer demand. Inventory optimization is easier to achieve because the whole company's position—all warehouses and factories—are considered together instead of as individual units; and the company-wide position can be reappraised whenever inventory action is indicated for any warehouse.

The inventory control and analysis problems described in this example are not unique; many companies have similar problems of processing data for and managing nation-wide inventories. As an outstanding example, airlines have developed the most elaborate solutions to the control of seat sales, since the stakes—the value of unsold or oversold seats—are high.

Selection of an Approach

Many factors enter into the selection of a suitable approach to systems design. Some of the important factors are (1) the skill of the designers in developing, devising, and inventing new methods, (2) the degree of satisfaction throughout the organization with the present information output and management decision policies, (3) the availability of important technical improvements in equipment, (4) increases in capabilities of people, (5) the possibility of inventing new design schemes, (6) time schedules, (7) financial considerations, (8) how recently an important change has been made and whether it is fully "digested," and (9) the receptivity of operating and management personnel to important changes.

Factors that contribute to substantial redesign of data systems and even the creation of entirely new concepts are management dissatisfaction with existing information and decision-making structures, important improvements in the capabilities of equipment and people, adequate financial budgets, and suitable lead times before a system must be operational. But, regrettably, there is no ready formula for relating these factors to the design approach selected in a particular situation.

ACCURACY AND AUDITING

The degree of accuracy of information supplied to management and operating personnel is another facet in choosing an approach to systems design. Accuracy is important enough, however, to deserve separate discussion. When outputs are not accurate—that is, when they are different from the true result obtainable by careful data gathering and processing—they may lead to erroneous management policies and incorrect operating decisions. In some cases, the sensitivity to erroneous information is small enough so that little or no harm is done; in other cases, errors may have important and far-reaching consequences. At the very least, erroneous output is likely to reduce the credibility placed in the system and necessitate doing additional work to patch mistakes.

The objective in raising the degree of accuracy for a system is to increase the value of system output faster than the associated costs increase. This is a two-way street, however, for though system outputs are usually considered not accurate enough, in some cases, too much may be spent to get a high degree of accuracy. The degree of accuracy is too high if processing costs can be reduced faster than the increase in other costs following a relaxation in the work done to get accurate output.

Inaccuracies can arise at many points in developing and operating a system: misunderstanding the management policies and rules for decision-making, faulty or deficient systems analysis, misunderstanding the logic of the system, incorrect or incomplete data origination, poor communication, and insufficient control over processing and output. While there are many ways in which inaccuracies may arise, there are also many techniques for combating them. Some of these techniques are covered here as they relate to systems design, processing, and auditing.

Design

Steps to achieve a high degree of accuracy must start in the systems-design phase. This means enough analysis must be done to understand the how and why of inaccurate results. The causes can be classified as *errors*—faulty logic because of misunderstandings, *mistakes*—blunders by people, and *malfunctions*—failure of machines to work properly. Knowledge about the cause, nature, importance, and effect of each type of inaccuracy should be obtained during the analysis stage so that safeguards can be designed into the new system to achieve the desired degree of accuracy.

Errors in understanding the logic of the existing and proposed system may be the greatest source of inaccuracy. The accuracy of the logic for a system can be improved with adequate investigation by competent analysts, careful design, review of design by experienced supervisors, and thorough testing of programs under a wide variety of conditions likely to arise in practice.

Emphasis can be put on improving areas that are important causes of mistakes: failure to originate data about a transaction, loss of documents and messages in the communication network, and erroneous data—for example, transpositions and shifts in catalogue and code numbers. The probability that data will be originated about every transaction can be improved by dividing the tasks of physical activity and data origination between two or more people. This is a fundamental idea of internal control which insists on having at least two people participate in every transaction. Also, data origination can be made a pre-condition of physical activity—for example, by preparing the material issuance papers before issuing material. Machines and pre-numbered forms help control document origination and assure a document for every transaction.

Data once originated should be safeguarded at each stage of communication and processing. Numbers assigned to documents at time of origination can be traced through each station to their destination to assure that all are accounted for. A compound number consisting of the original document number and a new sequence number assigned by each station handling a document increases the ability to control messages and detect when and where one goes astray and to resurrect it. Control totals for the usual data elements—dollar amounts, number of records, and units of similar product—are useful for guarding against loss of a document or a mistake in handling one. Similarly, "hash totals" for items of data not ordinarily added, such as catalogue numbers or number of units of dissimilar products, are useful in almost the same way as ordinary control totals. A control center may be set up to keep track of and calculate totals for controlling the accuracy of the data-processing center's work.

Processing

Transpositions and shifts in catalogue and code numbers can be reduced by the prepreparation of data whenever possible, as described in Chapter 4. Also, an additional "check digit" can be attached to each number according to certain rules and the same test applied each time the number is handled to reduce the risk of garbling it. One simple check-digit scheme makes all digits in a number add to 10 or a multiple of 10. For example, to the number 25630, which has a total of 16, the digit 4 can be attached to make the number 256304 with a total of 20: $2 + 5 + 6 + 3 + 0 + 4 = 20$. A mistake arising from changing one digit—for example, 259304— can be detected, since the total is 23 and is not a multiple of 10. But a switch between digits—for example, 253604—by a keypunch operator cannot be detected by this check-digit scheme since the total is still 20.

A slightly more elaborate check-digit scheme discloses transpositions between adjacent digits. One scheme is to multiply each alternate digit starting at the right by 2, add as before, and attach a digit to make the sum a multiple by 10. Thus, for 25630: $(0 \times 2) + 3 + (6 \times 2) + 5 + (2 \times 2) = 24$; therefore, if 6 is attached, the number is 256306. A switch between a pair of adjacent digits can be detected, since the sum, according to these rules, no longer adds to a multiple of 10. This rule will also detect a shift in a whole number—say, 256306 becoming 2563060. Simple rules merely detect mistakes, which require examination for correction. More elaborate schemes both disclose mistakes and permit easy correction of simpler mistakes.

The extended comments made about design for accuracy apply, of course, to the processing phase where such precautions are implemented. The possibility of tampering with data prior to processor handling can be detected by some of the methods described above and by others in the same vein. Assuring accuracy in pre-processing stages and during processor handling is facilitated by programming the processor to make checks for completeness of data in each message, the "meaning" of data as described in Chapter 1, the presence of all messages in a series, and for control and hash totals. Some manufacturers design the hardware and others rely on programming to make the processor print out on the console typewriter any changes made in the data or program during program execution. One copy of the log can be "locked" into the console for later removal as evidence of changes.

Equipment malfunctions are primarily the problem of the equipment engineer, but the programmer may be able to avoid or detect some of them by repeating arithmetical operations in a slightly different fashion, comparing results, and choosing the correct one. Some processors automatically perform selected operations via different circuitry and compare results to disclose malfunctions. Marginal checking, test routines, and systems checks help anticipate operating malfunctions or disclose them when they occur.

Possible loss of records and files through equipment malfunction or catastrophe is a real danger. Master files from the two previous processing cycles are commonly maintained as back-up against mishap until the next file-processing cycle is successfully completed. Periodically, copies of files may be stored elsewhere to permit reconstruction in case of disaster by using other machines that may be available.

Auditing

Auditing requirements of both the internal or company auditor and external or public auditor affect the design approach followed in any particular situation. Internal and external auditors are interested in the design of data-processing systems for several reasons. They want suitable safeguards designed into a system to be sure that it meets certain standards for accuracy and completeness. These standards cover procedures for complete and correct recording of all transactions, safeguards for assets, and realistic reporting of financial conditions and results of operations.

Auditing methods include examination of source data, methods of processing, and the contents of reports of *condition* and *operations* to draw conclusions about the credibility of such reports. Auditors obtain information from various sources to draw conclusions about validity of reports. The most important sources of information are examination of the books and records, survey of the internal audit and control scheme for separating and controlling the duties of recordkeeping and operating personnel, observation of inventory-taking and similar activities by company personnel, certificates from company management about areas that are difficult for auditors to appraise, and communication with outsiders—banks, customers and creditors—for completely independent data.

Auditors, especially internal auditors, are interested in systems analysis and approaches to design to assure that operations meet their standards when the system is implemented. In the simplification and mechanization approaches to system design, the problem of meeting the auditor's standards are relatively simple because only limited changes are made. More difficult problems of auditing arise with basic redesign to devise a new system because the link with "yesterday" is lost and there is little or no experience for "tomorrow."

Auditors are interested in the same problems described above to ensure accuracy for design and processing. They want to ensure that data are originated about every transaction, that the data on every document are processed to their logical and ultimate end, that neither the data nor program is tampered with during processing, and that there are adequate safeguards for reconstructing any files lost or destroyed. Internal auditors may participate in system design starting in the early stages. External auditors, on the other hand, are more likely to remain in an advisory position. Control over program modification and test-run procedures help ensure that the approved program is being used without any unofficial changes.

Each transaction handled in a paper-based system leaves an *audit trail* from the original event through input and files to final reports. Whatever the form of documentation and processing used, some form of evidence is necessary for an auditor to trace this trail. For many purposes, an auditor may prefer records in readable rather than machine-processable form because he is accustomed to working with readable records. File contents on tape may be printed for historical reference and for use by auditors. If print-outs are too bulky, they may be reduced to microfilm; and some equipment prepares microfilm records directly from magnetic-tape records without intermediate use of printed-paper records. No matter what scheme is used to supply information to auditors, there are two risks: (1) the audit trail may not be complete for the auditors' purposes; (2) the quantity of data may be overwhelming because of the ease of printing lists and the tendency to print detailed journal-type lists of transactions rather than highly condensed ledger-type summaries.

These comments about the interest of internal and external auditors in approaches to system design do not mean that they are in conflict with similar work by system designers and programmers. On the contrary, both designers and programmers usually include many safeguards in programs to assure control over data during processing; in fact, designers and programmers have taken the initiative in this area. Auditors should study the scope and caliber of such features in appraising the accuracy and control features developed by the people directly involved in making a system work. They can then add their audit procedures to this built-in foundation.

SUMMARY

There are four phases or stages in introducing a new system: analysis of the existing system, selection of a design approach, design of the new system, and implementation of the new system to displace the existing one. Initially, the plans may be to handle each phase in turn since they have a logical order, although they are closely interrelated. For example, the optimum amount of analysis depends on the possibility of implementing any system likely to be designed. Thus, each phase requires some consideration of the implications of other phases. After the first pass through all phases, it may be useful to recycle through one or more phases. At some point in introducing a new system, all four phases may be active.

The systems-analysis phase involves fact-finding and critical examination of the facts about a system. This requires determining the demands for data and information for operating and managing an organization, the sources of data, and the processing methods and files serving as a link between input and output. The organizational environment has important bearing on the kinds and volumes of information wanted for operating and control purposes. The objective of analysis is to learn enough about a system and the demands on it to serve as the foundation for designing and implementing a better system. Analysis is worthwhile if there is dissatisfaction with the outputs because they are late, insufficient, or inaccurate. Processing activities may be troublesome because of excessive costs or burdens placed on other departments to collect data. The timing and amount of analysis is geared to the prospective improvement in over-all operations after counting all costs of analysis, design, and implementation of any changes that are made. Some analysis is warranted whenever conditions either inside or outside the business change enough to offer some opportunity for potential improvements.

Systems analysis consists of five steps: (1) obtaining facts about the types, volumes, and timing of events that lead to the preparation of documents, maintenance of files, and other processing steps; (2) collecting sample copies of filled-in documents, file papers, and reports with facts to indicate activity volumes; (3) studying the how and why of every document each person receives or issues, the processing steps performed, the nature of files he keeps or uses, and the contents of reports; (4) organizing the facts about the flow of data arising from any event into lists or charts to disclose breaks in the event chain between origination and destination; and (5) interviewing document and report users in order to learn what information they use and what they think they need.

There are several ways to obtain and organize facts about the flow of data throughout an organization. AUTOSATE uses formal methods to gather facts about each event chain as it is reflected in messages, inputs, files, outputs, and reports. Formal methods have several desirable features; systems analysts and others with less training can prepare specification sheets about data flow for events, editors can scan the data for completeness and uniformity, and processors can manipulate the data to prepare the event chain reflecting the flow through the organization of the data related to an event.

Event-oriented analysis enables the analyst to develop numerical measures about the characteristics and relationships of stations— the points where similar data originate—and to determine what kinds and amounts of processing capability each station needs, and whether a station should be handled separately or integrated into a comprehensive system. File analysis indicates the nature of files and the need for different storage media and the nature and importance of redundancy. Redundancy is more than a simple matter of two or more files containing the data from one or more identical types of documents. File redundancy can be studied from the viewpoint of one document going into several files—the forms-to-files approach; or from the viewpoint of the documents that make up a file—the files-from-forms approach. Some redundancy may be planned to provide users with the desired combination and arrangement of data for quick reference. Network load analyses indicate the nature of processing work done at each station and its importance in relation to other work at that station and throughout the organization. People or processors can prepare flow lists showing the source and destination of each document throughout the whole event chain growing out of an initial event. Flow lists are desirable in that they quickly disclose gaps and inconsistencies in the event chain. Also, they are useful during design-planning stages to determine the consequences of various proposed changes. Flow charts can be prepared from the flow lists, if the graphics seem worthwhile.

Selecting a design approach is often considered part of either the analysis phase or the design phase. The design-approach phase is considered separately here in order to show that some important decisions should be made between the completion of the analysis and the start of the design phase. Knowing all about a system through careful analysis is only a foundation for systems design. An explicit statement of system objectives and selection of a design approach are equally critical to successful design and implementation.

The design approaches discussed here are simplification, mechanization, data system redesign, and information system design. Simplification is a suitable approach when the system produces the desired output and is basically satisfactory except that it is cumbersome or inefficient in certain limited respects. Simplification involves redesigning forms for easier preparation and use, elimination of unwanted data and files, and improvements in existing processing techniques. On the surface, little is changed, although big improvements may be made within the limits imposed.

The mechanization approach to design aims at introducing new equipment and processing procedures to develop a more efficient system while leaving data inputs and report outputs essentially unchanged. Emphasis is placed on mechanizing a system that requires only such moderate advance planning as run diagrams and flow charts for applications to be handled by new equipment, appraisal of system loads and information requirements to match against equipment capability, and planning and debugging to make the equipment operate efficiently. For example, integrated data processing, is built on the concept that data should be captured in machine-processable form when first originated and mechanically reproduced for later use, whenever possible. Integrated data processing uses ordinary types of office machines redesigned to punch and read either punched tape or edge-punched cards. Introduction of this version of integration increases the degree of mechanization but leaves unchanged the basic procedures of the office.

The data system redesign approach presumes a freedom to change both the inputs and processing methods yet still produce the same outputs. This freedom permits the designer to introduce entirely new equipment, develop novel data-origination schemes, and make almost any changes in processing that seem worthwhile. One example of data system redesign is the consolidation of files maintained throughout an organization to achieve functional integration. Other changes may be made in data origination—say, single-point origination of data about an event for dissemination of data to all users. Functional integration cuts across departmental boundaries and may result in merging some functions. Developing and installing a new data system involves large-scale equipment, personnel orientation and training, and intensive planning.

The management-information-system design approach implies essentially complete freedom to develop and produce entirely new kinds of information for management use in running the business. Such freedom may lead to complete overhaul of the present information system or to the design of a new one. The costs and benefits of any proposed system, considering all ramifications throughout the organization, should be estimated to appraise its merits. An example of a new management information system is the shift from warehouse data processing and resupply action to centralized processing and inventory management. The switch from the "pull" to the "push" control approach has important implications for company-wide inventory control and also for management; for example, how the skills and experience—the decision-making know-how—of local managers are utilized, since they are likely to feel left out when recordkeeping and most decision-making are done centrally. Ingenuity is required to make the best use of local management in the inventory-control area.

The degree of accuracy designed into a new data system depends primarily on the nature and importance of mistakes uncovered during the analysis phase and the consequences of inaccurate outputs for operating and managing the business. Inaccuracies creep into a system in many ways: misunderstanding management policies and rules for decision-making, incorrect or incomplete data origination, poor communication, and insufficient control over processing and output.

Design steps useful for increasing the degree of system accuracy include more intensive analysis of system logic and better control over the origination and communication of data by means of check-digits, message numbers and counts, control totals, hash totals, and semantics checks. Processing operations can be monitored by auditors participating in the design and modification of programs, by programmers documenting changes in programs, and by processors keeping a printed log of all changes made through the console.

Auditors are interested in the accuracy and completeness of records and reports, their usefulness for control purposes, and their relationship to the real world. Auditors may participate in systems design to assure that adequate safeguards are built into the system. More often, they can rely on the precautions taken by systems designers and concentrate on verifying the output by tracing the processing path and making tests of reality to prove the validity of the records.

CHAPTER 6

SYSTEMS DESIGN
AND IMPLEMENTATION

The steps following the systems-analysis work and selection of an approach to systems design are the design and installation of the proposed system. In order to design a proposed system, there must be agreement on the kinds of changes to be made—the outputs wanted, inputs needed, and the organization and content of files required to serve as connecting links between inputs and outputs. It is at the start of the design process that inventiveness and ingenuity offer the biggest pay-off in the development of new and different systems design.

SYSTEMS DESIGN

Systems design brings a proposed system much closer to reality by describing the nature of inputs, files, and outputs, and showing the processing procedures by which they are connected. The initial design of processing procedures can be *machine-independent*—they need not be related to particular equipment or even classes of equipment. But as design progresses further, classes and even particular

155

types of equipment must be selected, subject to later revision, of course.

Run diagrams and flow charts are useful for representing the flow of data throughout a business, the processing done at each stage, and the relationships between inputs, files, and outputs. Later, the diagrams and charts are used to prepare detailed routines for equipment and people to follow in implementing the system and making it operational.

The design of inputs, outputs, and files are discussed first; run diagrams, flow charts, and implementation are covered later in the chapter.

Input, Output, and Files

For the purposes of this book, *input* means the facts gathered about events that flow into the data-processing system. *Output* covers the reports, summaries, lists, documents, and answers to questions that the system furnishes to management, operating personnel, and outsiders. *Files* are the accumulated inputs still available to the system for use in preparing output. The data in files may be in their raw state or processed through one or more stages of condensation and summarization and organized in various ways.

Specifications. The development of suitable specifications for content and arrangement of inputs, outputs, and files is an important part of systems design. Output design is the most critical because outputs are the link between the data-processing system and information users—operating and management personnel and outsiders. Consumers do not really care about machines and procedures; they simply want results. The system outputs therefore should be designed to meet the users' requirements. The users may set criteria for content, degree of detail, format, timeliness, and accuracy. These factors affect file and systems design, since anything wanted as output must be *planned for* in designing files and data inputs and in setting up processing procedures that link inputs to outputs through files. Unless planned for, outputs are likely not to be available when and in the fashion they are wanted.

Summary reports—for example, total company sales for a year—may be readily prepared and these are adequate for evaluation of the organization as a whole. But a higher *degree of detail* is required for management purposes: sales by months or weeks, by products, by salesmen, to customers, by territories, etc. Each additional level or kind of detail requires finer classifications or rearrangement within files that may be most efficiently handled by setting up more files. Some higher-level requirements can be met by summarizing detailed-level files; for instance, territory sales are the total for all salesmen assigned to that territory. But the need for cross-classifications and intricate analyses can lead to files that contain the same data yet are not duplicative because they are organized differently. For example, sales may be classified once by salesman and once by customers, especially where the same customers operate in several sales territories, and a unique relationship does not exist between salesmen and customers.

Timeliness of reporting affects file and systems design in two ways. First, frequent reports at short intervals require the separation of events into successive *reporting periods* by setting up new records or by distinguishing between the several time periods within each record. To keep files from growing indefinitely in content, facts about earlier reporting periods may be purged from the record or the whole record transferred to less active storage. The second aspect of output timeliness is the *reporting delay*—the length of time between the close of a period and distribution of reports. Reporting delay needs special consideration when the reporting system is *event-triggered,* as when the event that a stock item reaches its reorder point triggers some action. Interrogations to learn file content require short-delay reporting because people want quick answers to their questions. Since the system must be designed with adequate capacity to process files and produce outputs within the permissible time, demands for extremely quick reporting lead to high peak loads for equipment, difficult scheduling problems, and elaborate equipment with large costs.

The *degree of accuracy* wanted in system outputs raises problems in designing an adequate data-origination scheme to obtain a high degree of completeness and correctness. Safeguards are also required throughout communication networks to preserve the fidelity of messages and during processing to achieve logical and arithmetical accuracy.

Careful planning for system outputs may permit the complete specification of all files to be maintained and the inputs entering such files. That is, anything wanted as an output must be planned for and obtained as an input; both files and inputs are limiting factors for output. Any output wanted must either be in the files or be derivable from the files, otherwise it is necessary to try to resurrect such facts from outside the system or wait until it is possible to gather the required data. Although it may seem a truism, many people overlook the limitation that a system cannot supply desired outputs unless it contains the necessary inputs. And to supply outputs quickly the inputs must already be in essentially the desired arrangement for output: content, degree of detail, classification, and time periods covered. Only minimal processing is permissible, if output is wanted quickly.

File Content. Of course, files and inputs may contain more, much more, data than reach the output stage. Efficient design depends on keeping excessive data at a minimum consistent with the ability to meet output demands planned in advance and a good probability of meeting demands that arise unexpectedly.

File content depends on input data and the methods of aggregation used in classifying, combining, and summarizing for products, different parts of the organization, and different periods of time. The structure and organization of files depend on the nature of demands for outputs. If output requirements are fully specified in advance, the files can be carefully structured, data inputs used to prepare the specified files, and the inputs discarded. In fact, there is only a limited need for files themselves, if output requirements are so carefully pre-specified that they can be filled and no further demand made for additional information. In such a case, it may be most efficient merely to produce the specified outputs and discard both inputs and the intermediate stages of summarization ordinarily saved as files. This extreme case—prepare reports and discard all else—is unusual. But for most operating situations, some of the utilize-data-and-discard feature is worth considering because it is costly to try to reanalyze raw data and relate them to the whole situation on a retrospective basis. So many pieces have to be fitted back together and people have so much trouble remembering all the circumstances for interpretive purposes that reanalysis may not be worthwhile.

If output requirements are only partly pre-specified and, therefore, depend partly upon new questions that may later arise, files cannot be quite so carefully structured and highly condensed. Files must contain more data than are immediately required in order to meet a high fraction of later demands for information. In fact, some input data may be retained in its raw form for processing on an *ad hoc* basis to meet output requirements when they arise. The most difficult case of file organization occurs when output requirements are so inadequately specified that it is impossible to design organized files to meet requirements. To cope with this uncertainty, much of the input data may be retained in their original form with little organization or condensation to await processing for output requirements when someone decides what he wants.

The practical approach to file design is likely to maintain more voluminous files than are needed for short-run requirements. This extra content assures that many unanticipated requests for output can be filled. In addition, raw input data may be retained for further analysis to prepare reports and answer questions not formulated initially but likely to arise later. Since usually it seems to cost little to obtain and store input data in raw form, the practical approach to gathering and retaining all potentially useful data has some merit. The difficulty lies in the high costs of retrieving and processing data to classify, summarize, and analyze to determine significant relationships. Masses of input data retained in their raw form are difficult to cope with and may result in excessive processing costs, both in money and elapsed time, when trying to prepare useful reports.

Example of File Content. In the work-a-day world, a routine record in a file for an inventory item is likely to contain several dozen data elements and several hundred characters. Cursory examination of the simpler inventory record in Figure 6-1 indicates it is useful for keeping a substantial, even though limited, quantity of data about each inventory item. It can be used for preparing catalogue lists, quantities on hand and on order, items with balances below the reorder point, contents of warehouses, stock values, and financial commitments on purchase orders. However, some data about inventory items may be available only in the original documents or handbooks; other desired facts may not be available anywhere in the company.

Run Diagram

A run diagram is a general or broad-brush picture of how files, transactions, and data are handled together. A simple example of a run diagram is one that shows how to update the inventory file and handle the reorder procedure on a periodic basis. File processing uses the master file from the prior run and new input transactions to produce several outputs: an updated version of the master file, lists of transactions applied, errors or discrepancies arising during processing, summaries or lists for use in subsequent processing runs, and documents for operating and management use. In this example of the mechanization approach to systems design, an electronic processor is being considered for handling inventory processing—file updating with the inputs, outputs, and files essentially

Stock Number | 1 4 3 0 7 5 3 1 3 9 | *Ten-digit number*

Stock name | GASKET | *Twenty alphanumeric*

Quantity on hand | 0 1 2 0 0 | *Five-digit number*

Quantity on order | 0 0 2 8 8 | *Five-digit number*

Reorder point | 0 1 3 9 0 | *Five-digit number*

Warehouse location

Building number | 3 7 | *Two digits*

Aisle number | A 5 2 | *One letter and two digits*

Bin number | 3 5 | *Three digits*

Unit cost | 0 0 1 5 0 | *Five digits, including cents*

Stock value | | *Seven digits, including cents*

FIGURE 6-1. *Inventory file master record (schematic).*

fixed. The degree of freedom open to the systems designer is simply to mechanize by introducing more equipment than is presently used. Inventory-control schemes, of course, may offer incentive for designing a superior system rather than merely mechanizing the existing system.

A simplified and condensed version of a weekly run diagram to update the inventory master file and prepare a reorder list is in

Figure 6-2. Each rectangular box represents a run—the processing of one set of inputs. The arrows show whether a file or document is an input to or output from a run and the numbers tell the volume of input or output records. In Run 1, the data in the inventory transaction file—receipts, issues, and orders—are first sorted into sequence by stock number to correspond with the master-file sequence.

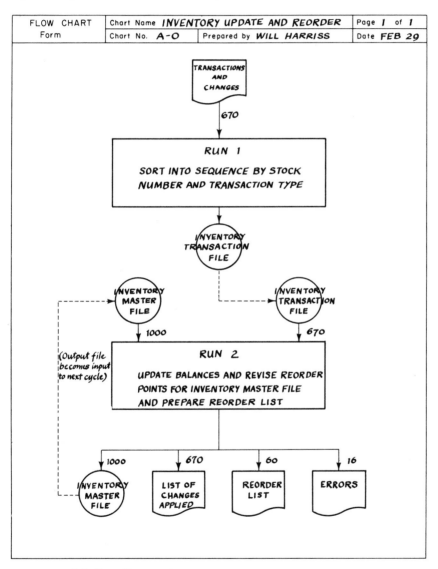

FLOW CHART	Chart Name *INVENTORY UPDATE AND REORDER*	Page *1* of *1*
Form	Chart No. *A-O*	Prepared by *WILL HARRISS*	Date *FEB 29*

FIGURE 6-2. *Run diagram for inventory updating and reorder procedure.*

The transactions are also sorted into a logical sequence for processing by transaction type. Each type of transaction must be processed in a certain order; for example, receipts are processed ahead of issues because processing an issue before a receipt for the same item may lead to an incorrect entry on the reorder list. Numbering the receipts, issues, and orders as transaction types 1, 2, and 3, respectively, makes it easy to sort transactions into the desired sequence in one operation. The combination of stock number and transaction type is used as the sorting key.

In Run 2, both the sorted inventory transaction file and the inventory master file are inputs to processing. The outputs from processing are the updated master file for use in the next cycle, lists of changes applied, a reorder list, and errors. Errors in this case consist of transaction records that lack corresponding master-file records, records out of sequence, negative balances, and other anomalous situations.

A point to observe is that even this extremely simple case contains two runs. First, the transactions are sorted into stock-number sequence corresponding to the master-file sequence and arranged in a logically correct order by transaction type for processing. Second, the sorted transactions and the master file are processed together to produce the desired outputs. If the inventory master file is stored on a media not requiring sequential processing, then sorting into stock number sequence can be omitted. But arrangement of transactions in a logical processing order by type is still required.

A master file is usually much longer than the transaction file. Each master record for an inventory item contains many data elements: stock number, name, quantity on hand, reorder point, location, unit cost, value, etc. But a transaction record for the same item need contain only a few data elements: stock number, transaction type, quantity, and, perhaps, the dollar amount. Also, a master file contains a record for every item in inventory, but transaction records arise for only the items that are active between processing cycles. The processor reads the master file and transactions to update each record that is affected. Unchanged master-file records are merely carried over to the new master file along with updated records to give a current and complete master file.

In designing a file run for magnetic-tape input and output, the work load can be estimated in terms of the length of the master-record file that the processor must read and write. The amount of processing time required to handle each transaction to update the master file should be estimated in terms of processor instruction steps. Since the program for updating each record is simple, a processor with concurrent read-process-write often can perform the whole operation within tape-reading time for the master file.

For another example, files for depositors' accounts can have appreciably different operating requirements than inventory files, although they are basically quite similar. The master file for depositors' checking accounts may be maintained in a bulk storage device with faster access than magnetic tapes to handle a high rate of change and permit immediate reporting. Possibilities for storage are disk, bulk drums, short tapes, or magnetic cards. Changes are processed to update the file soon after they occur; there is no need to wait for the weekly processing cycle. Reports can be prepared with any frequency wanted, whether weekly, daily, or after each change, and interrogations can be readily answered. However, reports and interrogations need careful appraisal since their preparation may interfere with routine processing.

FLOW CHARTS

Flow charts show the documents, conditions, actions, and outputs that make up a particular data-processing system. They contain various levels of detail below run diagrams. Unique symbols for each major class of items are connected by lines to represent the flow of documents, data, information, and action.

Structure Flow Charts

Structural flow charts are used in the general design of a system. They deal with the types, times, and quantities of input, processing, files, and output. They do not, however, indicate how jobs are performed. A flow chart of the system structure might show that inventory balances are required, for example, but not specify whether they are to appear on a typed list, punched cards, or magnetic tape. The structural flow chart represents, in basic terms, the information and data needs of an organization.

Only a few basic symbols are needed for flow charting; as illustrated in Figure 6-3, these are input-output document, operation, file, decision, connector, and line of flow. Card and magnetic-tape symbols are shown, in addition to a general symbol for files. The three-choice decision symbol is useful because three different possibilities often arise from making comparisons—for example, "greater than," "less than," or "equal to." The three-choice symbol, of course, can also be used for the two-choice—"yes" or "no"—decisions.

A sample flow chart at the system structure level is shown in

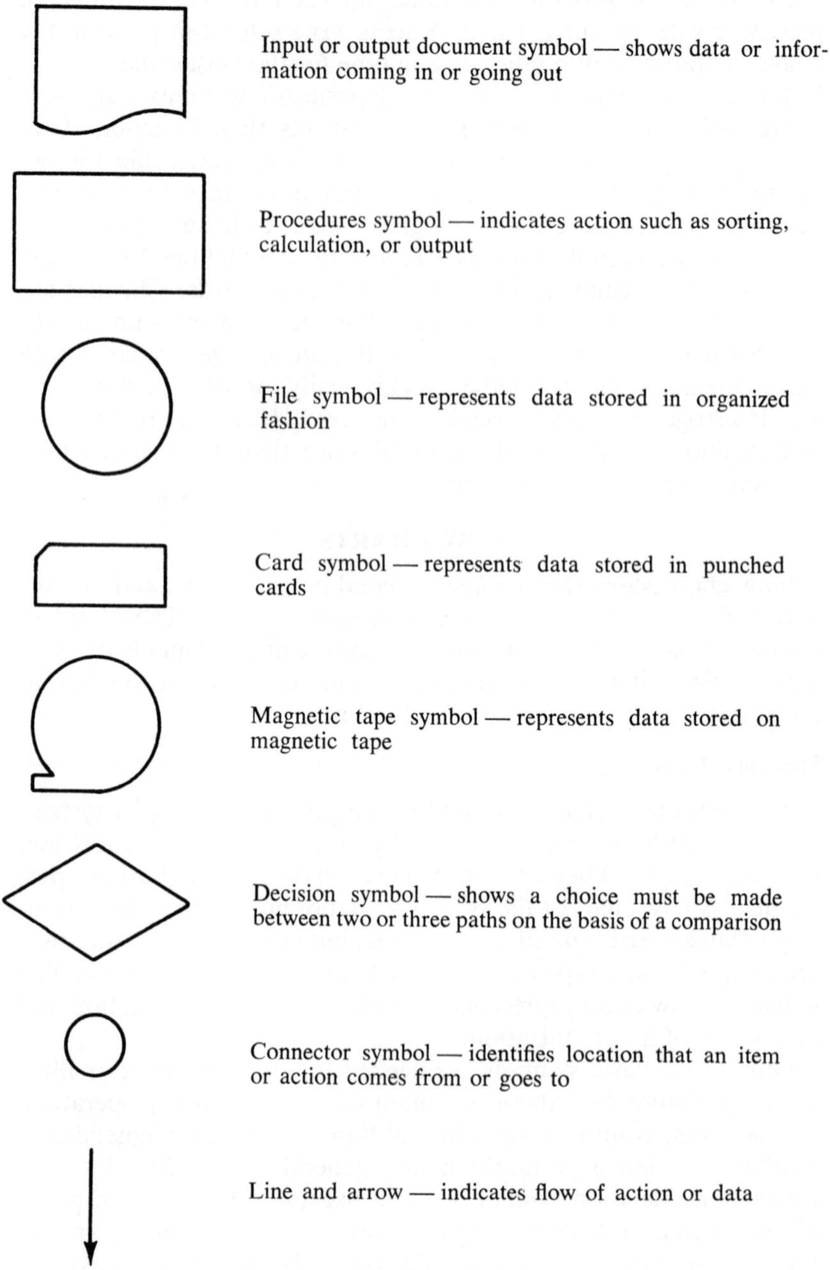

Input or output document symbol — shows data or information coming in or going out

Procedures symbol — indicates action such as sorting, calculation, or output

File symbol — represents data stored in organized fashion

Card symbol — represents data stored in punched cards

Magnetic tape symbol — represents data stored on magnetic tape

Decision symbol — shows a choice must be made between two or three paths on the basis of a comparison

Connector symbol — identifies location that an item or action comes from or goes to

Line and arrow — indicates flow of action or data

FIGURE 6-3. *Symbols for flow charting.*

Figure 6-4. It illustrates a scheme for updating the inventory master file and for writing a list of items that have balances below their reorder points. The *identification* names (or numbers) are given to major blocks, documents, and files. The same name or number should be used on all flow charts and sheets to identify the same

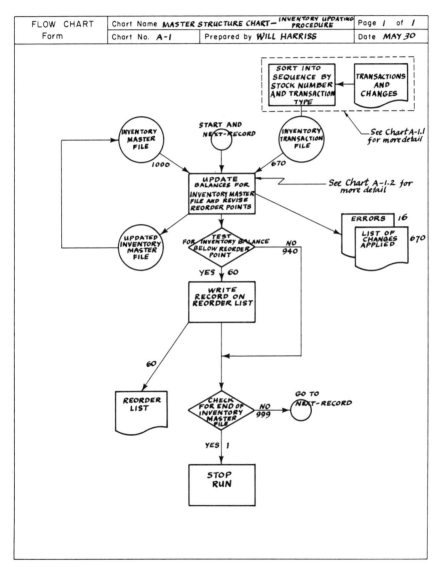

FIGURE 6-4. *Flow chart of structure for inventory updating and reorder procedure.*

item. Since keypunches and other machine-media devices produce only upper-case letters, it often is convenient to use all upper-case letters on flow charts. The INVENTORY MASTER FILE contains the complete record for each item in inventory: stock number, quantity on hand, reorder point, and other data elements shown earlier in Figure 6-1. The INVENTORY TRANSACTION FILE contains all the transactions received for processing since the INVENTORY MASTER FILE was updated in the prior processing cycle.

The *main flow* path of action is represented by lines and arrows entering at the top of a symbol and leaving at the bottom. Action lines may leave the points of the diamond-shaped decision symbol to indicate that the line of action branches into several choices, as shown here. Use of these conventions in flow charting makes the main action paths easier to follow.

Flow charts can show the volume of activity—the number of records or the times that each path is followed. The number 1000, which appears beside the line from the INVENTORY MASTER FILE, means that the inventory contains 1000 items. There are 670 inventory transactions, as indicated. The number 60 on the YES branch from the TEST FOR INVENTORY BALANCE procedure indicates that, according to systems analysis, an average of 60 items are below the reorder point and are written on the REORDER LIST. Volume figures are valuable for calculating work load and processing times.

At the TEST FOR INVENTORY BALANCE diamond, branching occurs when action lines split in two directions depending on whether an item is below the reorder point. The TEST procedure has only two branches, because the "equal to" and "greater than" cases are lumped together as NO. The "less than" case, YES, leads to the WRITE RECORD box. Branching at the CHECK FOR END procedure depends on whether more items are to be processed or the last item in the file has been handled. The CHECK procedure has only two branches because it is merely testing for the end-of-file condition after all records are processed. A line of action may branch into three lines, however, if all three possibilities of "greater than," "less than," or "equal to" are wanted from comparing one item with another.

Merging, the opposite of branching, occurs if the two lines of action that branched at some prior block come back together. Each branch may pass through one or more operations and then merge: In Figure 6-4, both the YES and NO branches of the TEST diamond come back together above the CHECK FOR END diamond. Other merging branches are shown in some of the illustrations that follow.

A loop may be indicated by an arrow to or from a small circle called a *connector*. The connector on the NO branch of the CHECK FOR END diamond contains the note GO TO NEXT RECORD and the NEXT-RECORD connector is located above the UPDATE BALANCE box. Therefore, each time processing is complete on one record, the path of action returns to the UPDATE BALANCE box and processing of the next record begins. The same action can be indicated by drawing a line from the NO branch of the CHECK FOR END diamond to the UPDATE BALANCE box; however, on complex charts the lines become too involved and hard to follow.

Flow charts disclose *common elements* that might be overlooked. The first chart drawn for the inventory reorder procedure might, for example, have an end-of-inventory test in two different paths. A flow chart should disclose that tests for the end-of-file condition are common elements in two lines of action, so that the designer can merge the two lines of action in his next draft of the chart and merely test once. Flow charts are tools for discovering and developing improvements. Thus a chart is only tentative when first drawn, and each new draft may reveal simplifications and improvements.

The precise method used to perform a job is not important at this stage. The INVENTORY MASTER FILE may be in a book, on punched cards, on magnetic tape, or in a random-access storage unit of a data processor. A clerk, punched-card equipment, or an electronic processor can update the file and prepare a reorder list. Because of the high degree of generality, a structural flow chart is useful to sketch the general design of a system.

Technique Flow Charts

Technique flow charts show data and information requirements and the particular methods proposed for filling them. These flow charts specify the media used for input and output and indicate the nature of files and types of processing equipment. A separate set of flow charts is required for each set of equipment considered. Selection of a particular technique may require modification of the structure already developed. Although a wide variety of symbols are sometimes used for technique flow charts of a proposed system, a limited set of symbols and brief explanations are often adequate.

Flow charts can be prepared with different *levels of detail*. A general outline, which concentrates on the major divisions of the operation and contains little detail, may be prepared first for designing the system and to help plan and control further design work. However, more details are required in flow charts as systems design progresses. Very detailed charts are useful when the systems designer wants to offer the programmer-coder more guidance in complex situations. One set of flow charts with only one level of detail may serve for small-scale operations, but many levels of detail are required for flow-charting large-scale operations.

The transaction-sequencing part of the structure flow chart for the inventory update and reorder procedure in Figure 6-4 is developed for one particular technique in Figure 6-5. Since the processor selected here takes only magnetic-tape input, the data on documents are first punched in cards and then converted to tape. The data on tape are then sequenced to produce the INVENTORY TRANS-ACTION FILE. Several other techniques might be used to handle these procedures, but each decision made restricts the freedom to make other choices. The programmer-coder responsible for preparing instruction routines will use the technique flow charts as a guide in his work.

Figure 6-6 is a technique flow chart for that part of Figure 6-4 covering master file processing—updating the inventory balances and revising the reorder points. Only four major procedures— READ, UPDATE, REVISE, and WRITE—and the associated files, input, and output are shown. But each procedure can be expanded to a detailed flow chart, since more details are required as systems-design work progresses. The connector above the IN-VENTORY TRANSACTION FILE shows that its preparation is explained on Flow Chart A-1.1 (Figure 6-5).

Figure 6-7 shows more detail for the READ and UPDATE operations. Essentially, it shows the sequence of operations involved in reading a record from the INVENTORY MASTER FILE and the INVENTORY TRANSACTION FILE, comparing them to determine whether they match, and updating the master record with data from the transaction record. Both a transaction record and master record are needed to start the process, so the first two boxes on the START path contain read instructions for both files. Several steps of this type, called "set up" operations, are required to prepare for a repetitive process. The START path is followed only *once*; thereafter a new record is needed from *either* the INVENTORY MASTER FILE or the INVENTORY TRANSACTION FILE.

After reading, the next step is to compare the stock numbers of

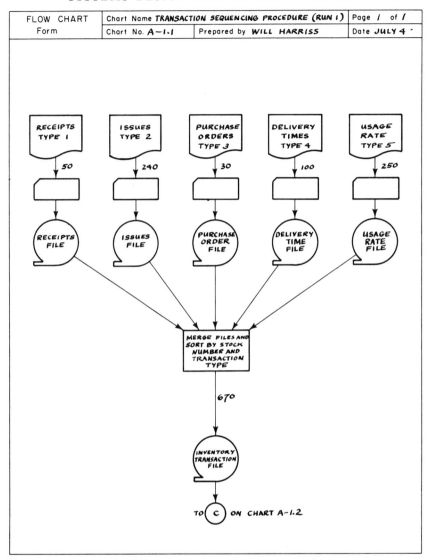

| FLOW CHART | Chart Name *TRANSACTION SEQUENCING PROCEDURE (RUN 1)* | Page *1* of *1* |
| Form | Chart No. *A—1.1* | Prepared by *WILL HARRISS* | Date *JULY 4* ˙ |

FIGURE 6-5. *Transaction sequencing procedure.*

the transaction and master records (TRANSACTION RECORD NUMBER : MASTER RECORD NUMBER). The three outcomes and their meanings are as follows:

1. *Greater Than* ($>$). The transaction has a larger stock number than the master record; therefore it should match a master record later in the file. The desired action is to write the existing master records

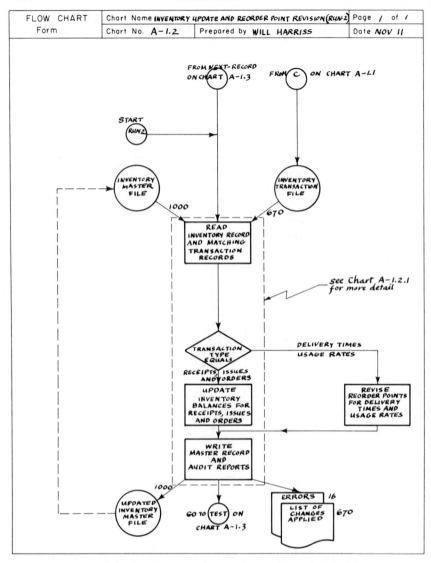

FIGURE 6-6. *Inventory update and reorder point revision.*

and read new ones until a master record matches the transaction record. The action path goes to the TEST procedure on Chart A-1.3.1 (not illustrated) and returns to this chart at the NEXT-RECORD connector.

2. *Less Than* ($<$). A transaction with a smaller stock number than the master record indicates an error in sequence.

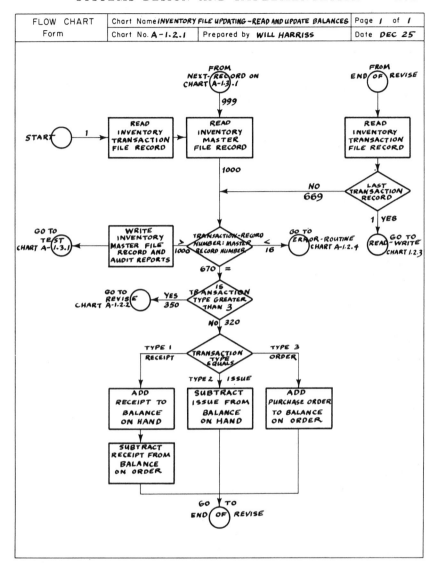

FIGURE 6-7. *Procedure for file reading and balance updating.*

3. *Equal To* ($=$). When both numbers are equal, the transaction will be used to update the master.

If the transaction is type 4 or 5, it is a change in delivery time or usage rate, respectively. The action path branches to the RE-VISE operation on Chart A-1.2.2 and returns to this chart at the

END-OF-REVISE connector. Transactions of types 1, 2, and 3 are processed as shown in Figure 6-7. If no transaction record remains (the YES branch of the LAST TRANSACTION diamond), no further processing is required and the action path goes to Chart A-1.2.3, which contains a special process to write the remaining INVENTORY MASTER FILE RECORDS on the output file. Otherwise, the next transaction record is read and the process repeated.

Many charts with the degree of detail shown in Figure 6-7 may be needed to cover the whole inventory updating and reorder procedure. The programmer may prepare charts with even more detail for his guidance.

Accuracy, simplicity, and understandability are prime considerations when preparing flow charts for systems analysis and design. "Simplicity" means that all relevant facts are presented as clearly as possible. Frequent explanatory comments, even brief ones, are helpful in developing and understanding a flow chart. Files, input, output, and operations should be labeled for flow-charting business problems. The flow-chart symbols used in this chapter are merely illustrative, and system designers can select the set or sets of symbols best suited to their needs and the problem at hand. However, a standard set for use by all programmers in an organization will help communications and reduce confusion.

Identification of all the inputs, outputs, operations, flow charts, and documents is useful in systems analysis and design. Documents and files should be named, numbered or given some other non-ambiguous identification for referring to them. Actions, files, or other items dealt with on two or more flow charts should be cross-referenced, and charts at various levels of detail for the same operation should be cross-referenced to each other. Extreme care is necessary to keep all the relations and details straight.

DECISION TABLES

An examination of detailed flow charts for processes such as inventory file updating reveals some severe deficiencies. First, flow charts are difficult and laborious to draw because of the symbols and spacing. Clarity presents a second and more serious problem. Conditions and actions of the type, IF Condition 1, THEN Action 1, are individually simple, but a series of condition-action phrases may become difficult to follow. There may not be a clear and obvious path from beginning to end through a flow chart, since action for any particular condition depends on all *prior* condition-action phrases. For example, the user might wish to determine from the flow chart in Figure 6-7 whether any master record is written before all the transactions affecting that particular record are handled. The answers to questions of this type are not obvious from a study of the flow chart, and it is easy to get lost while tracing an action path through several branches. If the designer must determine whether all conditions are covered or whether there exist alternative methods that may be superior, then flow charts offer little help. It is little wonder that people are willing to accept incomplete statements of a problem, quit trying to formulate the logic of an application, and stop searching for better methods. Instead, they simply skip to programming for the machine.

Decision tables are a design tool used to overcome some of the deficiencies of the flow-chart approach to systems design. These tables are similar in use and construction to flow charts, but they show conditions and operations in a more clear and orderly fashion, thus facilitating careful and complete development of the problem logic during both the problem analysis and programming stages.

Example of a Decision Table

Table 6-1 is a typical decision table. It parallels the flow chart in Figure 6-7 to facilitate comparison and understanding. The mechanics for constructing a decision table are simple. The table, as illustrated in Figure 6-8, is divided vertically into two parts— the stub and the body. All the *conditions* that are relevant to the problem are listed in the upper part of the stub in any order that is convenient. These conditions are the same as the contents of the diamond or branch symbols on a conventional flow chart. *Actions*— the contents of the rectangular symbols on a flow chart—are listed in the lower part of the stub in the sequence desired for execution.

The possible *outcomes* for each condition—such as the YES, NO, EQUAL, TYPE 1, and others used in conventional flow charts to identify the outgoing branches of a decision diamond—are listed in the upper part of the body. To conserve space, "Y" is used for YES and "N" for NO. A "–" indicates that the outcome is irrelevant and should be ignored. Each column in the body makes up a *rule*. When *all* the condition outcomes in the top half of a rule are satisfied, then the actions with an "X" opposite them in the bottom half of that particular rule are executed. A rule corresponds, therefore, to *one* of the several or many possible paths through a flow chart.

DECISION TABLE Form	Table Name	INVENTORY FILE UPDATE		Page 1 of 1
	Chart No. T-1.2.1	Prepared by WILL HARRISS		Date FEB 29

Stub	Body

	Rule Number														
Conditions	1	2	3	4	5	6	7	8	9	10	11	12	13	14	15
START	Y	N	N	N	N	N	N	N	N						
LAST TRANSACTION RECORD	–	N	N	N	N	N	N	N	Y						
TRANSACTION NO : MASTER RECORD NO	–	>	=	=	=	=	=	<	–						
TRANSACTION TYPE EQUALS	–	–	1	2	3	4	5	–	–						

Actions	1	2	3	4	5	6	7	8	9	10	11	12	13	14	15
ADD RECEIPT TO BALANCE ON HAND			X												
SUBTRACT RECEIPT FROM BALANCE ON ORDER			X												
SUBTRACT ISSUE FROM BALANCE ON HAND				X											
ADD PURCHASE ORDER TO BALANCE ON ORDER					X										
GO TO ERROR-ROUTINE TABLE								X							
PERFORM REVISE TABLE						X	X								
READ INVENTORY TRANSACTION FILE RECORD	X		X	X	X	X	X								
WRITE INVENTORY MASTER FILE RECORD		X													
PERFORM TEST TABLE		X													
READ INVENTORY MASTER FILE RECORD	X	X													
GO TO INVENTORY FILE UPDATE TABLE	X	X	X	X	X	X	X								
GO TO READ-WRITE TABLE									X						

TABLE 6-1. *Decision table for inventory file updating.*

Rule 1 handles the first cycle or set-up operations. For the first cycle, the START condition outcome is YES, and other conditions are immaterial. The action wanted for Rule 1 is to read a transaction record, read a master-file record, and return to the beginning of this table. Rules 2 through 8 handle the main body of processing. The NO's for these rules mean that this is *not* the start cycle. The last transaction record has *not* been used yet. In Rule 2, the transaction number exceeds the inventory master-file record number; therefore, either all transactions for this master record have been processed or there were none. The transaction type in this case is irrelevant. The resulting action is to write out the inventory master-file record, perform whatever action is specified in the test table, read in another inventory master-file record, and go to the beginning of this table. The action, GO TO INVENTORY FILE UPDATE TABLE, directs the processor to return to the *beginning* of this particular table and test the conditions again for the new master record.

The PERFORM TEST TABLE procedure in Rule 2 has some special features. This statement causes the action path to go to a subtable—the TEST TABLE—to find the appropriate rule, execute it, and return to the next action in the rule being executed in the main table—the INVENTORY FILE UPDATE TABLE. Therefore, after the appropriate actions in the TEST TABLE are executed, the path of action returns to the INVENTORY FILE UPDATE table and the last two actions of Rule 2—READ and GO TO—are then executed. The PERFORM statement, in effect, allows one table to contain other tables within it. Note that this PERFORM TEST TABLE process corresponds to the action path of Figure 6-7, which leaves at TEST and returns at NEXT-RECORD.

Rules 3, 4, 5, 6, and 7 apply to a transaction record and master-file record with matching numbers. Therefore, the transaction type —1, 2, 3, 4, or 5—determines the kind of action—ADD RECEIPT TO BALANCE ON HAND, etc.,—for updating the master-file record. Rules 6 and 7 contain PERFORM statements for the REVISE TABLE, which contains the processing logic for type 4 and 5 transactions. The next step is to read another transaction record and go to the beginning of the table to handle the new transaction. Rule 8 covers the out-of-sequence transaction because its stock number is less than the master-file stock number. The action, GO TO ERROR-ROUTINE TABLE, might result in punching a card for immediate study or writing the out-of-sequence transaction on a tape for printing. Action for a short error-routine might be included in the present decision table. Rule 9 deals with the condition in which *all* transactions have been handled, but more master-file records must be read and written on the output tape.

General Form for Decision Tables

Two important features of decision tables are described above. One is that conditions and actions are kept separate. Another is that all conditions are tested to find an applicable rule before any action is executed. Other features of interest in this method of problem analysis are (1) the uniqueness of rules, (2) the sequence of execution, (3) limited and extended entries, (4) the else-rule, and (5) the relationship of decision tables to programming.

Unique Rules.   The set of conditions specified by each rule must be unique to avoid ambiguity. Equivalent sets of conditions leading to different actions are erroneous. The converse—different conditions leading to the same action—is permissible and may be desirable. Often, however, careful examination of two or more rules leading to the same action will disclose that a redundancy exists and that either the problem logic is incorrect or one rule is contained in another. Several rules might be simplified to a smaller number of rules by, perhaps, using an "it doesn't matter" for one condition to cover YES in one rule and NO in another, or by broadening the limits of outcomes so that one outcome will cover another when no distinction was actually intended.

Sequence of Execution.   All conditions within a rule are tested at once to find if the rule applies to a particular situation in the data—in effect, parallel testing. The rules are sequence-numbered for convenience, as shown in Table 6-1; however, this does not imply that the rules must be executed in this sequence. If each rule is unique and does not have to rely on other rules or the sequence in which they are written, then that sequence which is most desirable— easiest to program, fastest running, or takes least high-speed storage —can be selected at the time of programming. The programmer can, for example, indicate the frequency of occurrence of each rule for processor guidance during the compiling pass to develop a faster-running program. But under these circumstances the programmer cannot be sure that rules will be executed in exactly the hoped-for sequence.

Each action desired for a rule is marked "X"; an action not wanted for a rule is simply marked "−" or left blank. Actions marked

"X" for a rule are executed in their *row-sequence*. Any desired sequence can be obtained by an appropriate listing; thus, the actions A and B can be executed in both the A-B and B-A sequences by listing A, B, and A, and then selecting A and B for one rule and B and A for another.

Limited and Extended Entries. The decision table in Table 6-1 has "limited entries" for all actions and for the START and LAST TRANSACTION conditions. Limited-entry rules are restricted to the notation "Y," "N," for condition outcomes, and "X" and "blank" for actions.

The two conditions involving transaction number and transaction type have "extended entries." Part of the record-number condition— the operators ">," "=," and "<"—extends into the rules column. For transaction types, the numbers "1," "2," and "3" are placed in the rule column as the second operand. The extended entry form is compact; one extended entry may have the capability of several limited entries. For example, the extended entry conditions of >, =, <, MASTER RECORD NO. requires the following limited entries (in the context of Table 6-1):

CONDITIONS	RULES								
	1	2	3	4	5	6	7	8	9
TRANSACTION NO > MASTER RECORD NO	–	Y	N	N	N	N	N	N	–
TRANSACTION NO = MASTER RECORD NO	–	N	Y	Y	Y	Y	Y	N	–
TRANSACTION NO < MASTER RECORD NO	–	N	N	N	N	N	N	Y	–

Similarly, actions can be written as extended entries to place either an operand or both an operator and an operand in the rules area. For example, acceptance of a customer's order on account may be conditioned on both credit bureau ratings and the amount of his account overdue. For the AMOUNT OF ORDER TO ACCEPT, the "<" is an operator and the amounts of $7000, $5000, and $2000 are operands.

Limited and extended entries can be used in the same decision table, but each row must be in one form only. Obviously, condition rules of YES and NO are incompatible with EXCELLENT, <30,000, and >20,000. Nor can X and blank for actions be mixed with ANY, <7000, and NONE.

STUB	BODY				
CONDITIONS	RULE NUMBER				
	1	2	3	4	5
CREDIT RATING	EXCELLENT	EXCELLENT	GOOD	GOOD	POOR
AMOUNT OVERDUE	<30,000	>30,000	<20,000	>20,000	–
ACTIONS					
AMOUNT OF ORDER TO ACCEPT	ANY	<7000	<5000	<2000	NONE

Else-Rule. The number of rules required to handle all possible conditions grows rapidly with the number of conditions. For the simplest case, in which each condition is filled by either YES or NO, as the number of conditions increases 1, 2, 3, 4, . . . n, the possible number of rules grows 1, 4, 8, 16, . . . 2^n. The complete set of rules soon becomes burdensome to write, and many are likely to have the same actions. The irrelevant, seldom-used, or logically-impossible rules may be omitted and an ELSE-rule with all conditions blank introduced to handle the situation when none of the other rules apply. The action associated with the ELSE-rule may be to halt processing, note the unanticipated case, or take some corrective action and return to this table, as appropriate. The ELSE-rule is executed when *none* of the other rules apply.

Relationship to Programming. Decision tables are described here as a method for organizing the logic for problem solution. However, they can also be used as a programming language. The brief coverage of decision tables here is consistent with the DETAB-X (Decision Table, Experimental) Programming Language, which is a combination of decision tables and COBOL, the Common Business Oriented Language discussed in Chapter 7. In the DETAB-X Language the contents of a decision table are treated as a single *procedure* and can be executed whenever desired in a COBOL program. The main processing program uses a PERFORM or GO TO statement to send program control to any desired decision table. When a PERFORM statement is used, the main program regains program control after all the data involved are handled by that table. One table can, of course, send program control to another table before returning to the main program. Viewed in this way, a program may consist of an executive control routine with a high fraction of the processing operations organized as decision tables.

IMPLEMENTATION

Implementation of a data-processing system extends from the systems-design phase to the successful operations of the new system and displacement of the existing system. The stages considered here in the implementation phase are (1) feasibility study, (2) applications study, (3) equipment selection, and (4) installation and review. Another phase, programming or the preparation, testing, and use of processor programs to carry out the applications, is discussed in Chapters 7 and 8.

Feasibility Study

A feasibility study rounds out the picture of systems analysis and design by considering the equipment available and determining whether new equipment and the proposed system are likely to be more efficient than the equipment and system already in use. Study of the feasibility of a system is important, for it affects all subsequent action. If the conclusion is negative, all further study may be shelved; if the conclusion is favorable, it is followed by an applications study and continued work toward the system's realization.

The first step in a feasibility study is to assign several competent people to a preliminary study group. Some group members should be familiar with the company operating environment for the areas under consideration. Other members should know the characteristics of the class or even type of equipment that may be used and the experience of other people in using it. From the beginning, the group should attempt to enlist the support of top management by suitable presentations, orientations, and briefings.

It is highly desirable to have a written charter to define the object and scope of the feasibility study. A charter can assure constancy of direction and serve as the basis for reviewing progress. A preliminary feasibility study should be completed in a few months, and should utilize the systems-analysis and design work described above and available knowledge about equipment in estimating the time and costs of completing the feasibility study. The preliminary study should also indicate the range of estimated costs and benefits that can be derived from carrying out the applications study and installing the proposed system. If the conclusion from a preliminary study is favorable, the study group should continue its work and make a full-scale study.

The design approach to be followed—whether simplification, mechanization, data-system redesign, or new management system—and the organizational objectives—reduced costs, improved information, faster processing, or maximum profit—should be spelled out in order to focus effort. Important users, processors, and suppliers of data should be listed as potential areas for further analysis. Other targets for analysis are areas with repetitive operations and high clerical costs, areas that presently have insufficient data for operating and management purposes, and those where newer equipment and techniques can have the greatest impact.

After the over-all picture of data-information requirements is developed, the most fruitful areas should be studied intensively. Factors to consider when evaluating an area are the history of the operation, experience of others with similar applications, expected benefits and costs, personnel requirements, relationships of various areas, resources of the organization, and the need for flexibility. Expected benefits are reduced costs, improved information, and the ability to handle large volumes with little increase in facilities.

The independence or interdependence of operations throughout an organization determines whether small areas can be tackled effectively or whether a broad-gauge attack on all related problems is required. Conducting a feasibility study involves determining the frame of reference for the system and the organizational structure involved. As pointed out in the discussion of systems analysis, it is necessary to examine the purpose and function of the system, catalogue internal functions and documents, and make flow charts or flow lists of operations. Whether it is necessary to develop a "blow-by-blow" description of what happens in a system depends on how much change will be made in the transition. To the extent that the new system is likely to be radically different, as in the management-system approach to design, the usefulness of detailed study of the existing system is reduced. Similarly, if the proposed changes are likely to be minimal, as in the simplification approach to design, detailed study has limited value. It is in the important intermediate design approaches, such as mechanization and data-systems redesign, that detailed study of the existing system is most valuable because changes are important but not radical.

Cost summaries should be developed for the factors likely to change with introduction of new methods. Changes may include more equipment, fewer personnel, and new methods for originating data, issuing reports, and controlling operations. Factors likely to remain constant deserve some analysis but need not be included in cost studies since they will not affect the *difference* between the costs of the old and new systems, and decisions are based on differences rather than absolute amounts. Changes in personnel costs may be an important factor in absorbing the cost of equipment. The costs, benefits, resources, conversion problems, and future plans for one or more systems—hardware and operating procedures—should be developed for each data-processing area that is studied.

Concluding a feasibility study requires a candid and complete report to management in order to gain acceptance for recommendations. A concise statement of conclusions and recommendations should be backed up by a detailed statement and supporting material. The range of uncertainty involved in estimates should be specified so that conclusions can be tempered by the range of estimates used.

Applications Study

The applications study group designs a system or set of procedures and establishes specifications for the equipment required by the system. The applications study group decides, in cooperation with others, on the methods and procedures to change, the files to set up or eliminate, the equipment to obtain or discard, and the organizational changes to make. This group takes the general proposals developed in the feasibility study and makes them specific. It also reviews the economic aspects of all proposals.

The applications study aims at creating the optimum operating-system design. Systems design involves developing inputs, constructing flow-process charts, integrating operations, determining personnel needs, and exploring equipment potentials. Fundamental to the applications-study functions are fact-finding, preliminary evaluation, systems design, and specifications development. Designing an efficient system requires providing for multiple use of common source data, minimum repetitive use of identical data elements, and careful selection of the most economical processor—manual or automated. The applications study develops specifications for input, files, data-handling, output, and special requirements.

Conducting an efficient applications study involves advance planning for time and money budgets, organization and personnel, systems analysis, systems design, new equipment evaluation, and correlation of system and equipment. An applications study schedule should be rigid enough to assure that work progresses, but flexible enough to permit more intensive coverage of selected areas or the exploration of promising new areas.

The personnel required for an applications study are the project supervisor, systems and project analysts, programmers, representatives of operating departments, clerks, and technicians. Some are recruited from the feasibility study group; others are chosen by aptitude tests, interviews, and supervisors' rating. A balance of people with knowledge about equipment details and system environment is desirable in the applications study group.

The design work, depending on the design approach selected, may involve inventing an entirely new information and management structure as well as obtaining new equipment. On the other hand, the design work may be limited to little more than the introduction of new equipment—merely mechanization. The cautious approach of introducing some new equipment and limiting initial changes in the existing system facilitates early conversion, although at the risk of postponing important equipment and systems changes until a later date. The rate and extent of change affect the scope and content of the applications study. The plans for introducing changes affect the final system since some changes are easier to make than others. And it is possible to get "locked in" at a particular stage so that further changes are difficult. The outputs required, inputs available, and files to link them are important factors in system design. The work load is determined by tracing inputs through files to outputs. Facts are organized on data sheets and flow charts or flow lists.

Equipment Selection

Equipment selection begins by obtaining facts about equipment and applications to make an informed choice. Specifications are developed to cover data inputs, processing, files, and outputs. Special requirements and features of installation and operation are also spelled out. Application descriptions are prepared in order to reduce manufacturers' discussions and negotiations to concrete terms. A well-planned description covers the user's requirements, answers questions about applications, and provides a fair basis for comparing equipment.

Manufacturers' proposals should be detailed and explicit enough to show that they understand the application requirements and are able to deal with them. Each proposal should cover the degree of automation anticipated, equipment needed, operating requirements, manufacturer's assistance, rental and purchase terms, maintenance, design changes, and expansibility for handling a growing work load. The evaluation of equipment determines how well the application requirements are met, the capability of equipment to handle applications, and the operating time required. The price of equipment is only one factor among many to consider in making a selection.

Although he must rely on the equipment manufacturer for help in the design, the user is responsible for determining the suitability and advantages of new equipment and the related operating system. Therefore, he must be aware of the margin of error in estimates and the biases introduced by various participants.

Installation and Review

The installation group is responsible for getting new equipment and the related system into operation. This includes making ideas and plans operational, ordering and installing equipment, educating and training people, converting operations to new procedures, discontinuing old procedures and equipment, and transferring personnel. The economic stakes are high in this phase, since large costs are involved in installing a big data-processing system.

It is necessary to plan the installation schedule, the operating organization, analytical and programming work, and site requirements before equipment is received. The user is often able to accomplish most of this work, since equipment delivery ordinarily takes a year or so. But experience indicates that programming and preparatory work may take longer than planned so that a last-minute rush and even a delay in starting operations is likely to occur.

Development and conversion may be divided into five broad phases: systems design; flow-charting, programming, and testing; elimination of bugs to get smooth operations; dual operation of both the new and old systems during final testing; and discontinuance of the old system. Deficiencies discovered during both parallel and solo operations should be corrected so that the new system will achieve its planned level of efficiency.

Organizational structures for data-processing activities are likely to require revision to reflect changes in operating methods, manpower, and concentration of responsibility. Personnel considerations involve keeping all people informed, selecting and training required personnel, and dealing with displaced personnel. Competent, enthusiastic personnel are as important as new equipment to the success of a system.

Programming in the broad sense—systems analysis, flow-charting, and coding the instruction routines—is likely to cost as much as the equipment itself and take many man-years for an important application. Advanced programming techniques and cooperative work by users and manufacturers can reduce programming costs for each user. Alternative facilities are valuable safeguards against long down-time or complete disability; jobs are given priority, use of other equipment is planned, and "grandfather files" and duplicate records and programs are stored elsewhere for safety and convenience. Continuing review and improvement should follow successful installation. Here, as elsewhere, hindsight is better than foresight for seeing how something should be done. Additional applications should make full use of any remaining equipment capacity and the manpower skills developed during the first application.

The sequential discussion of all the phases leading up to a system installation may give the impression that certain steps are done in one-two-three order without any difficulty. Actually, as was pointed out earlier, soon after a new system-project starts, two or more phases are likely to run in parallel. That is, analysts may continue work while others are selecting design approaches or doing design work.

Various phases are likely to occur in parallel instead of in an orderly sequence for several reasons. The first phase, systems analysis, may fall behind schedule and run in parallel with others after they are started. It is usually difficult to shut off an earlier phase, and may not be desirable to do so, because often more can be learned that may help later phases. Any important change in a later phase—say, adoption of a new design approach or the selection of a different class of equipment—may require more analysis to develop additional facts required for the new situation. Finally, and perhaps most important, developing a new data-processing system is a long and involved process that is best handled in an iterative fashion. The first pass through all phases merely leads to tentative results. One or more additional passes through all phases are required to assure that either the results of the prior round are still satisfactory or to make some improvement on them. Additional iterations may be made until the prospective improvement seems smaller than the cost of the next round of work. For these reasons, it may seem as hard to shut off any phase of systems work as to close Pandora's box.

SUMMARY

In the development of a new system, systems design and implementation follow the analysis and selection of the design approach. Designing a system involves making decisions about the kinds of changes proposed, the outputs wanted, the inputs and files needed, and the processing procedures that will be adopted to link input and output. Ingenuity and inventiveness, coupled with clear, sound thinking, have the biggest pay-off in the early stages of systems design.

The initial design is performed almost independently of the type of equipment that may be introduced. Attention is centered on the nature and content of inputs, files, and outputs, and on the kinds of processing required. Design decisions about outputs are critically important because they are the products delivered to system customers—management and operating personnel. System outputs can be appraised in terms of their content, organization, degree of detail, format, accuracy, and timeliness—the frequency of reporting and the delay in issuing reports. Careful planning may make it possible to specify in advance all the output requirements and thereby simplify the design of files and procedures. However, conditions are seldom so predictable that all required outputs can be pre-specified. Generally, many new demands for output arise that may be handled fairly well by gathering and storing additional data in files for possible later use. One measure of the efficiency of file design is the percentage of unusual requests for information that can be filled without having to cram the files full of data on the mere prospect of use. However, the cost of keeping excessive data in files is small compared to the cost of not having data when wanted. Therefore, the practical approach to file design of retaining large quantities of data is, within limits, a wise one.

Run diagrams are a broad-brush presentation of files, transactions, and data that are handled together. The treatment of data entering a run depends on the organization of files and the nature of processing. Sequenced master files require a similar arrangement of transactions for processing. Each kind of transaction must be handled in a logically correct sequence; for example, receipts of stock should be handled ahead of issues to avoid having transactions rejected during processing by illogical intermediate results.

The inputs to a processor run are the prior-run master file, new transactions, and a program. The outputs are an updated master file, list of transactions applied, errors, summaries or listings for use in subsequent runs, and reports for operating and management personnel. Even simple processing operations are likely to involve several runs for editing and sorting transactions, for updating the master file, and for preparing printing outputs. For a processor with concurrent read-process-write capability, processing times can be estimated as the longer of master-file read-write time or transaction processing time.

Structure flow charts are used in systems design to cover the types, times, and quantities of inputs, processing, files, and outputs. Structural flow charts are drawn without showing the equipment to be used or how jobs are performed. A small number of symbols, with explanations where needed, are adequate for drawing structural charts. There are many conventions to flow-charting that make preparing and understanding them easier: direction of flow lines, identification of files and procedures, volumes through each path, repetitive loops, branching into two or more paths, merging of several paths into one, and connections between different charts. Each version of a chart should be considered tentative and simplified, if possible, by combining common elements and eliminating unnecessary steps until an efficient final version is prepared.

Technique flow charts show data and information requirements and the methods for filling them. They specify data media and equipment for input, output, and operations. The level of detail in flow charts should be attuned to their use, and charts for guiding programmers and coders are the most detailed. Accuracy, simplicity, and understandability are prime considerations when preparing flow charts for systems analysis and design.

Decision tables are an alternative to flow charts for the description of problem logic. They show conditions and actions in a clearer and more orderly fashion than flow charts and thus facilitate careful and complete development during the problem specification and programming stages. DETAB-X is a programming language based on a combination of decision tables and COBOL. Implementation of a data-processing system extends from the systems-design phase through successful operation of the new system and displacement of the prior system. The stages in implementation are the feasibility study, applications study, equipment selection, system and equipment installation, and systems review. A feasibility study attempts to determine whether the equipment and processing scheme under consideration appear promising enough to warrant more intensive study. An applications study examines a particular area of the business in order to design a processing system with specialized equipment that will apply to that area. Equipment is selected and installed after much formal and informal discussion with equipment manufacturers. Installation requires thorough planning to cover both the hardware and "software" aspects of a new system. Review of the system following installation determines system efficiency, whether it meets design objectives, and what improvements should be made.

The task of improving systems is never-ending. As soon as a new system is installed, and even during the installation phase, analysis and design are likely to be going on to develop a superior system.

CHAPTER 7

PROGRAMMING—COBOL-1

A *program* consists of a set of instructions on how to perform a particular task. The nature and detail of instructions depends on many factors. These include the complexity of the immediate task, knowledge about performing this or similar tasks, the tools available, and the language the instructor or programmer thinks best for communicating on this particular occasion. Instructing a person to do a certain task has many facets, though most of them are taken for granted because of long practice in giving and using instructions, the wealth of languages available for communication between people, and the built-in experience of people in performing tasks.

Careful and explicit instructions are required when machines are used to perform tasks. At the present stage of development, machines have little capability to fill in missing parts of their instruction routines; in other words, they have limited learning power. But enough research work has been done to bring processors up to about the "cave-man" stage of development, and further advances in the ability of machines to adapt to their environment and solve problems will come.

189

PROGRAMMING

In more concrete terms, programming does and, for the foreseeable future, will consist of the following steps:

1. Analyze a problem area to determine what the problem is and to learn as precisely as possible the boundary conditions—what *outputs* are wanted, the *inputs* needed to produce the required outputs, and the *files* that relate input to output.
2. Formulate a plan or *program*—invent, improvise, or copy a solution—to produce the outputs from the inputs by appropriate processing techniques that will develop and maintain any files necessary. First develop the solution in broad terms and then in more detail as the occasion warrants.
3. Learn what *capabilities* are available—processing and communications equipment, people, and the organizational environment—how they operate, and how to communicate with them in a suitable language.

The important point from this broad-brush description of programming is the requirement to know the whole background situation in order to develop the instructions aimed solely at the machine. From this background it is possible to develop a solution that is detailed enough to put into operation. Implementation involves selecting equipment, people, and procedures, and preparing detailed descriptions of outputs and inputs and the processing steps for people and equipment to follow.

The Essence of Programming

In addition to the narrow, specific task of preparing machine instructions, the following background information must be developed: (1) precise descriptions of the information *outputs,* data *inputs,* and *files* used for organizing partially processed data; (2) *instruction lists to guide people and equipment* to carry out the required procedures; and (3) specifications of the available *equipment*—the central processor, high-speed and bulk storage, and input-output facilities— to run the program. In briefest terms, these points about programming might be called data description, procedure description, and equipment environment.

Example of a Program

Suppose you are going to see a friend; the set of directions for finding the friend's house is a program for the occasion of a visit. The objective—to reach his house—is explicit and both of you understand it, although he may need to identify the house for you by its appearance or street number and name. If you are resourceful, the address—street number and name, city, and state—is adequate to guide you to his house. You can, if you interpret his address into geographical location, plan a route from your starting point to his house, obtain a suitable means of conveyance, and execute your plan.

If your friend wants to help you by planning your route, several facts must be made explicit. You must agree where you will start from—*the input*—and what conveyance you will use, whether auto, bus, or on foot—*the equipment environment.* In order to describe an efficient route—*the procedure*—it is necessary to take into consideration simple and intricate routes, fast and slow roads, traffic conditions at that time of day, and miscellaneous factors such as road-construction obstacles.

Having answers to questions about the input point, equipment environment, and operating conditions, your friend probably visualizes he is driving from your house to his and says, "Go out Route 138, turn right at the second barn after the third house, and, at the end of the road, turn left and go to 2321 Sylvan."

Features of a Program

This brief program of instructions about how to reach a friend's house has features in common with processor programming that are worth noting.

1. The inputs, outputs and equipment environment are agreed upon before the procedures are prepared, but they are related to each other—any change in one may require some change in another.
2. An agreed-upon language is used—in this case, a subset of English suitable for giving instructions to people driving cars on highways. If two languages are involved—say your friend is a Frenchman—translation is required at some stage to convert French to English.
3. Instructions are at a macro or aggregate level—"go out," "turn right," and "go to"—for they say nothing about the details, such as how to make turns—slow down, signal, check traffic, get into the proper lane, check traffic, turn the wheel, check traffic, etc. Each instruction becomes many lower-level or detailed instructions upon execution. The instruction "second barn after the third house" requires the ability to count in the same way as intended by your programmer. Situations such as "end of road" and "Sylvan" must be recognized. A count-down or count-up to 2321 is required, de-

pending on whether you approach the house from the high- or low-number side.

4. The sequence must be followed as stated—go out, turn right, turn left, etc.—since a left turn before a right will spoil execution of the whole program and will spoil it completely unless you are able to detect you are off the route, stop, and call for further directions or return to a point you can identify as correct.

5. Execution of the program is up to you since your programmer will not be in the car with you. You can "interpret" each instruction as you go and take your chances. But in this particular case you have instructions in advance and can "compile" more detailed instructions by studying maps and by questioning your instructor. Does the "second barn after the third house" mean that the two barns are in succession with no intervening houses? Does "at the second barn" mean "before," "after," or "what?" Some of these ambiguities are resolved merely by reading the instructions and applying logical tests that you have developed by trying to follow similar instructions at other times. The most thorough test is to execute the program in advance so that after each mistake you can return to the last point you are sure about and repeat the erroneous parts until you *debug* the program or conclude it is unworkable and call for help or give up.

6. No provision is made for contingencies—engine failure, lack of gas, flat tire, or bridge out of use. Engine failure, like any central processor failure, may be near-fatal to the program. Others which may cause only minor annoyance on the road also have their equivalents in processor operations: out of cards, a magnetic-tape unit that doesn't work, or failure of a data channel to carry data.

PROGRAMMING LANGUAGES

Programming specialists have developed a rich variety of languages for writing instructions to data-processing machines. The earliest languages were *machine-oriented;* it was considered enough to operate processors without worrying about the niceties of the language itself. Subsequent programming research has focused on *problem-oriented* languages to ease the user's task of writing programs. Further schemes have been developed to make the processor handle many of the bookkeeping and clerical tasks required to make a program work. Thus, the program writer is free to concentrate on the essential features of his problem and do so in a language that he is familiar with.

Machine-Oriented Language

Actual processor instructions are expressed in numbers that indicate to the machine what operations to perform and what data to use. For example, the instruction to add regular pay to overtime pay giving total pay might look as follows in machine language:

$$10 \quad 100 \quad 101 \quad 200$$

The 10 indicates an ADD instruction. The 100 and 101 are addresses of storage locations that contain the numbers for regular and overtime pay; 200 is the storage location for the sum, overtime pay. The programmer must arrange to have the desired operands in the specified locations before the processor executes this instruction. It will add whatever is in location 100 to whatever is in location 101 and put the result in location 200 (displacing whatever is there). He must also plan to line up the decimal points and guard against overflow—numbers becoming too large to fit into storage locations. In short, machine-language programming places a large burden on the person writing the program to keep track of the details involved.

Problem-Oriented Language

Problem-oriented languages are designed around a language ordinarily used to solve the relevant type of problem. Engineers or scientists use mathematics and formulas to solve technical problems and hence have algebraic programming languages—for example, FORTRAN or *For*mula *Tran*slating System.

The use of English is natural when coping with business problems. Business applications often are described in English and detailed instructions are prepared in English for clerks. Similarly, English-language instructions are useful for people to communicate with business processors. The instruction to calculate gross pay, instead of using the numbers shown above—10 100 101 200—might be written as

ADD REGULAR-PAY TO OVERTIME-PAY GIVING GROSS-PAY

An instruction written in English is perfectly clear to any reader, whether programmer, programmer supervisor, payroll-department head, controller, or even the president. The burden of translating the instruction to machine form in order to execute it is placed on the processor in contrast to machine-oriented languages that place the burden on people. Programming specialists have developed schemes

—compilers—that enable the processor to convert English-language instructions to machine-language instructions. Other programmers are then able to concentrate on solving problems with English-language instructions that a processor will compile into machine language.

The COBOL Language

The problem-oriented language of major concern to business users is COBOL, the Common Business-Oriented Language. COBOL is near-English in form, represents a long chain of development from early languages, and is still developing as more refinements are added. COBOL-1961 (the 1961 version) was developed by a committee composed of government users, computer manufacturers, and other organizations. The language was first described in a report of the Conference on Data-Systems Languages (CODASYL), issued by the United States Government Printing Office in April, 1960. Each equipment manufacturer publishes detailed descriptions covering each processor for which he has implemented COBOL.

Since the processor shares in the programming job when COBOL is used, it must be given a considerable amount of data about each problem. The programmer must provide data about three facets of the program, just as are required for a trip to a friend's house: data division, procedure division, and environment division.

Data Division. The Data Division is a description of each item of data used in input, output, or temporary storage during processing. For each element of data, the Data Division includes a *data-name* such as EMPLOYEE-NAME, AMOUNT-ON-HAND, PAY-RATE, or TODAYS-DATE, and a description of its type—numeric or alphanumeric—and its length expressed in number of characters. The Data Division is a dictionary in which the programmer tells the processor that a particular set of characters, for example PAY-RATE, is used with a certain meaning in a problem. COBOL allows capital letters only, and has certain punctuation rules with special meanings. The programmer must conform to these rules even though their use upsets the rules for grammar and appearance of ordinary English text; COBOL is a programmer's English, not a grammarian's.

Procedure Division. The Procedure Division is the programmer's opportunity to specify what he wants done with the *data-names* described in the Data Division. The COBOL procedure statement, MULTIPLY PAY-RATE BY HOURS-WORKED GIVING

GROSS PAY, means just what it says. The data-name PAY-RATE—meaning "data identified by the name PAY-RATE"—is multiplied by the data-name HOURS-WORKED and the answer has the data-name GROSS-PAY. If the next instruction says, WRITE GROSS-PAY, the processor will write on magnetic tape the product resulting from the multiplication. PAY-RATE, HOURS-WORKED, and GROSS-PAY are data-names of items of data that the programmer wants to use in his program. A hyphen is used between words in a data-name since blanks are not permitted within a COBOL name. The programmer does *not* specify which storage locations should be used. The task of assigning a specific storage location to a data-name is handled by the processor in a *compiling* run; the compiled program can then be executed or carried out in a later *execution* run.

Environment Division. The Environment Division describes certain characteristics of the equipment that affect the way a program runs. For example the Inventory File may be a deck of punched cards in the card reader or a magnetic tape mounted on any one of twenty or so tape units. The Environment Division may specify the type and location of each file and other machine-related items. The precise form and content of the Environment Division depends on the equipment used at each of the two stages—compiling and executing—for a COBOL program. The equipment configurations may be different and more equipment capacity, especially storage, may be required for compiling than for executing a program.

COBOL-1

The remainder of this chapter describes COBOL-1, a programming language based on COBOL-61. COBOL-1 is a simplified version to facilitate learning the fundamentals of programming. It preserves the essential structure of a powerful business programming-language, but minimizes the number of rules and variety of options in the initial stage. The discussion of COBOL-1 is designed to communicate the fundamentals of programming without becoming enmeshed in details or esoteric features—enough of them will arise later.

COBOL-1 is a completely compatible subset of COBOL-61 in much the same way that the 800 or so words of basic English are a subset of the King's English of thousands of words. Programs written in COBOL-1 are real and operational, not just hypothetical. They will compile and run on any machine that has a COBOL-61 translator, *if* the additional instructions given at the end of this chapter are followed. COBOL-1 is, therefore, a realistic language, and experience with it is a valid introduction to writing in the full COBOL-61 language. There is much more to learn but nothing to unlearn.

THE DATA DIVISION

An important aspect of programming, briefly reviewed here, is the systematic organization of data for processing. First this section will consider files from the viewpoint of records on cards for manual processing, since most people are familiar with them. Then the organization of data will be discussed from the viewpoint of COBOL-1, which requires more careful organization for efficient processing.

Levels of Organization

As described in Chapter 2, data are organized into three levels, starting with a character—numeral, letter, punctuation mark, or symbol, as follows:

1. *Data element:* A group of characters to specify an item at or near the basic level—date, alphabetic name, address, order number, stock number, and quantity on hand. An item may be used as an elementary item or several may be grouped—a group item—for some purposes. For example, the group item "customer's address" contains the elementary items of the customer's name, street address, city and state.
2. *Record:* One or more data elements that are usefully associated with a person, thing, or place. A record for an inventory item includes a stock number, stock name, amount on hand, warehouse location (and, perhaps, building number, aisle, and bin number), unit price, cost, and as many other elements as seem useful.
3. *File:* One or more records concerning people, things, or places that are closely related in an operational sense—all records for inventory items can be grouped together as a stock-record file.

The following description of the stock-record file for the ABC Company is organized in outline form with an indication of the content of each data element:

Inventory File: A group of Stock Records; one for each of the several thousand parts stocked by the ABC Company. (Other files are kept for employees, customers, etc.)

Stock Record: One record for each stock item containing the following data-names.

Stock Number: A ten-digit number from the official catalogue.

Stock Name: Not more than twenty letters or numerals.

Quantity on Hand: Not more than five digits.

Quantity on Order: Not more than five digits.

Warehouse location:

Building Number: Two digits.

Aisle Number: One letter and two digits.

Bin Number: Three digits.

Unit Cost: Two digits for cents and not more than three for dollars.

Card Records

The stock-record file of the ABC Company is kept on cards, as shown in Figure 7-1. The maximum number of spaces permitted

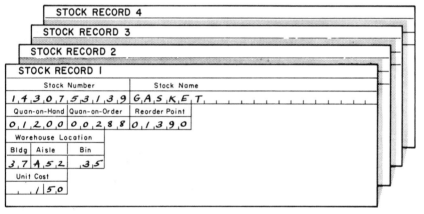

FIGURE 7-1. *Card layout for stock records in inventory file.*

for writing each data item is indicated and will guide the keypunch operator if the data are punched into other cards. The meaning of space allocations will become clearer when COBOL Data Descriptions are discussed.

This card record focuses on stock status, for it shows only the current quantity on hand, quantity on order, and unit cost. It does not show a prior balance or the transactions that resulted in the present balance. If these are wanted, the inventory card needs to be redesigned to show date, quantity, and type of each transaction. As presently designed, either a new stock record needs to be written after each receipt or issue in order to show current balances, or the recordkeeper must erase and write new amounts in place of old. In this respect—erase and rewrite—the card record corresponds to magnetic-tape or disk records.

The programmer, when designing a new or modified data-processing system, may rearrange or modify the contents of the existing records. Some of the items of data may not be relevant to his program; others, perhaps, can be fitted into less space or arranged for more efficient machine processing. For example, in analyzing the stock record shown earlier, the programmer may conclude that the reorder point is not needed and that bin numbers do not exceed two digits. He may also rearrange the items on the record to put them into a more efficient sequence for processing. The objective is to develop an efficient arrangement for the data actually used throughout the system.

COBOL Data Description

The stock record illustrated in Figure 7-1 is described in the proper form for COBOL-1 in Figure 7-2. The COBOL-1 rules for writing data descriptions must be carefully adhered to.

Data-Name. Data-names shown in Figure 7-2 are used to identify each piece of data during processing by a COBOL-1 program. When the program, for example, refers to STOCK-NUMBER, the data called STOCK-NUMBER is obtained and processed. The programmer's first problem, therefore, is what to call each kind of data that he wishes to process. The data-names used in COBOL-1 are arbitrarily selected by the programmer to suit his needs. It is often easier to use COBOL-1 data-names that are similar to normal business names, but any name that fits the rules is acceptable. After adoption, a name must be used consistently.

Names are formed in the following way. A name may use only the capital letters A through Z and the numerals 0 through 9. The length of a name is limited to 30 or fewer characters, as indicated by the space provided on the form: columns 12 to 41 for *data-name*. At least one of the characters must be a letter. Dashes may be used to separate the words or phrases in a name for easier reading, for example, STOCK-RECORD; but blanks are not permitted. Finally each data-name must be unique in that it differs from all other names used in the same program by one or more characters.

Level. The two digits in the column headed "Level" indicate the structure of the data. The description of each file used in a

Page 001	COBOL-1 Program Form	Program Name STOCK-VALUE CALCULATION		Page 1 of 1
		Program Number SVC-1	Prepared by WILL HARRISS	Date NOV 23

Line No.	Level No.	Data-Name	Picture
010	DATA	DIVISION.	
020	FD	INVENTORY-FILE	DATA RECORD IS STOCK-RECORD.
030	01	STOCK-RECORD.	
040	02	STOCK-NUMBER	PICTURE 9(10).
050	02	STOCK-NAME	PICTURE X(20).
060	02	QUAN-ON-HAND	PICTURE 99999.
070	02	QUAN-ON-ORDER	PICTURE 99999.
080	02	WAREHOUSE-LOCATION.	
090	03	BUILD-NO	PICTURE 99.
100	03	AISLE-NO	PICTURE XXX.
110	03	BIN-NO	PICTURE 99.
120	02	UNIT-COST	PICTURE 999V99.

FIGURE. 7-2. *COBOL-1 data division for stock record in inventory file.*

COBOL-1 program must begin with the level entry FD followed by the *file-name*—in this case, INVENTORY-FILE.

The *record-name* within a file has a level number of 01; therefore STOCK-RECORD is level 01. Each data-name contained within a record is given a larger number to indicate a lower level—02, 03, etc. The data elements, STOCK-NUMBER, STOCK-NAME, QUAN-ON-HAND, and QUAN-ON-ORDER are all part of the STOCK-RECORD and have, therefore, a level of 02. Figure 7-2 shows that a *group item*—WAREHOUSE-LOCATION—within the STOCK-RECORD also has a level number of 02. The *elementary items*—BUILD-NO, AISLE-NO, and BIN-NO that make up WAREHOUSE-LOCATION—have level numbers of 03. Level numbers are the COBOL equivalent of the indenting shown earlier in the description of the ABC Company inventory file. Note that UNIT-COST returns to the 02 level since it is not a subelement under WAREHOUSE-LOCATION. The general rules for assigning level numbers are as follows:

1. Level numbers consist of
   FD for a File
   01 for a Record
   Two digits—from 02 through 49—for data elements and subelements in a Record.
2. An item contains within it all items directly below it that have larger numbers for level.

Picture. A symbolic picture of each data element goes in the right-hand column of the COBOL-1 Form. The item with data-name QUAN-ON-HAND consists of five numeric characters and, therefore, has the description PICTURE 99999, which can be read "Picture is 99999." The character "9" in a PICTURE indicates the location of a single numeric digit. Any data element that consists only of numerals—numeric data—has an appropriate number of 9's in its picture to show its maximum size. If an item contains one or more letters or punctuation marks—alphanumeric data—its size is shown by "X's" in PICTURE. AISLE-NO consists of one letter and two digits in no specified sequence; therefore, PICTURE XXX properly covers it.

The STOCK-NUMBER was originally described in Figure 7-1 as a ten-digit number, so its description is 9999999999, or in shorthand form, 9(10). The number before the parenthesis tells the type of character—numeric or alphanumeric; the number within the parentheses specifies the number of these characters in the data element. Thus, 9(10) means that provision is made for ten numeric digits. This notation can also be used with the X symbol for letters.

All data used for computation must be numeric only. Alphanumeric data such as AISLE-NO consisting of three alphanumeric digits can be read into the processor, sorted into sequence, compared, or read out of storage, but such data cannot be used in an addition, subtraction, or other arithmetic operation.

The symbol "V" in a PICTURE indicates the location of the decimal point. PICTURE 999V99 for UNIT-COST means it has three numeric digits for dollars on the left of the decimal and two numeric digits for cents on the right of the decimal. The decimal point itself *cannot* appear in a number stored inside the processor for use in arithmetic operation. It is not a numeric character and, therefore, is not allowed in a numeric item used in arithmetic operations. If UNIT-COST is $127.13, the input data should contain merely the numerals 12713.

The PICTURE 999V99 for UNIT-COST instructs COBOL to assume that the decimal point is located two positions from the right and to treat 12713 as 127.13. COBOL will correctly align the decimal points of data elements indicated by a V before performing any arithmetic operations. The programmer need not worry about decimal-point location after the data description is written. However, he must assure that all input data has the appropriate number of digit positions. If UNIT-COST is to be $127.00 and PICTURE 999V99, the input then must be 12700 for correct handling. An input of 127 might be treated by the processor as though it were $1.27.

Pictures are used only with elementary items—items that do not contain any other items. The item with data-name WAREHOUSE-LOCATION is a group item (not a single element) of data and therefore does not have a PICTURE. STOCK-RECORD is a record-name containing several data elements and must rely on their description. Files need a special entry in place of a picture that identifies the records within the file. This entry has the general form of DATA RECORD IS *record-name*, and in Figure 7-2 is DATA RECORD IS STOCK-RECORD.

The rules for describing data in COBOL-1 are as follows:

1. The PICTURE shows the number and type of characters comprising each data element by means of the symbol 9 for each numeric

character, and X for each alphanumeric character. A number in parentheses indicates repetition of the preceding character.

2. A PICTURE is required only for elementary items (the lowest level); it is not permitted for group items, records, or files.
3. Data elements used for computation must be entirely numeric.
4. A V inserted at the appropriate place in a PICTURE indicates the location of an *assumed* decimal point. Input data for arithmetic operations must not contain an actual decimal point.

All data-names should be described in the Data Division *before* actually writing COBOL-1 procedures, but, of course, the data-names and procedures are closely interrelated and must be developed together.

PROBLEM EXAMPLE

The following problem example will be developed throughout much of the remainder of this chapter. Suppose that, in processing a file, the first requirement is to calculate the dollar value of one inventory item. Dollar value is equal to quantity on hand multiplied by unit cost. The input will be one STOCK-RECORD (Figure 7-2) and the output will be a VALUE-RECORD, as described below.

The Data Division for this example is shown in Figure 7-3. The upper part shows the INVENTORY-FILE, which is identical to the file described earlier. It contains the input data that are of special interest here: STOCK-NUMBER, STOCK-NAME, AND UNIT-COST. The bottom part of Figure 7-3, starting on line 140, is a second file identified as STOCK-VALUE-FILE. It is designed to receive the output data of stock number and stock value.

Since each data-name in COBOL-1 must be unique, the part number of an item is named STOCK-NUMBER in the INVEN-TORY FILE and STOCK-NUMBER-O ("O" might be thought of as Output) in the STOCK-VALUE-FILE, as shown on line 160. The data element STOCK-VALUE, line 170, is unique to the VALUE-RECORD, for it was not used in the STOCK-RECORD.

The STOCK-VALUE-FILE, lines 140 through 170, contains only two items: STOCK-NUMBER-O and STOCK-VALUE. If other information about a stock item is desired, it can be carried over from the STOCK-RECORD—for example, STOCK-NAME, QUAN-ON-HAND and WAREHOUSE-LOCATION. In each case the data-name in the VALUE-RECORD must be different by one or more characters from the corresponding data-name in the STOCK-RECORD.

Page 3	COBOL-1 Program Form	Program Name STOCK-VALUE CALCULATION	Prepared by WILL HARRISS	Page 1 of 1
001		Program Number SVC-1		Date AUG 17

Line No.	Level No.	Data-Name	Procedures / Picture
010		DATA DIVISION.	
020	FD	INVENTORY-FILE	DATA RECORD IS STOCK-RECORD.
030	01	STOCK-RECORD.	
040	02	STOCK-NUMBER	PICTURE 9(10).
050	02	STOCK-NAME	PICTURE X(20).
060	02	QUAN-ON-HAND	PICTURE 99999.
070	02	QUAN-ON-ORDER	PICTURE 99999.
080	02	WAREHOUSE-LOCATION.	
090	03	BUILD-NO	PICTURE 99.
100	03	AISLE-NO	PICTURE XXX.
110	03	BIN-NO	PICTURE 99.
120	02	UNIT-COST	PICTURE 999V99.
140	FD	STOCK-VALUE-FILE	DATA RECORD IS VALUE-RECORD.
150	01	VALUE-RECORD.	
160	02	STOCK-NUMBER-0	PICTURE 9(10).
170	02	STOCK-VALUE	PICTURE 9(6)V99.

FIGURE 7-3. COBOL-1 data division for stock-record and value-record.

203

THE PROCEDURE DIVISION

In the Procedure Division, the programmer specifies what he wants to do with the data described in the Data Division. As initially stated, the problem here is to calculate the value of inventory on hand for one item in the inventory file. The operation proceeds as follows. Read in a stock record, multiply the balance on hand for an item by its cost, and write out the value record.

The data required for both the input and output files was described in the Data Division in Figure 7-3. In actuality, the procedures and data descriptions are developed jointly since they are closely interrelated. Some procedures planning is often required to firm up the content of files.

Flow Chart

Figure 7-4 illustrates the value-calculation process in flow-chart form. The flow chart to handle one item is as simple as it looks. START identifies the beginning point for the program. Five steps are involved in processing and calculating the value of one inventory item. The first step, READ in a stock record, brings in one record. The second step, MULTIPLY quantity by unit cost, is the heart of the process, for it fulfills the original requirement for calculating stock value.

The MOVE operation simply copies the stock number that was read in from tape into another location, so that it is available for use with stock-value as part of the output records. The final two operations are WRITE out the desired record, and then STOP the operations.

The names used in preparing the flow chart can be any descriptive name that the programmer wishes. However, as shown here in Figure 7-4, it is highly desirable to use Data-Division names and COBOL-operation names when preparing the flow chart in order to reduce the risk of discrepancies when procedures are written. One good way to prepare a COBOL-1 program is as follows. A very general flow chart is drawn showing all known inputs and outputs and a brief description of each processing activity. This chart is essentially the run chart described in Chapter 6. The Data Division entries for inputs and outputs are next written up for each processing activity. Then a detailed COBOL flow chart is prepared using the data-names from the Data Division and COBOL operation names: READ, MULTIPLY, MOVE, WRITE, and STOP. When writing on the procedures form, the programmer must use the exact

| FLOW CHART | Chart Name **STOCK-VALUE CALCULATION** | | Page *I* of *I* |
| Form | Chart No. **X-1** | Prepared by **WILL HARRISS** | Date **JAN I** |

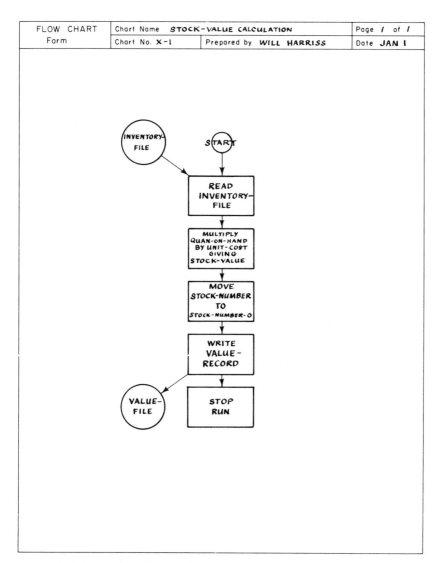

FIGURE 7-4. *Flow chart for calculating the stock-value of one inventory item.*

data-names from the COBOL-1 Data Description, as shown in Figures 7-2 and 7-3 and also in Figure 7-5. Although a programmer is free at the beginning to choose any file-names, record-names, and data-names that he wants, he must adhere to them after he selects them. No deviation in spelling, abbreviation, or punctuation is permitted.

COBOL - 1 — Program Form

Program Name: STOCK-VALUE CALCULATION
Program Number: SVC-1
Prepared by WILL HARRISS
Page 1 of 1
Date FEB 14

Page	Line No.	Level No.	Data-Name	Picture / Procedures
001	010		DATA DIVISION.	
	020	FD	INVENTORY-FILE	DATA RECORD IS STOCK-RECORD.
	030	01	STOCK-RECORD.	
	040	02	STOCK-NUMBER	PICTURE 9(10).
	050	02	STOCK-NAME	PICTURE X(20).
	060	02	QUAN-ON-HAND	PICTURE 99999.
	070	02	QUAN-ON-ORDER	PICTURE 99999.
	080	02	WAREHOUSE-LOCATION.	
	090	03	BUILD-NO	PICTURE 999.
	100	03	AISLE-NO	PICTURE XX.
	110	03	BIN-NO	PICTURE 99.
	120	02	UNIT-COST	PICTURE 999V99.
	140	FD	VALUE-FILE	DATA RECORD IS VALUE-RECORD.
	150	01	VALUE-RECORD.	
	160	02	STOCK-NUMBER-0	PICTURE 9(10).
	170	02	STOCK-VALUE	PICTURE 9(6)V99.
	180		PROCEDURE DIVISION.	
	190		START.	
	200		READ INVENTORY-FILE.	
	210		MULTIPLY QUAN-ON-HAND BY UNIT-COST GIVING STOCK-VALUE.	
	220		MOVE STOCK-NUMBER TO STOCK-NUMBER-0.	
	230		WRITE VALUE-RECORD.	
	240		STOP RUN.	

FIGURE 7-5. COBOL-1 procedure division for stock-value calculation program.

206

At the conclusion of flow-charting, the programmer should have a complete and integrated description of both logic and data. Writing COBOL procedures is then a relatively straightforward step.

Procedures Form

The spaces across the COBOL-1 form for use as a procedures form are headed Procedure-Name and Procedures. They are arranged in the following manner to guide the programmer when preparing the program for processor input:

> *Line number:* A line number identifies each line on the page. The programmer may number lines 010, 020, etc., to permit insertion of additional lines of program where desired by writing on a free line and assigning the desired intermediate number.
>
> *Procedure-Name:* A procedure-name is assigned to individual portions of a program so that one procedure statement can refer to another. The programmer selects and assigns a procedure-name to each paragraph and section of a program that he wishes to refer to so that he can use it in a different sequence. The broken line at Column 12 indicates that the procedure-name can run into the space for Procedures, if desired. Each procedure-name is followed by a period. The procedure-name START must always appear in each program before the first procedure to be executed.
>
> *Procedures:* Procedures specify action—program verbs—to be carried out by the program on the data when the program is executed, although a few verbs merely direct the processor. Notice that each statement is followed by a period.

Program Verbs

The way that the program verbs are used in this program, and also their general form, deserve discussion.

READ Instruction. The READ instruction on line 200 of Figure 7-5 causes the processor to read in the contents of the first STOCK-RECORD in the INVENTORY-FILE. The FD entry in the Data Description for INVENTORY-FILE, which says DATA-RECORD is STOCK-RECORD, indicates this is the record for the processor to work with.

The general form of the READ instruction is

READ file-name.

The processor executes this instruction by bringing in the next record from the file-name specified. The words in italics, *file-name,* indicate the number and kinds of data-names that a programmer can use with an instruction. The **READ** instruction can be used with any file-name that is correctly described in the Data Division of the program. A period is placed at the end of each COBOL sentence to indicate it is complete.

MULTIPLY Instruction. The instruction on line 210 is the multiplication instruction. The general form is

MULTIPLY *data-name-1* BY *data-name-2* GIVING *data-name-3.*

This instruction causes the data element described by *data-name-1* to be multiplied by *data-name-2;* it places the product at *data-name-3.* The data referred to by each *data-name* must be all numeric. Decimal point location is handled automatically, if the assumed decimal point is properly located in each PICTURE.

MOVE Instruction. An instruction to move data, such as that on line 220, copies the data into a receiving area. It does not destroy the original data. The general form of the MOVE instruction is

MOVE *data-name-1* to *data-name-2.*

Processor execution of the MOVE instruction causes the contents of the item, which may be an elementary item or group item, identified by *data-name-1* to become the contents of the *data-name-2* item also. In Figure 7-5 MOVE merely copies the contents of STOCK-NUMBER into STOCK-NUMBER-O. This transfer is needed to put the elementary item STOCK-NUMBER into VALUE-RECORD in order to identify STOCK-VALUE when it is written out.

WRITE Instruction. The WRITE instruction shown on line 230 is similar to the READ instruction, for it writes out one record from processor storage onto magnetic tape. The general form is

WRITE *record-name.*

The COBOL-1 compiler, as described later, is instructed by means of the Data Division for this program that the VALUE-RECORD goes in the STOCK-VALUE-FILE.

STOP Instruction. The STOP instruction on line 240 consists simply of two words, so its form is

STOP RUN.

DATA FLOW

Execution of the program for the problem example is illustrated by a series of figures that show the essential features at each step. Schematic diagrams are used here only for discussion purposes, for

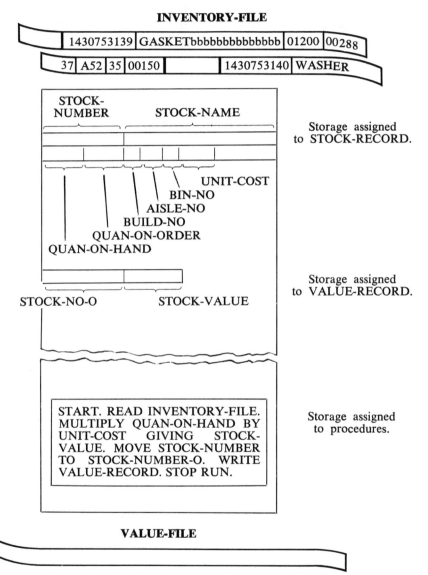

INVENTORY-FILE

| 1430753139 | GASKETbbbbbbbbbbbbbbbb | 01200 | 00288 |

| 37 | A52 | 35 | 00150 | | 1430753140 | WASHER |

STOCK-NUMBER   STOCK-NAME

Storage assigned to STOCK-RECORD.

UNIT-COST
BIN-NO
AISLE-NO
BUILD-NO
QUAN-ON-ORDER
QUAN-ON-HAND

Storage assigned to VALUE-RECORD.

STOCK-NO-O   STOCK-VALUE

START. READ INVENTORY-FILE. MULTIPLY QUAN-ON-HAND BY UNIT-COST GIVING STOCK-VALUE. MOVE STOCK-NUMBER TO STOCK-NUMBER-O. WRITE VALUE-RECORD. STOP RUN.

Storage assigned to procedures.

VALUE-FILE

FIGURE 7-6(a). *Files and processor storage after program read-in and storage assignment (schematic).*

this is not the way things really work. More careful descriptions are given later.

Assume that the procedure division (Figure 7-5) is read into high-speed storage as shown in Figure 7-6(a). The data descriptions for the Stock-Record and Value-Record (Figure 7-3) are used by the processor to assign storage locations for these two records, as is also shown in Figure 7-6(a). The amount of storage set aside here for each data-name is that specified by the PICTURE

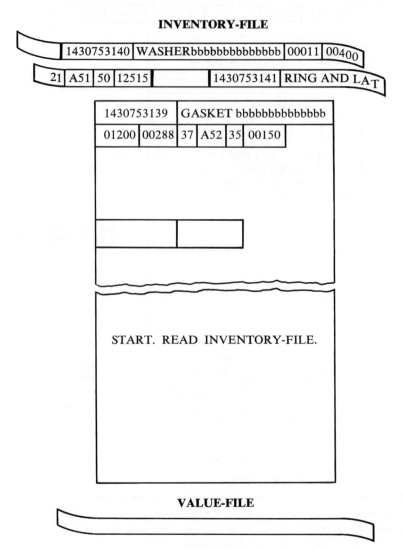

INVENTORY-FILE

| 1430753140 | WASHERbbbbbbbbbbbbbbbb | 00011 | 00400 |

| 21 | A51 | 50 | 12515 | | 1430753141 | RING AND LAT |

| 1430753139 | GASKET bbbbbbbbbbbbbbb |

| 01200 | 00288 | 37 | A52 | 35 | 00150 |

START. READ INVENTORY-FILE.

VALUE-FILE

FIGURE 7-6(b). *Files and storage content after read inventory-file.*

of the data element. The input file is ready for read-in at this point. Note that the data elements are stored exactly as wanted on tape and, for readability here, heavy rulings separate the items. The output file is merely a blank tape at this point.

When the READ instruction is executed the processor reads into the pre-assigned storage area the data contained in the first STOCK-RECORD, as shown in Figure 7-6(b). Observe the effect of this instruction by looking at the active parts, which are emphasized for readability. The data items, exactly fit the storage space assigned according to the data description. Alphabetical items are left-justified in the input stage to facilitate sorting, if required, and the remaining spaces are filled with blanks. The Stock-Name appears as "GASKETbbbbbbbbbbbbbbb" in storage, because it was described as 20 alphanumeric characters long by the PICTURE X(20). Each "b" indicates a blank character position. The numeric data items QUAN-ON-HAND, QUAN-ON-ORDER, and UNIT COST are right-justified to align their units positions and decimal points, if any, to perform arithmetic correctly. The inputs 01200, 00288, and 00150 correctly fit their PICTURES, as shown in Figure 7-6(b).

After the MULTIPLY instruction is completed, Figure 7-6(c), the product from multiplying QUAN-ON-HAND BY UNIT-COST is stored as the STOCK-VALUE. Note that use of these two operands in the MULTIPLY operation does not change their existence in the STOCK-RECORD; they remain just as before. Any number in the location identified by STOCK-VALUE, is replaced by the new product STOCK-VALUE. In general, data used as input to an operation also remain unchanged at their original location, and the results of an operation, when placed in storage, replace any data already in that location.

The MOVE instruction, as indicated in Figure 7-6(d) transfers the data called STOCK-NUMBER to the location called STOCK-NUMBER-O. Since the data-name STOCK-NUMBER is merely the operand copied into another location, it continues to appear unchanged as an item in the STOCK-RECORD. The result: STOCK-NUMBER, which is 1430753139 now appears in two locations in storage.

In the last stage, the WRITE instruction causes the processor to write out (by copying) the VALUE-RECORD. Operations STOP as indicated by Figure 7-6(e), and the program is finished. Both records—STOCK-RECORD and VALUE-RECORD—remain in high-speed storage. The VALUE-RECORD is written in the output file just as it appears in storage without any editing. It might be use-

ful to edit the STOCK-VALUE of 00180000, which has the PIC-
TURE 9(6)V99, as shown in Figure 7-5 to make it readable as
$1,800.00. Such editing would require suppression of leading zeros,
and insertion of dollar sign, comma, and decimal point. Editing
is described later in this chapter.

File Processing

The example described above shows how to calculate the value
of a single inventory record. But most business data processing deals
with many or all the records in a file; not merely a single record.

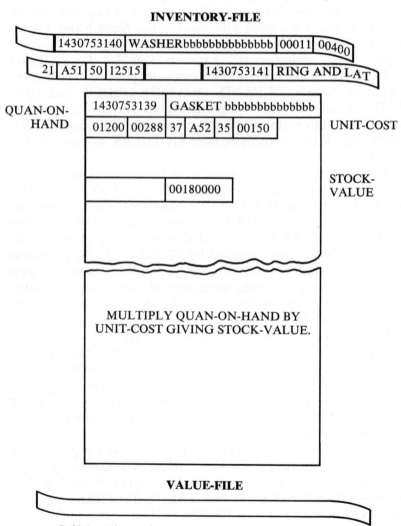

FIGURE 7-6(c). *Files and storage content after multiply order executed.*

Cycling. The brute-force approach to handling more than one record is for the programmer to repeat the set of instructions for each additional record. Such repetition may be efficient for a few records, but is intolerable for a large file. Since an identical set of instructions is used to process each record, one set of instructions should handle a whole file of records by performing the set one time

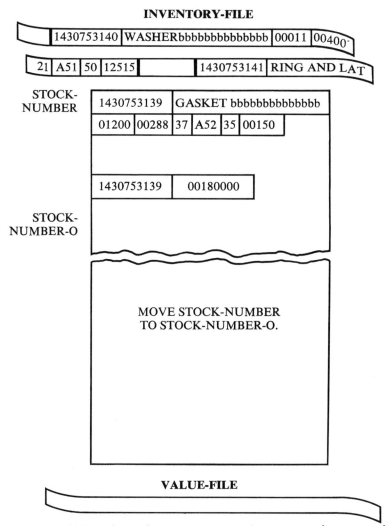

FIGURE 7-6(d). *Files and storage content after move order executed.*

for each record in the file. The idea of repeatedly using a single set of instructions to process numerous records in a file is called *cycling*. The program cycles through the data one time for each record and thereby greatly increases the usefulness of a program. Cycling is an essential and widespread programming practice.

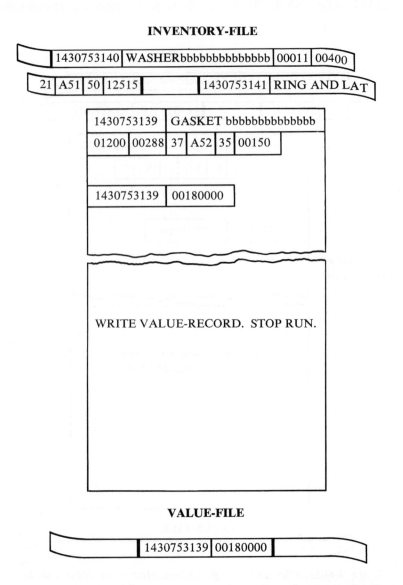

FIGURE 7-6(e). *Files and storage content after write order executed and stop.*

Figure 7-7 is a flow chart of the cycling procedure to calculate the value for each stock-record in inventory. It must, of course, stop when the end of file is reached. In the first cycle, the processor reads the first stock-record in the inventory-file, obtains a NO

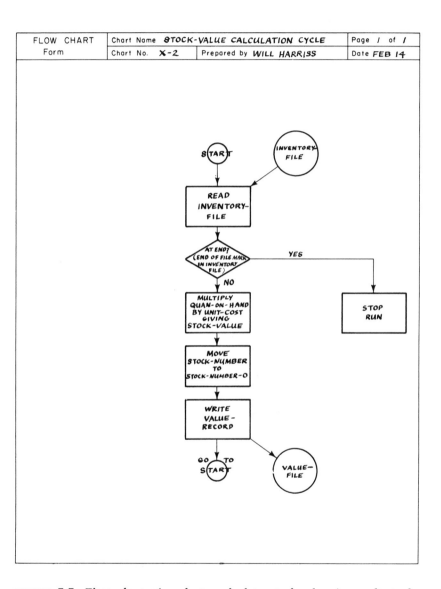

FLOW CHART	Chart Name STOCK-VALUE CALCULATION CYCLE		Page 1 of 1
Form	Chart No. X-2	Prepared by WILL HARRISS	Date FEB 14

FIGURE 7-7. *Flow chart of cycle to calculate stock-value for each stock-record.*

answer to the end-of-file question, and exits vertically. It multiplies quantity by cost to get value, and writes an output record containing the stock number and value of the first inventory item. Instead of STOP RUN, the next step is GO TO START. This GO TO transfer returns program control to the first operation, READ INVENTORY-FILE and the calculation process is repeated. From the flow chart in Figure 7-7, an instruction routine can be developed easily, as shown in Figure 7-8. It is similar to the routine for a single record in Figure 7-5 except that Line 240 is GO TO START instead of STOP RUN and the READ instruction is conditional, as discussed below.

COBOL instructions are executed in the same sequence as they are written, unless otherwise specified. The program sequence in Figure 7-8 is READ, MULTIPLY, MOVE and WRITE, with a new type of instruction: GO TO *procedure-name.*

GO TO Instruction. The GO TO instruction changes the normal sequence of executing instructions and causes the program to continue from the specified location. The general form of the GO TO instruction is

GO TO *procedure-name-1.*

The *procedure-name-1* is any valid COBOL name for a procedure section or paragraph as listed in the Procedure Division. The processor executes the GO TO instruction by finding the place in the program where *procedure-name-1* appears in the procedure-name column. It then executes the instructions starting at *procedure-name-1* and continues in normal sequence until it encounters another GO TO order to change sequence or encounters a STOP. In Figure 7-8, the GO TO START instruction on Line 240 causes the processor to go back to START on Line 190 to repeat the cycle of READ, MULTIPLY, etc. The program as written will cause the processor to continue processing records until it handles every record in the inventory file. It will then stop because of the conditional read instruction.

Conditional READ Instruction. The simplest plan for stopping the cycles—the repetitive execution of the program, described above—is to use a conditional READ instruction of the general form

READ *file-name-1* AT END *imperative-statement-1.*

The processor tries to read a record each time it reaches the conditional READ instruction in the program, which is basically similar

COBOL-1 Program Form

Program Name **STOCK-VALUE CALCULATION**
Program Number **SVC-2**   Prepared by **WILL HARRISS**

Page	Line No.	Procedure Name / Level No.	Data-Name	Procedures / Picture
001	010		DATA DIVISION.	
	020	FD	INVENTORY-FILE	DATA RECORD IS STOCK-RECORD.
	030	01	STOCK-RECORD.	
	040	02	STOCK-NUMBER	PICTURE 9(10).
	050	02	STOCK-NAME	PICTURE X(20).
	060	02	QUAN-ON-HAND	PICTURE 99999.
	070	02	QUAN-ON-ORDER	PICTURE 99999.
	080	02	WAREHOUSE-LOCATION.	
	090	03	BUILD-NO	PICTURE 99.
	100	03	AISLE-NO	PICTURE XXX.
	110	03	BIN-NO	PICTURE 99.
	120	02	UNIT-COST	PICTURE 999V99.
	140	FD	STOCK-VALUE-FILE	DATA RECORD IS VALUE-RECORD.
	150	01	VALUE-RECORD.	
	160	02	STOCK-NUMBER-O	PICTURE 9(10).
	170	02	STOCK-VALUE	PICTURE 9(6)V99.
	180		PROCEDURE DIVISION.	
	190		START.	
	200		READ INVENTORY-FILE AT END STOP RUN.	
	210		MULTIPLY QUAN-ON-HAND BY UNIT-COST GIVING STOCK-VALUE.	
	220		MOVE STOCK-NUMBER TO STOCK-NUMBER-O.	
	230		WRITE VALUE-RECORD.	
	240		GO TO START.	
	250			

FIGURE 7-8. *Procedure for cycling through stock-value calculation for the inventory file.*

217

to the READ instruction first described. But the conditional READ instruction differs in the following way. If one or more records remain in the file, the processor reads a record and continues with the following instruction. But, if no record remains in this file, the processor senses an end-of-file mark, previously placed on the tape. Since this mark indicates it is AT END of the file, the processor does whatever is directed by *imperative-statement-1*.

The READ-conditional instruction with an imperative-statement of STOP RUN will terminate the processing cycle when the end-of-file mark is encountered during execution of a READ instruction.

The programmer may want to perform some other operations—say, write out totals or perhaps go to another routine after processing all records in the file. For this purpose, the conditional READ instruction with an imperative GO TO statement is useful. The *procedure-name* TOTAL might identify the routine for writing out totals accumulated while processing the files. If so, the instruction READ STOCK-RECORD AT END GO TO TOTAL will cause the processor to execute the write-out routine that starts at TOTAL.

The conditional READ instruction enables the programmer to plan the processing of all records in a file without the bother of programming for the exact number in the file. The processor performs one cycle to handle each record in turn until the whole file is processed. A careful programmer is interested in how many records a file contains in order to control the accuracy of file processing, even though it is desirable to have instructions that save him the chore of testing after every READ operation to determine whether the last record was read. It is easier merely to count and check the number of records that are handled than it is to program for executing a cycle a specified number of times.

ADDITIONAL FEATURES

The COBOL programming language has many other features. Some of the basic features included in COBOL-1 are the standard arithmetic operations, special features for rounding and error control, branching or decision-making operations, and various data-editing operations to handle decimal points, commas, dollar signs, and zero suppression.

Arithmetic Instructions

The multiplication instruction was described above. COBOL-1 also has instructions for the other standard arithmetic operations—

addition, subtraction, and division. Examples in Figure 7-9 illustrate the operation of each of the arithmetic instructions, and a brief description is given below. Each operand may be viewed as

Instruction	Data-Name	Storage Contents	
		Before Execution	After Execution
ADD SELLING-PRICE AND TAX GIVING TOTAL-PRICE	SELLING-PRICE TAX	5100 204	5100 204
	TOTAL-PRICE	—	5304
ADD EACH-PURCHASE TO TOTAL-PURCHASES	EACH-PURCHASE TOTAL-PURCHASES	13200 62100	13200 75300
SUBTRACT DISCOUNT FROM GROSS-PRICE GIVING NET-PRICE	DISCOUNT GROSS-PRICE NET-PRICE	7300 73000 —	7300 73000 65700
SUBTRACT AMT-OF-CHECK FROM BANK-BALANCE	AMOUNT OF CHECK BANK-BALANCE	4521 2001	4521 -2520
DIVIDE NO-OF-ITEMS INTO TOTAL-COST GIVING AVERAGE-COST	NO-OF-ITEMS TOTAL-COST AVERAGE-COST	12 4836 —	12 4836 403

FIGURE 7-9. *Results of arithmetic operations.*

consisting of dollars and cents, although the "$" and "." are omitted because only numeric symbols can be present in data operated on arithmetically.

ADD GIVING Instruction. The addition instruction, ADD GIVING, provides for adding two numbers together and storing the total in another location. The general form of this instruction is

ADD *data-name-1* AND *data-name-2* GIVING *data-name-3.*

When the ADD GIVING instruction is executed, the processor adds the contents of *data-name-1* to the contents of *data-name-2* and stores the result at *data-name-3*. More simply, ADD A AND B GIVING C. By using more data-names, a series of items can be added—for example, ADD A AND B AND C AND D AND . . . AND Y GIVING Z. An example of this instruction is: ADD SELLING-PRICE AND TAX GIVING TOTAL-PRICE.

ADD TO Instruction. A second addition instruction, **ADD TO**, corresponds more closely to the desk-calculator or adding-machine scheme for adding each number to the prior total to get a new total. Remember that a desk calculator forms a subtotal after each addition operation and has only one total for a whole series of additions. More simply ADD A TO B. The general form of this addition instruction is

ADD *data-name-1* TO *data-name-2.*

This instruction is useful to accumulate individual items into a total—for example, ADD EACH-PURCHASE TO TOTAL-PUR-CHASES.

SUBTRACT FROM GIVING Instruction. There are two forms of subtraction operations, corresponding to the two instructions for addition operations. The SUBTRACT FROM GIVING instruction means: subtract *data-name-1* from *data-name-2* giving *data-name-3.* This operation retains the operands and the remainder resulting from a subtraction operation: SUBTRACT A FROM B GIVING C. The general form of this instruction is

SUBTRACT *data-name-1* FROM *data-name-2* GIVING *data-name-3.*

The two operands *data-name-1* and *data-name-2* are unchanged by this operation. The remainder is stored as *data-name-3.* An example of this instruction is SUBTRACT DISCOUNT FROM GROSS-PRICE GIVING NET-PRICE, which makes the three items available for printing as three lines on an invoice.

SUBTRACT FROM Instruction. The SUBTRACT FROM instruction places the remainder in the location of *data-name-2.* It corresponds to subtraction performed on a desk calculator that calculates a new remainder after each operation, but doesn't retain the prior amount. The general form is

SUBTRACT *data-name-1* FROM *data-name-2.*

It causes the processor to subtract the contents of *data-name-1* from *data-name-2* and store the result at *data-name-2.* An example is SUBTRACT AMT-OF-CHECK FROM BANK-BALANCE, or simply, SUBTRACT A FROM B.

DIVIDE INTO GIVING Instruction. The divide instruction simply causes the processor to divide A into B giving C. The general form of the instruction is

DIVIDE *data-name-1* INTO *data-name-2* GIVING *data-name-3.*

The processor divides the contents of *data-name-1* into the contents of *data-name-2* and stores the quotient as *data-name-3*. All three items are available after execution of the DIVIDE INTO GIVING operation since three storage locations are used. However, the remainder from the division operation is not available, though it can be calculated if wanted. An illustration of the divide instruction is DIVIDE NO-OF-ITEMS INTO TOTAL-COST GIVING AVERAGE-COST.

Decimal-Point Alignment

COBOL-1 handles decimal-point alignment automatically on the basis of information in the data description for each program. For example, the data description includes data-names and pictures as shown. At time of execution of an addition operation, the contents are as indicated:

Data-Name	PICTURE	Contents
QUANTITY-X	99V9	327
QUANTITY-Y	99V99	9165
QUANTITY-Z	9999V999	

The addition operation ADD QUANTITY-X, QUANTITY-Y GIVING QUANTITY-Z causes addition in the following manner. (Remember that the hyphen is used to avoid a blank space yet keep the name readable; it does not mean minus or negative when used with data-names such as X, Y, or Z, even though the value itself may be negative.) The data content identified by QUANTITY-X and QUANTITY-Y are aligned according to the assumed decimal point in their pictures, as indicated by the V's, and any unused space at either the left or right in the result is filled in with zeros. The result of addition from the machine and the programmer's viewpoint can be compared as follows:

Data-name	PICTURE	Processor Operation	Programmer's Viewpoint
QUANTITY-X	99V9	327	32.7
QUANTITY-Y	99V99	9165	91.65
QUANTITY-Z	9999V999	124350	0124.350

The processor stores the sum as 0124350 without a decimal point to conform to the PICTURE for QUANTITY-Z of 9999V999. The processor uses the picture 9999V999 to keep track of alignment during subsequent calculations and for inserting the decimal point by proper output editing to get 0124.350 for reports. The zeros will appear at both the left and right ends unless they are suppressed during editing to get 124.35 without unwanted zeros. A "$" sign can be inserted in any position wanted during the editing operation. Editing will be discussed in more detail later.

Size Error

The procesor will keep track of decimal points according to the PICTURE described for each item. But the risk arises that a PICTURE is not of appropriate length for the data it is supposed to store. A data-name described by a PICTURE that is too short to hold the results assigned to that data-name will discard some digits.

If the PICTURE for QUANTITY-Z were 99V9, the result from the addition operation would be stored as 243 instead of 0124350, as above. The PICTURE 99V9 is too short to hold the sum of 12435 so that one or more significant digits—the leading 1 in this case—are lost. There are two remedies for the leading digit(s) size error. The obvious one is to make the PICTURE for any result large enough to store the result. As a further precaution, each instruction that may result in a size error should be written with an option for size error to transfer processor control to another program point. The programmer may choose to stop processing or to take remedial action such as shifting the operands to the right (as described in Chapter 8) and repeating the arithmetical operation. The general form of the SIZE ERROR option in an instruction can be illustrated by the ADD GIVING instruction:

ADD *data-name-1* AND *data-name-2* GIVING *data-name-3*
ON SIZE ERROR *any imperative statement.*

The *imperative statement* corresponds to the *imperative statement* in the conditional READ instruction described earlier. It can be a STOP or a GO TO another point in the program to take remedial action. The size-error option can be used with any of the arithmetic instructions, and can also be used with the rounding option, as described below.

Rounding

Digits on the right-hand end of a result that exceed the picture field can be dropped with little or no harm. In fact, results should be shortened by dropping right-hand digits to get a suitable answer. Invoices, for example, are rounded to the nearest penny after adding taxes, deducting discounts, etc. Rounding is initiated by inserting the word ROUNDED in the instruction after the last dataname. The form of the multiplication instruction with the rounding and size error option is

MULTIPLY *data-name-1* BY *data-name-2* GIVING *data-name-3*
ROUNDED ON SIZE ERROR *imperative statement.*

The rounding option—increasing the right-hand retained digit by 1, if the left-hand discarded digit is 5 or more—can be used also for the addition and subtraction operations. The options for rounding and size error can be used independently, or together, if desired.

Decision-Making

Three basic types of operating instructions were discussed above:

1. *Input-output:* READ and WRITE
2. *Arithmetic:* MULTIPLY, ADD, SUBTRACT, and DIVIDE
3. *Rearrangement:* MOVE

The fourth type of operation of interest here is *decision-making.* The programmer uses it when he wishes to choose one out of two or more possibilities.

Two-Choice Situations. The READ AT END instruction discussed earlier can be rephrased into a two-choice situation for decision-making. The question can be stated as, "Is this record the end-of-file mark?" If the answer is no, then, as shown in Figure 7-7, the program should continue in normal sequence to process this record and read the next record.

If the answer is yes, then the whole file will have been read, as indicated by the fact that this record is the end-of-file mark following the last ordinary record. The imperative statement after READ AT END may be either STOP or GO TO another part of the program for additional processing—summaries, write out, or whatever.

An inventory reorder routine also illustrates a situation involving two choices within a program. The quantity on hand for each inventory item can be compared with the reorder point for that item. If BAL-ON-HAND is less than REORDER-POINT, a purchase order can be prepared. If the balance equals or exceeds the point, the order routine is skipped and the processing cycle continued.

The segment of a COBOL-1 program dealing with this decision-making aspect is shown in Figure 7-10.

IF Instruction. The instruction that starts IF BAL-ON-HAND in the inventory-ordering routine in Figure 7-10 is one version of the IF instruction. It is useful for situations that have two possible outcomes—action A or action B. Its general form is

> IF *conditional-expression-1* THEN *statement-1* OTHERWISE *statement-2*.

Conditional expression-1 is first set up and tested. If *conditional expression-1* is true—that is to say, the condition set up is filled—*statement-1* is executed and *statement-2* is ignored. But if *conditional expression-1* is false—not filled by the condition when the test is made—*statement-1* is ignored and *statement-2* is executed. That is, the option executed should correspond to the true condition. These rules can be expressed in decision table form, as follows:

	Conditional Expression-1	Statement-1	Statement-2
Rule 1	True	Execute	Ignore
Rule 2	False	Ignore	Execute

In the IF BAL-ON-HAND instruction of Figure 7-10, *conditional-expression-1* is BAL-ON-HAND IS LESS THAN REORDER-POINT, *statement-1* is GO TO ORDER, and *statement-2* is GO TO START.

Besides the conditional expression of the type *data-name-1* IS LESS THAN *data-name-2* discussed above, two others are available—the equal and greater conditions. The range of conditional expressions for the IF—THEN—OTHERWISE instructions is as follows:

> IF *data-name-1* IS GREATER THAN *data-name-2* THEN *statement-1* OTHERWISE *statement-2*
> IF *data-name-1* IS LESS THAN *data-name-2* THEN *statement-1* OTHERWISE *statement-2*
> IF *data-name-1* IS EQUAL TO *data-name-2* THEN *statement-1* OTHERWISE *statement-2*

Any one of these can be used, but some care is needed to make sure that the "equals" case is handled correctly. A test on greater

FIGURE 7-10. *Procedure to make a decision.*

| | COBOL – 1 Program Form | Program Name INVENTORY-REORDER PROCEDURE | Page 1 of 1 |
| | | Program Number IRP-3 | Prepared by WILL HARRISS | Date JUL 14 |

Page 3 001	Line No. 6	Procedure Name	Level No. 7 12	Data-Name	Procedures 41 Picture
	010	START.			
	020	READ INVENTORY-FILE AT END STOP RUN. IF BAL-ON-HAND IS LESS			
	030	THAN REORDER-POINT THEN GO TO ORDER OTHERWISE GO TO START.			
	040	ORDER.			
		NOTE THE ROUTINE TO GENERATE A PURCHASE ORDER STARTS HERE.			

225

condition, for instance, lumps the equal and less conditions together. In general, a test for one condition lumps the other two conditions into the OTHERWISE *statement-2*.

Comparison to Zero. A simple type of conditional expression is formed by testing the relationship of *data-name-1* to zero. The condition is stated in terms of whether *data-name-2* is positive, negative, or zero—in effect "sign" condition. These correspond to the conditional expressions IF *data-name-1* GREATER THAN *data-name-2*, etc., with *data-name-2* now equal to zero. The range of expressions to examine sign condition of a single data element A is as follows:

> IF *data-name-1* IS POSITIVE THEN *statement-1* OTHER-WISE *statement-2*
> IF *data-name-1* IS NEGATIVE THEN *statement-1* OTHER-WISE *statement-2;*
> IF *data-name-1* IS ZERO THEN *statement-1* OTHERWISE *statement-2*

As an example, the IF—NEGATIVE instruction can be used in processing checks against depositors' accounts to determine whether to reject them for nonsufficient funds. After subtracting the amount of a check from account balance the over-draft charge and rejection instruction are IF ACCOUNT-BALANCE IS NEGATIVE GO TO SERVICE-CHARGE OTHERWISE GO TO NEXT-CHECK.

Inclusion of Action Statements. The action statements associated with an IF instruction are commonly GO TO instructions, but any valid COBOL-1 imperative statement is allowed. That is to say, an operation can be incorporated with the IF instruction. For example, an instruction might be written as IF BALANCE IS GREATER THAN CHECK-AMT THEN SUBTRACT CHECK-AMT FROM BALANCE OTHERWISE WRITE BAD-CHECK-RECORD. In this expression, *statement-1* is a SUBTRACT command and *statement-2* is a WRITE command. Since each of the statements to be executed is an imperative command, both can be included in an IF statement. After the appropriate one of these commands is executed, the statement following the IF statement is executed next, since the processor is not sent to another procedure-name.

It is also proper to have a second IF instruction within an IF—THEN statement as the OTHERWISE clause. For an example, IF

BALANCE IS GREATER THAN CHECK-AMT THEN SUB-
TRACT CHECK-AMT FROM BALANCE OTHERWISE IF
CUSTOMERS-CREDIT-RATING EQUALS GOOD THEN
WRITE POLITE-BAD-CHECK-RECORD OTHERWISE WRITE
BAD-CHECK-RECORD.

Output Editing

The purpose of output editing is to present results in a format
useful to the reader. Output editing for alphanumeric elements
causes little trouble for they often can be used just as they were read
in. If changes are needed to select and emphasize certain items or
to improve readability, the output data descriptions can be used to
select and edit desired items.

Numeric output, on the other hand, poses a different problem.
First, the size of each item that is wanted in the output depends on
the calculations involved and cannot be determined in advance.
Second, the data description for each item must be long enough to
handle the biggest result likely to arise in order to minimize the
loss of digits at either end; however, this results in zeros filling in
excess spaces in numeric PICTURES. Third, arithmetic operations
will accept only all-numeric data. Special symbols—dollar signs,
commas, and decimal points—must be excluded from COBOL-1
input, for they cannot be present in data-names during computation.

The user, however, still insists on results in an attractive, readable
format. The current value of inventory is more comprehensible when
stated as $1,268,453 than as 0000126845302. It is unrewarding for
the processor to automatically keep track of the decimal point during a lengthy series of computations, unless it tells the user where the
decimal point belongs in the final result and gives him the right
number of digits.

Fortunately, COBOL provides the user with good facilities for
editing output data. The editing process consists of two parts. First,
when the Data Description is prepared for a program, certain data-
names are set up to serve as editing areas. The PICTURE of these
data-names will contain special editing symbols. The second part
of the editing process is included in the Procedures Division of a
program. The programmer writes program instructions to move data
to the desired data-name that serves as an edit-area. The MOVE
operation results in inserting editing symbols—decimal point, dollar
sign, and comma—in the data-name, shortening it to the desired
length, and suppressing any unwanted characters.

Decimal Point. Insertion of the decimal point is a common operation in editing. The *data-name* COST, for example, may have a PICTURE of 9999V99. The value of COST in one record in the input file might be 13726. This would mean $137.26 when used with the PICTURE 9999V99, although the "$" and "." are implicit from the digit positions in a card field and are omitted from the data when prepared for input. COST will appear as 013726 during processor computation in keeping with the PICTURE, and the V in the PICTURE tells the processor how to keep track of the decimal point. Thus the *data-name* COST may have the content 013726 from either data read-in or from processor calculations.

To insert the decimal point in the output data, an edit-area is set up by means of the Data Description, with a PICTURE containing a decimal point in the desired location. For example, COST-EDIT with the PICTURE 9999.99 may be set up as an edit-area for COST which was originally defined with the PICTURE 9999V99. Execution of the instruction MOVE COST TO COST-EDIT will make COST-EDIT contain 0137.26. The number now has the decimal point where it is wanted, but the "$" is missing, and there is an extra "0". These problems will be discussed shortly.

The important point about the editing operation, of which decimal-point insertion is a simple example, is that it involves two or more control stages as data move from input through processing to output. The input-file PICTURE controls input data. The PICTURE for each *data-name* that receives the results of calculations also controls the format of such results. The PICTURE for each edit-area controls the format and content of results before they go to output.

The symbol 9 in an edit-area PICTURE represents only a location for a numeric digit, which corresponds to the scheme for an input PICTURE—the actual content of the specified edit-area can be any numeric digit. The decimal point in the edit-area PICTURE is a *literal,* for it appears as the actual contents of a location and also indicates its position relative to others. When data are moved to the COST-EDIT area, with the PICTURE 9999.99, the characters fill the locations represented by the 9's and a decimal will occupy the third character-position from the right.

The processor will align the V-position of the source data (from read-in or from calculation) with the decimal point of the edit area, assuming that it exists in both cases. Figure 7-11 illustrates some of the possibilities that result from editing. Case 1 is the example described above in which the edit-area PICTURE and source

	COST		COST-EDIT	
	Input or Source		Edit-Area	
Case	PICTURE	Contents	PICTURE	Contents
1	9999V99	013726	9999.99	0137.26
2	9999V99	013726	9999.9	0137.2
3	99V9999	013726	9999.99	0001.37
4	9999V99	013726	99.99	37.26
5	999999	013726	99999.9	13726.0

FIGURE 7-11. *Result of moving data from the location described by input picture to the location described by edit-area picture.*

PICTURE correspond to the input data so that the edited result has the same decimal point and digits. In Case 2, the edit-area contains only one digit to the right of the decimal point, so the right-hand digit is dropped and rounding does *not* occur.

In Case 3, the source PICTURE indicates that the decimal point is located four digits from the right, which corresponds to 1.3726 as input. Since the edit-area provides for only two places to the right, the edited result is 1.37 and the 2 and 6 are dropped. Editing places zeros to the left of the decimal point to fill out the edit-area PICTURE.

Case 4 shows how leading digits can be lost by use of a short edit-area. The edit-area PICTURE has only two digits to the left of the decimal point, so that the leading 1 is dropped and the processor prints out a message on the console to indicate loss of a leading digit.

In Case 5, the input picture does not have a V, and the processor assumes that the source number is an integer—it consists of digits to the left of the decimal point only and none to the right. The edit operation correspondingly places the source data-item to the left of the decimal point, since the input PICTURE accepted all of it, and places a 0 to the right.

Dollar Sign and Comma. The other editing symbols, the dollar sign and the comma, are inserted in essentially the same way as the decimal point. First, the edit-area PICTURE is described in the Data Description with the dollar sign and comma in the character positions where they are wanted in the final output. The dollar sign, comma, and decimal point are three literals that also specify locations; each symbol both represents and is the location's content. The

9's in the PICTURE merely represent positions for numeric digits. The second step is to MOVE the data-name to be edited to the edit-area to associate the editing symbols with the data. Figure 7-12 illustrates some results from using these editing symbols.

	COST		COST-EDIT	
	Source Area		Edit-Area	
Case	PICTURE	Contents	PICTURE	Contents
1	9(5)	18710	$99,999.99	$18,710.00
2	9(7)	5371321	99,999,999	05,371,321
3	9999	0321	$9999	$0321
4	9999V99	132167	$9,999.99	$1,321.67

FIGURE 7-12. *Result of editing for dollar sign, comma, and decimal point.*

In summary, dollar signs, commas, and decimal points are inserted into numeric data by developing an appropriate set of symbols in an edit-area PICTURE, and moving the numeric data into the edit-area.

Zero Suppression. In Figure 7-12, both Cases 2 and 3 result in leading zeros that are undesirable; they interfere with quick comprehension and are unsightly. COBOL-1 has a zero-suppression editing symbol—Z—for replacing leading zeros with blanks. The Z, used in place of the 9 symbol in an edit-area PICTURE, has the following effect. When an item is moved into the edit-area, the digits fill in the Z locations just as they fill in the locations indicated by 9's. Leading zeros, however, become blanks. Examples of the use of zero suppression are shown in Figure 7-13.

The other editing symbols—dollar sign, comma, and decimal point—are usable with zero suppression in the same manner as described above for 9's. The comma, however, has an additional feature, for it disappears if suppression eliminates all digits to its left. But the dollar sign and decimal point used in an edit-area PICTURE remain after zero suppression with the dollar sign "floated" into the desired position (between the left and right $'s) if the edit-area PICTURE contains two or more $'s in the positions to the left of the digits that are wanted in the output.

The use of Z's alone in an edit-area PICTURE will result in all blanks for an item containing all zeros. If the programmer wishes to retain one or more leading zeros, he may use 9's to the right of the Z's. But 9's must not be written to the left of the Z's.

	COST		COST-EDIT	
	Source Area		Edit-Area	
Case	PICTURE	Contents	PICTURE	Contents
1	9(5)	17591	ZZZZZ	17591
2	9(5)	00018	ZZZZZ	18
3	9(5)	03040	ZZZZZ	3040
4	9(5)	03040	$ZZ,ZZZ	$ 3040
5	9999V99	001734	$$,$$$.ZZ	$17.34
6	9999V99	000000	$Z,ZZ9.99	$ 0.00

FIGURE 7-13. *Result of editing for zero suppression (with dollar sign, comma, and decimal point).*

The rules for editing data items for zero suppression, and insertion of dollar sign, comma, and decimal point can be summarized as follows:

1. [Z] Numeric data moved into an edit-area PICTURE fill in the spaces represented by the Z's. Zeros to the left of the first nonzero character become blanks and the decimal point does not stop zero suppression.
2. [9] Numeric data moved into an edit-area PICTURE occupy the spaces represented by 9's. Any 9's positions not filled by the source data become zeros.
3. [.] The V in the source data from input or calculations (or the right-most character if no V is present) is aligned with the decimal point in the edit-area PICTURE. The decimal point always carries through to the position shown by the picture of the edit-area.
4. [$] The dollar sign appears in the position shown by the edit-area PICTURE. Two or more $'s in the edit-area PICTURE "float" one $ to the position occupied by the right-most leading zero in the data that is indicated by a $.
5. [,] A comma in the edit-area PICTURE will appear in the edited result, *unless* zero suppression eliminates all digits to its left and it is then dropped.

TRANSLATING AND RUNNING A COBOL-1 PROGRAM

Programs written in COBOL-1 can, with minor modifications, be run on a data processor. Two phases are involved in using a COBOL program. First, a program written in COBOL, commonly called a *source program,* is translated into a program in machine language, called an *object program,* under the control of a special program called a *COBOL translator.* Second, the object program is run to process data. The idea that two processor runs and three programs are involved in writing, translating, and running a COBOL program is shown in Figure 7-14. Any processor that has a COBOL-61 translator can translate and run COBOL-1 programs.

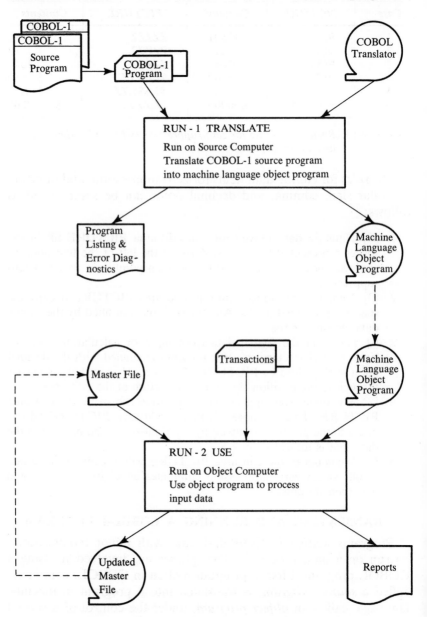

FIGURE 7-14. *Run diagram for translating and using a COBOL program.*

This section outlines the procedures required to prepare COBOL-1 programs in a form suitable for translating on a particular processor. The exact method for preparing source programs varies, of course, from one model processor to another and even between different configurations of one model.

COBOL Running Requirements

In order to translate and run a source program written in COBOL, a programmer must adhere to the COBOL rules for writing programs. Furthermore, he needs access to a computer that has a COBOL translator available *and* the particular machine he is working with must meet the manufacturer's minimum specifications for translating COBOL programs. In general, each equipment manufacturer provides a COBOL translator for his large and medium scale business processors. Table 7-1, at the end of this chapter, shows a list of manufacturers and their processors with COBOL translators, which are often called *compilers*.

Reserved Words. One of the rules a programmer must follow in selecting COBOL names is *not* to use any of the words reserved for all versions of COBOL-61 or any of the additional words reserved for the machine he plans to use for translating his program. Certain words have a special meaning in COBOL and may not be used as data-names, file-names, or procedure-names. COBOL defines a word as a group of letters written together without spaces, although the parts of a COBOL word may be separated by hyphens for readability. For example, INVENTORY-FILE is treated as one word in COBOL and is a legal name; FILE by itself is a reserved word; and INVENTORY FILE is illegal for it violates the rules by containing a blank. The words reserved for all versions of COBOL-61 are listed in Table 7-2 at the end of this chapter. The additional reserved words for the IBM-1401, which is used here to illustrate a COBOL-1 program, are as follows:

ADVANCING	NO-PRINT-STORAGE
BEFORE	1402-R
LINES	1402-P
VALUES	1403-P
ID	1403-CT
RETENTION-CYCLE	1403-P-CB
TAPE	1403-P-C9
TAPES	1403-P-CV
NO-RELEASE	1401-SS
NO-OVERLAP	

Source Computer.   A manufacturer specifies the minimum configuration of a computer, commonly called a *source computer,* for efficiently translating or compiling a source program written in COBOL into an object program in machine language. The minimum specifications for a source computer usually state the number of magnetic tapes needed, the size of high-speed storage, and the availability of index registers and other logic features. A data processor, commonly called an *object computer,* used to run the resulting object program is subject to few restrictions for minimum size. The fact that the source computer may have to be fairly large to operate efficiently reflects the fact that compiling a program is likely to be more difficult than running it. Big configurations of medium and most versions of large scale processors will compile COBOL source programs. For example, to use the IBM 1401 as a source computer requires that it have at least the following:

> 12,000 positions of magnetic-core storage
> Four magnetic-tape units
> A 1403 Printer, Model II
> A card-reader punch
> Advanced programming features (index registers)
> A high-low-equal compare instruction
> Sense switches
> A multiply-divide instruction.

Object Computer.   After the source program is compiled, the resulting object program will run on any IBM 1401 that has at least 4000 positions of magnetic-core storage. Even card systems—that is, systems without magnetic-tape units—can run COBOL object programs.

Sample Program

The sample program shown in Figure 7-15 brings together many subjects discussed in this chapter. The basic problem used here is the simple one for calculating stock value described earlier, but several new points are added to make the problem and program more realistic and interesting. Since the new points are simple, they can be discussed along with the program. Of course, a complete statement of the problem and flow charts in one place would be useful, but they are easily prepared. The program shown in Figure 7-15 is complete and, when keypunched, can be compiled and run on any IBM 1401 that meets the COBOL configuration require-

COBOL-1 Program Form

Program Name: STOCK-VALUE CALCULATION
Program Number: SVC-3
Prepared by WILL HARRISS
Date FEB 22

Line No.	12	Procedure-Name / Data-Name	41	Procedures / Picture
001	COBOL	RUN		
001	IDENTIFICATION	DIVISION.		
002	PROGRAM-ID.	STOCK VALUE.		
003	AUTHOR.	WILL HARRISS.		
010	ENVIRONMENT	DIVISION.		
020	CONFIGURATION	SECTION.		
030	SOURCE-COMPUTER.	IBM-1401		
040	MEMORY SIZE	12000 CHARACTERS		
050	NO-RELEASE	NO-PRINT-STORAGE.		
060	OBJECT-COMPUTER.	IBM-1401		
070	MEMORY SIZE	12000 CHARACTERS		
080	NO-OVERLAP	NO-RELEASE NO-PRINT-STORAGE.		
090	INPUT-OUTPUT	SECTION.		
100	FILE-CONTROL.			
110	SELECT	INVENTORY-FILE ASSIGN TO 1402-R.		
120	SELECT	STOCK-VALUE-FILE ASSIGN TO 1403)--P.		

FIGURE 7-15. Sample COBOL-1 program.

235

	COBOL-1 Program Form		Program Name STOCK-VALUE CALCULATION	Page 2 of 3
			Program Number SVC-3	Prepared by WILL HARRIS	Date FEB 22

Page 0012	Line No.	Procedure Name	Level No.	Data-Name	Picture / Procedures
	200			DATA DIVISION.	
	210			FILE SECTION.	
	220	FD		INVENTORY-FILE LABEL RECORDS ARE OMITTED DATA RECORD	
	221			IS STOCK-RECORD.	
	230		01	STOCK-RECORD.	
	240		02	STOCK-NUMBER	PICTURE 9(10).
	250		02	STOCK-NAME	PICTURE X(20).
	260		02	QUAN-ON-HAND	PICTURE 999999.
	270		02	QUAN-ON-ORDER	PICTURE 999999.
	280		02	WAREHOUSE-LOCATION.	
	290		03	BUILD-NO	PICTURE 999.
	300		03	AISLE-NO	PICTURE X.X.X.
	310		03	BIN-NO	PICTURE 999.
	320		02	UNIT-COST	PICTURE 999V99.
	330		02	FILLER	SIZE IS 28.
	340	FD		VALUE-FILE LABEL RECORDS ARE OMITTED DATA RECORD	
	341			IS VALUE-RECORD.	
	350		01	VALUE-RECORD.	
	360		02	STOCK-NUMBER-0	PICTURE 9(10).
	370		02	FILLER	SIZE IS 5.
	380		02	STOCK-NAME-0	PICTURE X(20).
	390		02	FILLER	SIZE IS 5.
	400		02	STOCK-VALUE	PICTURE 9(6)V99.
	410		02	FILLER	SIZE IS 5.
	420		02	STOCK-VALUE-E	PICTURE $222,229.99.
	430		02	FILLER	SIZE IS 68.

FIGURE 7-15. Sample COBOL-1 program (con't).

Page 003	COBOL-1 Program Form	Program Name STOCK-VALUE CALCULATION		Page 3 of 3
		Program Number SVC-3	Prepared by WILL HARRISS	Date FEB 22

```
500 PROCEDURE DIVISION.
510 START.
520     OPEN INPUT INVENTORY-FILE  OUTPUT STOCK-VALUE-FILE.
530 NEXT-RECORD.
540     READ INVENTORY-FILE AT END GO TO FINISH.
550     MULTIPLY QUAN-ON-HAND BY UNIT-COST GIVING STOCK-VALUE.
560     MOVE STOCK-NUMBER TO STOCK-NUMBER-O.
570     MOVE STOCK-NAME TO STOCK-NAME-O.
580     MOVE STOCK-VALUE TO STOCK-VALUE-E.
590     WRITE VALUE-RECORD.
600     GO TO NEXT-RECORD.
605 FINISH.
610     CLOSE INVENTORY-FILE  STOCK-VALUE-FILE.
620     STOP RUN.
```

FIGURE 7-15. *Sample COBOL-1 program (con't).*

ments. It can be used to demonstrate the operation of COBOL-1 and to gain actual introductory experience to COBOL-61.

A complete COBOL-1 program must have four divisions in the following sequence: Identification Division, Environment Division, Data Division, and Procedure Division.

Identification Division. The Identification Division is simple and has only three entries:

> IDENTIFICATION DIVISION
> PROGRAM-ID. *The program name.*
> AUTHOR. *The author's name.*

Each entry starts in the left-hand column under Procedure Name, as shown by the sample Identification Division in Figure 7-15 (lines 001 through 003).

Environment Division. The Environment Division describes the specific hardware to be used to compile and later to run this COBOL-1 program along with the assignment of files during the run phase. The Configuration Section specifies both the source computer and the object computer. It also includes an Input-Output Section to identify the particular piece of hardware—card punch, card reader, tape unit or printer—used for each input and output file; and it may also specify other equipment features. The exact content of this division depends upon the particular processor involved and is independent of the program except for the file names.

The Environment Division for the IBM 1401 processor to be used for the sample program is shown in the second part of Figure 7-15 (lines 010 through 120). The first two entries are the standard division and section titles. The *source computer paragraph* starts at line 030 to state the source computer is an IBM 1401. Line 040 specifies that it has 12,000 positions of core storage, which is the minimum permissible for use as a source computer. When a machine with 16,000 positions of core is used, the entry should be 16000 instead of 12000 in order to get more efficient compilation. The entries on line 050—NO-RELEASE, NO-PRINT-STORAGE— state that two special options available from the manufacturer— read-punch release and print-storage—are *not* included on this machine. If either of these features is available, the corresponding NO entry on line 050 is omitted. Note that a period follows the last entry in the paragraph for source computer.

The *object computer paragraph,* comparable to the source computer paragraph, specifies on line 060 that an IBM 1401 is the object computer to run the program. Line 070 indicates the object computer has 12,000 characters of core storage. The range of storage capacity for an IBM 1401 that can run COBOL programs is from 4,000 to 16,000 characters and the number actually available should be entered. Each NO entry on line 080 is omitted for each special feature that is available.

In the *Input-Output Section,* the programmer assigns each input and output file to a specific input-output unit. The section title appears on line 090 and the paragraph title FILE CONTROL appears on line 100. The general form for each line assigning a file to a piece of equipment is:

SELECT *file-name* ASSIGN to *device-name.*

The entry on line 110 assigns INVENTORY-FILE, the input file described earlier in this chapter, to 1402-R, which is the code name for the card reader in the 1401 system. The next line assigns STOCK-VALUE-FILE, the output file, to 1403-P, which is the code name for the printer.

As mentioned earlier, the exact contents of the Environment Division vary widely among different processors. The description given here is typical, but it is appropriate only to one configuration of the IBM 1401. A manufacturer's manual for the particular processor used should be consulted for a detailed description.

Data Division. The Data Division in Figure 7-15 corresponds to the Data Division for the stock value calculation problem given earlier in Figures 7-2 and 7-3. Some modifications are necessary to write it in correct form ready for compilation.

First, the title FILE SECTION must appear on the next line after DATA DIVISION (line 210). Second, after each FD and *file-name* entry the statement LABEL RECORDS ARE OMITTED must be inserted before the statement naming the data record (lines 220 and 340). Label records are special messages placed at the beginning and end of files that may contain an identification of the file, the date last processed, a record count, and other similar items. Label records are not used with punched-card files and are optional with magnetic-tape files. Two new data elements in the output record are STOCK-NAME-O (line 380), which is moved from the input record, and STOCK-VALUE-E (line 420), which will produce an edited version of stock value complete with a dollar sign, decimal point, comma, and zero suppression. For comparative purposes in this example, the program will print both the edited and unedited version of stock value in the output.

COBOL for the IBM 1401 imposes a special restriction on files that pass through the card reader or printer. These files must have a record length equal to the normal record length for the device that is used, which is 80 characters for the card reader or punch and 132 characters for the printer. The total number of data characters in STOCK-RECORD is 52. Since it must have a total of 80 characters, a pseudo-data element of 28 characters called FILLER is added to the STOCK-RECORD at line 330. Since FILLER is not a real data element, size is its only characteristic and is specified by a statement SIZE IS *number-of-characters*. The FILLER entry is used only for spacing and any number of elements with the same name, FILLER, can appear in the Data Division, but it must not be mentioned in any procedure statement.

The COBOL language implicitly assumes that output is in the form of magnetic-tape files, which can be printed later, if readable reports are wanted. As a result, general COBOL-61 makes little reference to printing, although specific processors may have COBOL instructions for line spacing, starting new pages, and so forth. When printed output is produced by a COBOL program, FILLER entries can be used to separate data elements. The entries on lines 370, 390, and 410 will each result in a blank space that is five characters wide during printing and make the report easier to read. The FILLER entry on line 430 is used to make the total characters in the Output record a full line of 132 print positions as required by the printer.

Procedure Division. The Procedure Division in Figure 7-15 corresponds to Figure 7-8, but several modifications are necessary to open the files only once for all records, to move three items (instead of one) to the output area, and to close the files after finishing processing.

The Procedure Division prepares files for use prior to executing a file READ instruction and for removal of file at the end of processing. The initial preparation is caused by inserting the following statement on line 520 as the first instruction:

OPEN INPUT *file-names* OUTPUT *file-names*.

The input *file-names* are written after INPUT and the output *file-*

names after OUTPUT. Before the STOP-RUN instruction, a file closing statement is written in the form:

CLOSE *file-names.*

All files are listed together regardless of type in the CLOSE instruction as shown on line 610.

The program reads many stock records, but it should OPEN the files only once. The *procedure-name* START, therefore, refers to the OPEN statement (line 520), and the record-processing part of the program (lines 540 through 600) is given the *procedure-name* —NEXT-RECORD (line 530). Finally, two new MOVE instructions are inserted (lines 570, 580) to transfer stock names from the input to the output record and to edit stock value.

At the last step of preparation for compiling, the COBOL-1 program is converted into punched cards or paper tape, depending on what media the source computer reads. The COBOL-1 programming form was designed to facilitate keypunching as well as to simplify writing the program. The data from each line filled in is punched as an entry on card or tape, but blank lines are ignored. For each entry, the page number of the COBOL-1 form is punched in the first three columns of a card (or characters on tape) and the rest of the entry copied intact from its line on the COBOL-1 form. Consequently, Line No. is punched in columns 4 through 6, Procedure-Name in columns 8 through 11; Data-Name in columns 12 through 41; and Picture in columns 43 through 49.

The maximum length of an entry depends upon the processor. For the IBM 1401, an entry is not permitted to exceed 72 columns because only the first 72 columns of an 80-column punched card are read by the IBM 1401 COBOL translator. Processors that accept punched paper tape can, of course, read entries of any length, although a limit is often imposed. When a COBOL-1 statement will not fit in one line on the COBOL-1 form, it is continued at the beginning of the *data-name* column on the next line. Therefore, one sentence may become two or more machine-media entries, but successive inputs are treated by the processor as a single statement until it encounters a period.

Most processors require some type of job or run card as the first card in the COBOL program. For the IBM 1401, this card is punched with COBOL in columns 6 through 10 and RUN in columns 16 through 18. The entry COBOL RUN is shown on the first line of Figure 7-15.

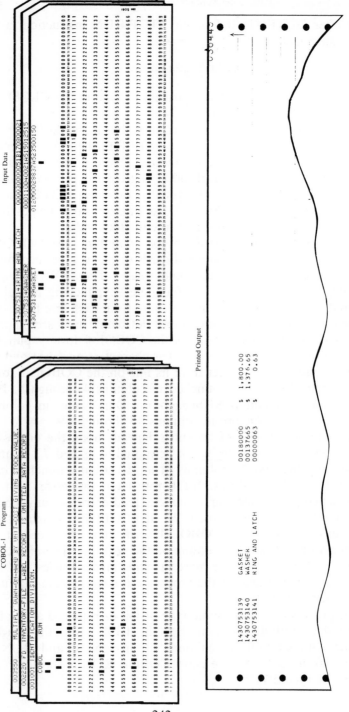

FIGURE 7-16. *Machine media: COBOL-1 program, input data, and output.*

242

Figure 7-16 shows part of this COBOL-1 program punched into cards and ready for read-in to a processor.

This simple program has many of the features of a typical file-processing application for it explains and illustrates each of the four COBOL divisions of a program. It shows how specific equipment is described and the data and procedures required. Although real COBOL programs are much longer, most of this length is due to more detail, not new features.

SUMMARY

When stated in ordinary terms, programming is a familiar subject to everyone. It consists simply of planning a solution and giving instructions for a way to do a particular task. The art of giving instructions to machines has much in common with that of giving instructions to people. However, more careful and explicit instructions in a special language are required for machines than is the case for people.

Programming consists of the following steps. First, define the *requirements*—inputs, outputs, files, and boundaries of the problem. Second, formulate a general *solution*. Third, identify available *capabilities*—people, organization, and hardware. Finally, match the general solution to the capabilities and arrive at a specific solution—a detailed set of *instructions* written in a particular language.

There are many types and varieties of programming languages. Machine-oriented languages reflect the engineering structure of a specific processor. Problem-oriented languages are designed with the symbols and format commonly used to solve a particular type of problem. Since English is commonly used in business, a language designed for solving business problems is built around English words and phrases.

The problem-oriented language described in this chapter is COBOL-1, a compatible subset of COBOL-61, the Common Business Oriented Language, which is planned for widespread use with different processors. COBOL-1 provides both an effective means of learning about programming and a practical tool for subsequent use, since COBOL-1 programs may be test-run on any of the many processors supplied with COBOL translators.

COBOL specifications require data descriptions in terms of *characters*—letters, numerals, and punctuation or special marks; *elements*—a set of related characters such as part name or stock number; *records*—a set of related elements, such as stock record; and *files*—a set of related records such as an inventory file. COBOL is designed primarily for *file processing*—reading a record, processing it, and writing it out, then repeating this cycle.

A COBOL-1 program contains four parts in the following sequence. First, the Identification Division simply identifies the program and the author. Second, the Environment Division describes the source computer for translating the COBOL program into machine language, and the object computer for running the translated program to process data. This division also specifies the particular media and device used for each file—cards, magnetic or paper tapes, or printer. Third, the *Data Division* describes each element, record, and file used in input, output or processing. Each entry in the Data Division consists of a *level number*—FD for files, 01 for records, and 02 to 49 for elements within records; a *file-, record-,* or *data-name*—a unique combination of 30 or fewer numbers and letters; and a *picture* that shows the type and maximum number of characters in each elementary item. Fourth, the *Procedure Division* specifies what operations the programmer wants to perform on the elements, records, and files described in the Data Division.

Instructions are available to read data in, move data inside the processor, and write out results. Arithmetic instructions provide for the operations of add, subtract, multiply, and divide. A third group of instructions are used to change the program sequence either unconditionally or depending on the outcome of a comparison. The order code for COBOL-1 is summarized in Table 7-3, at the end of this chapter.

After a programmer analyzes a problem and defines a solution, the process of writing a COBOL-1 program involves the following steps. First, a flow chart of the logic is drawn using COBOL data-names and instruction-names. Second, as each new data-name appears on the flow chart, its description is written in the Data Division. Third, the flow chart is translated into COBOL procedures using the exact data-names defined earlier. Both the description of data and the procedure statements are written on the COBOL-1 Programming Form. This form is designed for both writing programs and converting them to machine media.

COBOL is particularly well adapted to file-processing applications, which involve treating each record in a file in a similar manner—read the record in, perform some arithmetic or logic operations on it, and write out the results. Since this pattern of actions exists, one set of instructions can often be used repeatedly

Company	Model of Equipment
Bendix Computer Division	G–20
Burroughs Corporation	B–5000
Control Data Corporation	CDC–1604 CDC–924
General Electric Company	GE–225 GE–304B
International Business Machines Corporation	705–II 705–III/7080 709/7090 7070/7074 1410 1401
Minneapolis-Honeywell Regulator Company	MH–400 MH–800
National Cash Register Co. (Joint implementation effort with General Electric Co.)	NCR–315–Tapes NCR–315–CRAM NCR–304A NCR–304B
Philco Corporation	200 series computers (210, 211, & 212 main frames)
Radio Corporation of America	RCA–301 RCA–601 RCA–501
Remington Rand UNIVAC	UNIVAC II UNIVAC Solid State UNIVAC III UNIVAC 1107 UNIVAC 490
Sylvania Electronics Systems Data Systems Operations	9400 MOBIDIC

TABLE 7-1. *Equipment manufacturers and processors with COBOL-61 compilers.*

to process all the records in a file. This approach to repetitive use of programs is called cycling and is fundamental to programming.

The output-editing feature is of special interest in COBOL. Data used in computation must be numeric and not contain blanks, a decimal point, or other non-numeric symbols. Report users, however, want data in a readable and understandable format. COBOL editing features allow a programmer to suppress leading zeros and to insert dollar signs, commas, and decimal points.

Using a COBOL-1 program involves two steps. First, the COBOL-1 source program is translated into a machine language. Second, the resulting object program is run with data. With minor additions, a COBOL-1 program will compile and run on any machine that has a COBOL-61 translator and that meets the minimum configuration required for COBOL-61. The actual translation and execution of COBOL-1 programs should clarify its features and serve as an introduction to the operation of a typical business programming language.

ABOUT	CHARACTERS	END-OF-FILE
ACCEPT	CHECK	END-OF-TAPE
ADD	CLASS	ENTER
ADDRESS	CLOCK-UNITS	ENVIRONMENT
ADVANCING	CLOSE	EQUAL
AFTER	COBOL	EQUALS
ALL	COMPUTATIONAL	ERROR
ALPHABETIC	COMPUTE	EVERY
ALPHANUMERIC	CONFIGURATION	EXAMINE
ALTER	CONSTANT	EXCEEDS
ALTERNATE	CONTAINS	EXIT
AN	CONTROL	EXPONENTIATED
AND	COPY	FD
APPLY	CORRESPONDING	FOR
ARE	DATA	FILE
AREA	DATE-WRITTEN	FILE-CONTROL
AREAS	DECLARATIVES	FILLER
AS	DEFINE	FILLING
ASSIGN	DEPENDING	FIRST
AT	DIGIT	FLOAT
BEFORE	DIGITS	FORMAT
BEGINNING	DISPLAY	FROM
BEGINNING-FILE-LABEL	DIVIDE	GIVING
BEGINNING-TAPE-LABEL	DIVIDED	GO
BIT	DIVISION	GREATER
BITS	DOLLAR	HASHED
BLANK	ELSE	HIGH-VALUE
BLOCK	END	HIGH-VALUES
BLOCK-COUNT	ENDING	I-O-CONTROL
BY	ENDING-FILE-LABEL	IF
CHARACTER	ENDING-TAPE-LABEL	IN

TABLE 7-2. *Reserved words for all versions of COBOL-61.*

INCLUDE	OPEN	SEQUENCED
INPUT	OPTIONAL	SIGN
INPUT-OUTPUT	OR	SIGNED
INTO	OTHERWISE	SIZE
IS	OUTPUT	SOURCE-COMPUTER
JUSTIFIED	PERFORM	SPACE
LABEL	PICTURE	SPACES
LEADING	PLACES	SPECIAL-NAMES
LEAVING	PLUS	STANDARD
LEFT	POINT	STATUS
LESS	POSITION	STOP
LIBRARY	POSITIVE	SUBTRACT
LINES	PREPARED	SUPERVISOR
LOCATION	PRIORITY	SUPPRESS
LOCK	PROCEDURE	SYNCHRONIZED
LOW-VALUE	PROCEED	TALLY
LOW-VALUES	PROTECT	TALLYING
LOWER-BOUND	PROTECTION	TAPE
LOWER-BOUNDS	PURGE-DATE	TEST-PATTERN
MEMORY	QUOTE	THAN
MEMORY-DUMP	RANGE	THEN
MEMORY-DUMP-KEY	READ	THROUGH⎫ *Equivalent*
MINUS	RECORD	THRU ⎭
MODE	RECORD-COUNT	TIMES
MODULES	RECORDING	TO
MOVE	RECORDS	TYPE
MULTIPLE	REDEFINES	UNEQUAL
MULTIPLIED	REEL	UPPER-BOUND
MULTIPLY	REEL-NUMBER	UPPER-BOUNDS
NEGATIVE	RENAMING	UNTIL
NEXT	REPLACING	UPON
NO	RERUN	USAGE
NO-MEMORY-DUMP	RESERVE	USE
NOT	REVERSED	VALUE
NOTE	REWIND	VARYING
NUMERIC	RIGHT	WHEN
OBJECT-COMPUTER	ROUNDED	WITH
OBJECT-PROGRAM	RUN	WORDS
OCCURS	SAME	WORKING-STORAGE
OF	SECTION	WRITE
OFF	SELECT	ZERO
OMITTED	SENTENCE	ZEROES
ON	SENTINEL	ZEROS

TABLE 7-2. *Reserved words for all versions of COBOL-61 (cont'd).*

READ *file-name-1*. Read into the processor the record from the input file identified by *file-name-1*.

READ *file-name-1* AT END *imperative-statement-1*. If a record remains in the input file identified by *file-name-1*, then read it. If none remains, execute the instruction contained in *imperative-statement-1*.

WRITE *record-name-1*. Write the data identified by *record-name-1* in the output file set up to receive them.

MOVE *data-name-1* TO *data-name-2*. Move the data identified by *data-name-1* to the location called *data-name-2*.

ADD *data-name-1* AND *data-name-2* GIVING *data-name-3*. Add the data identified by *data-name-1* to the data identified as *data-name-2* and call the result *data-name-3*. Any number of *data-names* may be added together by placing them in the instruction between the ADD and the GIVING.

ADD *data-name-1* TO *data-name-2*. Add the data identified by *data-name-1* to the data identified by *data-name-2* and call the result *data-name-2*. Any number of *data-names* may be added to *data-name-2* by placing them in the instruction between the ADD and the TO.

SUBTRACT *data-name-1* FROM *data-name-2* GIVING *data-name-3*. Subtract the data identified by *data-name-1* from the data identified by *data-name-2* and call the result *data-name-3*. Any number of *data-names* may be subtracted from *data-name-2* by placing them in the instruction between the SUBTRACT and the FROM.

SUBTRACT *data-name-1* FROM *data-name-2*. Subtract the data identified by *data-name-1* from the data identified by *data-name-2* and call the result *data-name-2*. Any number of *data-names* may be subtracted from *data-name-2* by placing them in the instruction between the SUB-TRACT and the FROM.

MULTIPLY *data-name-1* BY *data-name-2* GIVING *data-name-3*. Multiply the data identified by *data-name-1* by the data identified by *data-name-2* and call the product *data-name-3*.

DIVIDE *data-name-1* INTO *data-name-2* GIVING *data-name-3*. Divide the data identified by *data-name-1* into the data identified by *data-name-2* and call the quotient *data-name-3*.

ON SIZE ERROR *imperative-statement-1*. If an arithmetic instruction with this phrase attached results in the loss of leading digits, follow the instruction in *imperative-statement-1*. Otherwise ignore *imperative-statement-1*.

TABLE 7-3. *COBOL-1 instructions.*

ROUNDED. When an arithmetic instruction with this phrase attached results in the loss of trailing digits, the right-most retained digit is increased by 1 if the discarded digit is a 5 or greater.

GO TO *procedure-name-1*. When this instruction is encountered, the program continues with the first instruction that follows *procedure-name-1*.

IF *conditional-expression-1* THEN *statement-1* OTHERWISE *statement-2*. If *conditional-expression-1* is a true statement, then execute *statement-1;* otherwise execute *statement-2*.

STOP RUN. This instruction marks the end of a COBOL-1 program and will cause the processor to halt.

TABLE 7-3 *(cont'd)*.

CHAPTER 8

PROGRAMMING—
MACHINE-ORIENTED LANGUAGES

This chapter deals with machine-oriented languages for programming data processors. In many ways machine-oriented language programming corresponds to COBOL. The problem-solving process is basically the same whether a machine-oriented or other programming language is used. Many of the principles of input, output, and cycling remain the same for any language, but the programmer works with them at a different level of detail in each language.

The machine-oriented languages discussed in this chapter are still one or more stages removed from basic machine languages. They use mnemonic operation codes—for example, ADD, PNC, and WT for "add a number," "punch data in a card," "and write a data record on tape," respectively. These codes are easier to remember and use than the numbers, such as 11, 32, and 24, to represent operations in near-machine language. The mnemonic instruction codes are converted to numbers on a one-for-one basis by means of the processor using an assembly program: ADD to 11, and PNC to 32. The assembled program consisting of numbers for operations and addresses is converted by the processor to binary for execution.

Absolute addresses are used for instructions in most of this chapter. Each instruction address refers to a certain location in the machine—for example, ADD 267—to deal with the *contents* of storage location 267. Results are developed in certain registers—the accumulator and M-Q—and can be returned to storage. Since instruction addresses are absolute, they refer to specific locations in storage and are ready to execute as written in a program without conversion, except for decimal to binary. The programmer deals with words and characters for machine-oriented languages instead of data elements as he does with COBOL.

A machine language is designed for a particular processor and exploits its unique capabilities better than COBOL does. COBOL, it will be recalled, is designed as an English-like language for data processing with a wide variety of processors. Thus a judicious mixture of languages may be most efficient: COBOL for most of a program and the particular machine-language for situations best handled by unique features of the processor. COBOL provides for transition between languages by use of the ENTER verb and the name of the desired language—the particular machine language or COBOL. This transition from one language to another makes programming bilingual, in a sense.

This chapter discusses machine-oriented language programming for both a *fixed*-word-length processor and a *field*- or variable-word-length processor. WORDCOM, a fixed-word-length processor, is covered in the first part of this chapter. FIELDCOM, a field processor, is treated briefly to cover programming for their unique features.

WORDCOM

WORDCOM (for fixed-*word*-length *com*puter) is a medium scale, internally-stored program processor. It is designed as a simplified machine to present machine-language programming for this important class of processors. It has arithmetic, control, and storage units as described in Chapter 3, and input-output units as described in Chapter 4. The features of WORDCOM of interest here are, briefly, as follows:

1. *Storage:* One thousand words of sign and seven alphanumeric characters each in high-speed storage. Addresses are 000 through 999 (999 is followed by 000).

2. *Arithmetic unit:* Accumulator and M-Q registers of sign and seven characters each.
3. *Control unit:* Instruction counter and three index registers.
4. *Input-Output:* One card read-punch machine and up to ten magnetic-tape units.
5. *Instruction repertoire:* Twenty-four different single-address instructions can be executed.

WORDCOM INSTRUCTIONS AND PROGRAMMING

As described earlier, a single-address instruction is a set of characters that specifies an operation and indicates a storage address or register that contains an operand. The address can also indicate where to put the results of an operation. The address part is used for special purposes in some instructions.

Instruction Repertoire

The list of instructions that WORDCOM executes can be described as follows. The instructions are defined in this chapter and a summary list is given in Table 8-1 near the end of the chapter.

1. *Input and Output*
   a. Read a card and place data contents in storage.
   b. Punch a card with data from storage.
   c. Read from tape a block of data and place in storage.
   d. Write on tape a block of data from storage.
   e. Rewind a tape.
2. *Cycling to repeat an instruction routine a desired number of times*
   a. Set an index register to prepare for counting the number of cycles.
   b. Increase an index register to count each time the cycle is executed.
   c. Compare an index register to a criterion to test whether the desired number of cycles is executed.
3. *Tests*
   a. Compare two items and, depending on whether the results are "less than," "greater than," or "equal to," jump to one of three locations.
   b. Jump, if accumulator is negative.
   c. Jump, if content becomes so large it overflows accumulator.
4. *Load and store accumulator and M-Q registers*
   a. Clear accumulator and add a number to it.
   b. Clear accumulator and M-Q register and add a number to M-Q.
   c. Store contents of accumulator.
   d. Store contents of M-Q register.

5. *Arithmetic*
 a. Add a number to contents of accumulator.
 b. Subtract a number from accumulator.
 c. Multiply a number in storage by a number in the M-Q register.
 d. Divide a number in the accumulator by a number in storage.
6. *Miscellaneous*
 a. Halt processor operations.
 b. Shift contents of the accumulator and M-Q to the left.
 c. Shift contents of the accumulator and M-Q to the right.
 d. Edit by combining contents of the accumulator and an edit word under control of an extractor.
 e. Unconditional jump in the program by transferring control to a specified instruction location.

Instruction Format

Each single-address instruction for WORDCOM consists of the following elements:

1. An instruction operation code of three characters which causes the processor to read, write, compare, add, subtract, and so forth, for a total of 24 different instructions.
2. A single-letter designation of index registers, which are special units of the machine.
3. Three characters for identifying (a) the address in storage of data to be operated on, (b) the location to store a result, or (c) the storage location of an instruction. These three characters may also be a special number—a literal that is used as such.

The format of an instruction written on programming sheets or punched in cards, for read-in to internal storage is as follows:

Sign	1	2	3	4	5	6	7
+	R	E	C		0	2	3

Positive sign for instructions	Operation code	Refers to an index register	Address or special constant

Input-Output Instructions

WORDCOM has one card read-punch unit and can have up to ten magnetic-tape units. Data are first punched in cards and either read in directly or converted to tape for high-speed read-in. Output is punched in cards or written on tape. Any readable copy desired is printed later by an off-line printer operating from cards or tape. Programming in machine-oriented language for WORDCOM requires complete format details for input and output.

Punched Cards. A card read-punch unit is connected to WORDCOM for on-line operation. Reading and punching are independent and operate on separate decks of cards. The REC xxx instruction activates the card reader to read 80 character positions of a card. The read operation stores the data in ten or fewer words of eight characters each (sign and seven alphanumeric) in consecutive storage locations starting with the address specified in the instruction. Read-in replaces anything previously in the storage locations used. The PNC xxx instruction activates the card punch to accept ten words of data in processor storage, starting with word location xxx, and punch them in a card without changing the contents of storage; read-out is nondestructive. The ten words will fill 80 characters in a card, with no option for the programmer, although blanks in storage are merely blanks in a card. The format and explanation of the instructions for WORDCOM to read or to punch a card are as follows:

Code	Explanation
REC xxx	*Re*ad the next *c*ard in card reader. Store the data in ten consecutive word locations starting with word xxx, where xxx is a three-digit number 000 through 999.
PNC xxx	*Pu*nch the next *c*ard in the card-punch unit with ten words from ten consecutive word locations starting with word xxx. Contents of storage unchanged.

A simple routine can be developed from these two instructions for reading into storage the data from one or more cards and punching the data into other cards. The program given below will read data from one card, punch the same data in another card, and repeat the read and punch operations. The program itself can be read in from punched cards and placed anywhere in storage by a read-in program described later in this chapter. For simplicity, it is assumed that this program will be read into storage locations 100 to 103. Execution of the read instruction will read data from each card into storage locations 150 through 159 and the data from the last card (the second in this case) will remain there after punching is completed.

Loc.	Content	Explanation
100	REC 150	Read ten words from the first card in the reader and place them in storage locations 150 through 159. The prior contents of these locations are replaced.
101	PNC 150	Punch ten words in storage locations 150 through 159 in the next card in the punch unit. Read-out does not change the contents of storage.
102	REC 150	Read ten words from the next card in reader into locations 150 through 159. The prior contents of these locations are replaced.
103	PNC 150	Punch ten words in the next card in the card-punch unit. Storage content is unchanged.

The repetition in duplicating cards becomes burdensome if many cards are involved. To avoid this, various program schemes are used to handle the cycle of read-punch, read-punch, as described later under cycling.

Magnetic Tapes. WORDCOM can have up to ten magnetic-tape units. Data can be read from or written on any tape mounted on a tape unit by addressing that tape unit, numbered 0 through 9. The reel of tape mounted on tape unit number 3, for instance, is available when tape unit 3 is addressed in an instruction. A file label can also be recorded as the first record on tape for identifying its contents.

Data on tape are handled in "record blocks" to facilitate movement between high-speed storage and input-output units. WORDCOM reads or writes magnetic tape in blocks of 60 words, which is much longer than the ten words handled for cards. The tape read, write, and rewind instructions are as follows:

Code	Explanation
RTt xxx	*R*ead the next block of data on *t*ape unit *t* and place the data in 60 consecutive words in storage starting with location xxx. Prior contents of these locations are destroyed.
WTt xxx	*W*rite on the tape in *t*ape unit *t* the block of data in 60 consecutive words in storage starting with location xxx. Storage contents unchanged.
RWt	*Rew*ind the tape on tape unit *t* and position for removal.

A simple program, similar to that for reading and punching cards, shows how card data can be read into storage and written on tape.

Loc.	Content	Explanation
010	REC 100	Read ten words from the first card in the card-
011	REC 110	read unit and place in storage locations 100
012	REC 120	through 109. Repeat for next five cards placing
013	REC 130	in succeeding locations ten words later: 110–119,
014	REC 140	120–129, 130–139, 140–149, 150–159.
015	REC 150	
016	WT4 100	Write on the tape in tape unit 4 the 60 words in storage locations 100 through 159.

The two input-output routines given here illustrate card duplication and conversion of cards to tape—read cards and write blocks of 60 words on magnetic tape. Data conversion and writing operations are used with other instructions for processing data.

Cycles

The simplified input-output routines given above appear inefficient because they contain almost identical instructions. Repetitive instructions for handling large volumes of input and output occupy too much storage. For example, to read 3000 cards and write them on tape would require 3500 instructions—six card-read and one tape-write instructions for each six cards—but WORDCOM has only 1000 words. More efficiently, this short seven-instruction routine can be repeated 500 times to handle 3000 cards. Both program steps and storage can often be saved by devising a cycle that the processor repeats the desired number of times. The steps a programmer might take to make the processor perform an operating cycle a certain number of times are as follows:

1. Before cycling starts, *set up* or initialize a cycle counter and a criterion for counting cycles and for testing when to leave the cycle.
2. *Perform* the desired cycle of read, write, or other operations.
3. Increase the *count* in the cycle counter.
4. *Compare* the contents of the cycle counter with the criterion to determine whether to repeat the cycle *or* to leave the cycle because the desired number of cycles has been completed.
5. *Jump* to the appropriate instruction in the program to repeat the cycle *or* go to another part of the program, depending on the results of the comparison.

Index Registers.   WORDCOM uses index registers identified as A, B, and C to count cycles. An index register is a counter that can be set to any desired number from storage, increased by a certain number, and tested to find whether the new number is equal to a criterion in storage that was set up before cycling started. Each index register can hold a three-digit number from 000 to 999 that can be set, increased, and tested whenever desired in a program by means of the following *indexing instructions:*

Code	Explanation
SISyxxx	*Set i*ndex register y (y designates index A, B, or C) with the three right-hand digits contained in *s*torage location xxx. Storage location xxx contents unchanged.
INCynnn	*Inc*rease the number in register y by the number nnn (nnn is the *number* itself and not an address).
CISyxxx	*C*ompare the number in *i*ndex register y to the criterion (right-hand three digits) in *s*torage location xxx. If index and criterion are unequal, take the next instruction in sequence, which should be a jump. If equal, skip one instruction and take the second instruction. Contents of index register and location xxx remain unchanged by the comparison operation.

The format of an instruction involving an index register is shown below. Character 4 identifies the register—A, B, or C. Positions 5 through 7 indicate a storage location whose contents are used to set a register initially in a SISyxxx instruction, or the location of a criterion for comparisons in a CISyxxx instruction. For an INCynnn instruction, positions 5 through 7 contain *the number* used for increasing index contents.

Sign	1	2	3	4	5	6	7
+	S	1	S	y	3	2	0

Positive sign for instructions	Operation code	Identifies register A, B, C	Address or special constant

Sequence Changes.   One more instruction is required to complete the cycling scheme. A jump instruction is placed after the comparison instruction to return program control to the beginning of the cycle, if it is supposed to be repeated. If the cycle is not completed enough times when the CISyxxx is executed—as indicated by the contents of index register y and storage location xxx *not* being equal—the next instruction should be executed in sequence, a jump. If the cycle is complete—contents of the index register and location x are equal—the jump instruction should be skipped and the main program path continued. The jump instruction (also called *branch* or *transfer*) merely changes the sequence of program execution.

Code	Explanation
JMPyxxx	Change the content of the instruction counter to xxx. The result is to *jump* unconditionally and take the next instruction from storage location xxx, indexable.

The instruction required to halt operations at a desired point, and always at the end of a program, is defined as follows:

Code	Explanation
HLT xxx	*Halt* unconditional. Processor halts after this instruction with instruction counter set to address specified by xxx. Leave unchanged at next sequential instruction location if xxx is blank.

Indexed Read-In. The instructions for setting, counting, and comparing index registers can be illustrated for the simple read-write program given earlier. Assume that a cycle is run for reading cards containing ten words each and writing the 60 words in one block on tape. To read 3000 cards, this cycle will be repeated 500 times. The flow-chart for this operation is in Figure 8-1.

Before the cycle starts, the programmer provides for initializing the index register used for cycle counting and placing a criterion of 500 in storage. During each cycle the program should increase the index register count by 1 and test the index-register number against the criterion of 500 to find whether the cycle has been performed 500 times. If the cycle has not been performed 500 times—the index-register number *is not equal* to the criterion—the program repeats the cycle. If performed 500 times—the index register number *is equal* to the criterion—the processor exits from the cycle and continues with the main program. The instructions to repeat the card

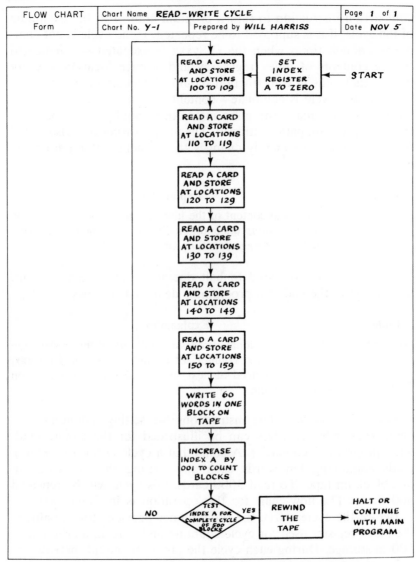

| FLOW CHART | Chart Name **READ-WRITE CYCLE** | | Page **1** of **1** |
| Form | Chart No. **Y-1** | Prepared by **WILL HARRISS** | Date **NOV 5** |

FIGURE 8-1. *Flow chart of read-write cycle using indexes.*

reading cycle 500 times, rewind tape, and halt the processor are as follows:

Loc.	Content	Explanation
011	+0000500	Criterion for counting 500 tape blocks (500 blocks × six cards per block = 3000 cards).

Loc.	Content	Explanation
012	+0000000	Zero used to set index register.
013	SISA012	Set index register A to 000 from contents of location 012 and use for counting 500 tape blocks.
014	REC 100	Read next card in reader and store in ten consecutive word locations: 100–109, 110–119,
015	REC 110	etc., to 150–159.
016	REC 120	
017	REC 130	
018	REC 140	
019	REC 150	
020	WT9 100	Write on the tape mounted on tape unit 9 the block of 60 words in locations 100–159.
021	INCA001	Increase the number in index A by 001 from 000 to 001 on first cycle, 001 to 002 on second, and so forth, to 500.
022	CISA011	Compare number in index register A and criterion in storage location 011. If contents unequal, take next instruction in sequence; if equal, skip one instruction and take second instruction.
023	JMP 014	Arriving here means cycle for writing 500 blocks on magnetic tape not complete; go to location 014 to read six more cards.
024	RW9	Arriving here means 500 blocks written on tape; rewind tape on tape unit 9.
025	HLT xxx	Halt processor with instruction counter set to any desired program location xxx to start other operations (or omit the HLT xxx and continue the main program).

The program to read 3000 cards and write their content in 500 blocks on tape deserves brief examination from the viewpoint of length and use. Three instructions are used for initializing, increasing, and comparing index A with the criterion. One jump returns to the beginning of the cycle. Only seven instructions—six read-card and one write-block-on-tape—are used directly to perform the card-to-tape conversion operations. Two instructions close up by rewinding tape and halting. While the seven *operating* instructions seem outnumbered by the eight *housekeeping* instructions and constants, the routine is efficient, for it repeats each instruction in locations 014 through 023 to perform the read-write cycle 500 times, although 023 is not executed in the last cycle. Instructions in locations 013, 024, and 025 are executed only once each. Thus thirteen instructions in locations 013 through 025 result in executing 5002 instructions. Written as straight-line coding without the use of a cycle, 3500 instructions would be required for this card-to-tape conversion. Cycling means less work for the programmer and less space in storage, but more operations for the machine to do the same work.

Effective Addressing. The card-to-tape conversion can also illustrate the idea of effective addressing with index registers, because the card-read instruction is used six times with merely different addresses: 100, 110, . . ., 150. A second or inner cycle can be set up to handle this repetitive operation by using one indexable read instruction: RECy100. In order to gain this dual use of the read instruction, the programmer associates index register B with the read-card instruction and writes the instruction as RECB100. Instructions, such as this one, that can have their addresses, as written, modified by the number contained in index register to get an effective address during program execution are called *indexable* instructions. The programmer writes the program so that index B contains 000 in the first cycle, 010 in the second cycle, etc., up to 050 in the fifth cycle in order to get the desired number for effective addressing. The effective address, when the RECB100 instruction is executed, is the sum of the number in register B and the 100 in the read instruction. The effective address is thus 000 + 100 = 100 in the first cycle, 010 + 100 = 110 in the second, etc., and 050 + 100 = 150 in the sixth cycle. The jump following the comparison test is made five times to execute the inner cycle a total of six times. Note that it is executed once before the operations for increase and compare index B are first executed. *After* the sixth card-read cycle, index register B is increased to 060, and comparison of index B and the criterion of 060 sends program control to the second following instruction to write the block on tape.

The tape-write operation is followed by counting and testing index A, as in the prior example, to determine whether 500 blocks have been written. If not, program control is returned to the beginning of the read cycle to *reset* index B to zero and repeat the inner cycle to read six more cards. Executing the outer loop the 500th time causes program control to skip one instruction and continue operations. The program using a second index register for counting card-reading cycles and for effective addressing to store card data, is given below. Only new instructions introduced into the prior example are explained.

Loc.	Content	Explanation
011	+0000060	Criterion for counting 60 words read from six cards containing ten words each.
012	+0000500	
013	+0000000	
014	SISA013	
015	SISB013	Set index register B to 000 and use for *counting* 60 words read from cards *and* for *effective addressing* to put card data in desired storage locations.
016	RECB100	Read next card and put data in storage at *effective address* equal to number in index B plus the 100 in this instruction. This is an *indexable* instruction because the address of 100 as written is modified by the contents of an index register to get an effective address each time the instruction is executed. The other instructions involving index registers in this example are *indexing* instructions because they initialize, increase, or test an index register and do not involve another instruction.
017	INCB010	Increase the number in index B by 010 in each cycle: from 000 to 010, 010 to 020, . . ., to 060. (But B is reset to 000 after the sixth cycle, when the instruction in 015 is repeated.)
018	CISB011	Compare number in index register B and criterion of 060 in location 011.
019	JMP 016	Arriving here from the comparison instruction means that the card-reading cycle has not been completed six times to get 60 words. Return to the read instruction.
020	WT9 100	Arriving here from the comparison instruction indicates six cards have been read to get 60 words; write a tape block.
021	INCA001	
022	CISA001	

Loc.	Content	Explanation
023	JMP 015	Less than 500 blocks have been written on tape; go to 015 to reset index B to 000 and repeat the card-reading cycle.
024	RW9	
025	HLT	

A program using two index registers for the card-to-tape conversion routine happens to occupy the same storage space but results in *more* instruction executions than the first conversion scheme using only one index. That is to say, six instructions are not a long enough loop to deserve using the inner cycle. A longer and more varied instruction loop warrants use of cycles and indexes to save programming work and processor storage space, as a later example will show. An index register can be used with as many instructions as desired to get a different effective address for each one. It is important to understand that effective addressing *per se* changes neither the instruction nor the index register. The use of indexes for effective addressing is similar to chemical catalysts: they make operations possible but are not themselves affected.

Arithmetical Instructions

The WORDCOM instructions discussed above were limited to input-output and cycling instructions. These types of operations make up a large part of many business data-processing programs. Along with them, the arithmetical operations of add, subtract, multiply, and divide are used to calculate bills, inventories, sales forecasts, and production schedules. Arithmetical operations are explained briefly and their use in programs illustrated.

Addition and Subtraction. Addition and subtraction operations are performed in the processor's arithmetic unit and the results are located in the accumulator. The sequence of instructions is as follows: The accumulator is cleared to remove any prior result, the first number is added from storage, each desired number is added or subtracted, and the result placed in storage for further use or for read-out. The instructions to clear the accumulator, add, subtract, and return the results to storage are as follows:

Code	Explanation
CAAyxxx	Clear the accumulator and add contents of location xxx, indexable; contents of location xxx unchanged. (This starts the addition operation *and* adds the first number.)

Code	Explanation
ADDyxxx	*Add* contents of storage location xxx, indexable, to contents of accumulator, which will contain the sum.
SUByxxx	*Sub*tract contents of storage location xxx, indexable, from contents of accumulator, which will contain the remainder.
STAyxxx	*St*ore *a*ccumulator contents in storage location xxx, indexable. Accumulator contents remain unchanged, but prior contents of location xxx are destroyed.

Addition and subtraction operations may be started by a clear-accumulator-and-add instruction, which corresponds to clearing a desk calculator *and* adding the first number from location xxx. Each number is added to the number in accumulator by an ADDyxxx instruction, or subtracted by a SUByxxx. These instructions might be used for posting receipts and issues to inventory-control accounts, for summarizing inventory on hand, or for myriad other purposes.

WORDCOM operates on a whole word from storage when performing arithmetical operations. The programmer is responsible for aligning operands for decimal points and coping with overflow of accumulator capacity. Alignment can be handled by punching each number in the appropriate positions on a card when preparing input, so that the *assumed* decimal point will occupy the desired position within a word in storage. A WORDCOM storage word consists of a sign and seven characters that occupy eight positions on a card. Ten words punched in a card can be read directly into ten words in storage. For example, a money amount with three positions for dollars and two for cents can be punched in a card, as $+0036742$ with two zeros for filler. The decimal point is assumed (as was true for COBOL) and is not punched in a card or represented in storage for amounts used in arithmetical operations. If a plus sign and seven-digit money amounts are punched in a card starting in columns 1, 9, 17, etc., to 73, each one will occupy a whole word when read into storage. Other numbers to be added or subtracted from these must be similarly positioned. Of course, the card-reader plug board can be wired to arrange the words and characters in the card in various ways—spread them out, compress, or resequence them—during read-in to WORDCOM storage. The program can also shift a word in the accumulator and M-Q to the left or right to discard unwanted parts and to align decimal-point positions. Such operations are covered later in this chapter under packing and shifting.

Overflow. Continued addition or subtraction of numbers may give an answer that is too large for the accumulator to hold. For example, adding $+6000000$ to $+7000000$ gives an eight-digit total of $+13000000$. The eighth digit results in an *overflow* condition, when addition is tried in WORDCOM. To indicate overflow in a yes-no fashion, an extra bit is available in the accumulator. Whenever overflow is likely to occur in a routine, the programmer should test immediately, and if the overflow bit is on, go to a correction routine. One correction scheme is to shift the operands one position to the right before repeating the operations that caused overflow, continue with the main program, and later make adjustment for the shifting. Another scheme is to split each word into two parts in separate storage locations, operate separately on the two parts—double-precision arithmetic—and later join them together. A third scheme useful in some cases, such as adding a series of numbers, is to save the subtotal just prior to overflow, start afresh, and later combine all the subtotals. If an overflow occurs and a test is not made in the next instruction, the processor halts and indicates the condition on the console. The jump-on-overflow instruction to test occurrence of overflow and go to a correction routine, if required, is defined as follows:

Code	Explanation
JOV xxx	*J*ump on *ov*erflow, if one occurs, to take the next instruction from storage location xxx. If no overflow, continue regular sequence of operations. The processor halts if an instruction causing overflow is not followed by a JOV xxx instruction.

Multiplication. The multiplication of two seven-digit words gives a fourteen-digit product, although many of the left-hand digits may be zeros. The accumulator and M-Q registers are used together for multiplication in the following way:

1. The accumulator and M-Q registers are cleared to zero and the multiplier placed in the M-Q by the CAMyxxx instruction.
2. The multiplicand is obtained from location xxx, indexable, and the multiplication operation performed by the MLTyxxx instruction.
3. The product is stored from the M-Q register alone, if seven digits or less, by means of the STMyxxx instruction. If more than seven digits, the product extends into the accumulator and that part can be stored by a STAyxxx instruction.

The M-Q clear and add, multiplication, and M-Q storing orders are defined as follows:

Code	Explanation
CAMyxxx	*C*lear accumulator and M-Q and *a*dd to *M*-Q register the contents of location xxx, indexable; contents of location xxx unchanged.
MLTyxxx	*Mul*tiply contents of location xxx, indexable, by contents of M-Q. Low-order digits of the product will be in M-Q, and high-order in accumulator, although many may be zero. Storage-location contents are unchanged.
STMyxxx	*St*ore contents of *M*-Q register in location xxx, indexable. (Use STAyxxx to store accumulator contents.)

The programmer is responsible for keeping track of the decimal point in the operands and the product. For example, multiplying the unit cost of $1.50 each by 1200 items on hand can be summarized as follows:

Multiplicand	+00001V50	Location x, indexable
Multiplier	+0001200	M-Q register
Product	+000000001800V00	Accumulator and M-Q

The desired answer of +01800V00 can be placed in storage by a STMyxxx instruction and, in this case, the accumulator content of +0000000 ignored.

Example of Inventory Calculation.   From the earlier example of converting inventory records from 3000 cards to 500 blocks of data on tape, an example of arithmetic operations can be developed. Suppose that the problem is to read in a block of data on tape containing six stock records, calculate stock value for each item (quantity on hand times unit cost) to complete each record, write out each completed record, and summarize stock value to find total stock value. For the six records in each of the 500 blocks on tape, the calculations must be repeated six times.

Since individual words in each record are handled here, the record format must be considered. The inventory-record layout used is similar to that for the COBOL-1 example in Chapter 7, but some changes are made to facilitate WORDCOM processing. A WORD-COM word consists of a sign and seven characters; therefore, ten words fill a card, as shown in Figure 8-2. Positions 1, 9, 17, etc., are reserved for signs, although they are needed only with numbers used for arithmetic operations. The record layout is designed so that the three words used here—quantity on hand, unit cost, and stock value—occupy whole words 6, 9, and 10, respectively, on each card, thus making these words directly available for use. Packing and shifting operations to handle elements not precisely fitting WORD-COM words are covered later in this chapter. The cards in Figure 8-2 also illustrate the stock records.

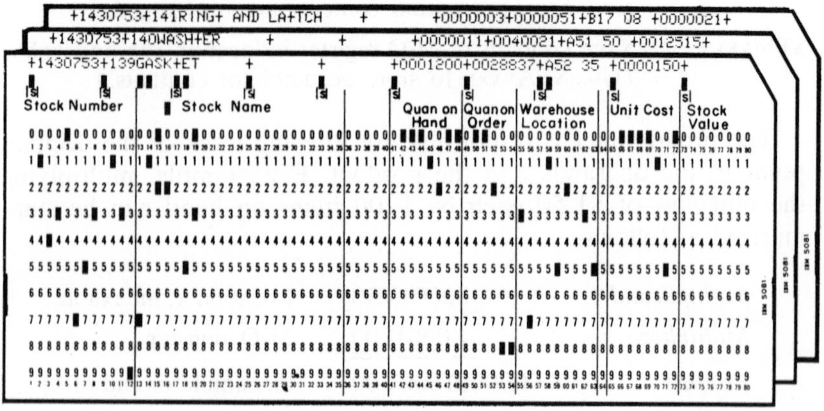

FIGURE 8-2. *Sample stock record for WORDCOM processing.*

Each tape block of six records read into storage occupies 60 words starting at, say, word 201 with the three desired words of the first record occupying locations 206, 209, 210, of the second record locations 216, 219, 220, etc., and of the sixth record locations 256, 259, and 260. The program is given below for reading in a block from tape, calculating the stock value for each of six records in storage, subtotaling stock value, testing for overflow, writing the block, repeating the cycle 500 times and punching the total value:

Loc.	Content	Explanation
010	+0000000	Constant for setting and resetting index registers.
011	+0000000	Zero at first; use to hold stock-value subtotal.
012	+0000060	Criterion for testing completion of tape-block-processing cycle.

Loc.	Content	Explanation
013	+0000500	Criterion for testing completion of file-processing cycle.
014	SISB010	Set to zero and use to count tape blocks read—the outer loop.
015	SISA010	Set to zero and use to count record-handling cycles and for effective addressing of records—the inner loop.
016	RT3 201	Read a tape block from tape unit 3 into locations 201–260 inclusive.
017	CAMA206	Clear accumulator and M-Q and add quantity on hand to M-Q from location 206, indexed by register A: 206 first cycle, 216 second cycle, etc., to 256 in the sixth.
018	MLTA209	Multiply unit cost in 209, 219, etc., to 259 in following cycles by quantity on hand to get stock value.
019	STMA210	Store stock value in 210, 220, etc., to 260 in following cycles. (Assuming that only seven digits are wanted in product.)
020	CAA 011	Clear accumulator and add contents of location 011, which contains zero on first cycle and thereafter the subtotal of stock value.
021	ADDA210	Add stock value from 210, 220, etc., to 260 in following cycles to get new subtotal.
022	JOV 035	If addition causes overflow, jump to location 035 to punch the previous subtotal and restart operations for the record causing overflow. Overflow total not stored.
023	STA 011	Store stock-value subtotal in 011 after each addition.
024	INCA010	Increase index A by the number 010 for the spacing of data in records in storage since each record is ten words long.
025	CISA012	Compare index A to criterion 060 in location 012 to test completion of arithmetic operation cycle six times. (Criterion of 60 instead of 6 because index A is also used for effective addressing for *words* as well as for *record* counting.)

Loc.	Content	Explanation
026	JMP 017	Return to repeat arithmetic cycle, if not completed six times.
027	WT9 201	Write block on tape, if six records handled.
028	INCB001	Increase index B by the number 001 to count tape blocks handled.
029	CISB013	Compare index B to criterion 500 in location 013 to test completion of block read-write cycle.
030	JMP 015	Return to read next block, if not all blocks handled.
031	PNC 011	Punch total stock value in a card (or subtotal if prior overflow occurred) after all records handled.
032	RW9	Rewind output tape.
033	RW3	Rewind input tape.
034	HLT 001	Halt with instruction counter set at 1 to indicate program completion.
035	PNC 011	Punch stock-value subtotal for all records handled prior to overflow.
036	CAA 010	Clear accumulator to zero.
037	STA 011	Reload location 011 with zero, use to hold stock-value subtotal.
038	JMP 017	Return to repeat calculation for stock record that caused overflow and continue main program.

Division. WORDCOM also does division. Division is performed, from the programmer's viewpoint, in the following way. The accumulator is cleared by a CAAyxxx instruction and the dividend added. The divisor in storage location xxx is divided into the dividend in the accumulator by use of the DIVyxxx instruction. The quotient can be stored by a STMyxxx instruction and the remainder, if wanted by STAyxxx.

In essence, the division operation subtracts the divisor from the dividend as many times as possible, places the count in the right-hand position of the M-Q and shifts the contents of both the accumulator and M-Q one position to the left. The subtract, count, and shift operations are repeated seven times to form the quotient in the M-Q and leave the remainder in accumulator. Division has a special rule: the divisor "as stored" must be larger than the dividend to avoid stopping the machine in a "divide-halt" condition. The programmer is responsible for anticipating relative sizes of the dividend and divisor and making adjustments to avoid a divide-halt condition. The division instruction is defined as follows:

Code	Explanation
DIVyxxx	*Div*ide the dividend in the accumulator by the divisor in location xxx, indexable. Quotient is formed in M-Q register and remainder is left in the accumulator.

Comparisons

The program illustrated earlier in this chapter for card-to-tape conversion accepted the sequence of records as given and simply wrote them on tape. Two choices exist, if data must be in sequence for efficient processing. The first is to leave the cards unsorted, convert them to tape, and use a processor program to sort the records into sequence by one of the schemes to be described in Chapter 9. The second is to sort the cards into sequence on a card sorter and merely check their sequence by comparing the numbers on each two successive cards during the conversion for subsequent processing. If the cards are in the correct sequence, the read-in should be continued; if out of sequence, the read-in operation halted. For cards almost in sequence, the sequence should be rechecked with a card collator and any cards out of sequence manually refiled. Cards in badly-mixed sequence should be rerun through the card sorter. After correction by either method, the cards will be ready for processor read-in and a second sequence check.

Comparison and Three-Way Exit.   The comparison instruction with a three-way exit is useful for card-sequence checking and many other purposes. The comparison operation determines whether one number is less than, greater than, or equal to another. For names, the outcome is expressed in alphabetic-sequence terms: earlier, later, or same. To perform the comparison operation, the key word from one record is first placed in the accumulator and compared to the key word of another record in a specified storage location. The flow-chart block for the comparison operation, with the colon indicating the comparison operation, is as follows:

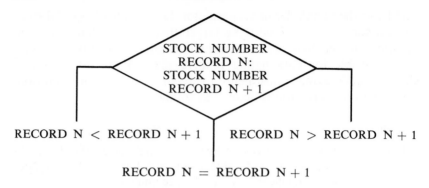

RECORD N < RECORD N + 1 | RECORD N > RECORD N + 1

RECORD N = RECORD N + 1

WORDCOM is designed to go to the first instruction following the comparison instruction for the *less-than* condition. In that location the programmer should place a jump instruction to send program control to the desired point in the program to handle that condition. The less-than condition can indicate that the card-read instruction just executed should be repeated, because the card examined is in sequence.

The second jump after the comparison is reserved for the *greater-than* condition. This outcome indicates a card is out of sequence and a jump instruction in that location can send program control to an error routine, which will either halt the processor, merely duplicate the out-of-sequence card and return to the main program to read the next card, or take other action.

The third location after the comparison instruction is reserved for the *equal* condition. If this condition indicates the main processing path should continue, the programmer can place the first instruction in the subroutine here.

The comparison instruction is defined as follows:

Code	Explanation
CMPyxxx	*Compare* content of accumulator with content of storage location xxx, indexable.

Go to *next* instruction, if content of accumulator < content location xxx.

Go to *second* instruction, if accumulator > content location xxx.

Go to *third* instruction, if accumulator = content location xxx.

Content of accumulator unchanged. For alphabetic comparisons, <, >, and = mean "earlier than," "later than," and "same," respectively.

File Sequence Checking. The use of comparison operations for sequence checking can be illustrated for the stock record card-to-tape conversion described earlier. Assume that the cards were sorted on the first seven digits that are the sequence part of the stock number. As a further check on card sequence before processing, the first word of one card may be put in the accumulator and compared with the first word on the next card. For the purposes of this example, each in-sequence card may be written on tape, each out-of-sequence card punched into another card for examination, and duplicate cards in the input deck ignored. The accumulator is first filled with blanks to act as a "prior card" before making the first comparison, so that the first card is correctly treated as in-sequence.

The simplified routine to read cards, check for numerical sequence, write in-sequence stock records in blocks on tape, punch out-of-sequence cards, and ignore duplicates is given in Figure 8-3 on a programming form. This routine is similar to the routine for card-to-tape conversion given earlier, so only new instructions are explained here.

Test Negative and Two-Way Exit. The comparison instruction described above involves contents of the accumulator and a specified storage location. The jump-if-negative instruction is simpler. It tests the accumulator *sign* alone and branches in one of two ways for the negative or nonnegative condition. The jump-if-negative is useful for determining whether one number is smaller or larger than another. For example, quantity on hand minus reorder point quantity, if negative, indicates an order should be placed, but, if positive, no action should be taken. The jump-if-negative instruction is executed *only* if the sign of the accumulator is negative. It is defined as follows:

Code	Explanation
JINyxxx	*J*ump *i*f content of accumulator is *n*egative, to location xxx, indexed, for next instruction; otherwise continue regular sequence of instructions. Accumulator content unchanged.

Packing and Shifting

The input-output, cycle, arithmetic, and comparison instructions operate with whole words. Shifting instructions, however, operate on individual characters within a word. To save input preparation and read-in time, it is sometimes useful to pack two or more *data items* into seven characters when preparing input. The seven characters can then be stored as one WORDCOM *storage word* to save

WORDCOM	Program Name		FILE SEQUENCE CHECKING			Page *1* of *1*
Program Form	Program No. **WC-1**			Prepared by **WILL HARRISS**		Date **MAY 5**

Location	S	1	2	3	4	5	6	7	Explanation
	Sign	Op Code			Index	Address			
050	+	0	0	0	0	0	0	0	Constants.
051	+	0	0	0	0	0	6	0	
052	+	0	0	0	0	5	0	0	
053	+	C	A	A	A	0	5	0	Set accumulator to zero initially so that the first comparison will treat the first record as in-sequence.
054	+	S	I	S	B	0	5	0	
055	+	S	I	S	A	0	5	0	
056	+	R	E	C	A	I	0	0	Read card and store in locations 100-109, indexed, to build an in-sequence block of 60 words from six cards.
057	+	C	M	P	A	I	0	0	Compare stock number in accumulator (zero in the first comparison) with stock number in location 100, indexed.
058	+	J	M	P		0	6	I	Arriving here indicates card in sequence; go to load accumulator with stock number for next comparison.
059	+	J	M	P		0	7	I	Indicates out-of-sequence; go to punch card.
060	+	J	M	P		0	5	6	Indicates duplicate; ignore by reading next card (without changing index) into same storage locations over the duplicate cards.
061	+	C	A	A	A	I	0	0	Put current stock number in accumulator for next comparison.
062	+	I	N	C	A	0	I	0	
063	+	C	I	S	A	0	5	I	
064	+	J	M	P		0	5	6	
065	+	W	T	9		I	0	0	
066	+	I	N	C	B	0	0	I	
067	+	C	I	S	B	0	5	2	
068	+	J	M	P		0	5	5	
069	+	R	W	9					
070	+	H	L	T					
071	+	P	N	C	A	I	0	0	Arrival here means out-of sequence card in location 100, indexed; punch a card for later examination.
072	+	J	M	P		0	5	6	Return to read the next card without increasing index A, which makes the new card read into storage over the prior card.

FIGURE 8-3. *Sample WORDCOM program for file sequence checking.*

internal storage. *Shifting* operations can be used to *unpack* the storage word to separate the individual data items for processing. Processed results that occupy less than a whole word can be packed together for storage or read-out and punching in a card or writing on tape.

Shifting is the simplest method for unpacking and packing data. It uses the accumulator and M-Q registers together as a "shifting register" but ignores their sign positions. For shifting data, the M-Q register can be considered as simply an extension of the right-hand end of the accumulator, as follows:

Shifting Register

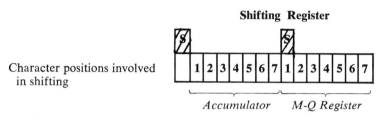

Character positions involved in shifting

Accumulator   *M-Q Register*

An example of utility billing shows use of the shifting register. A utility punches a card with the following word, which consists of three different facts about a customer's meter reading:

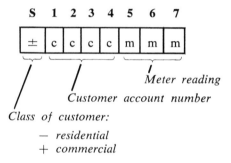

Meter reading

Customer account number

Class of customer:
    — residential
    + commercial

One word of new input, along with the master-file record is enough (with an appropriate program, of course) to compute a customer's bill. The master file is kept in customer account-number sequence in two blocks: residential ahead of commercial accounts, since minus numbers are smaller than plus numbers. For the four-digit numbers, the sequence is -9999, -9998, $\ldots$, -0001, $+0001$, $\ldots$, $+9999$. The cards punched with customer class, account number, and meter reading are sorted into sequence on sign and digits 1 to 4 before processor read-in. After read-in, the program checks sequence by using the whole word consisting of sign and seven characters to avoid the trouble of extracting the account number. The processor compares whole words, but meter reading in the low-order positions is minor to account number (which is major) and does not affect the sorting sequence. For shifting to unpack, as shown schematically in Figure 8-4, first clear both the accumulator and M-Q registers, and add the meter-reading word to accumulator.

Shifting Register

Accumulator   *M-Q Register*

	S								S						
Character positions		1	2	3	4	5	6	7		1	2	3	4	5	6	7
Contents after clearing	+	0	0	0	0	0	0	0	+ 0	0	0	0	0	0	0
Add meter-reading card (c for customer account; m for meter-reading digits)	+	c	c	c	c	m	m	m	+ 0	0	0	0	0	0	0
Shift right three positions	+	0	0	0	c	c	c	c	+ m	m	m	0	0	0	0
Shift left seven positions	+	m	m	m	0	0	0	0	+ 0	0	0	0	0	0	0
Shift right four positions	+	0	0	0	0	m	m	m	+ 0	0	0	0	0	0	0

FIGURE 8-4. *Shifting register to unpack customer meter reading.*

To Unpack	Explanation
Customer account number	Shift right the shifting-register contents three character positions, so that customer account number is in accumulator positions 4 to 7. Store for later use as a separate word.
Meter reading	Next, shift left seven positions to discard customer account number. Meter reading is then in accumulator positions 1 to 3, unpacked. Store meter reading for later use or shift right four positions to 5 to 7 of accumulator for calculating consumption.

Instructions used in shifting the contents of the shifting register are defined as follows:

Code	Explanation
SHL nn	*Sh*ift *l*eft the contents of shifting register nn places, where nn is 01 through 13, inclusive. Sign positions of accumulator and M-Q unchanged. Discard any characters shifted

Code	Explanation

out of left end of accumulator; fill with zeros the spaces vacated on right.

SHR nn *Sh*ift *r*ight the contents of shifting register nn places. Discard any characters shifted out of right end of M-Q; fill with zeros the spaces vacated on left.

Data Read-In

To simplify the earlier discussion of programming, any program written was assumed to be available in the processor whenever wanted. Actually, the programmer must arrange to load his program into storage for processor use. The first step is to get enough instructions into the processor by manual means to make the processor bring in other instructions. Thus, a few instructions are used to "bootstrap" in more instructions.

General Scheme. The essential features of the four stages in loading WORDCOM with a program already punched in cards, and illustrated later are as follows:

1. Use the console and card reader switches to read the first card in the program load-routine into a desired location in high-speed storage.
2. The first card bootstraps the second into storage.
3. The load routine on the first two cards will read in an indefinite number of program cards.
4. The last program card makes a transfer to the start of the program, which includes data read-in and execution of the program itself.

The bootstrap load-routine cards, the program cards, and transfer-card to start execution of the card sequence-check program described above are shown in Figure 8-5. The program cards are discussed first here because their format affects the design and operation of the bootstrap load routine. Each program card will have from two to ten words on it. The first word on each card, called *word-count and location,* is used solely for guiding the processor in storing the other words and has the following format:

S	1	2	3	4	5	6	7
−	0	0	0	w	x	x	x

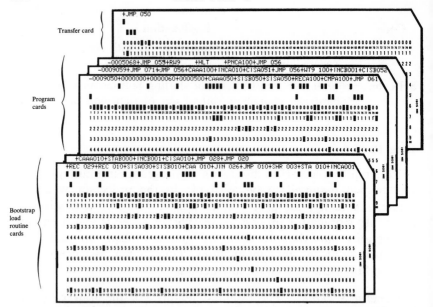

FIGURE 8-5. *Bootstrap load routine, card sequence-checking routine, and transfer card.*

The word-count character "w" indicates that one to nine words are to be read in from that card, corresponding to the number of instruction words in the card. The location part xxx, indicates where the second word on a card (the first program word on that card) will be put in storage. Other words on that card are stored in sequential locations.

The last card to be loaded, called a *transfer card,* contains +JMP xxx. The plus sign, instead of a minus, distinguishes the transfer card from the program cards to execute the +JMP xxx instruction. Execution of the +JMP xxx instruction transfers control to location xxx where the main program starts. Its format is:

S	1	2	3	4	5	6	7
+	J	M	P		x	x	x

Bootstrap Load Routine. The load routine starts from manually-set console switches to read one card into the locations specified in the program for the first card—say, 019 through 028, in this case. The processor is directed to execute the instruction in location 019. The instruction in location 019 causes the processor to read one more card, which contains the rest of the bootstrap load routine. The load routine of 16 instructions punched into the first two cards illustrated in Figure 8-5 is listed under Card Content below, with the location in storage and explanation added for clarity. The plus or minus sign that should be used with each word in WORDCOM has been omitted from instructions illustrated earlier, but is included here. The sign is used to indicate whether a card contains more program steps or all the program has been read in and program execution should start.

Loc.	Card Content	Explanation
		Use console switches to read first card into storage locations 019 to 028 and then transfer control to the first instruction in 019 for the processor program to take over the load routine.
019	+REC 029	Read second load-routine card into locations 029 through 038.
020	+REC 010	Read a card from main program into locations 010 through 019 for temporary storage while examining the first word to determine what to do with the other words. (The instruction in location 019, +REC 029, is not needed again and is destroyed when the first main program card is read into locations 010 through 019.)
021	+S I S A030	Set index register A with the three right-hand digits of location 030 which are 000. The 000 is taken from another instruction word, which contains 000, to economize storage.
022	+S I S B 010	Set index B with the right-hand three digits of the first word of a card in location 010—the word-location digits.
023	+CAA 010	Clear accumulator and add the first word from a card in order to get its sign.
024	+J I N 026	If sign of accumulator is negative, the accumulator contains a word-count and location for the other words on the card.
025	+J M P 010	If sign of accumulator is positive, then the word in location 010 is the transfer word to the first program instruction for execution. Make two jumps—one to location 010 and a second to execute the jump instruction there.

Loc.	Card Content	Explanation
026	+S H R 003	The word-count and location word wxxx loaded into accumulator by the CAA 010 operation above is shifted right three places to put the "w" in the right-hand position. The location digits were set in index B by the SISB010 operation above and need not be retained here.
027	+S T A 010	The word-count in the right-hand position of the accumulator is stored in the right-hand position of the word-count, as follows: —000000w. Prior contents destroyed.
028	+I N C A001	Increase index register A by 1 to count the number of words stored from the current program card.
029	+CAAA010	Clear accumulator and add the word in effective address location 010, indexed: 011 in first cycle, 012 in second, etc., to 019 in ninth cycle, if there are nine words to be stored from the card.
030	+S T AB000	Store accumulator content in effective address of 000 plus the content of index register B set in operation 022 with the desired location for the first word to be stored.
031	+I N C B001	Increase index register B by 1 to load program words into consecutive storage locations when repeating the cycle.
032	+C I S A010	Compare the count of words stored as contained in index register A with the number of words to be stored, which was placed in location 010 by instruction 027 to determine completion of word-storing cycle.
033	+J M P 028	Contents of index register A and location 010 are not equal; therefore, go to location 028 to repeat loop for storing a word.
034	+J M P 020	Contents of index register A and location 010 are equal; therefore, go to location 020 to read the next card.

A load routine of sixteen words punched in two cards, as illustrated here, can read in an indefinite number of other program cards and start execution of the program. Loading a program and starting its execution is similar to a chain reaction. If everything is ready, a small event triggers the whole operation for loading and executing the main program. Use of the load routine illustrated above precludes storing any part of the main program in locations 010 through 034, except for temporary storage of the data from each card in locations 010 through 019 to examine them before transfer to desired locations. Anything else stored in locations 010 through 034 will either destroy the load routine or be destroyed upon reading the next card. A similar load routine can be stored elsewhere, if these locations are required for the main program. After the main program is read in, the load routine area can be used for other purposes. The point is that storage must be allocated among load routine, main program, data, and working storage so that they do not interfere with each other.

Locations 000 to 009 are not used in the load routine shown above. They may be reserved for jump instructions after a halt occurs in order to start the program running again. Certain halt instructions (HLT xxx) in the program may specify a storage location from 000 to 009 for setting the instruction counter when the processor halts. A JMP xxx instruction stored in one of these locations can transfer control to an error-correction routine, when the processor is restarted. Used in this way, the jump instruction serves to connect the program halt and the error-correction routine with a temporary stop. The fact that the program arrives at location 003, for instance, indicates that HLT 003 was encountered in the program and may give some indication of the nature of the halt.

Editing

Programming WORDCOM for output of alphanumeric data items is simple. An alphanumeric data item occupying a whole word in storage, including blanks used to fill out the item, is ready for printing on the high-speed printer after writing on tape or punching in cards. If two or more items of data are stored in one seven-character word, each can be isolated by unpacking. Unpacking involves placing a word in the shifting register—accumulator and M-Q registers—and shifting left, right, or both to isolate the desired data item and discard others. During shifting operations, the desired item should be right- or left-justified as wanted for printing.

Editing numbers ready for printing with suitable symbols is more involved. It requires the use of an edit word containing editing symbols and an *extractor* to control editing these symbols into the data word. Two operations are involved for a data word that is already unpacked. First, zeros are placed in the data item to pro-

Instruction		Explanation

Op.
Code   Address

Input and Output

RECyxxx	Read a card and store contents in location xxx and following, indexable.
PNCyxxx	Punch a card with ten words from storage at location xxx and following, indexable.
RTtyxxx	Read a block of 60 words from tape on tape unit t and place in storage location xxx and following, indexable.
WTtyxxx	Write on tape t a block of 60 words from location xxx and following, indexable.
RWt ——	Rewind tape on tape unit t.

Indexing

SISyxxx	Set index y from contents of storage location xxx (not indexable).
INCynnn	Increase contents of index y by the number nnn (not indexable).
CISyxxx	Compare index y to contents of storage location xxx (not indexable). Next two instructions in sequence are used for "not equal" and "equal" exits.

Tests

CMPyxxx	Compare contents of accumulator and contents of location xxx, indexable. Next three instructions in sequence are used for exits for accumulator $<$, $>$, and $=$ location xxx.
JINyxxx	Jump, if accumulator negative, to xxx, indexable
JOV xxx	Jump, on overflow condition in accumulator, to location xxx.

TABLE 8-1. *Order code for WORDCOM.*

vide spaces for inserting the desired edit symbols of "$," "," and "." or perhaps others. Second, the data item is placed in the accumulator and the edit word is extracted into it under control of the extractor. The result of the operation is to give the edited data item in the accumulator ready for use. To *extract* means to remove from a word all the characters that meet some criterion and replace them with other characters.

Instruction	Explanation

Op.
Code   Address

Load and Store Accumulator and M-Q

CAAyxxx — *C*lear *a*ccumulator and *a*dd contents of location xxx, indexable.

S TAyxxx — *St*ore contents of *a*ccumulator in location xxx, indexable.

CAMyxxx — *C*lear *a*ccumulator and *M*-Q registers and add contents of location xxx into M-Q, indexable.

S TMyxxx — *St*ore contents of *M*-Q register in location xxx, indexable.

Arithmetic

ADDyxxx — *Add* contents of location xxx to accumulator, indexable.

S UByxxx — *Sub*tract contents of location xxx from accumulator, indexable.

MLTyxxx — *Mult*iply contents of location xxx, indexable, by content of M-Q register.

D I Vyxxx — *Div*ide the dividend in accumulator by divisor in location xxx, indexable.

Miscellaneous

HLT xxx — Unconditional *halt*, with instruction counter set to xxx. (Leave unchanged at next sequential instruction, if xxx is blank.)

S HL nn — *Sh*ift combined contents of accumulator and M-Q registers nn places to the *l*eft.

S HR nn — *Sh*ift combined contents of accumulator and M-Q registers nn places to the *r*ight.

EXOyxxx — *Ex*tract *o*dd replaces characters in the accumulator with characters from storage location xxx that have *positions* corresponding to odd-value characters in extractor, indexable; nothing else changed.

J MPyxxx — Unconditional *jump* to location xxx, indexable.

TABLE 8-1. *Order code for WORDCOM (cont'd).*

A data item in storage to be edited, 0068429, which should read $684.29 for printing, is opened up and zeros inserted by shifting and addition operations to give 0684029. Editing by extracting works in the following way. An extractor, say 1000100, consisting of 0's and 1's or any "even" and "odd" characters is read into processor storage. An edit word consisting of $——— . — is read into, say, storage location 379. The conditions just before extraction are as follows:

Edit word in location 379	$——— . —
Data item in accumulator	0684029
Extractor	1000100

The extract *odd*-character order, EXO 379, will replace the characters in the accumulator with characters from location 379 that have *positions* corresponding to the odd-value characters—the 1's—in the extractor, without changing anything else. The result of an extract odd order is to give $684.29 in the accumulator but not change the edit word or extractor. The extract *odd*-character order is defined as follows:

Code	**Explanation**
EXOyxxx	*Ex*tract *o*dd replaces characters in the accumulator with characters from storage location xxx that have *positions* corresponding to the odd-value characters in extractor, indexable; nothing else changed.

This scheme for editing is closely akin to the manual process, but it is less adroit than the COBOL-1 editing operation in which the EDIT order causes the processor to assemble the instructions to do the work.

The orders that WORDCOM executes (see Table 8-1) serve as a brief, simplified guide to the operation of internally-stored program processors with word-organized storage.

FIELDCOM

FIELDCOM (for *field com*puter) is similar to WORDCOM in many respects, for it is a medium scale, internally-stored-program processor. But FIELDCOM storage is organized differently: it consists of 8000 individual characters, each identified as xxxx here, without organization into words. This means a programmer must plan the use of *each character* in storage to hold instructions or data for processing. Actually, a compiling program handles most of the details of storage assignment, but the brief comments here about FIELDCOM indicate the nature of the scheme.

FIELDCOM is a character machine with storage and logic designed for the programmer to *select* the length of each field for a data element. This corresponds to the selectable-length feature of data on punched cards. Any number of card columns can be assigned to an item of data, but after a particular length is selected to cover the longest instance likely to occur, it must be used for that item in all records. Chapter 2 discussed the selectable-length organization of records.

Data Organization.   The programmer organizes storage for data and instructions as selected-length fields to suit the requirements of each application, instead of trying to fit the application to the word-lengths designed into a machine, such as WORDCOM. He might select a field of ten characters for a stock number, twenty for stock name, five for quantity on hand, etc.

The left character of each operand in FIELDCOM storage is indicated by a fieldmark. The programmer sets fieldmarks—the eighth bit in a character—wherever required in storage, by means of the instruction FM xxxx in a program either before or after reading in data. The address of an operand is ordinarily its right character, but some other character can be used that will shorten the field and give the effect of shifting when copying a field. The left end is indicated by its fieldmark in either case. The characters in storage between the address used in an instruction and the first fieldmark to the left, inclusive, make up a unit of data for processing and may range from one to hundreds of characters. For example (see Figure 8-6) the quantity on hand of 1200 units from a stock record might be stored in a five-digit field, to provide for numbers up to 99999. The address here is 1035 and the fieldmark is indicated by "–" in location 1031. The "b" indicates a blank in an alphanumeric field.

The operand 01200 is addressed by its right-hand character, 1035, which is its high-numbered storage location. Processing starts with the character addressed and extends leftward through the location with the fieldmark. An instruction, such as add or copy with an address of 0134 would be executed with 0120 as the operand. Dropping one character position by addressing in this way "shifts" the operand one position to the right and, in effect, divides a number by 10.

Logic.   FIELDCOM has add-to-storage logic so that an operand in another field—say, units received—can be added to the quantity-on-hand field. The addition instruction format is AD xxxx xxxx

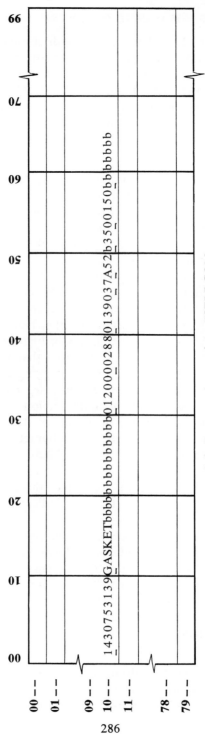

FIGURE 8-6. Layout of record in FIELDCOM storage.

286

to add the contents of A address, identified by the first xxxx, to contents of B address, the second xxxx, giving the total at the B address. This corresponds to the ADD TO operation in COBOL.

Continued addition to the contents of address 1035 will give a sum exceeding five digits that attempts to go beyond the fieldmark in 1031. The result is a field mistake corresponding to an overflow in WORDCOM. A field mistake sets a "switch" in the processor which is one of a number of elements used to indicate the occurrence of certain conditions. In this particular case, a switch identified as "F" is used to indicate that a field mistake occurred. The condition of the "F" switch can be tested by a conditional jump instruction—JS xxxx F—which will, if the switch is on, send program control to an appropriate correction routine at xxxx. The point is that even in FIELDCOM with selectable-length fields, a programmer must consider how long an operand is likely to be and allocate enough storage for it in most cases. He should check for the possible occurrence of unusually large numbers and take corrective action. FIELDCOM eliminates many problems of assigning storage to data, but others merely recur in a different framework.

Instruction Format.   The FIELDCOM instruction format is variable in length. Simple instructions have no address whereas others have one or two addresses. Instruction format showing the instruction add field A, address 2376 to field B, address 4895 (and modifiers "c" and "d," as explained below, but blank here) is as follows for FIELDCOM:

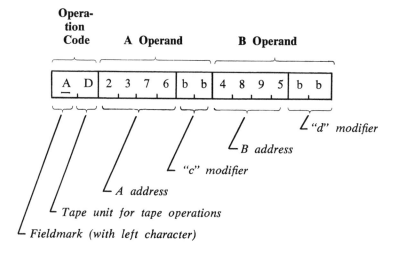

Some examples of FIELDCOM instructions illustrating the variations in number of operations handled are given below.

Op. Code	Instruction Addresses				Explanation
	A	c	B	d	
HL	xxxx				Halt with instruction counter set to xxxx.
Tt					Tape rewind, unit number t, ready for removal.
JS	xxxx	F			Conditional jump, if field mistake switch "F" is on, to the A address.
CP	xxxx		xxxx		Copy contents of A address into B address.
AD	xxxx		xxxx		Add contents of A address to contents of B address.
CM	xxxx		xxxx		Compare contents of A address with contents of B address. Sets switches E, H, L, N for equal, high, low, negative that can be tested later in the program by a JS xxxx — instruction.

Each instruction requires a fieldmark in the left-hand character position in storage and is addressed by the left-hand character. Instruction execution on a character-by-character basis is stopped when the next fieldmark is encountered. That is, an instruction is terminated one character before the next fieldmark. A "c" modifier is used to indicate a switch condition to be tested for a conditional jump instruction, such as the JS xxxx F above.

Either the "c" or "d" modifier can be used to modify the A and B addresses, respectively, as written in an instruction to get an effective, shifted address to the left or right of the address as written for that particular field. Called *field shifting,* minus 1 to 9 shifts the address to the left and plus 1 to 9 shifts the address from 1 to 9 positions, as specified, to the right. Field shifting is useful to shorten a field or divide by 10, 100, etc., and also to lengthen or multiply by 10, 100, etc. Field shifting is more useful with symbolic addressing (using letters and numerals for addresses as shown later in an example in this chapter) than for absolute addressing, since the absolute address of the whole field, and therefore the location of certain characters in it, is not known when the program is first written in symbolic form.

Instruction Repertoire. The FIELDCOM order code is given in Table 8-2. Most of the orders correspond to WORDCOM instructions, but there are some important differences. Card or paper-tape read-in goes to specified locations 0001 through 0080, and output uses locations 0101 through 0180. Specifying these spaces in storage eliminates the need to include addresses in card and paper-tape input-output operations.

The FM xxxx instruction sets a fieldmark in any desired location. A fieldmark, as explained earlier, is used with the left-hand character of each operand or instruction. The CS xxxx xxxx instruction clears fieldmarks and characters from storage at the B address downward to the A address, inclusive. The CP xxxx xxxx instruction copies the contents of the field at the A address into the field at the B address. The fields at A and B addresses should be the same length to avoid a field mistake, unless it is desired to shorten a field. The copy and edit instruction—CE xxxx xxxx—copies a data field into another field containing editing characters—for example, $$,$ZZ,ZZ9.99—to perform leading-zero suppression in positions represented by blanks down to the X position. The dollar sign is "floated," between its left and right limits, to the first position before the number being edited.

Arithmetic instructions address operands directly since FIELD-COM has add-to-storage logic. The add instruction, AD xxxx xxxx, adds the contents of the A address to contents of the B address and places the sum at B address. The subtraction operation has similar addressing. The multiplication operation in FIELD-COM with its add-to-storage logic is a bit tricky since it does not have an accumulator and M-Q register, as such. Any field in storage can be used as a *multiply field* for performing multiplication, but it must be as long as the two factors involved plus one extra position. The sequence of operations is as follows: the multiply field is cleared, the multiplier is copied into the *left* end of this field, and the multiplication instruction—ML xxxx xxxx—is then executed. Of course, the multiplier may already be in the left-hand end of the multiply field so that only the right-hand end need be cleared before executing the multiplication order. The multiplication instruction A address is for the multiplicand anywhere in storage, and the B address is the right-hand position of the multiply field containing the multiplier. Upon completion, the product is in the right-hand end of the multiply field. All of the product can be used or some right-hand digits may be cut off by addressing the right-most digit wanted when storing the product in another field.

Instruction				**Explanation**
Op.	**Addresses**			
Code	**A**	**c**	**B**	**d**

Input and Output

RC		Read a card or punched tape and store contents in storage locations 0001–0080.
PC		Punch a card or paper tape with contents of storage locations 0101–0180.
Rt	xxxx	Read a block of data from tape *t* and store in A address in high-speed storage downward to blockmark.
Wt	xxxx	Write a block of data on tape *t* from A address downward through first blockmark in high-speed storage.
Mt		Mark tape *t* with filemark to indicate end of file on reel.
Tt		Rewind *Tape t* ready for removal.
PT		Print a line of 120 characters from high-speed storage locations 0201–0320.
RD	xxxx	Read the disk sector specified by the six-character address—uddtts—for unit, disk track, and sector, in high-speed storage at the A address indicated by this instruction and place the contents in the 100 positions of storage preceding the sector address.
WD	xxxx	Write the disk sector specified by the uddtts address in high-speed storage at A address in this instruction using the contents of the 100 preceding positions of high-speed storage.
SD	xxxx	Seek disk sector specified by uddtts at the A address in this instruction.

Load and Store

CS	xxxx	xxxx	Clear storage of fieldmarks and characters from B position through A position and fieldmark A position.
FM	xxxx		Fieldmark one position at A; contents undisturbed.

TABLE 8-2. *Order code for FIELDCOM.*

Op. Code	Instruction Addresses A	c	B	d	Explanation

Instruction Addresses / **Explanation**

Op. Code | A | c | B | d

CP xxxx ±n xxxx ±n — *Cop*y contents of field at A address to B address; stop with first fieldmark, can shorten but not edit a field; —n shifts the field address n positions to the left; +n to the right.

CE xxxx ±n xxxx ±n — *C*opy and *e*dit whole content of A address into B address, erasing any fieldmarks in B address. B address may contain, for example, \$\$\$Z,ZZ9.99. Leading zeros and commas suppressed from left to right down to first 9; float \$ within its left and right limits as indicated by the series, "\$\$\$." The five characters, dollar sign, comma, "Z," "9," and decimal, each count in the edited field as a character position.

ZR xxxx — Set contents of field at A address to *zero*.

BM xxxx — *Block*mark one position at A for indicating low-order end of block for writing on tape or of a sector (100 characters standard) for writing on disk.

Arithmetic

AD xxxx ±n xxxx ±n — *Ad*d contents of A address to B address, stopping at first fieldmark; if length of B field exceeded, mistake occurs; field shiftable.

SB xxxx ±n xxxx ±n — *Sub*tract contents of A address from B address, stopping at first fieldmark; if length of B field exceeded, mistake occurs; field shiftable.

ML xxxx ±n xxxx ±n — *M*ultiply contents of A address by B address giving product in B address, the "multiply field," which must be as long as multiplicand (A) and multiplier (B) field +1. Multiplication starts with multiplier in *left* part of B and zeros to the right; product obtained in right end of multiply field; field shiftable.

TABLE 8-2. *Order code for FIELDCOM (cont'd).*

Op. Code	Instruction Addresses				Explanation
	A	c	B	d	

Tests

CM xxxx			xxxx		Compare contents of A address with B to first fieldmark and set a switch to indicate conditions tested by jump switch instruction, described below.
JS xxxx	C E F H L N R U				Jump if switch is *on* indicating condition resulting from comparison: C, last card condition—preceding read operation not executed because hopper empty; E, (A = B); F, field mistake; H, high (A > B); L, low (A < B); N, negative sign from the first preceding arithmetic operation; R, last record read from tape in preceding read operation; U, unconditional.

Miscellaneous

HL xxxx					Halt, with instruction register set to A address; can be the start of program if it is to be repeated; or address of the halt instruction itself to insure halt if processor restarted.
NP xxxx			xxxx		No operation; ignore this operation even though it contains addresses; use as "dummy" to form an instruction later.
AL xxxx	±lll	 l			Assign literal "ll...l" written in "c" columns and following to the address A, relative, absolute, or symbolic; the literal can be alpha, numeric, alphanumeric, or blank ("b" indicates a blank) up to 30 characters.
AA xxxx			ssss		Assign A address, relative or absolute, to symbolic address "s" shown in the B address.

TABLE 8-2. *Order code for FIELDCOM (cont'd).*

The comparison instruction has two addresses to compare contents of A address with B address, CM xxxx xxxx, and sets switches that can later be tested by a conditional jump instruction,

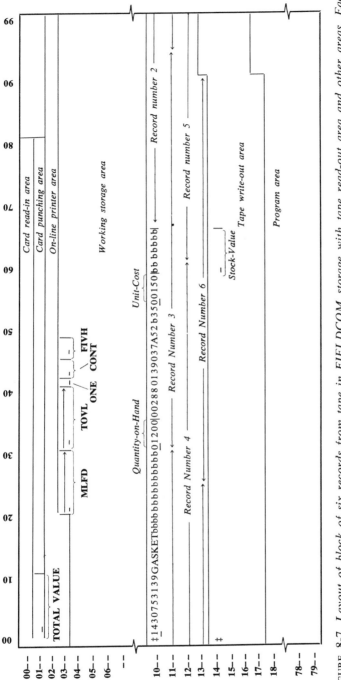

FIGURE 8-7. *Layout of block of six records from tape in FIELDCOM storage with tape read-out area and other areas. Each fieldmarked location is indicated by "‾" under the character involved. The right-hand end of each field—the address—is indicated here by "|" for clarity.*

293

JS xxxx ——, which transfers program control to the appropriate part of the program.

Excerpt from a Program. A brief excerpt from a FIELDCOM program is given here to illustrate some aspects of selectable-field programming. The problem, corresponding in some ways to a WORDCOM example given earlier, is to calculate the stock value for each of 3000 records stored on tape, write the new file tape, and punch a total card. Assume that the records, each 65 characters long on cards, were previously converted to tape blocks containing six cards each for a total of 390 characters per block and 500 blocks. The layout of storage for reading, processing, and writing tape records is shown in Figure 8-7. Areas are indicated for card read, card punch, and on-line printing as specified by FIELDCOM design. It also shows the areas assigned for use in this program: working storage, tape read-in, tape write-out, and the program. The tape read-in area indicates the result of reading in the first block and shows the first record of 65 characters in detail. Fieldmarks required for only the three items used in the first record are indicated, but similar fieldmarks would be required for the other records. Fieldmarks are not needed in the tape write-out area, but a blockmark "‡" is necessary at location 1400 to terminate the block when writing the record on tape. Fieldmarks are also indicated in the card-punching and working-storage area with an indication of the use of these areas in this example.

The FIELDCOM program to calculate each stock value and summarize the value for all records is briefly shown and described here with symbolic location addresses, which are assigned specific locations during a compiling run through the processor before executing the program.

Inst. Addr.	Op.	Addresses A	c	B	d	Explanation
STRT	CS	0 1 0 1		0 1 8 0		Clear the card-punch area of fieldmarks and characters.
	FM	0 1 0 1				Fieldmark the field in punching area to receive the total value. Also fieldmark the positions shown in working storage and 18 positions in tape read-in, of which three are shown in Figure 8-7. Fieldmark position 1459 in the tape write-out area for stock-value field. Also fieldmark similar positions for five other records in block.
READ	R2	1 3 9 0				Read a tape block of 390 characters into locations 1390–1001 from tape unit 2.

Inst. Addr.	Op.	A	c	Addresses B	d	Explanation
	ZR	MLFD				Zero the field with address MLFD consisting of 11 character positions 0331 down to 0321 to use as multiply field. (MLFD assigned address 0331 during program assembly.) Also ZR TOVL (0341), for total value field.
	CP	1 0 3 5		MLFD	−6	Copy quantity on hand, address 1035, into *left* end of multiply field, MLFD −6 positions. (MLFD assembled with address of 0331, therefore 0331 − 6 = 0325, the "−6" indicates field shifting of 6 positions left.)
	ML	1 0 5 8		MLFD		Multiply unit-cost, address 1058 by quantity on hand in multiply field, address 0331, giving stock value.
	CP	MLFD		1 4 6 5		Copy the seven right-hand characters from multiply field to stock-value field in tape write-out area. Copy operation terminated by fieldmark at 1459.
	CP	1 0 5 8		1 4 5 8		Copy unit cost, address 1058 into tape-write area. Copy next two fields, which completes the copy of the first record. Since both addresses follow in sequence for the second and third instructions, they could be omitted if desired and "chained" together.
	CP	1 0 5 3		1 4 5 3		
	CP	1 0 3 0		1 4 3 0		
ADDX	AD	MLFD		TOVL		Accumulate stock value "current subtotal" in address total value.
	JS	MSTK	F			If subtotal in address 0341 causes field mistake (it set the "F" switch), jump to MSTK for instruction to punch the "prior subtotal" in address 0110.
	CP	TOVL		0 1 1 0		Arriving here means no field mistake, copy "current subtotal" to "prior subtotal" in address 0110, the punching area, to make current. Since FIELDCOM does not have index registers, one way to advance through the six records in a tape block is to rewrite the preceding instructions five more times and use higher A addresses for the CP 1035, MLFD −6, and ML 1058, MLFD and a higher B address for the CP MLFD, 1465 instruction. Increase by 65 positions each time, corresponding to the spacing between similar items in storage.
	W3	1 7 9 0				After handling six records, write a block on tape from address 1790 through blockmark in 1400 onto tape unit 3.

Inst. Addr.	Op.	A	Addresses c	B	d	Explanation
	AD	O N E		CONT		Add "ONE," for name of address containing 1, to "CONT" for name of counter to count number of tape blocks handled. (Assigned addresses 0342 and 0345 later in program.)
	CM	CONT		FIVH		Compare CONT to "FIVH" for name of address containing 500.
	JS	WNDP	E			If 500 cycles performed (CONT equals FIVH) jump to WNDP to wind up the program.
	JS	READ	L			If less than 500 blocks of tape handled, jump to READ to read next block and process it.
WNDP	PC					Punch a card with total value; or the final subtotal, if a field mistake occurred previously and a subtotal card was punched.
	T2					Rewind input and output tapes.
	T3					
HALT	HL	HALT				Halt with instruction counter set to HALT.
MSTK	PC					Arriving here from the JS MSTK F instruction means a field mistake occurred. Therefore punch a card with "prior subtotal" from address 0110.
	ZR	TOVL				Zero the fields at addresses TOVL and 0110 to eliminate "current" and "prior subtotals."
	ZR	0110				
	JS	ADDX	U			Return to ADDX to add stock value still in address 0331 to zeroed address 0341.
	AA	0 3 3 1	11	MLFD		Assign the address 0331 to an 11 position field 0321–0331 and give it the symbolic name MLFD.
	AA	*	10	TOVL		Assign the next 10 free positions in storage and name it TOVL for total value. This is an example of relative addressing.
	AA	*	1	O N E		Assign the next 1 free position and name it ONE. Similarly for CONT (counter) and FIVH (five hundred) assign 3 free positions to each.
	AL	FIVH	5	0	0	Assign the literal 500 to symbolic address FIVH. Similarly assign 1 to ONE and 000 to CONT.
	AA	1 8 0 0		STRT		Assign first instruction in program to location 1800; others follow in sequence.
	ND	STRT				End of program, program to start at STRT.
	b					Blank and fieldmark to terminate last instruction.

SUMMARY

The precise instruction format devised by engineers must be adhered to by programmers. The format specifies the use of each character position for operation code, index register, and address or special constant.

A program to read the data from one deck of cards or a tape, and punch another deck of cards or write on tape is trivially simple, but it shows address modification for cycling through instruction loops to cut the number of program steps to be written and stored. *Index registers* are special counters that can be set and increased or decreased by specified numbers—an increase by 995 is equivalent to a decrease of 005 in WORDCOM, since storage 999 is followed by 000. A register is tested to determine its contents during each loop in a cycle. An indexable instruction uses the content of an index register to form and use an *effective address* at the time of instruction execution instead of the address as originally written in the program.

Comparison orders are at the heart of the decision-making process. Various comparisons can determine, for example, whether an inventory balance is larger or smaller than the reorder point, whether one item belongs ahead of another in a sequence, and whether a cycle has been performed the desired number of times. *Jump* instructions are used after comparison instructions to transfer processor control to that part of the program appropriate for each result from a test.

Instructions for addition, subtraction, multiplication, and division are used to perform arithmetical operations, but arithmetical instructions are only a small fraction of the operations performed in business processing. The programmer has many responsibilities for arithmetical operations. He must keep track of the decimal point, deal with the possibility that results will overflow the accumulator, and edit results for dollar signs, commas, and decimal points. *Shifting operations* are used to line up characters before comparison or addition operations and to isolate desired characters during processing.

Processor storage may be designed so that the programmer is restricted to fixed groups of characters called *words* for both operands and instructions. Or the machine may be designed to handle characters grouped as *selected-length fields* that just fit each data element. WORDCOM and FIELDCOM illustrate some aspects of each type machine and its programming for business data processing.

CHAPTER 9

PROCESSING PROCEDURES—EDITING, FILE PROCESSING, AND SORTING

The preceding chapters dealt with the fundamental building blocks of business data processing—machine-processable data, data organization, processing equipment, systems analysis and design, and programming. This chapter combines these building blocks to illustrate three major facets of business data processing: editing, file processing, and sorting. Editing and file processing are basic to nearly all business data processing; sorting is essential for processing files not maintained in addressable bulk storage.

Editing is done at two stages of data processing: first, during input to ensure that the data are accurate and in suitable form for the processor to handle, and second, during output to prepare understandable and useful reports for people.

Business record file *maintenance* introduces new records into a file and deletes old records from a file. File *processing* changes the content of individual records in a file to reflect transactions involving each record. Although file maintenance and processing frequently are handled together in one file run, treating them separately ensures more careful control over the opening and closing of records in the file. Bank officers, for example, try to guard against an employee's improperly opening or closing depositors' accounts in order to reduce the risk of internal embezzlement. For inventory control, on the other hand, the risk of loss is small from each account incorrectly opened; for example, a transaction for a non-existent stock number can lead to opening a new account and posting it with that transaction. While this mistake doesn't really facilitate fraud, it does mean that another account—the correct stock record—is not posted and therefore is incorrect. Ways of guarding against these problems will be discussed later.

Sorting is the arrangement of items into sequence on a *key*—one or more selected data elements in each record—that consists of alphabetic or numeric characters. Customarily, files consist of a homogeneous class of records that are sequentially ordered. This organization means that transactions must be separated by class, each class sorted into sequence on the same key—say, stock number—used to organize the file, and all transactions affecting a record must be ordered for logically correct processing, as described in Chapter 6. But in many cases, the data-system requirements and the equipment available for use are such that nonsequential processing is preferable to sequential. When random-access processing is used, transactions need only be classified by type for handling in a logically correct order—for example, receipts ahead of issues—without regard for key sequence.

EDITING

Input editing is done during the initial stages of data handling or read-in. Input editing makes the transaction data conform to the format and standards of quality of data already in files in order to facilitate processing. Output editing is done during the write-out operation or at a later stage to select and arrange the desired information in usable form. Editing is approached here primarily from the viewpoint of its *operational aspects*. From the user's viewpoint, the meaning of data is more important than its form and the operations performed, but the question of *meaning* depends strongly upon the particular circumstances.

Input Editing

Input editing ensures, or at least increases the probability, that data being processed are what they are supposed to be. For example, input editing, in broadest terms, might be used to determine whether an inventory file about to be updated is the current version of that file and not some prior and obsolete copy of it or some entirely different file.

File Labels. One way to check whether the desired file is being used is to identify the tape or card files by written labels that people can read. In addition, a file label that identifies or describes the contents of a file can be included as the first record in a file. Then, before using a file, the processor program reads the file label and checks it against the file wanted for processing, as specified by the label in the program being run.

Although this kind of input editing sounds complex, the reader may understand this by an analogy with his check book. File-label checking corresponds to making sure that you have your *check book* (the file) to write a check (the program), because it must be written in the check book and not on a desk pad, blackboard, or in some other check book. The file label on the check book is implicit in its appearance, for a check book seldom has "check book" printed on it. The "file label" in your check-writing "program" is your remembrance of how a check book looks. This sounds trivial, but imagine the problem if you could not perceive general shapes by visual examination or touch, and all labels were omitted. Electronic processors don't see or feel; they must be instructed by means of the program to call for the necessary file *and* have a way of identifying that the wanted file is available for processing. Programmed checking of file labels is more effective than visual inspection of written labels by machine operators because processors follow programs more consistently than people do.

Input-Editing Operations. Input editing deals primarily with the transactions that cause changes in files and only secondarily with the files themselves. If good control is maintained over all inputs, then the files are bound to be satisfactory. Input-data editing includes several kinds of tests and operations:

1. Field content: input editing determines whether alphabetic and numeric characters are where they are supposed to be and not elsewhere.
2. Accuracy of numeric data *per se*: check-digit, check-sum, and "hash-totals" rules are tested against totals summed at a prior stage for checking purposes to determine whether data meet them.
3. Completeness of data: the presence of all data elements in each transaction record and all records required for the particular type of transaction is ascertained by examining each record, counting

records, and testing for gaps in the numerical sequence of records
originated and transmitted through the communications network.

4. Code compatibility: editing determines whether input-data code—
   say, punched-card alphanumeric—differs from processor code, in
   which case a conversion is made to seven-bit code during read-in.
5. Rearrange data element sequence: data elements in an input record
   are put into suitable sequence for efficient file processing.
6. Expand or compress data: characters are introduced or deleted to
   make data element and record length of input data correspond to
   lengths in files for efficient processing.
7. Remove non-numeric data: money amount symbols—decimal
   points, commas, and dollar signs—are removed from input data
   that will be used in arithmetic operations.
8. Examine internal consistency: several data elements within one
   record or a data element within the record and an external constant
   are examined for the existence of a specified relationship.
9. Check for correspondence of data with files: proper names, descriptors, and numeric amounts are compared to see whether they
   correspond with file content.

Editing and Files.   Most of these input-editing operations are
handled by programmed subroutines or features built into the machine. In either case, the processor—or, perhaps, a satellite processor—examines the data and performs operations on individual
data elements, each transaction record, or on all transaction records. The first eight types of editing—field content, accuracy, completeness, code conversion, rearrangement, expansion or compres-
sion of data, non-numeric extraction, and internal consistency—
can be performed by a processor without reference to the master
files that the transactions will later update. Most of these editing
operations can be performed during the first pass of data—perhaps
input conversion—through the main processor or satellite because
files are not needed.

To determine whether an input record corresponds to the content of its related record in the master files—say, employee pay-
rate action and employee master-record, the transaction must, of
course, be compared with the master-file record. Proper names,
numbers, descriptors, and even amounts in the input data can be
compared with file content to determine whether they correspond.

Conversion of data code often is handled automatically by the
machine during data read-in, especially in processors using a seven-
bit code for each alphanumeric character. For processors using pure
binary for numbers, the conversion from, say, decimal on cards to

binary inside the processor may require a programmed computation. Newer machines handle these conversions automatically and the programmer need not worry about them.

Card Format and Editing

A brief description of card input illustrates some of the features of editing listed above. Compatibility of the processor and peripheral card equipment can be achieved either by editing devices associated with the peripheral units or by editing techniques programmed for the processor. In the case of punched-card equipment, limited editing may be done after reading the card and before transferring the data to storage in the processor.

Data Rearrangement. Data from several fields on a card—columns designated for particular purposes—can be combined into one processor word for a "word" machine. On the other hand, data from card fields containing fewer than the number of characters specified for a word in processor storage can be filled out with zeros or blanks. Of course, variable-field processors can deal directly with fields of any length in the input data, since there is no need to fit characters into words. It is also possible to shift, transpose, or suppress digits within a field and to rearrange fields with input-edit devices. Blanks, zeros, and plus or minus signs are supplied where wanted in a word by the editing unit during input. Any vacant positions not wanted in a numeric word must be filled with zeros (not blanks) during read-in so that the word can be manipulated arithmetically. The card reader may check for field content—alphabetic or numeric characters only where specified—and for format and completeness in a rudimentary way by means of double-punch and blank-column detection.

Other editing operations are programmed for the processor to perform. Since each type of transaction has a specified format, elaborate editing programs are possible on the input data *per se* and, especially, in conjunction with the file records affected by the transaction.

The edit operations for expanding or compressing and rearranging input data to correspond to file records are much simpler in a programming system designed specifically for business data processing. Both the input data and master files are organized as files, records, and data elements. By appropriately defining the data elements in records in both the input and the files as either elementary items or group items, the processor automatically handles the expansion-compression and rearrangement phases of editing. Many of the other phases of editing, however, must be handled by tailor-made programming.

Some processors have a *scatter read* feature for rearranging the individual data elements of each transaction anywhere desired in processor storage. In this way the 80 characters or less of data that are read from each card can be formed into processor words or fields and stored (under simple program control) in the locations that are most convenient for subsequent processing. Without scatter read, the characters read from each card probably would be stored in sequential locations and rearranged in subsequent operations. This pattern is true unless record descriptions organize the characters as words, fields, or data elements (depending upon the design of the machine and the programming system used), and place them wherever wanted in storage.

As discussed in preceding chapters, most processors cannot perform arithmetic operations on data that contain such non-numeric characters as decimal points or dollar signs. If input data does contain these symbols, then an edit routine is required to extract them. In most instances, these symbols are omitted when numeric data are first converted to machine media and the need for subsequent editing thereby is eliminated.

Editing for internal consistency is a powerful means of checking input. Often several data elements within a record bear a known relationship to each other. For example, the start time of a production order must be earlier than the finish time. Other data elements within a record can be compared to a known constant. The issue date on an inventory transaction must not be later than the day of processing and should not be older than, say, one week. An issue dated in the future is clearly a mistake; however, other kinds of comparison may give *unreasonable* but not necessarily wrong answers. An order from a retail customer for 100 suits needs further investigation. He might want 100, but more likely he wants one or ten.

Sequence Checking. The arrangement of instructions on a card may leave some spare columns that can be used to hold identifying data or remarks. For example, if there are six remaining columns after punching as many instructions as possible in a card, they might be used to identify a program deck, such as LOAD 1 and LOAD 2 for the load-routine cards and SEQCHK for each card in a sequence-check routine. Furthermore, two columns might be reserved (if available) for sequence-numbering the cards (00 through 99) to help keep them in sequence for input. The total of these sequence numbers can be punched into the transfer card to allow a check on peripheral equipment during read-in to assure that all cards are loaded. The processor can, by a small loop in the load routine, also check card sequence within the program or data. A simple check scheme for serially numbered cards might be the comparison of the card number with the contents of a counter, and accepting the card if the two numbers correspond. A 1 should be added to the counter, of course, before comparing the counter contents and next card number. Slightly more elaborate schemes are required if the interval between card numbers is not uniform. Similar schemes can be used for identifying and sequence-numbering input data cards to guard against loss of cards or mixups within and between decks.

Devices. A plugboard wired for input of a particular card format is kept for reuse to avoid the trouble of rewiring the board each time. Clever editing saves card-reading time and processor time for packing or unpacking characters that need to be rearranged for efficient processing. Similar plugboard devices are used for editing data for card-punching units.

Magnetic-tape-handling units lack editing facilities, and using a large processor to perform editing may be expensive. Instead, a satellite processor is often used to edit and rearrange data. In some cases, peripheral equipment, such as card-to-tape converters and off-line printers operating from magnetic tape, do limited editing operations. Processor programs are also used for further editing and rearranging input data during read-in and for editing results during output processing.

Edit Limitations. Some input, such as certain instruction words for a program kept on cards, are difficult to edit for accuracy. The first word—the word-count and storage-location word—on a program load card may have a format different from other instructions and be numeric with a *minus* sign. Two cards to load the routine and the transfer card (to initiate program execution at the desired starting instruction) can start with an instruction word and a *plus* sign to indicate the different use made of the cards. Since the first word on most cards may be used in any one of several ways, this word cannot be edit-checked during read-in. If a plus is erroneously marked a minus on a program card, the program will not run correctly when execution is attempted. In fact, an erroneous sign may prevent loading the whole program and cause a premature attempt to execute the program.

Output Editing

Output editing is actually done after file processing, which is discussed later in this chapter; however, it is desirable to cover output editing at this point, for it has many similarities to input editing, and it bears on file layout and processing. The quantity and quality of information issued by a data-processing system depend upon the caliber of both the input- and output-editing schemes.

User Requirements. Output editing is required because people need their information in a different form than is most efficient for processing. People are accustomed to short documents and reports containing only a few items and to longer reports of orderly rows and columns of names and numbers on sheets of paper with appropriate headings. Common types of reports are statements, statistical summaries, checks, payroll, and cost distributions—lists or summaries about any facet of a business.

The most important questions about report preparation are, "What information should this report contain?" and "How should it be arranged?" The answers depend on several factors. Content of a report depends on *transaction events*—what and how many transactions are being reported. The intended *audience*—who will read and use the report—determines format, and, to some extent, content. And the *management operating plan*—how the organization responds to reports about what has occurred—influences the content, arrangement, emphasis, and distribution of reports. The exact content and format of any report depends on bargaining between report users and people who operate the data-processing system.

In more concrete terms, and viewed at the operational level of data processing, the desired content of reports needs to be selected from records in a file and arranged for printing as separate words in a readable format in reports. Specifically, this includes the following: editing individual words for spacing; inserting punctuation, special symbols for dollars or units of weight, and abbreviations; and suppressing leading zeros or other symbols in order to improve readability. Also, spacing (or breaks) by minor and major classes must be planned for, headings supplied, and totals and subtotals computed for printing.

In short, output editing bridges the gap between, on the one hand, the most efficient data layouts for processor storage and manipulation and, on the other, the presentation of lengthy reports or merely selected facts to people. Processors have limited primary-storage space; therefore, to economize storage, the format arrangements and redundancies that make data more readable for people are usually eliminated from the input data during read-in. These special format arrangements and redundancies are then restored during output editing so that people can readily use the results without being distracted by the make-up of reports.

If the processor output is used by equipment instead of people, then the output, of course, is edited for machine usage. Examples of machines using processor output are automatic devices for machine or process control in the plant, communication networks to disseminate results, or the processor itself during the next processing cycle.

Output Format. Output editing concentrates on selecting data elements from files, rearranging them—perhaps by *scatter write,* the opposite of scatter read—expanding data elements into separate visual words for readability, and developing attractive page layout. Processors perform several operations, and some in parallel, when handling files to prepare reports:

1. Select desired items or groups of items from specified records (ignore others) in a file and organize them into readable words.
2. Assign desired words to one report output on tape or cards or to several report outputs—say, payroll and earnings report—if wanted in each report.
3. Sort the items for each report into sequence by name, number, quantity involved, or other elements of data, as desired.
4. Develop "breaks" in the data on major and minor classifications and calculate subtotals and totals for each category.
5. Introduce report titles, page headings, page numbers, and special symbols; delete repetitive descriptions and unwanted leading zeros; plan horizontal and vertical spacing and alignment; and select a suitable amount of printing per page.
6. Count the number of records and calculate the totals for all items going into each report and proved against the items selected from files for report preparation.

Some of the critical problems concerning input data—field content, data accuracy, completeness of data, and correspondence of data with files—are most efficiently handled during input editing. During output editing, it is generally assumed that these problems were handled correctly earlier, because little or nothing can be done efficiently about them at this stage. This is true except for the discovery of mistakes that cast doubt on input editing and lead to further investigation. But relationships among items in files can be determined by testing their validity in terms of *standards,* past *actual* results, or even *reasonableness* according to an intuitive feel of the situation. If, for example, purchase orders for a particular item have been issued for quantities ranging from 100 to 350 during the past two years, an order for either 1 or 1000 units deserves investigation. The unusual quantity may arise from a special order or a change in the production schedule, but it is probably an error. Such testing augments input editing by concentrating on the meaning of the output. The *meaning* of the output depends on the logic of processing— whether the program was designed to do what was actually wanted —and on an understanding of the nature of the input data and file content at any point in time and during any stage of processing. These are vastly broader problems, and more difficult to deal with at the procedural level than input editing, for which many techniques are available.

Report Programming. Programming all of the editing required for report preparation can be extremely time consuming, if done at the level of machine language. Report generators represent an advanced form of programming and are often more efficient than tailor-made report-writing programs. These generators provide a simplified means of preparing statistics—totals, averages, and standard deviations—and setting up format—titles, spacing, and special symbols. Assuming the availability of a report generator prepared by the equipment manufacturer or other programming specialist, the user must first learn how to work with it, which may be nearly as onerous as writing a program afresh. After he comprehends the generator and still feels that it fulfills his requirements, he specifies certain facts about the data arrangement in the records to be used and the content and layout of reports. The processor, first, *generates* the report-writing program and, second, *executes* the report-writing program to process the files and prepare the desired reports.

FILE MAINTENANCE AND PROCESSING

Business data processing involves huge files of records on employees, material in stock, customers, production scheduling, and other items. These files are *maintained* or updated to reflect non-arithmetical changes in records and *processed* to change the contents of individual records by means of arithmetical operations.

File Maintenance

File maintenance is the modification of a file to incorporate additions, deletions, transfers, and substitutions. Emphasis is placed on the whole record rather than the data elements. The following types of changes in an inventory stock file illustrate the transactions involved in file maintenance.

1. Addition of new stock items to the approved list
2. Deletion of discontinued items
3. Transfers from one section of the file to another because items are reclassified or switched between warehouses
4. Substitution of new identification data—part number, part name, item cost—for old.

If the master file is stored on tape in catalogue-number sequence, the changes are sorted into the same sequence in order to maintain the file. If the file is kept in random-access storage, preliminary sorting of file changes is not required. However, for both file-processing techniques, transactions affecting each record must be handled in a logical sequence.

Inputs and Outputs. In addition to the processor program, the inputs for file maintenance are the master file, new changes, and pending changes left over from the prior maintenance cycle. The outputs are an updated master file, change list, pending changes, and mismatches. The *updated master file* will reflect additions, deletions and transfers of stock items, and substitution of new facts for stock items that are otherwise unchanged. A *change list* is useful for keeping track of the kinds of changes made in the master file and for tracing them, if necessary.

Pending changes is a type of output peculiar to maintaining files that are kept in sequence. In one file run, an item can be transferred forward by removing it from its original location and inserting it in the file at a later point. The reverse is not possible because the desired insertion point is passed before reaching the item to be moved. To move the record for an item to an earlier point in the master file, the record for the item is taken out of the file during one cycle and inserted at an earlier point in the next cycle. The fact that records to be moved upstream are extracted from the master file and kept in a pending-change file between two cycles may require that the different types of transactions be handled in a certain order. Otherwise, futile attempts will be made to process the item while it is temporarily out of the master file.

Accuracy Control.   *Mismatches* arise in file maintenance whenever the key for an item is incorrect. An attempt to delete, transfer, or substitute an item in the file will end up on an error tape or console print-out, if the input-item key does not match the key of a file item. On the other hand, an incorrect key that happens to match the key of another item will update the wrong record. In one amusing example, a mail-order house reported extremely high sales of fur coats because keypunch operators introducing input data tended to transpose the stock number for another item and punch the number for fur coats. Daydreaming and wishful thinking outfoxed the processing system, and an inventory count and reconciliation was required to correct the records.

A new record can be introduced into a file even though it has an erroneous key. A record with a key 23451 that is erroneously punched as 12345 and used during a file maintenance run will be introduced at the wrong place. The next transaction processed against item 23451 will be rejected as a mismatch (because the earlier item was introduced as 12345) and written out on an error tape for examination.

The accuracy of file-maintenance operations can be controlled, to some extent, by keeping track of the number of records in the file. The initial number, plus introductions, minus deletions equals the final number of records. Transfers within the file change the number of records in a category, but not in total. Obviously, control over modifications within individual records requires more thorough techniques.

Housekeeping Runs.   The file-maintenance requirements of an application affect the initial selection of equipment, modes of storage, arrangement of master-file data, conversion and housekeeping programs, and amount of processor time devoted to nonproduction runs. Systems analysts tend to concentrate on getting tangible output from production programs without giving careful consideration to housekeeping runs—that is, to the sorting, merging, extracting, editing, and updating programs that must be written and run regularly in order to make a production run possible. A single production run can grow into a half-dozen preparatory programs and a like number of one-time file conversion and editing programs.

File Processing

File processing updates a file to incorporate changes involving arithmetical operations. Examples of inventory transactions handled by file processing are:

1. Purchase and use commitments
2. Receipts
3. Issues
4. Financial accounting.

These transactions require arithmetical operations to update the quantity or value of a stock item available or on hand. The transactions are sorted into the same sequence as the master file and processed, by means of suitable programs, against the master file. A program can process many kinds of transactions in the same run if each type is properly identified and handled in a logical sequence.

The essence of processing files kept on tapes—which has been touched on in several earlier chapters—is basically simple. First, a suitable file-processing program is read into the processor. Second, the program directs the read-in of one or more transactions and master-file records (depending upon the length of the records and quantity of processor storage available) to compare them for identity on stock-number or other key until a match is found. Third, each master-file record without a transaction match (inactive file record) is copied onto the new master file. And each transaction lacking a corresponding master-file record—incorrect sequence, or invalid stock number—is written out on a mismatch tape. Fourth, when a match on stock number is found, the program directs the processor to handle all transactions affecting that record to update the master file. Fifth, the updated record is written out on the new master-file tape, and the cycle is repeated starting at the second step.

For files kept in random-access storage, file processing is simpler because transactions need not be sorted into stock-number sequence (although each type has to be handled in a logical sequence) and each updated file-record merely takes the place of the old record in storage; the file is not rewritten. Mismatches are written out for analysis and correction.

Transactions and Subroutines. The transaction identifier is used in the following way to calculate instruction addresses and execute the required subroutine. Assume, for simplicity, that a subroutine of 100 program steps is required to process each of the four types of transactions that occur for the stock file: purchase, receipt, issue, and financial accounting. These subroutines are in processor storage starting at locations 100, 200, 300, and 400, respectively. The main program first takes the transaction type—1, 2, 3, or 4, for the four classes of transactions—from the input record for each transaction. Next, the program multiplies the transaction type number—1, 2, 3, or 4—by 100 to obtain a number indicating the starting point of the subroutine for that kind of transaction. The calculated result—100, 200, 300, or 400—is then inserted into a program jump instruction that can then be executed. When executed, this instruction step makes processor control go to the correct starting point to execute the subroutine. The last step in each of the four subroutines—storage locations 199, 299, 399, and 499—contains a jump to return program control to the main program and handle other transactions in a similar way or continue with other parts of the program.

An important feature of the addressing scheme outlined above is the creation of an address by calculation in order to complete an instruction. Several important aspects of this feature should be noted. The address of the branch instruction is omitted when the instruction is written—that is, it is a *dummy* instruction. Three program steps are used to fill in the address of the dummy instruction. First, the transaction type number is obtained. Second, this number is multiplied by 100. And, third, the product—100, 200, 300, or 400—is incorporated in the dummy instruction by copying or moving it to the blank part of the instruction without changing the instruction code. In the next cycle, a new address is merely written over the address that was copied into the dummy-instruction address. This cycle can be repeated indefinitely to operate correctly on any and every example of the four types of transactions. This is a simple example of the ability of a processor to modify an instruction to fit conditions encountered in the data.

Other schemes, which vary in nature depending on the processor's features, are available for using the desired subroutine in the program. Machines with *indirect addressing* can do this more simply, as follows. The starting points 100, 200, 300, and 400 of the subroutines for the four kinds of transactions are placed in the corresponding storage locations—1, 2, 3, and 4, respectively. Upon reading in each transaction, the transaction class number is used to form the address of an instruction which will obtain from location 1, 2, 3, or 4, as directed, the address of the starting point—100, 200, 300, or 400—of the required subroutine. Thus, in two steps, one address, which corresponds to the type of transaction, is used to find the address of the subroutine starting point. This indirect-addressing scheme of using storage at one address to find another address is carried through several stages by some processors. Corresponding to clues in a "treasure hunt," two (or more) steps are required to reach the goal.

Although this example of how a transaction code may be used to direct the program to a selected subroutine is highly simplified, it should convey the idea of how a program develops, or at least completes, some of its own instructions. The reader may see how transfers to subroutines that have different numbers of instructions can be set up without wasting storage space by padding them out to the same length. It may also be visualized how less orderly-looking schemes for coding transactions can be coped with.

Trial Runs for Processing. On the surface, file processing seems to be a simple, straightforward process in which all that needs to be done is to process the transactions and carry out the related physical actions—fill orders, pay workmen, or whatever. However, many factors make processing complicated; one factor, which bears on the sequence used for processing, is the fact that it is possible to substitute one stock item for another. More important, a trial run with calculations and perhaps tentative update of the file may be required where reciprocal effects are involved. After deciding what action to take, the file can be updated.

Assume that when stock item A is ordered by customers, if it is not available, then B is the first substitute, and D the second. Substitution of an alternate color or a higher-priced item for the one ordered may be made. A wag once said that mail-order houses try to maximize substitution by sending the alternate or wrong item to each and every customer even though they could fill every order as placed. Ignoring the possible intention of that remark, it is nevertheless possible that every order could be filled "correctly," according to some definition, yet every customer get a substitute. Similar patterns of choice may exist for machine-assignment in a factory and for selection of transportation routes.

A matrix can be developed to show how one item can be substituted for another:

Item Wanted	Substitution Choice					
	A	B	C	D	E	F
A		1		2		
B	1				2	
C	No substitutes					
D		1				
E			1			2
F	2				1	

The matrix means that, if A is wanted but is not available, B is the first choice and D is the second choice as a substitute. When processing requests for issues, the decision rules might be to (1) try to fill all orders with the items requested, (2) then fill any un-filled orders with first substitutes, if possible, and (3) fill any re-maining orders with second substitutes, if possible.

In the simple case, supply equals or exceeds demand, and every order can be filled with the item wanted. The situation is more com-plex if supply of some items falls short of demand. Two or more attempts may be made to fill orders—initially, with the item wanted; next, with the first substitute; and, finally, with the second substi-tute. If the demand for A exceeds the supply, the remaining de-mand is filled with B and D, but only after the primary demands for those items are filled, and so on.

Another rule for filling orders might be to fill all the orders for A—use A and substitutes B and D, if necessary, before going to B, etc. Obviously, the outcome of this scheme depends on whether the order-filling procedure starts with orders for item A and works through to F, or vice versa. More intricate rules might be developed to keep the frequency of substitution at a minimum or to maximize the quantity ordered that is filled by the item wanted or its first substitute.

Two important points are involved in applying substitution rules to maximize the number of orders filled by first-choice items, if the supply of some items is short: (1) the allocation requires a trial run involving *all* orders, and (2) some rules are needed to de-cide how to allocate items in short supply. The allocation rules, once formulated, can then be applied as part of the data-processing rou-tine to update files and initiate shipping action.

Controls.   File maintenance and file processing have enough in common so that they might be handled in the same processor run. Joint treatment may cause some difficulties because control over each kind of operation becomes more difficult. For example, a bank found that checking-account transactions, which were processed in the same run as file changes, sometimes resulted in opening new accounts because of mistakes in account numbers. File-maintenance procedures, it will be recalled, handle insertion of new accounts, and an erroneous transaction account number may either open up a new account or post the transaction to another depositor's ac-count. Erroneously opening a new account causes some difficulty, but posting to the wrong account is at least twice as bad, for it affects two depositors and both may be annoyed by the mistake. One remedy is to handle file maintenance and processing in two separate runs so that tighter control can be kept over the opening and closing of accounts.

The fact that file processing leaves unchanged the number of records in a file facilitates control over a file to guard against erroneous gain or loss of a record. Money amounts can be controlled by keeping control totals—today's balance equals yesterday's balance plus additions and minus deductions—for proving the total of individual account balances. Quantities can be controlled on a unit basis by adding all items to get a control total, even though dissimilar items are involved.

File Handling

Maintaining and processing files kept on magnetic tape usually require reading and rewriting the whole file during each processing cycle. There are several ways to cut down the work of reading and recopying the whole file at each cycle just to update the small fraction of active records.

Fractional Updating.   One way is to update a fraction—one-fifth or one-twentieth—of the master file each day so that the whole file is updated once in a week or a month. The whole file is never really current but, on the other hand, it is almost current, for it averages only two days old, if one-fifth is updated each day. On any given day, one-fifth is current or zero days old, and the other fractions are one, two, three, and four business-days old, respectively. Many billing operations—charge accounts, utility bills, insurance premiums—operate in this fashion.

A second way to keep files current without rewriting the master tape completely is to retain the master tape intact and accumulate the changes on a change tape. This approach can save much time for a processor lacking the feature of concurrent read-process-write. Modifications to the master file are accumulated on the change tape until it becomes unwieldy. Finally, the change tape is processed against the master file to update it, the change tape is discarded, and the cycle started afresh. At any time, both the master tape and the change tape must be considered together to find the current status of a record. Although writing time is reduced, the entire master file must be read during each cycle.

The use of addressable bulk-storage devices—mainly disk or drum—is a third approach to the problem of reducing the time used to read and rewrite whole files to change a few records. These devices read a master record only if a transaction is present and provide for writing the revised record in the space occupied by the original and leaving the other records unchanged. Precautions are necessary, of course, to keep the new record within the space occupied by the old and to ensure that data are available for reconstruction in case of mishap. Maintaining files on disk or drum storage offers several advantages, therefore, for large files with low activity.

Retention Period. After setting up, maintaining, and processing a file the question arises, "How long should the file and transactions be kept before they are discarded?" A commonly-used plan is to keep three "generations" of files. For example, Monday's output is retained until Wednesday's output is successfully used as input on Thursday. Then Monday's files can be discarded, leaving the files for Tuesday and Wednesday for back-up in case Thursday's output is defective. Wednesday's file alone may be sufficient back-up for Thursday in most cases. Certain files—those for the end of each month, for example—may be retained longer to prepare reports and answer unexpected questions. The ability to reconstruct all records from a specified date to the present may be wanted as protection against mishap. If so, copies of the master file for that date and all interim transactions must be kept.

The general rule for deciding when to discard output files, and even raw data, is easy to state: discard the file when the cost of keeping it exceeds the probable value of having the data on hand. However, application of the rule is difficult because it is not possible to forecast accurately when and what demands will be made on the files that are saved and when a discarded file will be wanted.

Magnetic-tape files pose problems similar to those of retaining paper records, but some problems are accentuated. The tendency to save data and processed results is stronger for magnetic tape than for other media because of the high density of data and the possibilities of economical reprocessing. Furthermore, the possibility of selectively rewriting tape files to eliminate or consolidate some of the detail, while keeping the more consequential facts, is a plus factor in retaining tape files. Selective condensation may be done one or more times before the files are discarded and the tape reused. Economic analysis would predict that a higher fraction of data in magnetic-tape files will be saved than is the case for paper and card records. This is true even though tape is reusable. As the cost of an item decreases, the quantity used is likely to increase. For example, the Bureau of the Census reports that many *thousands* of magnetic tapes of data are being stored for statisticians and others who may want to process them at some future date to answer questions that are not yet formulated. Of course, if all future questions likely to be asked about data in the files could be formulated now, the questions could be answered and the files discarded.

SORTING

The obvious, immediate objective of sorting data is to arrange records according to rules. The basic reason for sorting data, which is inefficient *per se,* is to make subsequent processing more efficient considering the equipment available and the data-information system requirements. Records are classified by category, sorted into file sequence, and logically ordered by type before processing. Sorting into sequence by numeric or alphabetic key is of primary interest here.

Off-line data-flow plans that use serial storage require sorting transactions by class, sequence, and type to facilitate processing. Most data-processing equipment can more efficiently handle one class of transactions—as viewed from the standpoint of programs and files—than several classes of transactions. Furthermore, an orderly sequence is often easier to deal with than a jumbled sequence.

Random-access equipment operating on-line works more efficiently with one class, or a small assortment of classes, of data than with a wide variety. Arrangement in some orderly fashion may be easier to handle than a disordered mass. The classification and sorting of data into sequence will continue to precede processing until equipment with much larger, low-cost storage capacity is used in business.

An inventory record might contain these data elements along with dozens of others:

Stock Number	Stock Name	Size	Quantity
35079	Truck tire	650-16	12,327

Inventory records are commonly sorted by stock number or name. If the records are to be sorted by stock number, then the key is five digits—35079. Sometimes inventory records are sorted on the basis of stock name, location, size, quantity on hand, or even the number of days overdue for outstanding orders. The point is that any data element in a record can be used as a key. A file sorted into sequence on one key may require rearrangement for further processing. Rearrangement on another key can be avoided if processing that would seem to require resorting can be done by other processing schemes, such as searching, extracting, tallying, or summarizing.

Records are generally sorted into sequences on their keys so that they form either an ascending or a descending string. Each key in an ascending string is larger than the preceding key: 1, 2, 5, 12, 27, 28. Each key in a descending string is smaller: 50, 13, 5, 2, 1.

Alphabetic sorting treats "A" as the smallest (or earliest) letter and "Z" as the largest letter in the alphabet. The assignment of codes to numerals and letters during machine design determines the sorting sequence, which makes up a collation table for the particular processor being used.

Three methods of sorting are discussed here: digital, comparison of pairs, and merge. People, tabulating equipment, and electronic processors can do digital sorting, but comparison- and merge-sorting is restricted, for practical purposes, to electronic processors.

Digital Sorting

Digital sorting starts by sorting records on the right-hand digit in the key and finishes with the left-hand digit; it might be called "minor-major" sorting. The output for sorting on digital keys is ten classes. Each class contains items with the same right-hand digit, but with different left-hand digits. For two-digit keys, the result of the first pass of digital sorting is ten classes: 00, 10, 20, ..., 90, 01-91, 02-92 and so on through 09-99. The classes can be abbreviated as X0, X1, X2 through X9, with X any digit or digits.

The ten classes from the first pass of digital sorting can be combined in ascending sequence and sorted on the second digit from the right. When the ten output classes are "stacked," the items are then in sequence from 00 to 99 on the two right-hand digits. The process can be repeated until all digits in longer keys are handled and the items are in sequence on all digits 0...0 to 9...9. A schematic diagram of digital sorting is shown in Figure 9-1.

A simple example shows how to sort records with a three-digit key (for each additional digit, it is necessary merely to repeat the third step below) into ascending sequence. This procedure can be done either by hand or by machine, depending on whether the data media are paper, cards, or tape, as follows:

1. Sort on the right-hand or units digit.
2. Stack or combine in ascending sequence on the units digit—X0, X1, X2, . . ., X9—and sort on the second digit from the right, or tens, digit.
3. Stack in ascending sequence on the tens digit—0X, 1X, 2X—and sort on the third from right, or hundreds, digit.
4. Stack in ascending sequence on the hundreds digit and the sequence is 000 to 999.

Alphabetical Sorting

Ten output pockets are useful for sorting digital keys one digit at a time, if a simple decimal code is used. An eleventh pocket takes rejects—cards not punched in that position. Two more pockets are included to accept cards punched in the "11" and "12" positions (above the 0 to 9 positions) to sort alphabetical keys using a combination of zone and numeric punch. In short, most card sorters have twelve pockets for alphanumerical sorting, which takes two passes to handle the combination of zone punches—10, 11 and 12—and the numeric 1 through 9 punches in each column.

Any number of output pockets, from two upward, can be used for sorting, but a small number requires more passes to get the items into sequence. Sorters have been built with dozens of pockets for checks and even hundreds of output pockets for ordinary letter mail, because the availability of more output pockets permits sorting with fewer passes of the items through the sorter.

Physical handling of each separate item is an important feature of manual and mechanical sorting. A slip of paper, a card, or an ordinary envelope used for letter mail contains both the key and record. When sorted on its key, the record itself is also sorted. On the other hand, some records cannot be separated for sorting. High-density storage makes records so small that physical separation for sorting is not feasible, and such records are usually recopied during sorting.

Electronic Sorting

Sorting records in electronic data-processing systems using magnetic-tape storage involves recopying data from one tape to another. The essential feature is the comparison of two or more items to find which one should be recopied first to build a sequence. Since records on long magnetic tape cannot be sorted by physical rearrangement in the same way that paper or punched cards are sorted, they are transferred into processor storage for sorting and rewriting on

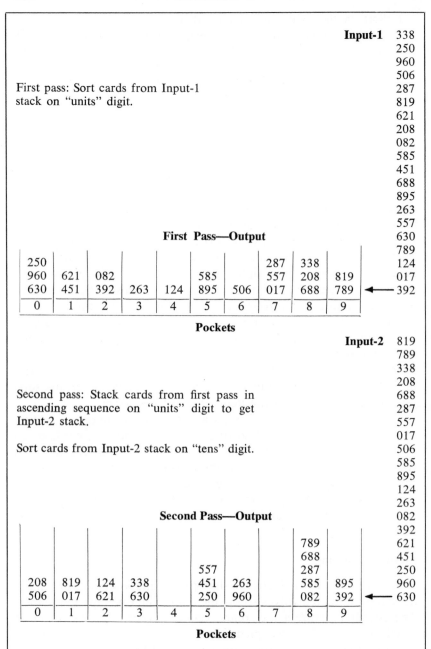

First pass: Sort cards from Input-1
stack on "units" digit.

First Pass—Output

250							287	338	
960	621	082			585		557	208	819
630	451	392	263	124	895	506	017	688	789
0	1	2	3	4	5	6	7	8	9

Pockets

Second pass: Stack cards from first pass in
ascending sequence on "units" digit to get
Input-2 stack.

Sort cards from Input-2 stack on "tens" digit.

Second Pass—Output

								789	
								688	
					557			287	
208	819	124	338		451	263		585	895
506	017	621	630		250	960		082	392
0	1	2	3	4	5	6	7	8	9

Pockets

Input-1	338
	250
	960
	506
	287
	819
	621
	208
	082
	585
	451
	688
	895
	263
	557
	630
	789
	124
	017
	392

Input-2	819
	789
	338
	208
	688
	287
	557
	017
	506
	585
	895
	124
	263
	082
	392
	621
	451
	250
	960
	630

FIGURE 9-1. *Digital sorting.*

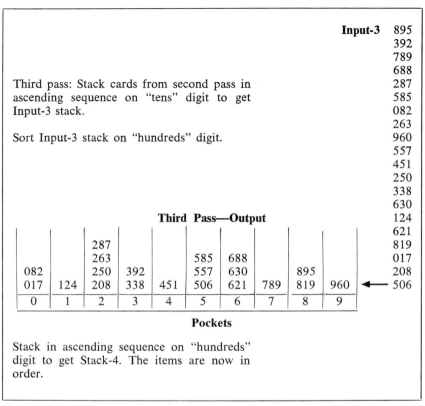

FIGURE 9-1. *Digital sorting (cont'd).*

tape. Many schemes exist for sorting records with electronic equipment: comparison of pairs, merge sorting, and digital sorting. Each is discussed briefly here.

Comparison with Exchange. There are several ways to sort records by comparing their whole keys at one time and exchanging them in storage at each step. By one plan, the keys of the first two items are compared to select the record with the smaller key. The smaller key from the first comparison is then compared with the key of the third record. Whichever record-key is smaller is saved for the next comparison, and the other record is placed in the storage location of the second. Comparison of the keys of two records at a time with exchange at each stage continues until the record with the smallest key is the one saved at the end of the cycle. This record is either placed at the end of the space originally occupied by the file or removed from the set and placed in a separate block in storage. Completing the compare-and-exchange loop for all records in the file merely puts the record with the smallest key at the end of the file. The loop is repeated from the beginning to get the next record in sequence. As the ordered sequence gets longer, the number of records remaining to be sorted in the next loop gets smaller.

The scheme for sorting by comparison of pairs obviously involves many comparisons. To sort 100 records into sequence involves 99 comparisons in the first cycle, 98 comparisons in the second cycle after one record is selected, and so forth. Only one comparison is needed in the last cycle when two records remain. If provision is made for immediate recognition of the end of the sorting operation—it is reached when no record moves toward the small end of the sequence—the number of cycles performed can be reduced.

Sorting by comparison may be used with automatic equipment when all items are kept in internal storage throughout the process. The location of items can be exchanged after each comparison, if desired, so that only the original storage occupied by the items is used during sorting. If the item selected after each pass is put into another section of storage, additional space is required, although programming is simpler.

Sorting by comparison of pairs is limited to the number of items in internal storage at one time. If desired, the sorted items can be read out, storage reloaded, and the sorting process repeated. The result is to sort into sequence the block of items that just fills the working space available in internal storage. Separate blocks of items are not related so that the whole set is not in sequence. A plan is needed to merge individual sequences together into one over-all sequence.

Merge Sorting.   Business records usually involve so many items that internal storage capacity is exceeded, and the sequences developed in storage must be merged into longer sequences. Furthermore, it is highly desirable that any sequences in the original data should be exploited. The merge-sorting scheme takes advantage of whatever sequence exists in the data when the operation starts. A set of data already in sequence is handled only once, and the sorting operation merely checks the sequence. Data in the worst possible sequence—completely inverted order—are passed through the processor many times to merge into sequence. Most situations actually lie in between these extremes, for there is usually some order in the data. If two or more sequences exist in the data, each sequence should, of course, be saved and then merged into an over-all sequence.

The basic feature of merge sorting is that it produces a single sequence of items from two or more sequences that are already arranged by the same rules. Viewed in simplest terms, the number of sequences is reduced in each merge-sorting pass corresponding to the number of input tapes used—for example, reduced to one-half for two input tapes—until all the data are arranged in one sequence.

The merge-sorting scheme is frequently used for sorting data stored on magnetic tape. The mechanics of merge sorting are the reading of data from two or more input tapes, arranging the data in sequence on the desired key, and writing the data on output tapes. Longer sequences, which are not limited by processor storage capacity, are developed in each pass through the processor until all items are in one sequence. Merge sorting is easier to follow in detail if only two input and two output tapes are used, and one item at a time is read from and written on a tape as soon as its place in the sequence is determined. The processor follows an instruction program to compare the keys of items received from each input tape with the key of the item just written on the output tape. Actually, longer strings are developed internally and written as a block on tape.

The procedure for merge sorting can be stated simply: build the longest string possible at each stage on an output tape. This requires comparing the preceding item written on that tape and the two items that are available which may be added to the sequence. As each item is written on an output tape, another item is read from the input tape that was the source of the item just written. If it is not possible to continue building the string on one output tape—because both items available are too small—switch to the other output tape and start a new string. In short, a three-way comparison is made each time between two items in storage and the item just added to the sequence.

Merge sorting into ascending sequence is illustrated in Figure 9-2. For simplicity, only the key is shown for each item, but the remainder of the record is assumed to follow the key at every stage. This is not to say that handling the rest of the item is trivial, because considerable detail is involved merely in keeping a record associated with its key. Data movement involved in making internal comparisons can be minimized by forming *key-location* records that consist solely of the key and storage location of each record. The key-location records are sorted into sequence on the key alone, and

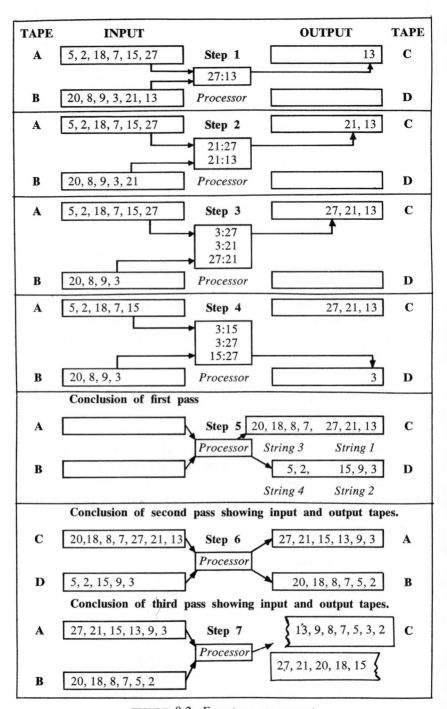

FIGURE 9-2. *Four-tape merge-sort.*

324

the location part is then used to get the record with the corresponding key and write it on tape.

Four-Tape Merge. Merge sorting with four tapes—two input tapes, A and B containing items to be sorted, and two output tapes, C and D—can be illustrated for the following initial conditions:

>**Tape A:** 5, 2, 18, 7, 15, 27
>**Tape B:** 20, 8, 9, 3, 21, 13
>**Tape C:** blank
>**Tape D:** blank

The steps involved in the four-tape merge sorting shown in Figure 9-2 can be described as follows:

1. Read in the first key, 27 and 13, from tapes A and B. Compare 13:27 and write the smaller, 13, on tape C. (See Step 1.)
2. Read in the next key, 21, from tape B and compare with 27 already in storage to find the smaller. If the smaller, 21, is larger than the key, 13, just written on tape C, then write 21 on tape C. (See Step 2.)
3. Read in the next key, 3, from tape B and compare with 27 to select the smaller of the two. If the smaller key, 3, is larger than the key, 21, just written on tape C, then write 3 on tape C. Since 3 is smaller than 21, do not write it, but compare 27 with 21, and write 27 on tape C since 27 is larger than 21. (See Step 3.)
4. Read in the next key, 15, from tape A and compare with 3 to select the smaller. Since 3 and 15 are both smaller than the last number written on C, neither can be used to build that sequence. The smaller, 3, is transferred to tape D to start a new string. (See Step 4.)

The procedure described in Steps 2 and 3 is repeated to build the longest possible sequence on tape D. When the available keys will not increase the sequence, a new sequence is started on the other tape. The first pass is completed when all the items on tapes A and B are transferred to tapes C and D. The first pass gives two strings on each output tape. (See Step 5.)

The output tapes for one pass are input tapes for the next pass. The second pass (tapes C and D are now input) yields one string on each tape. (See Step 6.) The third pass, with tapes A and B as input, arranges the items in one sequence. (See Step 7.)

Alternate output is used to get the same number of strings (plus or minus one) on each tape, but it is not necessary to build each sequence on the alternate tape. For a huge number of items, strings can be written on one tape until it is filled. The other tape is then filled. About the same number of sequences is built on each tape, if there are enough items to fill two or more tapes.

A decision table for the logic of four tape merge-sorting is shown in Table 9-1. The three conditions of the problem—input-key-1 is smaller than input-key-2, input-key-1 will build the sequence on the output tape, and input-key-2 will build the sequence on the out-

DECISION TABLE Form	Table Name **MERGE-SORT**		Page **1** of **1**	
	Chart No. **DT-1**	Prepared by **WILL HARRISS**	Date **OCT 10**	

Stub	Body														
	Rule Number														
Conditions	1	2	3	4	5	6	7	8	9	10	11	12	13	14	15
INPUT-KEY-1 < INPUT-KEY-2	Y	Y	Y	N	N	N									
INPUT-KEY-1 > PRIOR-OUTPUT-KEY	Y	N	N	N	–	Y									
INPUT-KEY-2 > PRIOR-OUTPUT-KEY	–	Y	N	N	Y	N									
Actions															
SWITCH OUTPUT TAPE			X	X											
WRITE INPUT-1 ON OUTPUT TAPE	X		X			X									
READ NEXT-RECORD ON INPUT-TAPE-1	X		X			X									
WRITE INPUT-2 ON OUTPUT TAPE		X		X	X										
READ NEXT-RECORD ON INPUT-TAPE 2		X		X	X										
GO TO MERGE-SORT TABLE	X	X	X	X	X	X									

TABLE 9-1. *Decision table for four-tape merge-sort.*

put tape—are listed at the top of the stub. Here, "input-key-1" means the key of the record read from input tape 1. The actions —write the appropriate input record to build the sequence on the active output tape, read a new input record to replace the one written out, and switch to the inactive output tape when neither input will fit into the sequence on the active output tape—are listed at the bottom of the stub. After each set of actions is completed, the action path returns to the beginning of the table to process the new set of inputs. In actual practice, the complete sorting process would need some tests and actions for the end-of-file conditions on one or both inputs, but such parts are omitted here for simplicity.

In Rule 1, INPUT-KEY-1, the smaller key, is larger than the prior key on the output tape; so INPUT-1 is written and a new record brought in to replace it. Since, in Rule 2, the input with the smaller key will not build the sequence on the output tape, the input with the larger key, which will fit, is written. Rules 3 and 4 cover the case in which neither input record belongs on the current output tape, so the processor switches to the other output tape and writes the input with the smaller key. Rules 5 and 6 are similar to Rules 1 and 2 except that INPUT-2 has the smaller key.

This simple table clearly specifies what actions to take for each set of conditions. It is unnecessary to trace the action path through a series of branches which would be true if flow charts were used. After all the conditions are identified for a particular set of inputs, the correct set of actions follows directly. This particular table is complete in that all possible rules are stated. Since there are three binary conditions, a complete table contains eight rules ($2^3 = 8$). Although the table shown appears to contain only six rules, each rule with a blank for one condition counts for two rules—one rule with a "yes" and one with a "no" for that condition—so the effective total is eight. For analyzing processes of this type, decision tables are likely to be clearer and more consistent than other means.

Three Tapes on First Pass. The merge-sorting example given above assumes that the items are originally stored on two tapes. If the items are on one tape, they are separated or dispersed in the first pass. Two items are read in and comparisons are made to build strings as before. The output of the first dispersion pass starting with one tape corresponds to the result obtained in the illustration involving two tapes. After the first pass, similar procedures are followed for subsequent merge passes.

The merge-sorting procedure described here uses only one item from each tape. A three-way comparison is made between these two items and the item just added to the sequence on one tape. In a processor with fast internal speeds in relation to input-output speeds merge sorting is faster, if more items can be compared at one time because longer strings can be built at each stage. The ultimate, for a machine with fast internal-operating speed and large storage, might be to put all items in storage, sort them into one sequence, and write them in one pass.

Available storage may be filled with the items to be sorted, and later refilled as items are written out in sequence. In this way, the length of each string, counting both key and record, can be about twice as big as the available storage on the first pass. Developing longer strings on the first pass reduces the number of passes required, but increases the number of comparisons. The number of items handled simultaneously depends on available storage, record length, number of tape units, input-output speeds, and programming complexities. Input-output speeds become crucial when data are read in and out through many passes.

More Inputs, Fewer Passes.   Using more than two input tapes permits building sequences faster and reduces the number of passes required for the case where only two inputs are available. With n input tapes (and n is two or more), each pass builds longer strings so that the number of sequences on all the tapes is divided by n. Sorting is complete, of course, when only one string remains. The exact number of passes required depends on the arrangement of data before the sorting operation starts.

The easiest sorting problem occurs when checking the sequence of data from cards sorted into sequences and converted to tape for further processing. The first processor operation may check the sequence of data on tape because of the risk that some cards were out of sequence before conversion. Each tape starts through the merge-sorting procedure and if the input is in sequence, only one output string is obtained, and the sequence is checked. If the input is out of sequence because cards were not correctly sorted before conversion, two or more output strings are obtained from the first pass. Additional passes are then required to build one sequence.

Digital Sorting.   Records on magnetic tape can also be sorted by the digital scheme—as described above for punched-card equipment. One plan is to use a single input tape and ten output tapes corresponding to the ten outputs of a punched-card sorter. On the first pass, items with the right-hand digit 0 are put on one tape, with 1 on another tape, and so forth. Outputs are consolidated in order from 0 to 9 and resorted on the next digit. When ten outputs are combined, the sequence is XXX00 to XXX99 where X represents any digit from 0 through 9. After three more passes, items with five-digit keys are in sequence from 00000 to 99999. One pass is required for each digit in the key regardless of the number of items, when one input and ten output tapes are used. If the key is short and the number of items large, digital sorting may be fastest.

Other Techniques

One approach to the problem of electronic sorting is to arrange items in sequence at an earlier stage—*pre-sorting*. Although this approach does not really solve the sorting problem, the idea of presorting has some merit. Input data might be kept in order as they originate or be sorted before they are put on magnetic tape. Sequence checking might still be desirable, but it can be handled as part of the input-editing routine.

On-line and in-line data-flow plans also eliminate the need for internal sorting during processing since the original sequence of transactions is adhered to.

Items on magnetic tape might be converted to punched cards, sorted by conventional methods, and reconverted to tape for further processing. This scheme involves the cost and time of two conversions. It also increases the possibility of mistakes during sorting, for punched-card sorting is less accurate than processor sorting. Experience shows that one or more cards may be lost or a stack dropped or misplaced in some fashion when numerous cards are involved. Some people say it is impossible, or at least nearly so, to sort a huge number of cards into perfect sequence because too many things can go wrong in the process.

Some data-processing systems avoid sorting by using random-access storage. Data in the master file are quickly available by means of one of several plans. The key for an item may indicate where the record is located in storage. A *table look-up* or *index* may be used to find where a record is stored in order to obtain it. Another plan for placing items in storage and later finding them is to use the *item number* itself as a locator. Some calculations may be performed on the number; for example, squaring the identification number to get a random-like number and selecting the center digits. This approach will convert, say, twenty-digit identification numbers into four-digit numbers and facilitate compact storage.

System Selection

A system designer may want to minimize either the time or the cost of sorting. An efficient system depends on the equipment available, the sorting scheme employed, and the application involved. Important factors about the application are the number of items, length of record, and number of keys—since the items may have to be sorted several times on different keys. Also important are the sequence of the original data, the manner in which data are processed before and after sorting, the speed with which results are wanted, and other functions—editing or checking—that can be combined with sorting.

Sorting data on punched cards is slower, but may be less expensive, than on magnetic tape. Processor sorting is more nearly automatic than punched-card sorting. Less manual effort is involved, which reduces the risk of mistakes. Punched-card sorting may be preferable if data are already on cards and need be sorted only once.

Sorting data one time merely to count one type of item or resorting to accumulate another item is not necessary when a processor is used. Several items can be counted and accumulations made in one pass by the processor with the data arranged in any sequence.

After the data are analyzed, merge-sorting plans can be programmed to take advantage of any sequence already in the data, and partially-ordered data can be sorted with fewer passes than completely unarranged data. A study might show that a set of items wanted in ascending order is already in descending order. Inverting the sequence would be faster than sorting to rearrange, if it is possible to read the input tape while it is moving backwards and write the items out in the desired sequence on another tape, or more simply, merely to process the tape by read-reverse.

Digital sorting, on the other hand, ignores any order in the data and treats every set of items in the same way—any sequence that does exist is destroyed on the first pass. Digital sorting takes the same number of passes whether items are in the desired, inverse, or random order.

The number of merge-sorting passes depends on the number of items and their initial sequence, regardless of the length of the key. Digital sorting, on the other hand, depends on the length of the key, so that lengthy keys increase the number of digital-sorting passes.

An efficient balance is needed between the number of tape units, their arrangement for input and output, programming costs, and processor operating time. Having more input units reduces the number of merge-sorting passes but increases the number of processor comparisons and other operations on each pass. Each pass takes more machine time, but fewer passes are required. Generator routines can analyze the records and "generate" a sorting routine tailored to the application.

SUMMARY

This chapter discusses three major facets of business data processing: editing, file processing, and sorting. Editing during input operations increases the probability that the data are accurate and in suitable form for the processor. Input editing concentrates on getting input transactions into a suitable condition for processing. Thereafter, the input, having been carefully edited during its first processing, ranks as part of the file; and tape-label checking alone is considered adequate for files, unless mistakes are discovered.

Input editing deals with the following facets: field content, accuracy of numeric data, completeness of data, code conversion, item sequence, data field-length, non-numeric symbols in numbers, internal consistency, and the correspondence of new data to data already in files. The first eight types of editing can be done in a pre-processing stage without reference to files, although specifications about the data format and the checking schemes are needed. Checking for correspondence between transaction data and files— say, customer's name and address are identical—requires, of course, availability of the master file.

Elaborate techniques are available for manipulating data on cards to do certain kinds of editing during conversion operations or during read-in to a processor. More often, satellite processors serve as general-purpose converters and editors for data before reaching the main processor. The main processor still performs any editing requiring availability of the master file.

Output editing focuses on the preparation of reports with content and format suited to the users' needs. This involves selecting desired data elements from files and making them readable for people, assigning data elements to appropriate reports, sorting items into sequence, developing major and minor classifications, calculating subtotals and totals, introducing titles and headings, deleting repetitious and distractive elements, and proving the number of items and their values against prior totals. Values in the output can be tested in terms of standards, actuals, or even reasonableness on an intuitive basis. Report generators, which the processor follows in compiling a report-writing program for later execution, facilitate report preparation.

File maintenance is the modification of a file to incorporate additions, deletions, and transfers. Examples are additions to an approved stock list, deletion of discontinued items, transfers between warehouses, and substitution of new facts for old. Inputs for file maintenance are a master file, new changes, pending changes and, of course, a processor program. Outputs are an updated master file, change lists, pending changes, and mismatches. The number of records within a file can be controlled, since the prior number of records, plus records introduced, minus records deleted, equals the current number of records.

File processing is the modification of a file to incorporate changes involving arithmetical operations. A processor program controls operations to read in transactions and master-file records, compare them for stock-number identity, update active stock records and write out a new master file consisting of both active and inactive records. File updating for random-access storage is easier than for tape records because transactions need not be sorted into sequence; and each updated record merely occupies its same space. A variety of transactions can be processed against a file in one run because the transaction-type identifier directs the processor to go to the correct subroutine in the program. Calculation, indirect addressing, and other schemes are used to select the desired part of the program. File maintenance and file processing are often done together.

Preliminary processing is useful, or even vital, in some situations to determine what action to take. For example, a trial pass of all orders against stock files may be needed to develop decision rules about how to fill customers' orders. Then it is possible to process the orders against the file to update it and prepare shipping documents.

The maintenance and processing of magnetic-tape files usually involves recopying the whole file each time some records are changed, but some processing schemes accumulate changes for a few cycles and then rewrite the whole file. Interesting problems arise concerning how long to keep files to enable reconstruction of files lost through erroneous processing at the next cycle and to make analyses for unexpected questions at any time in the future.

Classification of a transaction in terms of the program or file needed for processing—as payroll, stock transactions or the collection and payment of money—is often done before sorting. *Sort-*

ing consists of arranging items into sequence on their keys—fields of characters used to identify or locate an item. Any data element in a record—part number, size, or location—may be used as a key. Records may be sorted on one individual key or on two or more keys—one major and one minor. Commonly-used sorting schemes are block, digital, comparison, and merge sorting. Punched-card equipment uses a digital plan and also "block" to break up large quantities of cards into manageable quantities. Processors generally use the comparison and merge-sorting schemes.

A processor merge-sorts by reading items held in external storage, comparing them in internal storage, and writing them out in longer strings. The process is repeated in succeeding passes until one continuous string is developed. The number of passes required is related to the number of items sorted, regardless of the length of the key. Merge-sorting often uses two or more tapes for input and two or more tapes for output. Satellite processors are useful for sorting if the main processor is heavily loaded and the volume of special types of work is high. High-speed sorting of records in disk storage is possible by using multiple-access arms according to the "cylinder" concept, in which the read-write heads handle all records in all the tracks in one reading position before moving to a new position.

The selection of equipment and sorting scheme depends partly on whether the objective is to minimize the cost of sorting or the time required. Important factors in system selection are the number of items, length of key, length of record, sequence of original data, processing required before and after sorting, available time, and whether other editing or processing functions can be combined with sorting. Sorting with electronic processors is faster and more accurate than punched-card sorting, but it may be more expensive unless the equipment, sorting scheme, and application are closely attuned.

APPENDIXES

Appendix I

QUESTIONS AND PROBLEMS

CHAPTER 1

1. a. Why are data processed? **b.** What is the most important reason? **c.** What operations are included in the processing of data?

2. a. What is the distinction between *data* and *information*? **b.** How can this distinction be used in designing and operating a system?

3. a. Why is it so difficult to solve the problem of deciding precisely what data to gather and store for use in the future? **b.** What is a rational approach toward answering the question, "How much data should we obtain now and save on the chance that we will need it someday"?

4. a. Describe briefly some reporting system with which you are familiar and then answer the following questions. **b.** How satisfactory is the structure of reports judged by the definition of "information" given in the chapter? **c.** Suggest improvements in the report structure. **d.** How much back-up data are retained and how long are they retained primarily for the purpose of dealing with unexpected requests for information? **e.** How frequent and important are such requests? **f.** In view of the frequency and nature of such requests and the penalty that results from not being able to fill them, would it be better to reduce the quantity of back-up data and shorten the retention period?

5. a. What data-processing capabilities does a trained clerk have? **b.** What arithmetical and logical operations can a clerk perform? **c.** How would you reply to the supervisor who demands that clerks originate perfect data—either they should be trained thoroughly and work hard enough to reach perfection, or more checking must be done to make the data perfect?

6. a. What determines the form and method for originating data? **b.** Why not originate data in the precise form and media wanted for input to the processing unit?

7. a. Why verify data? **b.** What are the different kinds of verification and how are they performed? **c.** Does verification assure perfection? If not, why bother to do it? **d.** Would it be feasible to do all the steps in verification when data are first originated so that no problems— errors, incomplete data, etc.—will arise in later stages of processing?

8. What equipment and support are necessary for an electronic data-processing system?

9. **a.** What steps should be taken to evaluate a data-processing system? **b.** What changes in the way business operations are organized and carried out are likely to accompany the introduction of electronic data-processing systems?

10. One proposal for report preparation is to use the same format every time so that the location of an item will not change in each edition of a particular report. A second proposal is to include in a report only those items that have a suitably high information content and omit all other items. Answer and explain the following questions. **a.** Are fixed format reports compatible with high information content? **b.** Which scheme for preparing reports is more efficient? **c.** Which type of report is more efficient for the user? **d.** Which scheme uses the least quantity of paper to print?

11. **a.** Since sorting anything—invoices, checks, or vouchers—into sequence seems such a chore for people or equipment, why not merely avoid doing it when processing data? **b.** What changes would be required in the equipment and techniques used for processing?

12. **a.** Since advanced data-processing systems are likely to accelerate the growth of scientific decision-making and take over routine decisions, the question arises, "What kinds of education and training should be given to a prospective manager?" **b.** Where and how will a junior manager get any practical experience in order to grow into a bigger job by first making small decisions, if the system makes all small decisions but leaves important decisions to senior managers?

13. Random-access files are often claimed to be superior to magnetic-tape files, which are sequential. **a.** What do the terms "random access" and "sequential" mean in this context? **b.** Since random-access files cost more to operate than sequential files, how would you go about selecting the type most suited for an application? **c.** Does it seem compatible to use both kinds of files within one data-processing system? Explain.

14. **a.** What are the differences between historical reports, forecast reports, and action documents? **b.** Name an example of each drawn from the area of production for a company that you are familiar with and describe their content and use. **c.** Similarily, from the area of marketing for a company.

15. **a.** Explain why it is necessary to distinguish between these two facets of time for reports: (1) the frequency of report preparation, and (2) the length of time available after the close of a period (or when a request is made for information) before reports have to be submitted. **b.** What is the practical effect of trying to get immediate or up-to-the-minute reports on everything that is happening throughout an organization? **c.** Why do unexpected and even unscheduled

requests for information pose a difficult problem for a data-processing system? **d.** Why should one turn the question, "Look, we have these kinds of facts on file, what useful reports can we get out of them?" over to statisticians or researchers to try to answer rather than attempt to develop a solution to the question and immediately incorporate it into the data-processing system?

16. An electronic data-processing system reads in its instruction program in just the same form as the data to be processed, whereas a clerk reads (or already knows) operating instructions expressed in words and handles documents containing words and numbers. **a.** How do the processor and the clerk keep the instructions and data separate so that they correctly use each? **b.** What happens if they switch the instructions and data before they use them? **c.** How does a clerk modify the instructions as he works through the data and finally reaches the end? **d.** How does a clerk know which set of instructions to use on the next stack of documents that he receives? **e.** What does a clerk do if a document does not fall within any of the categories that he knows how to handle? **f.** What does an electronic processor do in the unique-document situation?

CHAPTER 2

1. It is possible to punch a hole in any of twelve positions in each column of a punched card. **a.** How many different symbols can be represented by one punch in a column? **b.** How many different symbols can combinations of not more than two punches in a column represent?

2. Packing density is the number of bits or characters in a unit of media. **a.** Compare the packing densities in characters per linear inch for paper tape, magnetic tape, and a track on a magnetic drum. **b.** What is the ratio of the packing density of punched cards to magnetic tape in characters per square inch?

3. Observe the arrangement of alphanumeric characters on a telephone dial. **a.** How many three-letter exchange names can be formed using any combination of letters? **b.** How many three-digit exchange names can be formed? **c.** What increase in the number of possible exchanges is gained by changing from alphabetical to numeric exchange names? **d.** Repeat (a), (b), and (c) for two-letter and two-digit exchange codes. **e.** If numeric exchange names are used, is there any need to keep the letters on the dial? **f.** Will elimination of letters from the telephone dial occur as quickly as the initial introduction of automatic dialing on a local basis? Explain.

4. a. Explain the purpose and use of parity-bits. **b.** How does a simple-parity-bit scheme operate to detect malfunctions? **c.** How does an elaborate scheme operate to detect and correct malfunctions? **d.** Explain how parity-bits might be used on ordinary punched cards.

5. a. What is the relationship of characters, data elements, records, and files for organizing data? **b.** What is the purpose of dividing an item of data into two or more parts (for example, the data element "city-state" can be redefined as "city" and "state")? **c.** Give five other examples of redefinition of one data element into two or more sub-elements that are useful in processing data.

6. a. Is English the "natural" language of an electronic data-processing system? **b.** How might a processor be modified to read and print the 32 characters of the Russian alphabet? **c.** How would the processor sort the Russian characters into sequence?

7. a. Sort the following characters into ascending sequence by using the code collating sequence illustrated in the chapter: P, K, End Data,), #, O, A, $, and *. **b.** Why should numeric data be right-justified and alphabetical data left-justified before sorting? **c.** What scheme would you suggest for a processor to keep the decimal point straight in performing addition operations? Remember that decimal points are not ordinarily shown in punched cards used for data read-in, and even if they were, a processor cannot add numbers containing nonnumeric characters.

8. What sequence of accounts—numeric, alphabetical, or random— will result from the sorting operations performed on customers' accounts in each of the following cases? **a.** Use account number as the key when account numbers are merely assigned sequentially to accounts when they are opened. **b.** Use account name and number (name is major, number is minor) as a combined key for the account number scheme described in (a). **c.** Use account number as the key when account numbers are assigned from a table designed to keep names in alphabetical sequence. The scheme works 99.6 per cent of the time, but 0.4 per cent of the time a pre-assigned number block becomes filled with names, which requires the assignment of numbers from a reserved block at the end of the whole series. **d.** Use account name and number as a combined key for the account numbering scheme described in (c).

9. a. How are items separated on tape and in processor storage when the processor is designed to handle variable-length items? **b.** What kind of addressability of storage is required for a processor designed to handle fixed-length fields? **c.** Variable-length fields? **d.** Selectable length fields?

10. The address element of a customer's record on magnetic tape using the code scheme illustrated in the chapter is given below:

**Channel
number**

7	0 0 0 0 1 0 1 1 1 1 1 1 0 1 1 1 0 1 1 1 1 1 1 0 1 0 0 1 0 1 0
6	1 0 1 0 0 0 1 1 1 1 1 1 1 1 0 1 1 1 0 1 1 1 0 1 1 1 1 0 0 0 1
5	1 1 1 1 1 0 1 0 0 1 1 0 1 1 0 0 0 1 0 0 0 0 1 0 1 0 1 0 0 1 1 1
4	1 0 1 1 1 0 0 1 1 0 0 1 0 0 0 0 0 0 1 0 1 1 0 0 1 1 0 1 0 0 1 1
3	1 1 0 0 0 0 1 1 1 0 1 1 0 0 1 0 0 1 1 0 1 1 1 0 0 1 0 0 0 1 0 1
2	1 1 0 1 0 0 1 0 0 1 1 1 0 1 1 0 0 0 0 0 0 1 0 0 1 0 1 0 0 1 0
1	0 0 1 0 0 0 0 0 1 1 0 0 1 1 1 0 0 1 0 0 1 0 0 0 0 0 1 0 0 1 1 1

There are, for purposes of illustration here, five single-bit errors in recording the address data element.

a. Detect as many errors as you can by means of the column or vertical parity rule (row parity is not used here).

b. Correct as many errors as you can by applying the parity rule.

c. How many more errors could be corrected by means of the row parity rule (in addition to column-parity) if it were used?

d. Correct as many errors as you can by decoding the message (determine each character from the code illustrated in the chapter) and applying what you know about the composition of addresses.

e. What conclusions would you draw about the accuracy of the system—equipment and people—if you were told that this element of a record was the customer's name?

11. The following numbers have a decimal base:

2	64	.5	64.25
4	260	.25	324.75
9	4096	.375	4356.33
17	32768	.4375	36864.9375

a. Convert each number from the decimal to the binary base. (In most cases, one may do the conversion by inspection. Start from the brief description in the chapter and build from your own solutions; e.g., $4356 = 260 + 4096$.)

b. Convert the binary numbers from part (a) to octal. (Octal uses the digits 0, 1, ... 7 to represent binary digits taken three at a time on either side of the binary point: $1_{octal} = 001_{binary}$, $3_o = 011_b$, $7_o = 111_b$, etc.)

c. Convert the numbers from the decimal base to binary-coded decimal. (Each decimal digit, 0, 1, ... 9 is converted to bcd (8421): $3_{decimal} = 0011_{bcd}$, $9_d = 1001_{bcd}$, etc.)

12. What changes will probably occur in data representation, input-output, and processing methods, if data processors and physical operations—selected machines, individual processes, or even a whole factory—are more closely linked as another step toward the "automatic factory"?

13. **a.** Given the following description about manpower data for a manufacturing organization, show how they can be organized from lowest to highest level as data elements, records, and files by using the outline form given below. Show the level numbers similar to those in ordinary outlines, and indicate the *class* (numeric, alphabetic or alphanumeric) and the *size* (average number or range of characters) of each item. For each item that may be repeated, merely describe it once and indicate how many times it may occur. Each possible occurrence must be counted to determine size. Indicate the class and size for only the lowest level description of each item—which may be a data element, sub-element, etc.—so that there is no duplication of description in the outline.

b. Calculate the estimated size of each file that is required and the total file content. Make any reasonable assumptions required about the number of characters in each element and the number of times that each repetitive element occurs—for example, ten children, etc.

I. Name of file.
   A. Name of record.
      1. Name of data element with class, and size (if lowest level).
         a. Name of sub-data element with class, and size (if lowest level).
            (1) Name of sub-sub element with class and size.
               (a) Etc.

The ABC organization has 2600 employees on the active payroll, 1800 work in the main plant located in state *A,* 500 in plant 2 located in state *B,* 100 in sales throughout the United States, and 200 in general administration in state *A*. In addition, there are 150 retired employees still on the employee newsletter mailing list (pensions are handled through a trust); two-thirds reside in state *A* and the others in state *C*. For each active employee, the data on file, although not arranged in any particular order, covers name, address (in the usual detail), social security number, sex, birth date and place; marital status, name of spouse (usual format), sex, birth date and place; name, birth date and sex of each child; number of dependents claimed for tax purposes; participation in medical and hospital plans, family coverage, and amount of deduction each month; savings bond deduction amount for specified weeks in each month, and denomination to purchase when enough is deducted; deduction for specified organizations, amount, and pay periods for deduction (repeated for ten possible deductions); name and address of bank to mail check to, if so requested; department employee assigned to and date assigned; rate of pay and date of change to that rate (repeated for all work assignments and rates for the past ten years or five work assignment changes or rate changes whichever is longer).

Each record for a retired employee consists of his current address and the presently useful part of his active payroll record (which you are to select for purposes of this question) at date of retirement. It also lists his annual total earnings for each of the last five years.

CHAPTER 3

1. **a.** What are the major components of data-processing systems? **b.** What is the flow-path of data among them? **c.** How much freedom does the user have to choose the equipment that he wants at each stage? What is available and how compatible is it with equipment used at other stages?

2. Draw a block diagram showing the relationship between the following elements of a data processor: **a.** input; **b.** internal storage; **c.** arithmetic function; **d.** control function; **e.** output.

3. **a.** What are the control functions in a processor? **b.** How are instructions given to a processor? **c.** Which method is most flexible and why? **d.** If an externally-stored program is difficult to change, why is an internally-stored program not equally difficult?

4. Instructions and data are said to have the same appearance in storage and either can be stored anywhere in an internally-stored program processor. **a.** How can you distinguish between instructions and data to avoid confusion? **b.** What is the meaning of the sentence, "It is useful to modify instructions but it is not meaningful to execute data"? **c.** How can the address part of an instruction be modified? The operation part? **d.** Why is it useful to modify either part of an instruction? **e.** Give an example of address modification and show how it can be used in programming and processing.

5. **a.** For the instruction "SUBTRACT 200, 300," what is the meaning of the explanation, "Subtract the contents of location 200 from the contents of location 300"? **b.** Is the result 100; if not, what is it exactly? **c.** Where is the result located? **d.** Develop an example to show the operation.

6. **a.** What is an *operand*? **b.** How is an operand related to storage locations and the instruction command in one-address instructions? Three-address instructions?

7. a. Explain what function is performed by the following: (1) accumulator; (2) M-Q register; (3) instruction counter; (4) instruction register? **b.** How are the accumulator and M-Q registers used in performing addition and multiplication instructions? **c.** Would it be possible to use both the accumulator and M-Q registers together to perform double-precision addition—addition of operands twice as long as the usual word in storage—by having each register handle one half of an operand?

8. a. What are the steps in an operating cycle to execute one instruction? **b.** Can the console be used efficiently to monitor the execution of one instruction? **c.** What is the function of the console in debugging on the machine, and preparing traces and post-mortems?

9. a. What are the similarities and differences between arithmetical and logical operations? **b.** Give three examples of logical operations and show how they can be used.

10. a. How is it possible to make decisions within a program since it is essentially sequential—instruction-after-instruction—but decision-making may result in skipping forward or backwards ("jump" or "go to") various parts of the program because of conditions that are encountered in a program? **b.** Draw a simple flow chart to illustrate decision-making for joint conditions. For example, accept customer's order *if* no bill exceeding 10 per cent of credit rating is overdue *and* the value of this shipment will not cause his new balance to exceed credit limit. **c.** Draw a simple flow chart to cover the order-credit case described in (b), if the rule is to grant credit to a customer who meets one of the two conditions. **d.** Ambiguity is raised by the condition, "No bill exceeding 10 per cent of the credit rating is overdue." How should you cope with it? (Flow chart symbols are illustrated in Chapter 6.)

11. Explain why it is necessary to eliminate the symbols "$", "," and "." from an item of data before read-in to a processor, if used for **a.** arithmetic operations; **b.** decision-making operations; **c.** merely forming part of the output record?

12. a. What are concurrent operations? **b.** How are they achieved? **c.** What is the practical effect of concurrent operations for processor operations? **d.** What is the importance of trapping from the programmer's viewpoint? **e.** From the program execution viewpoint?

13. Describe and appraise the efficiency of the various schemes used to represent stored data.

14. Define: **a.** stated storage capacity; **b.** effective storage capacity; **c.** access time; **d.** volatility; **e.** word time; **f.** transfer rate.

15. a. What scheme is used to address an element of data in storage organized as fixed-word? **b.** As character-addressable storage? **c.** Under what conditions are absolute addresses useful? **d.** How can symbolic or name-addresses be used in programming since a processor works with numerical addresses only when executing instructions? **e.** What are *data-names* and *procedure-names* and how are they used in addressing data in a program?

16. What is the nature and importance of each of the following for evaluating storage-unit characteristics: **a.** data representation; **b.** addressing scheme; **c.** operating mode; **d.** capacity; **e.** access time?

17. a. For a magnetic drum, how are packing, access, and capacity affected by revolver loops? **b.** Why is it possible for magnetic cores and thin films to operate a hundred or more times as fast as magnetic drums? **c.** Why are combinations of storage used for a processor instead of only one type of storage throughout?

18. a. What are the chief differences between high-speed and bulk storage? **b.** Under what conditions is each useful for processing data? **c.** What is the relationship of bulk drum to high-speed drum storage and to disk in terms of access speed, capacity, and function within a system?

19. a. What storage requirements do disks fill for file processing? **b.** For on-line processing and interrogations that require quick answers to routine questions? **c.** How is access time to records on disk storage reduced by the cylinder concept of data storage when each diskface has one or more read-write heads? **d.** How might disks be used in conjunction with tapes for efficient sorting of large volumes of data by means of the cylinder concept?

20. a. What is the purpose and the effect on data density, read-write speeds, and organization of data in blocks of the inter-block gap on magnetic tape? **b.** Explain how the following contribute to tape operating efficiency: read-write speed, density, transfer rate, read backwards, rewind speed, tape swaps, search.

21. Explain how the following factors affect the selection of storage equipment: **a.** type of processing; **b.** size of file; **c.** time limit for processing and interrogation rate; **d.** cycle up-dating; **e.** retention period and selective condensation and discard.

22. Internal storage capacity has increased over the years while access times have decreased. **a.** What is the effect of this dual change on practical capabilities of processors? **b.** One might speculate that a suitable design objective is to keep the product of storage capacity and access time roughly constant. Would keeping this product constant mean that effective storage capacity of processors for handling data will remain almost constant? Explain.

CHAPTER 4

1. **a.** What are the steps in the chain of activities leading up to data input to a processor? **b.** What is the distinction between *symbols* and *data* in this context? **c.** Why is an *event* the basis for starting the data input operation?

2. **a.** Describe an example of data origination that you are familiar with to illustrate the steps in the activities leading to data input to a processor. **b.** Show how the performance of each of these steps can be improved. **c.** How much combining of these steps is feasible if important changes in system design are permitted?

3. **a.** What are the advantages of originating data in a form suitable for processing as a by-product of another operation? **b.** What is the net effect on system efficiency? **c.** What are the audit control features of remote by-product preparation of data when the machine operator is excluded from the tape room (the input keyboard is wire-connected to a tape punch in a central room) and therefore never sees the by-product output?

4. **a.** What is meant by *prior* or *advance preparation* of data?
b. Under what conditions is prior preparation of data input useful?
c. What is the feasibility of prior preparation when your organization has sole control over the data media at all stages (for example, time cards and inventory tags), and when your organization shares control with others (for example, checks and public utility bills)?
d. What spoilage rate and reconstruction costs are permissible, yet can still make prior preparation worthwhile?

5. **a.** What are the advantages of on-line data input? **b.** What problems does on-line input pose in trying to keep processors operating at capacity?

6. **a.** Since equipment is available, or can be developed, for converting data from one medium to almost any other, or a satellite processor can be used, why should a system designer worry about data incompatibility? **b.** What are the merits of direct data conversion—as from punched cards to processor—instead of an indirect scheme—punched cards or tape to magnetic tape and then to processor?

7. **a.** Obtain copies of bank checks printed for MICR (magnetic-ink character recognition) and study them to determine what characters are specially printed on a check when first issued by the bank and after it is paid by the bank. **b.** Are the characters readable in both cases? **c.** What are the chief features of the MICR scheme? **d.** How much advance preparation of checks is possible with this approach to bank automation? **e.** What features would an optical character-

reading system need to have in order to compete with the magnetic-ink system? **f.** What combination of circumstances, as you view the situation, caused bank automation to become a reality only in the 1960's in view of the fact that punched cards were widely used starting about 1920 or 1930?

8. a. What features are required in a data-collection system to make it suitable for use in a job shop factory? **b.** What are the merits of installing and using a factory data-collection system? **c.** How many other features would have to be built into a data-collection system in order for it to be able to communicate operating instructions about the next job to the machine operator? (Consider the central processor's capabilities to store data about men, machines, and jobs in order to calculate what to schedule next.) **d.** How closely does a factory data-collection system approach the automatic factory? **e.** What else would be required to warrant the name "automatic factory?"

9. a. What is the relationship between a satellite processor and the main processor? **b.** What are the merits of a satellite processor for input-output conversion instead of a number of specialized media converters to handle conversions between the processor, cards, magnetic tapes, and printers?

10. a. Assuming typical densities and inter-record gaps, how much tape is required during the initial card-to-tape conversion to record the content of 30,000 cards punched in all columns, if the card-to-tape converter writes the data from each card as a separate record? **b.** If the satellite processor used for conversion has 10,000 characters of storage for data and program and it forms long data blocks before writing on tape? **c.** If blocked records are superior to unblocked records, why not combine all records into one super-block? **d.** What determines the practical upper limit to block length?

11. Explain the implications for processing speeds of each of the following features of magnetic tapes: **a.** long or short interblock gaps; **b.** unblocked and blocked records; **c.** vertical parity-bit for each character; **d.** horizontal-parity check word for each record or block; **e.** concurrent "read-process-write" or "overlapped" operations; **f.** high-speed rewind; **g.** read-reverse; **h.** back-space in order to read a prior record (but no read-reverse feature); **i.** back-space and reread a faulty record as many as five times before halting operations.

12. People are sometimes considered too slow and unreliable to operate on-line keyboards for data input. **a.** How does multiplexing cope with the speed and accuracy problems? **b.** What functions do special devices—agents' desk sets, bank tellers' machines, and others—perform to facilitate manual inquiry and output? **c.** What is the purpose of providing remote interrogation of, and data input to, a processor file via a communication network?

13. **a.** What part does the document or report format—headings, lines, number of characters, sub-totals, and blank spaces—play in determining the speed of editing, output, and printing? **b.** What is the effect on report format and printing speeds of adopting a perfectly uniform format so that the same item will appear in just the same position on every report to facilitate the reader's finding the item that he wants to study? **c.** How would you choose between the constant report format described in (b) and a variable format that emphasizes off-standard performance and omits items that are on-standard? (Consider the user's problems of reading voluminous reports or searching through shorter reports that may not contain the desired items.)

14. Explain how the following factors are balanced out in trying to design an efficient communication scheme: **a.** volume of data to be transmitted; **b.** number of origin and destination points; **c.** time limits within which data must be transmitted; **d.** degree of reliability required; **e.** media containing the data at origin point and media wanted at destination; **f.** capacity of the communication channel; **g.** the need for on-line processing and immediate reply of current information to interrogators.

CHAPTER 5

1. **a.** What are the steps in systems analysis? **b.** Why is it any more important or difficult to determine the outputs that users want than it is to do the other steps?

2. Explain the meaning of each of the following terms related to systems analysis: **a.** event; **b.** event chain; **c.** station; **d.** data collection sheet; **e.** editing; **f.** station characteristics; **g.** network load analysis; **h.** document activity analysis.

3. **a.** What are the objectives of systems analysis? **b.** How do they differ from the objectives of any other kind of analysis? **c.** What factors determine how much analysis is worthwhile for a company that has just completed installation of a radically new and improved system? **d.** How much analysis is suitable for a company that has not made any important changes in its system in twelve years?

4. **a.** What work is involved in the systems analysis and approaches to design phases of developing a new system? **b.** Since the selection of a design approach may be important for guiding systems-design work, why not choose a design approach first in order to minimize the analysis work that is done for no useful purpose? Explain. **c.** If

the design approach is selected in advance with no possibility of change, can the new system be designed immediately without analyzing the existing system? Explain.

5. Some observers say that initial estimates of new system benefits are usually too high and costs too low. **a.** What is the meaning of this statement and under what circumstances is it likely to be true? **b.** If you were responsible for appraising and selecting proposals to develop new systems, how would you apply this observation in accepting or rejecting individual proposals? **c.** How does the statement, "Note that the criterion for continuing or stopping analysis and design work is not how much has been spent to date; but is how much will be spent to completion," correspond with what you know about decisions to continue or stop systems work?

6. Systems analysts were told that the frequency of processing was "as required" for certain kinds of documents. Document activity analysis and file analysis indicated a disproportionate fraction of as-required processing. Further investigation disclosed that people meant documents were not processed if there were no documents either because of a delay in receipt or because no transactions had occurred, and that a daily or weekly schedule was ordinarily followed.

a. How is it possible to describe processing schedules when replies of this type are obtained?

b. What would be the effect on system design if this unusual definition of "as required" was not discovered?

c. What is the practical effect of the two no-processing situations upon the workload for the following day or week?

d. Should delayed processing be adopted so that a small backlog of transactions of each type awaiting processing can be built to help keep the processing load steady by filling the gaps in receipt of transactions? Explain.

e. If a small backlog is used to keep the processor workload steady, what is the effect on timeliness of reports?

7. a. What is a *flow list*? **b.** How is it related to events, documents, files, outputs and stations? **c.** Why is a flow list superior to a flow chart when one picture is often said to equal ten thousand words? **d.** Can flow charts be developed from flow lists? Flow lists from charts? Explain. **e.** How are gaps or breaks in the event chain discovered from flow lists? From flow charts?

8. a. What are the important features of automated analysis of a system? **b.** How does automated analysis differ from traditional systems and procedures analysis? **c.** Why go to all the bother of interviewing people and obtaining copies of forms when it is possible to analyze a system automatically?

9. Two definitions of file redundancy are that it exists (1) if two or more files make common use of the same document(s), and (2) if they are based solely on an identical set of documents.

a. What is the nature of forms-to-file redundancy?

b. Reconcile these two definitions.

c. Is it possible for two files based solely on an identical set of documents not to be redundant from the user's viewpoint? Explain.

d. Why, and under what conditions, does file redundancy have merit for operating purposes?

e. Would it be possible and feasible to eliminate file redundancy by having only one file that contains all transaction data in original raw form for analysis and presentation when information is wanted? Explain the merits and demerits of this scheme.

10. a. Why is it important to consider selecting an approach to systems design before starting the actual design work? **b.** What are the essential features of each of the four approaches to design discussed in the chapter? **c.** What are the consequences for the system designer of a broad degree of freedom when selecting an optimum approach to design? **d.** What is the optimum approach if freedom is small or nil?

11. Describe in moderate detail the analysis and design-approach selection work for a system that you have first hand experience or some familiarity with. Answer with explanations the following questions:

a. Was the analysis group set up with a sufficiently high-level and explicit charter and enough manpower and money to cover the work it was supposed to do?

b. Did the analysis group adequately examine all fruitful areas? Over-examine any?

c. Did the approach to system design most likely to be selected have any bearing on the initial analysis phase? On subsequent phases?

d. Were the facts obtained by analysis efficiently organized in flow charts, tables, or other forms for use in selecting a design approach and later designing the system?

e. How much analysis work was wasted because improvements were not possible in a particular area or a prior decision had been made to proceed along a certain path?

f. What steps should and could have been taken to make the analysis and design selection work more efficient?

12. Explain the effect on systems analysis and design of the following changes: **a.** Important improvement in communication techniques or data-processing equipment. **b.** Increase in complexity of the business by acquisition of new factories, introduction of new products, and expansion into new markets. **c.** Increased competition from improved services on products and lower prices of competitors.

d. Reduction in the data-processing budget because management believes the company cannot afford the usual outlay.

13. A company packs its four-digit-product code number full of information; one digit indicates material, another the season the product was introduced, and two indicate style. Some near-duplicate numbers occur occasionally—for example, 6435 and 4435—which leads to much confusion when a mistake occurs in the original code number that causes it to become another legitimate number. The cards used for order processing and stock control are full, so there is no spare column to introduce a check digit.

    a. What changes can you suggest to increase accuracy in handling customers' orders to minimize mistakes in keypunching product code numbers, quantities ordered, and other numeric items?

    b. How can processing operations be controlled to guard against the loss of cards or the erroneous duplication of any cards spoiled in the card reader or in other machines during processing?

14. The head of the systems department for a company with nation-wide sales outlets suspects that local and state sales and excise taxes are probably calculated incorrectly in branch offices and overpaid.

    a. What kind of mistake is involved?

    b. How would you obtain facts to answer his suspicions?

    c. What action should be taken if he is correct and taxes are overpaid?

    d. If he is incorrect and taxes are paid correctly or underpaid?

    e. The company is planning to consolidate order-processing and invoicing on a nation-wide basis at its new data-processing headquarters. One analyst suggests that the center follow existing methods and simply ignore any inaccurate calculation of local taxes. Appraise this suggestion for feasibility and practicality.

    f. What points concerning when and how much systems analysis and the accuracy of data are illustrated by this small facet of a system? For example, how much should the company spend in cases (c) and (d) to determine the true situation?

15. **a.** What is an audit trail? **b.** What changes in auditing procedure are likely to accompany the widespread use of processors? **c.** Can you visualize processing procedures that do not use or make any hard copy? **d.** What changes in auditing procedures would be required to cope with the lack of hard copy? **e.** What is the relationship of the audit trail to manual, punched-card, and electronic-processing methods?

16. A new check-digit scheme is proposed for detecting and correcting mistakes in any digit and transpositions of adjoining or alternate digits. The plan is simply to multiply each digit in a number by its digit position counting from the decimal point to the left 1, 2,

3 . . . *n,* sum the products, and attach the total to the number.
a. Illustrate the scheme for the number 728643 and show how long the check digit(s) need to be for ten-digit numbers.
b. Show how this scheme will detect and permit correction of the number 738643.
c. What control does the scheme furnish over accuracy of the check digits themselves?
d. Does this scheme have the detection and correction features that are described for it?
e. Compare this scheme with a roughly similar one described in the text and appraise their merits and weaknesses.

CHAPTER 6

1. a. What bearing do input and output requirements have on systems design? **b.** Do output requirements or the available inputs deserve more emphasis in systems design? Explain. **c.** If a system can be described precisely in terms of its inputs and outputs, why is any consideration given to the processing operations between input and output?

2. a. What is the relationship between reporting requirements and file design?
b. Explain *timeliness* of reports and show how it affects file design.
c. What factors should be considered in designing an efficient file structure?

3. a. How are unexpected requests for information planned for in designing files? **b.** Develop an example to illustrate the definition of "efficiency of file design" described in the chapter. **c.** Develop and illustrate a better measure of efficiency, if possible.

4. a. Evaluate the following statement: "Concentration on data inputs, when designing a system, is incorrect because it is based on the assumption that if enough data enter a system, the desired results are *pushed* out. Instead, concentration on outputs is correct because their careful definition will cause the necessary data to be *pulled* into the system." **b.** If not satisfactory, develop a superior statement of the design relationship between inputs and outputs.

5. a. Why should long-run systems objectives be spelled out when starting design work? **b.** What are the sources of information about systems objectives? **c.** Who establishes systems objectives?

6. a. What is a *run diagram*? **b.** What is the function of run diagrams? **c.** What level of detail does a run diagram have? **d.** Draw a run diagram for an application you are familiar with.

7. a. What is the purpose of *structure flow charts*? **b.** What is the relationship between run diagrams and structure flow charts? **c.** How can a structure flow chart be drawn without taking equipment into account and still be useful in systems-design work?

8. Explain how each of the following is shown on flow charts: **a.** main flow of data; **b.** identification of blocks, documents and files; **c.** quantity of items handled at each stage; **d.** repetitive loops; **e.** branching; **f.** merging; **g.** connectors; **h.** reuse of a file in a following run.

9. a. Study the run diagram and flow charts in the chapter and describe the ambigous situations, mistakes, or duplications in them. **b.** Redraw any flow charts that you can clarify, correct, simplify or improve. State your assumptions in making any changes.

10. A manager of a programming and analysis staff says that one of his most difficult problems is to get people to document their work so that program maintenance work can be done easily several months later by the same programmer or by another one, in case the original programmer is not available. What suggestions can you offer to solve this almost-universal problem?

11. a. Why does the number of flow charts required at each successive level of detail increase so much? **b.** Can this number be reduced efficiently? **c.** How big (or small) a gap should exist between the most detailed flow chart and the program to be prepared from the flow chart?

12. a. What is a feasibility study? **b.** What are the differences between feasibility studies in data processing and another area, such as the acquisition of plant machinery and equipment? **c.** How does a feasibility study differ from a casual or once-over-lightly examination?

13. a. What are the advantages of including representatives from different areas of the organization in the feasibility study group? **b.** Why should a feasibility study group divide its attention between new equipment and the data-processing system? **c.** Under what conditions would you expect to find a feasibility study group rationally concentrating almost exclusively on either new equipment or the data system?

14. a. When considering proposed changes for a system, why are cost reductions much easier to appraise than improvements in the value of information obtained for management and operating purposes? **b.** Devise general rules for the introduction of a new system and equipment when cost reductions seem almost certain, but it is unlikely that the information obtained from the data system will be improved. **c.** Show how these rules apply to some representative applications.

15. Two plans exist for introducing a new system. One scheme is to select one area at a time, convert it individually and, finally, integrate all areas. A second scheme is to start with a small fraction of all areas, convert them at the same time and, finally, expand them to handle the whole load in all areas.
a. What are the merits of the two plans during initial stages of system conversion?
b. Which plan is better for coping with the problem that continuing changes in business policy and operating practices usually plague systems design and installation work?
c. Which plan is better for building solid, practical experience in the organization? Explain.

16. a. What is the purpose of an applications study? **b.** What is involved in making an applications study and selecting equipment? **c.** How are the feasibility study and the applications study related?

17. a. Why is an applications study focused on specific data-processing jobs? **b.** Is it possible and useful to make an applications study in general terms or for a hypothetical situation without regard to actual applications? Explain.

18. Explain what consideration should be given to each one of the following points in the manufacturer's proposal: **a.** rent or purchase option; **b.** maintenance service; **c.** education and training of user's staff; **d.** equipment-design changes before and after installation; **e.** precise units, models, and capacities of equipment proposed; **f.** "software" package—compilers, generators, utility routines, etc.; **g.** machine time for testing user's programs before and after delivery of equipment.

19. a. What factors must be considered in evaluating equipment? **b.** How can various excesses and deficiencies in equipment capabilities be weighed to select the best-suited equipment? **c.** Where does the ultimate responsibility for equipment acquisition rest within an organization?

20. a. What steps are involved in selecting equipment? **b.** How should a prospective user communicate his requirements to a manufacturer? **c.** What should an equipment manufacturer cover in his proposal? **d.** How are a user's *desires* for certain features in equipment separated from his *demands*? **e.** Who is responsible, the user or equipment manufacturer, if the systems—both hardware and "software"—do not meet the time schedules and performance standards agreed upon when equipment was ordered?

21. a. Why should a review of operations be started soon after conversion to a new system? **b.** Evaluate the following statement: "Our system doesn't need to be reviewed because, with the aid of the equipment manufacturer and experienced consultants, we designed the most efficient system possible before we ordered our equipment."

22. Test the flow chart in Figure 6-7 for inventory-file reading and balance updating by tracing through its application to several different situations. Determine the number of times that each path is followed and balance these against the number of master records and transactions. (One way to do this is to simulate the processing operations and tally on the chart each path as it is used.) Master-file contents to use in each of these cases are limited to stock record numbers: 1, 2, 3, 5, and 8.
Case **a.** Stock transactions for stock record number and type: 2 issue, 5 receipt, 5 issue, and 8 purchase order (in that sequence).
Case **b.** Transactions: 2 issue, 5 receipt, 5 issue, 3 receipt, and 8 purchase order.
Case **c.** Transactions: 2 issue, 5 issue, 5 receipt, 5 purchase order, and 7 receipt.
Case **d.** What other master record and transaction situations should be tested through this flow chart to determine its validity?
Case **e.** Redraw the flow chart to eliminate any bugs that you can find.

23. Explain the meaning of each of the following terms related to decision tables: **a.** condition; **b.** action; **c.** rule; **d.** limited entry; **e.** extended entry; **f.** Else-rule.

24. **a.** How can the sequence numbers assigned to rules be used to simplify the writing of rules and the order of execution? **b.** In what sequence are actions performed? **c.** How do rules relate conditions and actions?

25. This question pertains to the decision tables illustrated in the chapter: **a.** What effect would switching ">" and "<" in Rules 2 and 8 have on the solution logic? **b.** What effect would omission of Rule 5 have on the solution logic? **c.** Omission of Rule 9? **d.** If an Else-rule should be included in this table, what conditions and actions would be appropriate for it?

26. Calculate the number of rules needed to handle all the possible combinations of C conditions in a decision table, each of which may have entries of "Y" or "N": **a.** $C = 2$; **b.** $C = 4$; **c.** $C = 7$; **d.** $C = 10$. Repeat if three entries "Y," "N," and "–" are permissible for **e.** $C = 2$; **f.** $C = 5$; **g.** $C = 10$.

27. Revise the decision table illustrated in the chapter to write two output master-file records, one for the updated active-inventory-item records and a second for the inactive-inventory-item records.

28. Revise the decision table illustrated in the chapter to handle insertion of new catalogue items, transaction type 6, in the master-file record.

29. A fire completely destroyed building 10 and its contents. Building 11 was damaged with complete loss of contents from aisle 25 upwards and 60 per cent smoke and water damage to the remaining contents. The insurance company wants a detailed listing based on the inventory master-record form in the chapter: stock number, name, quantity on hand, unit cost, fraction of loss, and dollar amount of loss for each stock item suffering a loss of 100 dollars or more. For items with smaller losses, the insurance company requests that merely the number of items and dollar amount of loss occuring in each building be accumulated. Prepare a decision table to make the fire-loss listings, as specified.

CHAPTER 7

1. a. What are the essential steps involved in programming? **b.** How do they differ from the steps in merely preparing instructions telling an experienced person how to do the job?

2. For the program on how to reach a friend's home given in the chapter, many points are implicit.
a. Rewrite the program with a *completely explicit* data description and procedures description. ("Completely explicit" means that all details are handled for the level of detail that is selected as suitable, not that every conceivable detail or contingency is covered.)
b. What details and contingencies are likely to cause your program to fail to work and when will they be discovered?
c. Show how these weaknesses can be handled: higher degree of detail, cover more contingencies, pre-test the program yourself, ask your friend to pre-test it, or let him try it and call for help in case of trouble.

3. Explain what the following terms used for programming mean: **a.** subset of English language; **b.** macro-level; **c.** translation; **d.** sequence; **e.** execution; **f.** interpret; **g.** compile.

4. a. What is a problem-oriented language and how does it differ from a machine-oriented language? **b.** How is a problem-oriented language useful since there are many different kinds of problems and many different kinds of machines?

5. Explain the meaning of each of the following terms used with COBOL: **a.** data division; **b.** procedure division; **c.** data-name; **d.** procedure-name; **e.** compiling run; **f.** execution run.

6. The level numbers assigned to a stock record are the same as in the chapter, except as follows:

02	WAREHOUSE-LOCATION
04	BUILD-NO
05	AISLE-NO
06	BIN-NO
03	UNIT-COST
04	STOCK-VALUE

a. What effect do these differences have on the organization of data? **b.** What changes occur in the single-element, group-element arrangement? **c.** What element(s) will be obtained by an instruction that refers to (1) BUILD-NO; (2) UNIT-COST; (3) WAREHOUSE-LOCATION; (4) BIN-NUMBER; (5) UNIT-VALUE?

7. **a.** If a programmer can select and use any data-names and procedure-names he wants, what prevents confusion within each group and between the two groups? **b.** What are the rules for writing pictures of data? **c.** Why must data used for calculations have numeric pictures?

8. Prepare a data description for customer-account records containing the following elements (in no particular order) on a COBOL-1 programming form and making necessary assumptions that are compatible: (1) customer name; (2) address for billing purposes; (3) address for shipping purposes (if different); (4) salesman; (5) sales territory; (6) sales to customer for "season history" (each season in current and preceding year); (7) date and amount of first order for season history; (8) returns in units and dollar amount for season history; (9) two most recent credit ratings by Dun & Bradstreet and by the company's own credit department; (10) account-balance high and low amount for season history; (11) dollar-days (dollar amounts X days overdue) for invoices now overdue 30 days and 90 days; (12) current balance of account; and (13) open-to-buy balance—that is, credit authorization minus current balance of account minus orders on hand to be filled.

9. Show the general form and illustrate the operation by means of simple numerical examples using appropriate data-names for each of the following instructions: **a.** ADD GIVING; **b.** ADD TO; **c.** SUBTRACT FROM GIVING; **d.** DIVIDE INTO GIVING; **e.** MULTIPLY.

10. **a.** How is decimal-point alignment handled in input data and inside the processor? **b.** How are the decimal points handled in the three numbers involved in the multiplication operation? **c.** What steps are used to assure that the desired number of digits are retained in a result without losing any significant digits?

11. **a.** How are decision-making choices written in a program? **b.** Show how the three conditional expressions—greater than, equal to, and

less than—can be used in the format of the IF-THEN instruction, which has only two outlets. **c.** What is the relationship between conditional expressions, truth or falsity of expressions, and statements in an IF—THEN instruction? **d.** Why and how are imperative statements included in IF—THEN instructions?

12. For the example discussed in the chapter, develop a program—flow chart, data description, and a procedures description—to determine the following:

a. Number of stock records in the inventory file.

b. Total number of all units on hand for all inventory items ignoring the differences in unit of measure.

c. Total value of all stock items.

d. Number of stock items with unit-cost below $10.00 and above $100.00.

e. Calculate a "hash total" of all stock-record numbers in the inventory file. Show how the total can be updated during file-maintenance runs (when catalogue changes are made) to prove against a new hash total calculated before the next processing cycle to guard against incorrect entry or elimination of a file record.

13. a. For the stock-record file described in the chapter, design an output record to show the number of line items on hand, total number of inventory units on hand, and average dollar value on hand per stock item. **b.** Prepare a program to produce this output record.

14. a. Redesign the stock-record file described in the chapter to contain reorder point and reorder quantity. **b.** Design an output message format (assuming new order can be placed at prior unit cost shown in record) to show the following:

ITEM ORDERED _____ QUANTITY _____ EST-COST _____

c. Write a program to prepare this output message for each stock item below the reorder point. **d.** Describe how to modify the program to restrict the placing of orders to the first X items that should be ordered. **e.** Describe how to modify the program to restrict placing orders for those items resulting in the largest dollar-cost orders, yet remain within a financial limit set by the controller.

15. a. Design a simple customer-account record. **b.** Write a program to check whether the file is in order (assume the file is prepared in an appropriate medium and sorted into sequence). Write out a message FILE IN ORDER or count the number of records out of order (in relation to the immediately preceding record) and prepare the following record:

_____ RECORDS OUT OF ORDER.

16. a. Starting with the stock-record description in the chapter, develop appropriate data descriptions for receipts and issues transactions. **b.** Assuming that the two types of transactions are available as two files, each in sequence, draw a flow chart for updating the stock record, if not more than one receipt and one issue have occurred for each stock item. **c.** Prepare a program to update the stock record.

17. **a.** Design a master record for employees to contain name, number, department, starting date, rate, and 200 other alphanumeric characters. **b.** Design a "new hires" transaction record with appropriate data elements. **c.** Draw a flow chart to merge hires records into master-record file. (Assume any sequence wanted for each file.) **d.** Write a COBOL program to merge hires into the master file.

18. This question makes use of the employee master record required for the preceding question. **a.** Design an employee termination record with appropriate data elements. **b.** Draw a flow chart to eliminate terminated employee records from master-record file and write them in a termination-record file. (Assume any sequence wanted for each file. Provide for erroneous employee numbers in termination records.) **c.** Write a COBOL program to eliminate terminated employee records from master file.

19. **a.** Draw a flow chart to handle new hires and employee terminations described in the preceding two questions to update the employee master file in one pass. **b.** Write a COBOL program to update the master file.

20. **a.** How are files organized into three levels for COBOL purposes? **b.** Describe a record you are familiar with that contains at least twenty data elements and show two ways that these elements can be organized for file processing. **c.** How are single and group elements related to a record for file organization purposes?

CHAPTER 8

1. **a.** What is the instruction format for WORDCOM? **b.** What is each character used for in an input-output instruction? **c.** In an indexing instruction? **d.** In an arithmetic instruction?

2. Explain the operation of the following instructions from the programmer's viewpoint: **a.** RECyxxx; **b.** WTtyxxx; **c.** CAAyxxx; **d.** ADDyxxx; **e.** JMPyxxx; **f.** RWt.

3. The following instructions are supposed to make WORDCOM read in 120 words of data from tape and 20 words from cards and then duplicate them in the same media so that two copies are available:

RT3 160	PNC 180	
REC 170	RW3	
REC 180	WT3 160	
PNC 170	WT3 220	

a. What will this program procedure actually do?
b. Point out the mistakes in the intended routine.
c. Write the routine correctly.

4. **a.** How are index registers used to control the number of times that cycles are performed? **b.** What causes a program to leave the cycle after it is executed the desired number of times? **c.** Which instructions can a programmer use to alter, and in what way, the contents of an index register in WORDCOM?

5. **a.** What is an effective address? **b.** How is an effective address formed? **c.** Why and how are instructions written with effective addresses? **d.** What does effective addressing do to the instruction and to the index register involved?

6. A routine using an index has five elements: set up or *initialize* index, *compare* index to a criterion, *increase* the index count, *perform* the operations specified in the main program, and *go to* the location specified for repeat or exit from the loop.
a. In what sequence are these elements used in the illustrations involving cycle counting in the chapter?
b. A program is supposed to add ten numbers that are available on ten cards—one number per card. Write two different logical versions of a program with different sequences for the indexing and operating elements after setting the index, such as (1) increase, count, operate, test, and jump; and (2) operate, test, jump, and count.
c. If a loop in the main program is occasionally supposed to be performed zero times (that is, not at all), what sequence of elements and what criterion should be used to guard against performing the main program one time before testing the index content?

7. **a.** List the conditions necessary for the use of each kind of comparison instruction described in the chapter. **b.** State the instructions that must follow each kind of comparison instruction in order to handle each condition.

8. **a.** What are the three types of jump instructions? **b.** Give an example of each. **c.** What provision is required in a program to make the jump operate?

9. Answer the following questions about the multiplication operation for WORDCOM: **a.** What set-up operation is required? **b.** Where is the multiplier placed initially and how is it used during multiplication? **c.** How long is the product and where is it located? **d.** How is the product stored?

10. **a.** Where is the assumed decimal point located in the product after a multiplication operation? **b.** Develop a general rule for the location of decimal points for the multiplication operation.

11. a. Write a program to read and punch ten cards. **b.** Draw a flow chart for the program to read and punch 2000 cards. **c.** Write the program for (b).

12. a. Write a program to read two blocks of data on tape that contain records of ten words each and punch cards containing one record each. **b.** Draw a flow chart for the program to read 10,000 blocks of data from tape and punch a ten-word record in each card. **c.** Write the program for (b).

13. Suppose the problem is to find the total value of 200 stock items on cards with the stock value punched in word 6. **a.** Write a program to summarize the stock value and punch in word 2 of a new card. **b.** What will the program do, if there are only 199 instead of 200 cards? **c.** If there are 201 cards instead of 200?

14. For a deck of cards containing stock number, quantity, and unit cost in words 1, 2, and 3, respectively, the problem is to calculate the value on hand for each item and punch a new deck containing the original three words plus stock value in word 4. Also, punch a summary card with the *number* of stock-record cards processed in word 3 and the *total value* of stock on hand in word 4.
a. Draw a flow chart for the program.
b. Write the program. State any compatible and consistent assumptions you need to solve the problem.

15. Repeat the prior question but restrict the calculation, card punching, and summarizing to items having a value on hand exceeding $100 each. **a.** Draw a flow chart for the program. **b.** Write the program with provision for the possibility of overflow.

16. Write a program to unpack each of the following items stored together in one word:

> JR 3 782 S
> *Storage location in warehouse*
> *Quantity in stock*
> *Item description*

17. The following three versions of a program procedure are supposed to total the quantity of units in stock where the item record contains five words with the quantity in the third word. There are 110 inventory items stored in locations 200 and following. Location 099 contains zero, location 100 contains 550, location 101 contains 110, location 102 contains 445, and the main program continues in location 125.

Location	Version 1	Version 2	Version 3
060	SISA099	SISA100	SISC102
061	CAAA200	CAAB204	INCC005
062	ADDA205	ADDB209	CISC099
063	INCA005	CISB099	JMPC125
064	CISA099	INCB004	CAAC203
065	JMP 060	JMP 062	ADDC208
066	JMP 061	JMP 065	

a. Trace through one cycle of each version of the program.

b. Describe the plan in each version for dealing with each item in turn.

c. Revise the nearest correct version of the program so that it is correct.

d. Draw a flow chart and write a program following a different plan to meet the problem requirements.

18. This question deals with the program example in the chapter to read tape records, calculate stock value, summarize stock value, write tape records, and punch a summary card.

a. Why is provision made for accumulator overflow and what will cause it to occur in this program?

b. What are the operating consequences of overflow?

c. If overflow occurred three times before the end of program was reached, how many subtotal or total cards would the program punch?

d. Write a program just to summarize these total cards to find total value. (Hint: Shift each total right one place, summarize and adjust for the shift. Or split each total into two parts, summarize the two parts and put them back together—double-precision addition.)

19. This question deals with the card sequence-check example in the chapter.

a. How many cards will the program handle if all are in sequence?

b. What is the effect on the number of cards read and converted to tape if one card in fifty is out of sequence and one card in a hundred is a duplicate?

c. Revise the program to use an index register to count the number of duplicate cards.

d. Can WORDCOM unload the content of the index register used in (c) so that the number of out-of-sequence cards is available for use? If not, define a new instruction for the designers to build into WORDCOM II to unload an index register.

e. Revise the program to use a storage location for keeping count of the number of duplicate cards. (Hint: Assign a storage location to keep count, and initially load it with zeros. Then include the following steps in each cycle involving a duplicate card: Clear accumulator and add the prior count, add 1, and store current count back in the same location.)

20. This question deals with the load-program example in the chapter.
a. What is the merit of using the contents of location 030 to set index register A?
b. What are the risks involved, since location 030 has an active instruction?
c. Can this load program be run a second time (for another program) without another read-in? Explain.
d. What will happen, if the transfer instruction in the main program being run is punched "—" instead of "+"?
e. Rewrite the load program to cure any real risk pointed out in (b) above and also relocate the whole load-program in the high end of storage—locations 999 and immediately below.

21. Explain the relationship between the following features of FIELD-COM and WORDCOM: **a.** storage capacity; **b.** organization of storage; **c.** length of a word and length of a field; **d.** number of addresses per instruction.

22. a. Why must a programmer worry about fieldmarks for FIELD-COM? **b.** How does a fieldmark indicate the end of an instruction, since the controlling fieldmark is in the next instruction? **c.** How does a fieldmark terminate operations involving an operand?

23. Storage contains fieldmarks at positions 1001 and 1201. Explain the result of each of the following instructions: **a.** $\underline{CP}$ 1010 1210; **b.** $\underline{CP}$ 1010 1205; **c.** $\underline{CP}$ 1005 $\underline{1}$210; **d.** $\underline{RC}$ 1080 1280; **e.** $\underline{PC}$ 1280 1080.

24. Explain the result of executing the following instructions: **a.** $\underline{R}$3 4567; **b.** $\underline{PT}$; **c.** $\underline{CM}$ 1234 4321; **d.** $\underline{FM}$ 2345; **e.** $\underline{ZR}$ 2345; **f.** $\underline{CP}$ 4567 890$\underline{1}$; **g.** $\underline{AD}$222 3333; **h.** $\underline{HL}$ HALT; **i.** $\underline{NP}$ WRITE; **j.** $\underline{AA}$ 0321 STRT; **k.** $\underline{JS}$ READ U.

25. Explain what determines the amount of data handled in each of the following operations: **a.** card read; **b.** print; **c.** tape write; **d.** add; **e.** copy; **f.** copy edit; **g.** disk read.

26. a. What is the sequence for handling characters in an instruction? **b.** Sequence of character handling in an operand? **c.** What is the setting of the address registers for the A and B addresses after executing an instruction? **d.** How is this feature of address registers used in "chaining" instructions? **e.** What are the merits of chaining addresses in instructions?

27. a. Write a program to clear storage, set fieldmarks, read, and print two cards with the following changes in sequence of the data from the cards:

Card Columns	Print Positions
1–5	101–105
6–20	16–30
21–30	6–15
31–70	31–70
71–75	discard
76–80	1–5

b. Reprogram the read and print operations for two cards using only the one fieldmark obtained from the clear storage instruction; that is, do not use any fieldmark instructions as such.
c. Rewrite (b) to use "chaining" so that only two B addresses are used in the copy instructions.

CHAPTER 9

1. a. Explain why data are edited during both input and output operations and what the chief differences are in the edit operations?
b. What is the nature, purpose, and use of file labels?

2. a. What kinds of input editing can be done without reference to the master file? **b.** What assurance does such editing give that input data are correct? **c.** How does further editing by use of the file improve accuracy of input data?

3. a. What do the terms *proof totals* and *hash totals* mean? **b.** Develop an example of proof totals and hash totals. **c.** Under what conditions is each type of total suitable? **d.** How is each type of total obtained most efficiently under operating conditions?

4. a. What are the special problems involved in editing input data on cards and how are they handled? **b.** What are "explicit data" on cards and why is it not possible to edit them? **c.** How is it possible to assure that cards are in sequence during read-in, when they are subject to mishandling during sorting and feeding? **d.** How is it possible to ensure that the card sequence is correct if the processor's card-reader accepts only 74 columns of data?

5. a. What are the objectives of output editing? **b.** What operations are performed during output editing? **c.** How is *scatter write* used during output editing?

6. a. Evaluate the statement, "During output editing, it is generally assumed that these problems were handled correctly earlier, because little or nothing can be done efficiently about them at this stage." **b.** If this statement is true, would it be suitable to omit either input or output editing? Explain. **c.** What is the relationship between report generators and editing operations?

7. a. What is the difference between *file maintenance* and *file processing*? **b.** What are the arguments for combining or for separating file maintenance and processing? **c.** Why and how do pending changes arise in file maintenance? **d.** How does the quantity of available processor storage affect efficient file maintenance and processing methods?

8. Explain the meaning of the following items related to file maintenance: **a.** master file; **b.** change list; **c.** pending changes; **d.** mismatches; **e.** number of records in files; **f.** housekeeping runs; **g.** logical sequence of transactions; **h.** transfers between sections of the file; **i.** insertion point.

9. a. What is *trial processing*? **b.** Why is it necessary and under what conditions is it useful? **c.** Describe an example of data processing with which you are familiar that does use or could advantageously use trial processing.

10. Explain the meaning of the following items related to file processing: **a.** key; **b.** orderly sequence of transactions; **c.** match; **d.** random-access storage; **e.** subroutines; **f.** dummy instruction; **g.** indirect addressing; **h.** retention period; **i.** fractional updating.

11. a. Why and under what conditions is it necessary to rewrite files during updating operations? **b.** What is the smallest fraction of a file that can be updated during each file pass and still give efficient file processing?

12. The following file-maintenance plan is proposed for file updating: Accumulate all transactions that occur over a period of time and organize them in a suitable fashion for use with master files to permit determination of current results whenever wanted.
a. How should the files and transactions be arranged and stored for this scheme to make any sense?
b. What storage media are implied?
c. Over how long a period of time is it feasible to accumulate transactions before updating the master file?
d. What processing and calculating operations are required to answer each file interrogation?
e. How would you appraise such a scheme, if file activity is low and inquiries are few; if activity is high and inquiries are numerous?

13. a. Why are data sorted? **b.** How does sorting facilitate the subsequent stages of data processing? **c.** How can data be processed efficiently if they are not sorted? **d.** Some people object to the term *sort,* since no item is eliminated (unlike sorting bad apples from good) but prefer the term *marshall,* or *sequence.* Evaluate the argument.

14. **a.** Explain the steps involved in digital sorting on a five-digit key. **b.** Why is digital sorting called *minor-major?* c. What are the similarities and differences between digital and alphabetical sorting of data on cards? **d.** What is the relationship between the number of output pockets, the base for the number scheme (or alphanumeric scheme) used, and the number of passes required to sort a large number of items? Develop a general rule or use several examples to show the relationship.

15. You are told that a series of items is sorted into ascending sequence when you receive them. **a.** How can you check their sequence most efficiently? **b.** How much work is involved, if you conclude they are not in sequence and try to sort them into ascending sequence by the digital scheme and by the merge scheme? **c.** What sorting schemes exploit any existing sequence in the data? **d.** What scheme is most efficient for sorting into descending sequence a series of items that is in ascending sequence?

16. Define and distinguish between the following schemes for sorting data:
    a. digital;
    b. comparison with exchange;
    c. merge.
    Suppose you are given records with the following keys:

    13, 39, 35, 43, 11, 28, 04, 26, 32, 30, 37, 98
    38, 60, 07, 43, 19, 11, 75, 31, 36, 82, 95, 46.

    Show how records with these keys would be sorted by each of the following schemes:
    d. digital;
    e. comparison with exchange;
    f. merge.
    g. Describe the effect on each of these sorting schemes, if some additional records with alphanumeric keys are included: 8G, AF, ML, B4.

17. **a.** What is the relationship between digitally sorting data on cards and on tape? **b.** How is it possible to sort digitally if there are fewer than ten output pockets or tapes for each digit position?

18. A manufacturing company codes each master-file record to indicate its origin—for example, customer or stock number—and its destinations—for example, list of delinquent customers or of stock items depleted. In order to prepare reports, each record is repeated once

on tape for each report in which the item will be included. One way to arrange the items for report preparation is to block-sort the items for each report and fine-sort each subset into report sequence. Another method is to devise a combined report and item code so that all items can be sorted directly into one over-all report and item sequence.

a. What are the advantages of sorting a large set of items into one over-all sequence instead of block-sorting first and then fine-sorting into individual sequences?

b. Devise a combined report and item-code classification useful for the second method of arranging items for report preparation.

c. What are the implications of each method for report editing and printing operations?

19. Explain the effect on merge-sorting operations of the following: **a.** Using larger internal storage to develop longer sequences on the first pass. **b.** Using three tapes instead of four on the first pass. **c.** Using four input and four output tape units on each pass. **d.** Using six input and two output tape units on each pass (with swaps on the output units for filled tapes).

Appendix II

GLOSSARY

This glossary is intended for people without special training who are interested in business data processing. Therefore, it attempts to define only the terms most often used in data processing and to provide a useful meaning for these terms. It does *not* ordinarily include instructions, for which the order codes for individual machines should be consulted, nor does it generally deal with technical words related to equipment design.

To reduce the over-all length of the glossary, cross-referencing has been minimized by listing most multiple-word entries under their first word. In some cases it is necessary to look under the more important word to find a desired entry.

Access Time—Time required to read or write a character, word, or field in a particular location. Frequently used to mean average access time for all locations in a particular storage unit.

Accumulator—A register in the arithmetic unit in which operands are placed and in which arithmetical results are formed.

Accuracy—The degree of correspondence between data, files, and outputs and the true results obtainable by extremely careful data gathering and processing. Accuracy is measured in terms of either the number of items that are different or the amount of difference between the calculated and true result.

Action—The processing steps to take when the related conditions are satisfied.

Add-to-Storage Logic—Processor logic designed to add any operand in storage to any other; an accumulator, as such, is not available.

Address—A label consisting of numeric or alphanumeric characters which identifies a storage location, register, or device containing data.

    Absolute Address—Actual location in storage of a particular unit of data; an address that the control unit can interpret directly.

    Symbolic Address—A label assigned to a selected word in a routine for the convenience of the programmer. The label is independent of the location of a word within a routine; it identifies the field of data to be operated on or the operation to be used rather than its storage location. Before the program is executed, the symbolic address is converted to an absolute address.

Align—Placing operands within words so that operations can be performed correctly; for example, shifting numbers to put the units values (and others) in corresponding positions before adding.

Alphabet—Sets of letter symbols—for example, A through Z—used to form words. More broadly, any set of symbols used to represent data.

Alphanumeric—A coding system capable of representing alphabetic characters, numerals, and other symbols.

Applications Study—Design of a system and related procedures plus development of equipment specifications to perform a certain job.

Arithmetic and Logic Unit—The part of a processor that performs the arithmetical operations of adding, multiplying, etc., and the logical operations of comparing one number or name with another.

Auditing—Examination of source data, methods of processing, and contents of reports to draw conclusions about the validity of the system and credibility of reports; auditors use many sources of information and various techniques for verification.

Automatic Data-Processing System—A system that makes maximum use of an electronic data processor and related equipment for processing data.

Automatic Programming—A way of writing programs based on a problem-oriented language and a translator routine for translating this language to machine language.

Automatic Transaction Recorder—Systems for recording several of the facts about a transaction with minimum manual input. For example, in a job shop the recorder will pick up the worker and job identification from plates or cards and the start-stop times from a built-in clock, so that only the quantity completed is punched into the keyboard or set up in dials for recording.

Batch Processing—Collection of data over a period of time for sorting and processing as a group during a particular machine run.

Binary-Coded Alphanumeric—A scheme for representing all alphabetic characters, digits, and special symbols in binary notation. The use of six bits for each character is common since $2^6 = 64$, which is generally adequate for the alphabet involved.

Binary-Coded Decimal—A system for representing *each* decimal digit by a code written in binary notation. Among the several systems are the 8-4-2-1 and the Excess 3 schemes.

Binary Number—A number with the base 2 having the following positional values: 64, 32, 16, 8, 4, 2, 1, ½, ¼, ⅛, etc.

Bulk Storage—Large-volume storage used to supplement the high-speed storage; may be addressable, as with disks and drums, or nonaddressable, as with magnetic tapes. Also called "secondary" and "external storage."

Business Data Processing—Processing of data for *actual* transactions—purchases, sales, collections—involving file processing, calculations, and reporting; also includes processing *planned* transactions for budgeting and operating control purposes. Characterized by large volumes of input and output with limited amounts of computation during processing.

Card Punch—A device for punching data in cards. Examples are simple hand punches, keyboard print-punches, paper tape-to-card converter punches, and high-speed punches for magnetic tape-to-card conversion or for direct output from the processor.

Changes, Pending—Transactions not successfully processed against the file because of mistakes in data, program errors, records not yet established or already deleted from file, account "frozen," or record was moved within the file and, therefore, was not available in the expected sequence.

Channel—A path along which data, particularly a series of digits or characters, may flow or be stored either in a particular set of equipment or a communications network. In storage that is serial by character and parallel by bit (for example, a magnetic tape or drum in some coded decimal processors), a channel comprises several parallel tracks.

Character—(1) One of a set of elementary symbols, such as those corresponding to the keys on a typewriter. The symbols may include decimal digits 0 through 9, the letters A through Z, punctuation marks, operation symbols, and any other single symbol that a processor may read, store, or write. (2) a binary representation of such a symbol.

Character Reader—A device for scanning and identifying characters on documents that can also be read by people. *Magnetic-ink* readers work with specially-shaped characters printed in metallic ink that is magnetized before reading. *Optical* readers use ordinary characters printed in ordinary inks.

Check—A means of verifying the accuracy of data transmitted, manipulated, or stored by any unit or device in a processor.

COBOL—*Common Business-Oriented Language*; an English-like programming language designed primarily for business-type applications and implemented for use with many different data processors.

Code (noun)—A system of rules for using a set of symbols to represent data or operations.

    Instruction Code—The symbols, names, and descriptions for all the operations that a processor executes.

    Mnemonic Code—An instruction code using abbreviations, instead of numeric machine code, to permit easy recognition. For example, "subtract" is represented by "SUB" instead of the number "12." Mnemonic code must be converted to machine code before a program is executed.

Code for Processor (verb)—To express a program in a code that a specific processor was built or programmed to interpret and execute, or by means of a code that can be translated into machine code.

Collate—To produce a single sequence of items, ordered according to some rule from two or more similarly ordered sequences. The final sequence need not contain all of the data available in the original sets. If, for example, two sets of items are being matched, items that do not match may be discarded.

Common Language—A single code used by several different devices—for example, typewriters, calculators, transmitters—manufactured by different companies.

Communication Channel—Messenger, voice, mail, telegraph, telephone, and microwave available for transmitting business data over short or long distances.

Telegraph Channel—A low-capacity communication channel with a maximum data-transmission rate of ten characters per second.

Telephone Channel—A medium-capacity communication channel with a maximum data-transmission rate of 300 characters per second.

Telpak or Microwave Channel—A high-capacity communication channel with data-transmission rates up to 100,000 characters per second.

Computer—Any device capable of accepting data, applying prescribed processes to them, and supplying the results of these processes. The word "computer" usually refers to an internally-stored-program data processor; the term "processor" is preferable for business applications.

Condition—(1) An expression that, taken as a whole, may be true or false. A *simple* condition has only one element—for example, "if account balance exceeds credit limit, reject customer's order." A *compound* condition has two or more elements—for example, "if account balance exceeds credit limit but account is current and the new order will not cause balance to exceed twice the credit limit, then accept order." (2) The result of a test—for example, greater than, negative, overflow. (3) A value that an item may have.

Console—Equipment that provides for manual intervention and for monitoring processor operations.

Control Field—The field used to edit data before output for printing. For example, $$$Z,ZZ9.99 will result in the insertion of a "$", a ",", and a "." as well as the suppression of leading zeros in the number 000345678 to give an edited field such as $3,456.78.

Control Sequence—Normal order of selection of instructions for execution. In some processors, one of the addresses in each instruction specifies the control sequence. In most processors the sequence is consecutive except when a jump is made.

Cycle (verb)—To repeat a set of operations a prescribed number of times including, when required, supplying necessary address changes by arithmetical operations, by an index register, or in other ways.

Data—Figures, words, or charts that refer to or describe some situation.

Data Description—An entry in the data division of a COBOL program describing the characteristics of a data item in terms of level, name, length, and alphanumeric content.

Data Division—A division describing the characteristics of data: files, records, and data elements.

Data Element—A group of characters that specify an *item* at or near the basic level. An *elementary* item—for example, "month"—contains no subordinate item. A *group* item—for example, "date," which consists of day, month, and year—contains items that may be used separately and therefore treated as elementary items.

Data Density—The number of characters that can be stored per unit of length, area, or volume. Specifically, for magnetic tape, the number of bits in one row per inch of tape where one bit in each row across the tape makes up a frame representing one character.

Data Processing—Rearrangement and refinement of data into a form suitable for further use; often involves file processing to update files for transactions that occur.

Debug—To test a program by running it with test, simulated, or live data on a processor to find whether it works properly, and, if mistakes are revealed either in the final answer or at various stages of processing, discover the source and make corrections.

Decimal—Pertaining to the number ten. A number system whose base is the quantity 10; a system of notation utilizing ten symbols 0, 1, . . ., 9.

Decision Table—Organized tabular representation of relationships between variables, sets of conditions and the related sequences of action that make up rules.

Delay—The length of time after either the occurrence of an event for individual event reporting or the close of a reporting period for summary reporting before reports are made available. Delay covers the time needed to process data and to prepare and distribute reports.

Design Approach—The view that the designer takes of the restraints on the design process; his freedom may range from nearly none to almost carte blanche to design whatever seems most useful for the organization.

Simplification Approach—Stresses better forms, elimination of useless data, more efficient flows of data, consolidated files, and improvements in existing techniques.

Mechanization Approach—Stresses the introduction of new equipment and processing procedures with the current inputs, files, outputs, and data flows.

Data System Redesign Approach—Stresses redesign of files, inputs, data flows, but outputs and management procedures are viewed as fixed. New equipment is introduced when appropriate.

Information System Redesign Approach—Stresses complete freedom to redesign both management decision rules and the entire data system.

DETAB-X—Decision Tables; Experimental; a programming language that combines decision tables with COBOL.

Disk—A circular metal plate with magnetic material on both sides, continuously rotated for reading or writing by means of one or more read-write heads mounted on movable or fixed arms; disks may be permanently mounted on a shaft or, as a package, they may be removable and others placed on the shaft.

Display, Direct—Television-like tubes that display various alphanumeric or graphic results from a processor for viewing or photographing for the record. More simply, a desk set on which selected facts—for example, availability of a seat for a desired airflight—may be viewed.

Division (noun)—The parts in which a COBOL program is organized. *Identification* division provides information to identify the source and object programs. *Environment* division specifies the equipment to use for translating and running a program. *Data* division contains entries to define the nature of the data to be processed. *Procedure* division consists of the processor program to be run with data.

Dump—To record the contents of internal storage at a given instant of time, usually to help detect program mistakes or errors, or to remove a program and data from the processor to permit running another program.

Edit—(1) To arrange or rearrange information for the output unit of the processor to print. Editing may involve deletion of unwanted data, selection of pertinent data, and application of standard processes, such as zero-suppression. (2) To examine raw data to check or improve their accuracy and relevance before keypunching. (3) To examine data during the input operation or at other stages of processing for completeness and correctness.

Electronic Data-Processing System—A machine system capable of receiving, storing, operating on, and recording data without the intermediate use of tabulating cards. The system is also able to store internally at least some instructions for data-processing operations, and to locate and control access to data stored internally.

Entry—A notation written in a stub of a row or in a cell of a decision table. Any row must be in the form of either a limited entry or an extended entry.

    Extended Entry—A notation other than a limited entry with part of the condition or action written in the cells—for example, "less than," "greater than," or "equal to" an amount; "excellent," "good," "poor," "none," "any."

    Limited Entry—A notation restricted to "yes," "no," "X," and "blank" in a cell in a decision table. Conditions and actions are restricted to the stubs of the rows.

Error—The difference between an accurate quantity and its calculated approximation. *Errors* occur in numerical methods; *mistakes* are human blunders that occur in programs, coding, data transcription, and operating; *malfunctions* occur in equipment.

Event—Any action that gives rise to data that affects the contents of the files of a business—for example, purchase, shipment, or sale.

Event Chain—A trace of the series of actions—preparing documents, processing data, and updating files—that result from one initial event.

Exception-Principle System—An information system that reports on situations only when actual results are outside a "normal range"; results within normal range are not reported.

Exit—A possible outcome from comparing items of numeric data—equal to, smaller than, larger than, or zero, negative, positive—or from comparing alphabetic data items: same, earlier, or later. An outcome from checking the truth of a condition statement: yes or no. Each outcome may be used to send program control to a different, appropriate subroutine.

Field—A set of one or more characters treated as a unit of data. Used for the organization of data on punched cards where enough columns are assigned to each item to handle the longest case likely to occur. Similarly applied to character-addressable processors, although often called "variable word."

FIELDCOM—*Field Com*puter, a hypothetical processor used to illustrate the features of and programming for a processor with character-addressable storage that handles data as fields.

File—One or more records concerning people, things, or places that are closely related and handled together for processing.

    Change File—A list of the transactions effectively processed against a master file. May also include selected parts or all of each changed record from the master file.

    Master File—A file of records containing a cumulative history or the results of cumulation, updated in each file-processing cycle, and carried forward to the next cycle.

    Transaction File—The transactions occurring over a period of time and accumulated as a batch ready for processing against the master files that are affected.

File Analysis—A study of file characteristics to locate file redundancies or similarities and to list documents affecting a file and data elements contained in a file.

File Maintenance—Modification of a file to incorporate changes that do *not* involve arithmetical operations—for example, insertions, deletions, transfers, and corrections.

File Processing—Modification of a file to incorporate changes that involve arithmetical operations—for example, receipts, issues, returns, and losses of stock items.

Flow Chart—A systems-analysis tool consisting of a graphical representation of a procedure.

    Structure Flow Charts—General flow charts showing types, times, and quantities of input, processing, files, and output but *not* indicating how jobs are performed.

    Technique Flow Charts—Specific flow charts showing data and information requirements and the methods proposed for filling them.

FORTRAN—*For*mula *Tran*slating system; consists of a language and translator designed for programming problems expressed in a mathematical-type language.

Frame—The group of bits across magnetic tape, usually seven, consisting of one from each row that make up a character; also five, six, seven, or eight punches across punched paper tape.

Hardware—The electric, electronic, and mechanical equipment used for processing data; consists of cabinets, racks, tubes, transistors, wires, and motors.

Hash Total—Sums of data items not ordinarily added, such as the stock numbers of units shipped, which are used to control the accuracy of the data at each stage of processing.

Implementation—The steps involved in installing and starting successful operation of a system and related equipment. These steps include feasibility study, applications study, equipment selection, systems analysis and design, physical installation, operation, and review.

Index Register—A register to which an integer, usually one, is added (or subtracted) upon the execution of certain machine instructions. The contents of a register are used with other instructions to get effective instruction addresses during execution. The register may be reset to zero or to any desired number.

Information—Knowledge that was not previously known to its receiver. Information can be derived from data only to the extent that the data are accurate, timely, unexpected, and relevant to the subject under consideration.

Information Flow Analysis—A technique for organizing and analyzing the facts obtained about the flow of documents throughout an organization; can be performed manually or on a processor. One mechanized version is called AUTOSATE.

Initialize—Preparatory steps required *before* executing a repetitive cycle in order to get it started correctly; performed initially and not repeated within the program unless the cycle is started afresh.

Instruction—A set of characters that defines an operation together with one or more addresses (or no address) and which, as a unit, causes the processor to operate accordingly on the indicated operand. *Single, double,* and *triple* address instructions have one, two, and three operand addresses, respectively.

Integrated Data Processing—A business data system designed as a whole so that data are initially recorded at the point of origin in a form suitable for subsequent processing without manual recopying.

Internally-Stored Program—A program prepared by programmers and converted to a suitable input medium—cards, paper tape, magnetic tape—for reading into the processor and storing for execution when data are read in. Instructions in the program itself can be manipulated in much the same way as data and the whole program can be replaced by merely reading in another program.

Jump—To transfer control by executing an instruction that specifies the location of the next instruction to be executed by the program. Also called "branch" or "transfer". An *unconditional* jump is made to occur whenever the jump instruction is encountered in the program. A *conditional* jump transfers control only if some specified logical condition is satisfied; if the condition is not satisfied, the next instruction is taken in normal sequence.

Key—A field used for identification of a record; a selected element in each record used for sorting records into a desired sequence.

Language—Expressions used to define the operations of a processor.

Machine-Oriented Language—A language intelligible to a processor with little or no translation—for example, the programs written in WORDCOM and FIELDCOM order codes. Mnemonic order codes need to be translated into the machine's numeric order code on a one-for-one basis and the symbolic addresses need to be converted into absolute addresses.

Problem-Oriented Language—A language designed for solving a particular class of problems—for example, COBOL for business and FORTRAN for mathematics. Requires elaborate translation or compiling—each program instruction becomes several machine instructions—before the program can be run on a processor.

Level—In COBOL, the status of one data item relative to another; indicates whether one item includes subsequent ones or whether, as reflected in the numbering scheme which must follow certain rules, data items are independent of each other.

Literal—One or more characters used to represent the value "literally" expressed.

Magnetic-Core Storage—A storage device consisting of magnetically permeable binary cells arrayed in a two-dimensional matrix; a large storage unit contains many such matrices. Each core is wire-connected and may be polarized in either of two directions to store one binary digit. The direction of polarization can be sensed by wires running through the core.

Magnetic-Disk Storage—A storage device consisting of magnetically-coated disks accessible to a read-write arm operating similar to records in an automatic record player. An arm is moved mechanically to the desired disk (unless there is an arm for each disk) and then to the desired track on that disk. The arm reads or writes data sequentially as the disk rotates.

Magnetic-Drum Storage—A device that stores data on tracks around a rotating cylindrical drum surfaced with a magnetic coating. A magnetic read-write head is usually associated with each track so that the desired track can be selected by electric switching. Data from a given track are read or written sequentially as the drum continually rotates.

Magnetic-Ink Character Recognition—A system using specially shaped characters printed in magnetizable ink for machine reading; originally developed for commercial check processing.

Magnetic-Tape Storage—A storage device consisting of plastic tape or metal coated with magnetic material. A read-write head is associated with each row of bits on tape so that a frame can be read or written at one time as the tape moves past the head.

Management Information System—A data-processing system designed to supply management and supervisory personnel with information consisting of data that are accurate, timely, and new.

Master Record—The official updated record for use in the next file-processing run. The master record is usually on magnetic tape or cards, but a card copy of it may be used as a visual file for reference purposes.

Merge—To produce a single sequence of items, ordered according to a certain rule from two or more sequences previously ordered according to the same rule, without changing the items in size, structure, or total number. Merging is a special kind of collating.

Microsecond—A millionth of a second; "μs."

Millisecond—A thousandth of a second; one thousand microseconds; "ms."

Modular—Standardization of processor components to permit combining them in various ways.

Modulate—Conversion of one form of signal to another suitable for transmission over communication circuits. For example, a modulator converts the bits representing a frame of data on punched-paper tape or magnetic tape from the parallel mode to the serial mode for transmission over a communication circuit.

M-Q Register—A register used in conjunction with the accumulator for performing arithmetical operations. For example, in multiplication, the M-Q is first loaded with the multiplier. After multiplication, the

M-Q contains the low-order digits of the product; the high-order digits are in the accumulator and the multiplicand remains in its storage location.

Multiplex—A technique for transferring data from several storage devices operating at relatively low transfer rates to one storage device operating at a high transfer rate in such a manner that the high-speed device is not obliged to wait for the low-speed units. The high-speed device is time-shared by offering service to each low-speed device in turn.

Nanosecond—A billionth of a second; a thousandth of a microsecond.

No Operation—A "dummy" operation inserted in a program which, depending upon conditions encountered in the program, can be replaced by a specific instruction formed by the program itself. Also sometimes used at intervals throughout a program written with absolute addresses to provide space to write additional instructions with minimum rewriting of other instructions. A "no operation" instruction *per se* is skipped and not executed.

Object Program—A program in machine language resulting from the translation of a source program by a source computer. For example, a source program written in COBOL and compiled into machine language results in an *object* program ready to run on an object computer.

Off-Line Equipment—Equipment *not* connected directly to the central processor but working through an intermediary device. For example, a processor can write output on an on-line magnetic tape that is *later* used as input to an off-line printer for printing reports.

On-Line Equipment—Equipment connected directly to the central processor to furnish or receive data—for example, card readers, high-speed printers, inquiry stations, and direct-display devices.

Operand—Any one of the quantities entering into or arising from an operation. An operand may be an indication of the location of the next instruction or a result from computation.

Order Code—The complete set of instructions that a processor can execute; also called "instruction repertoire."

Pack—To combine two or more different items of data into one machine word. For example, the three fields of employee pay number, weekly pay rate, and number of tax exemptions might be stored together in one word. To *unpack* is to separate the individual items for processing by means of shifting or partial-word logic.

Parity Bit—A bit associated with data bits to get some specified relation such as an odd or even total number of bits for each character. A parity bit is usually associated with the frame for each six-bit character on tape; also parity bits may be placed at frequent intervals to associate them with the seven rows of bits (six for data and one for parity) along the tape.

Picture—In COBOL, a symbolic description of each data element according to certain rules concerning numerals, alphanumerics, location of decimal point, and length.

Printer, High-Speed—High-speed printing that makes use of rotating print wheels or a chain with raised type faces and fast-acting hammers to press the paper against the desired character at the instant it is in the correct position.

Processor—Any device capable of accepting data, applying prescribed processes to them, and supplying the results of these processes. Usually internally-stored program, but may be externally-stored or built-in.

Programming—The process of creating a program; includes applications analysis, design of a solution, coding for the processor, testing to produce an operating program, and development of other procedures to make the system function.

Punched Card—A card of standard size and shape in which data are stored in the form of punched holes. The hole locations are arranged in 80 or 90 columns with a given pattern of holes in a column representing one alphanumeric character. The data content is read by the mechanical, electrical, or photoelectrical sensing of the hole positions.

Punched Tape—Tape, usually paper, in which data are stored in the form of punched holes arranged in a frame across the tape. There are usually five to eight channels with data represented by one or more holes in a binary-coded alphanumeric system.

Random Access—Access to storage under conditions in which each set of data is directly addressable. Access to data at random—in any desired sequence. More commonly used to mean bulk storage having access within several milliseconds to several seconds to data at any location.

Read-Process-Write—To read in one block of data, while simultaneously processing the preceding block and writing out the results of the previously processed block. Some processors concurrently perform any two of the three operations; others are restricted to concurrent read-write.

Real-Time Operation—Processing data in synchronism with a physical process rapidly enough so that results of data processing are useful to the physical operation. Sometimes called "on-line, real-time control."

Record (noun)—A set of data elements closely related in the sense that they pertain to the same person, place, or thing.

Report—Data-processing system output that has high information content; more broadly, any planned and organized output from a system.

Routine—A set of coded instructions arranged in proper sequence to direct the processor to perform a desired operation or series of operations. *See also* "Subroutine."

Compiler Routine—A routine that, *before* the desired processing is started, translates a source program expressed in a problem-oriented language into an object program in machine code.

Post-Mortem Routine—A routine that either automatically or on demand prints data concerning contents of registers and storage locations after the routine stops in order to assist in locating a mistake in coding.

Trace Routine—A routine used to observe how the object program operates while it is being executed.

Translator Routine—*See* "Compiler."

Run—The act of processing, under the control of one program, a batch of transactions—for example, the inventory receipts, issues, etc., for the week—against all the files that are affected to produce desired outputs consisting of updated files and reports.

Run Diagram—A generalized graphic presentation of the files, transactions, and data that are handled together under program control to produce an updated file, list of changes, and errors.

Runs, Housekeeping—The sorting, merging, editing, and operating runs required for file maintenance; the nonproduction runs. In a limited sense, the set-up and clean-up parts of a program as opposed to production processing.

Scatter Read-Write—A *scatter-read* operation performed under program control reads a block of data from tape and breaks it up into processable elements that can be placed where wanted in storage. A *scatter-write* operation picks up the dispersed data elements in storage and writes them on tape as a block.

Sequence—In sorting, the ordering of items on an element—for example, records on a selected key—according to some rules that utilize the processor's collation table.

Alphanumeric Sequence—A sequence developed for records containing alphanumeric characters. The exact sequence depends on the binary value assigned to each alphabetic and numeric character—whether alphabetic precedes numeric or vice versa—by the machine designer.

Numeric Sequence—A sequence developed for records with keys containing numerals only; usually ascending, but may also be descending.

Random Sequence—A sequence that is not arranged by ascending or descending keys, but which actually may be arranged in an organized fashion. For example, each record may be placed in bulk storage in a location determined by some calculations performed on its key to develop an address; the calculations are repeated in order to get the address and locate the item.

Software Package—The programming aids supplied by the manufacturer to facilitate the user's efficient operation of equipment. Includes assemblers, compilers, generators, subroutine libraries, operating systems, and industry application programs.

Sorting—The arranging of records so that they are in ascending or descending sequence for some data element used as a key.

    Comparison-of-Pairs Sorting—To compare the keys of two records and put the record with the smaller-valued key ahead of the other to get the two items into ascending sequence; or to put the smaller behind to get a descending sequence.

    Digital Sorting—A procedure for first sorting the records on the least significant (right-hand) digit in their keys and resorting on each higher-order digit until the records are sorted on the most significant digit in their keys. A commonly used punched-card technique.

    Merge Sorting—To produce a single sequence of records, ordered according to some rule, from two or more previously ordered (or perhaps even unordered) sequences, without changing the items in size, structure, or total number. Although more than one pass may be required for complete sorting, during each pass items are selected on the basis of their entire key to build the sequence.

Storage—A device capable of receiving data, retaining them for an indefinite period of time, and supplying them upon command.

    Addressable Bulk Storage—Storage with the primary function of augmenting capacity of internal storage for handling data and instructions. Data from addressable bulk storage must be transferred to internal storage in order to use them in operations.

    High-Speed Storage—The quickest access internal storage of a computer; this is composed of magnetic cores in most computers, although some use special cores or thin-film elements for limited amounts of ultra high-speed.

Storage Capacity—Number of units of data that can be stored in a device at one time; variously expressed in terms of bits, characters, or words, depending upon the method of organization.

Storage Location—A storage position holding one machine word and usually having a specific address; the character position used to address a data field in a character-addressable machine.

Structure (of a System)—Refers to the *nature* of the chain of command, the origin and type of data collected, the form and destination of results, and the procedures used to control operations.

Subroutine—A set of instructions in machine code to direct the processor to carry out a well-defined mathematical or logical operation; a part of a routine. A subroutine is often written with symbolic relative addresses even though the routine to which it belongs is not.

Suspense File—A file of transactions or records that are awaiting some anticipated event. For example, rejected transactions are retained in a suspense file for control purposes until corrections are returned for another attempt at processing.

System—Any regular or special method or plan of procedure. In a broader context, a system consists of an organization, people, hardware, and procedures that operate together to perform a set of tasks.

Systems Analysis—An orderly study of the detailed procedure for collecting, organizing, and evaluating information within an organization, with the objective of improving control over its operations.

Systems Design—Formulation and description of the nature and content of inputs, files, and outputs in order to show how they are connected by processing procedures, and for the purpose of developing a new or improved system.

Tape Unit—A device for reading data from magnetic tape and writing new data (after erasing prior data) on tape; some tape units read in either direction, although they write in only the forward direction. The device also rewinds tape ready for removal and replacement by another reel.

Technique (of a Data-Processing System)—Refers to the *method* used to collect data inputs, to process them, and to convert processed data into reports or other usable form.

Teledata—A device for introducing parity bits and transmitting over telegraph circuits data already punched in five-, six-, or eight-channel paper tape. The receiving unit at a distant point checks parity for code accuracy, and reperforates valid data into paper tape.

Teletypewriter—Basically an electric typewriter that can be operated manually or by reading and reperforating paper tape; it is connected to a leased or dial-switched telegraph grade circuit for transmitting text and also data messages in readable form.

Thin Film—An ultra high-speed storage device consisting of a molecular deposit of material on a suitable plate.

Track—A sequence of binary cells arranged so that data may be read or written from one cell at a time in serial fashion. For example, a track on a magnetic drum is a path one-bit wide around the circumference of the drum; the bits in several tracks make up a character.

Transceiver—Card-reading, modulating, and punching equipment for card-to-card transmission of data over telephone or telegraph grade circuits.

Verb—In COBOL, an instruction word that specifies one or more operations to be performed by a data processor.

Word—A set of characters occupying one storage location; it is treated by the processor circuits as a unit and transported as such. Ordinarily,

the control unit treats a word as an instruction, whereas the arithmetic
unit treats a word as a quantity.

WORDCOM—*Word Com*puter, a hypothetical processor used to illustrate the features of, and programming for, a processor with storage
organized into words.

Write—To cause the contents of one or more storage locations to become the contents of other locations after erasing the contents of the
location to receive the data; for example, to write a block of data on
magnetic tape after erasing the previous contents at the block written.

Zero Suppression—Elimination of nonsignificant zeros to the left of the
integral part of a quantity before printing as part of the editing routine.

Zone—(1) In processors, two bits used in conjunction with four numeric
bits to represent alphanumeric characters. The zone bits may be used
separately to represent signs, to identify index registers, and for other
purposes. (2) For punched cards, the 11 and 12 punches used with
numeric punches 0 through 9 to represent alphabetic and special symbols. Zone punches may be used independently to indicate signs and
for special control purposes.

Appendix III

GUIDE TO THE LITERATURE

The books and magazines listed here represent a brief guide to literature of interest in the field of business data processing. It is divided into two sections: books and periodicals. The periodicals are devoted to computers and data processing; in addition, professional and trade journals are available to anyone interested in particular fields. Manufacturers should be consulted for descriptive bulletins about equipment and for literature about "software" packages available.

BOOKS

Baumes, Carl G., *Administration of Electronic Data Processing, Business Policy Study,* No. 98. New York: National Industrial Conference Board, 1961; 136 pages.
Based on a survey of 124 companies, this report covers the planning, the feasibility study, and the systems study. It also deals with the study of electronic equipment, organizing the data-processing operation, defining jobs and selecting personnel, evaluating performance and progress, and gaining employee cooperation.

Canning, Richard G., *Electronic Data Processing for Business and Industry.* New York: John Wiley & Sons, Inc., 1956; 332 pages.
This book, a classic in its field, discusses electronic data processing as a management tool; it covers the patterns of data processing, equipment characteristics, programming, systems study, initial design, and detailed design.

Chapin, Ned, *Programming Computers for Business Applications.* New York: McGraw-Hill Book Company, Inc., 1961; 279 pages.
Directed at programming for business data processing, this book discusses how to prepare programs for two different situations: where the problem is carefully defined in advance, and where the problem must be developed by the programmer. A chapter each is devoted to special problems of programming such as saving storage, improving accuracy, and increasing speed. Subroutines and library programs are also discussed.

COBOL—1961: Revised Specifications for a Common Business Oriented Language. Washington, D.C.: U. S. Government Printing Office, 1961; 175 pages.
This manual gives the official specifications for COBOL-1961. It covers the general structure of COBOL, details of format and notation, and available features, including both optional and required

ones. Equipment manufacturers use these specifications to prepare a COBOL language for their machines.

Computer Applications—1960: Proceedings of the 1960 Computer Applications Symposium. Armour Research Foundation, New York: The Macmillan Company, 1961; 193 pages.

A symposium dealing with both business-management and engineering-scientific applications of computers. The business and management applications cover a wide range of topics: subscription fulfillment, library usage, economic research, brokerage accounting, and mail-order house operations.

Conway, B., J. Gibbons and D. E. Watts, *Business Experience with Electronic Computers.* New York: Controllers Institute Research Foundation, Inc., 1959; 191 pages.

This report surveys the experience of a number of companies in introducing electronic data processing. The topics covered are the decision to introduce the system, company education and the programming group, development of the applications and conversion from prior methods, operating electronic equipment, and relations with manufacturers. Also included is a discussion of some unresolved matters and some thoughts on the next five years.

Data Processing Today: A Progress Report. New York: American Management Association, 1960; 143 pages.

Conference proceedings dealing with management and data processing, advances in data-processing technology, computer applications, and an intensive study of information processing at one company.

Electronics in Action: The Current Practicality of Electronic Data Processing. New York: American Management Association, Inc., 1957; 156 pages.

A report of an early AMA Conference containing thirteen papers dealing with feasibility studies, electronics at work, and new frontiers.

Gallagher, James D., *Management Information Systems and the Computer.* New York: American Management Association, Inc., 1961; 191 pages.

This book undertakes to put the management information system into perspective by showing how to organize a system for management planning and control and develop the relationship between systems work and the management information system. It contains case studies of the American Airlines SABRE system and the experience of Sylvania Electric Products, Inc. with business data processing.

Gatto, O. T., *Autosate: An Automated Data Systems Analysis Technique* (Memorandum RM-3118-PR). Santa Monica, California: The RAND Corporation, 1962; 50 pages.

Describes an organized, automated technique that provides information on data system flows and characteristics in a more usable form and more economically than usual manual methods.

Gregory, Robert H. and Richard L. Van Horn, *Automatic Data-Processing Systems: Principles and Procedures,* 2nd ed. Belmont, California: Wadsworth Publishing Company, Inc., 1963.

This book covers orientation, automatic equipment, programming and processing procedures, principles of processing, systems design, and equipment acquisition and utilization.

Haskins and Sells, *Introduction to Data Processing.* New York: Haskins and Sells, 1957; 107 pages.

This book discusses the principal methods and devices used in data processing and relates them to the basic operations they perform: classifying, sorting, calculating, summarizing, recording, and communicating. Chapters are devoted to punched-card equipment and to electronic data-processing equipment.

Hattery, Lowell H., *Executive Control and Data Processing.* Washington, D. C.: Anderson Kramer Associates, 1959; 92 pages.

A short guide to the executive in meeting the challenge of using new data-processing tools for more effective control. Heavy emphasis is placed on reporting systems, data for management systems, and human resources.

Kaufman, Felix, *Electronic Data Processing and Auditing.* New York: The Ronald Press Company, 1961; 180 pages.

This book focuses on the problem of control in electronic data processing and shows how data flow through an organization by means of two examples: (1) payroll and sales functions, and (2) accounts receivable, purchases, and disbursements. The book will be of interest to auditors and others concerned with controlling the accuracy of data processing, since it covers redundancy and the reliability of data and the effects of data processing systems on internal control and audit-trail conditions. It also raises some of the control problems associated with the use of data processors.

Malcolm, Donald G., and Alan J. Rowe, *Management Control Systems.* New York: John Wiley & Sons, Inc., 1960; 375 pages.

The proceedings of a symposium that dealt with the concepts of management control, the impacts of computers on the design of management controls, research in systems design, new approaches to future possibilities in management control, and information systems. It contains some examples of automated management controls.

McCracken, Daniel D., Harold Weiss and Tsai-Hwa Lee, *Programming Business Computers.* New York: John Wiley & Sons, Inc., 1959; 510 pages.

In 21 chapters, this book covers the structure of files, flow-charting, data-processing equipment, programming (arithmetic operations, address computation, loops and index registers, subroutines, and input-output devices) and verification of program accuracy. Also covers machine-aided coding, sorting, operating techniques, steps in planning and programming computer applications, and auditing.

McNerney, John Peter, *Installing and Using an Automatic Data Processing System: a Case Study for Management*. Boston: Division of Research, Graduate School of Business Administration, Harvard University, 1961; 314 pages.
A case study of a manufacturing company converting from punched-card equipment to the installation of a small computer for sales control and inventory control. The areas covered are background and systems evaluation, investigation and results, and evaluation of equipment.

Optner, Stanford L., *Systems Analysis for Business Management*. Englewood Cliffs, New Jersey: Prentice-Hall, Inc., 1960; 276 pages.
This book deals with systems analysis focused on business data-processing systems. Part I covers the systems concept in business, fundamentals of systems design, postulating data-processing systems, preparing for the systems study, and evaluation and cost estimation for data systems. Part II contains ten case studies covering a wide range of business problems.

Proceedings, 1962 Joint Computer Conference, American Federation of Information Processing Societies—AFIPS. Palo Alto, California: The National Press, 1962; 392 pages.
Proceedings of one conference in a continuing series covering a wide range of topics of interest to systems designers and users; some coverage of business and other applications.

Saxon, James A., and William S. Plette, *Programming the IBM 1401*. Englewood Cliffs, New Jersey: Prentice-Hall, Inc., 1962; 208 pages.
A self-instructional book covering programming for the IBM 1401 in 42 lessons.

Sprague, Richard E., *Electronic Business Systems: Management Use of On-Line—Real-Time Computers*. New York: The Ronald Press Company, 1962; 168 pages.
As the preface states, this book undertakes to show that "by 1970, all electronic data-processing systems will be of the on-line—real-time variety." The book covers the effect of pressures upon system requirements, developments in data processing and communications, and current potential developments in on-line real-time systems. Chapters deal with the impact of data systems on industrial manufacturing and the organization structure.

Wallace, Edward L., *Management Influence on the Design of Data Processing Systems: a Case Study*. Boston: Division of Research, Graduate School of Business Administration, Harvard University, 1961; 259 pages.
An intensive case study of a shoe manufacturing company's prod-

ucts, management organization, and methods of planning; some discussion of its previous mechanization of data processing. The proposed system for automatic data processing is covered and comments are made about the company study group's proposal for new system development with an alternative proposal for information handling.

PERIODICALS

Business Automation. OA Business Publications, Inc., Room 1716, 100 East 42nd Street, New York 17, New York.

This monthly magazine contains articles of general interest in business data processing. The topics range from self-checking numbers to background material on successful new firms.

Business Automation News Report. OA Business Publications, Inc., Room 1716, 100 East 42nd Street, New York 17, New York.

This nontechnical publication is a weekly newsletter. It covers data processing applications, announcements of new equipment, financial status of manufacturers, contract announcements, meetings, and similar items.

Communications of the ACM. Association for Computing Machinery, Mt. Royal & Guilford Avenues, Baltimore 2, Maryland.

Published monthly by a professional society, the Association for Computing Machinery (ACM), this magazine informs subscribers on such topics as standards, techniques, and applications in the areas of scientific and business data processing. Most of the articles are of a specialized and technical nature. An ACM member also receives *Computing Reviews* (a comprehensive, bi-monthly abstract of literature in the field) and the *Journal of the Association for Computing Machinery* (a quarterly journal that describes new research).

Computers and Automation. Berkeley Enterprises, Inc., 815 Washington Street, Newtonville 60, Massachusetts.

This monthly magazine has articles on the construction, applications and implications of data processors. One of the regular features is a computer census giving for each computer the number of installations, unfilled orders, average monthly rental, and date first installed.

Computer Characteristics Quarterly. Charles W. Adams Associates, 142 The Great Road, Bedford, Massachusetts.

Salient features of all general-purpose stored-program electronic data processors that are actively used in the United States are described in this quarterly report. It covers typical price, internal speed, storage capacity, input-output equipment and special features for each system. New equipment or changes are added as they appear.

Data Processing. Iliffe Production Publications Ltd., Dorset House, Stamford Street, London, S.E. 1, England.

This British journal has articles on data-processing equipment—both American and European—punched-card equipment, applications, and new ideas or techniques. A complete subject index is provided yearly.

Data Processing Digest. Data Processing Digest, Inc., 1140 South Robertson Boulevard, Los Angeles 35, California.

A monthly abstract service, this digest reviews most of the articles and books relevant to business data processing. Articles of interest in such related fields as management science are also covered. In addition to abstracts, each issue may contain a brief article on a topic of special interest. The contents of the *Computer Characteristics Quarterly* are also reprinted here. A comprehensive index to past abstracts classified by subject is available as the *Data Processing Digest Fact Finder.*

Data Processing for Management. American Data Processing, Inc., 22nd Floor Book Tower, Detroit 26, Michigan.

This monthly publication covers a variety of business data processing topics in a nontechnical fashion. Regular features include sections on equipment, forms, books, and coming events.

Datamation. F. D. Thompson Publications, Inc., 141 East 44th Street, New York 17, New York.

A basic source of current information in the data processing field, this monthly magazine discusses controversial topics as they arise. Sections are included each month covering meetings and new literature and products.

EDP Weekly. Industry Reports, Inc., 1327 F Street, N.W., Washington 4, D. C.

This bulletin contains nontechnical news reports on subjects of general interest in data processing—equipment, applications, contracts, meetings, and people.

Journal of Machine Accounting. Journal of Machine Accounting, 1750 West Central Road, Mt. Prospect, Illinois.

Published under the auspices of the Data Processing Management Association (DPMA), this journal covers data-processing equipment and applications related to accounting and financial management. Activities of the DPMA are also covered.

Office Automation. OA Business Publications, Inc., 288 Park Avenue West, Elmhurst, Illinois.

This handbook contains extensive and detailed specifications by manufacturer and model of data-processing equipment—punched-card devices, electronic data processors, transmission facilities, and peripheral equipment of all types. A monthly updating service provides information on changes and newly-announced equipment. Other volumes are available from this publisher on selected applications of data-processing equipment.

Systems Management. Data Processing Publishing Corporation, 200
Madison Avenue, New York 16, New York.

Articles in this magazine are oriented toward the recording, re-
trieval and reproduction of data, although articles on other aspects
of data processing also appear in each issue. Regular sections are
included for such areas as microfilm topics and reproduction techniques.

ACKNOWLEDGMENT FOR COBOL

The COBOL-1 chapter of this publication is based on the COBOL
System developed in 1959 by a committee composed of government
users and computer manufacturers. The organizations participating in
the original development were:

> Air Materiel Command, United States Air Force
> Bureau of Standards, United States Department of Commerce
> Burroughs Corporation
> David Taylor Model Basin, Bureau of Ships, United States Navy
> Electronic Data Processing Division, Minneapolis-Honeywell
>   Regulator Company
> International Business Machines Corporation
> Radio Corporation of America
> Sylvania Electric Products, Inc.
> UNIVAC Division of Sperry Rand Corporation

In addition to the organizations listed above, the following other
organizations participated in the work of the Maintenance Group:

> Allstate Insurance Company
> The Bendix Corporation, Computer Division
> Control Data Corporation
> E. I. du Pont de Nemours and Company
> General Electric Company
> General Motors Corporation
> Lockheed Aircraft Corporation
> The National Cash Register Company
> Philco Corporation
> Standard Oil Company (New Jersey)
> United States Steel Corporation

This COBOL-61 manual is the result of contributions made by all of
the above-mentioned organizations. No warranty, expressed or implied,
is made by any contributor or by the committee as to the accuracy and
functioning of the programming system and language. Moreover, no
responsibility is assumed by any contributor, or by the committee, in
connection therewith.

It is reasonable to expect that many improvements and additions will be made to COBOL. Every effort will be made to insure that improvements and corrections will be made in an orderly fashion, with due recognition of existing users' investments in programming. However, this protection can be positively assured only by individual implementors.

Procedures have been established for the maintenance of COBOL. Inquiries concerning the procedures and the methods for proposing changes should be directed to the Executive Committee of the Conference on Data Systems Languages.

The authors and copyright holders of the copyrighted material used herein: FLOW-MATIC (Trade-mark of Sperry Rand Corporation) *Programming for the UNIVAC® I and II, Data Automation Systems* © 1958, 1959, Sperry Rand Corporation; *IBM Commercial Translator,* Form No. F28-8013, copyrighted 1959 by IBM, have specifically authorized the use of this material, in whole or in part, in the COBOL-61 specifications. Such authorization extends to the reproduction and use of COBOL specifications in programming manuals or similar publications.

Any organization interested in reproducing the COBOL report and initial specifications in whole or in part, using ideas taken from this report or utilizing this report as the basis for an instruction manual or any other purpose is free to do so. However, all such organizations are requested to reproduce this section as part of the introduction to the document. Those using a short passage, as in a book review, are requested to mention "COBOL" in acknowledgment of the source but need not quote the entire section.

ACKNOWLEDGMENTS OF ILLUSTRATIONS

We are indebted to the following organizations for supplying material for the figures indicated:

Ampex Corporation, Figure 4-5.
Burroughs Corporation, Figure 4-1.
Commercial Controls Corporation, Figure 4-1.
International Business Machines Corporation, Figures 2-1, 2-2, 2-4, 3-3, 4-2, 4-3, 4-5.
Monroe Calculating Machine Company, Figure 4-1.
The National Cash Register Company, Figure 4-1.
Pacific Telephone and Telegraph Company, Figure 2-3.
Pan American Air Lines, Figure 4-6.
Radio Corporation of America, Figures 2-5, 4-3, 4-5.
The RAND Corporation, Figures 5-1, 5-2, 5-3, 5-4, 5-5.
Remington-Rand UNIVAC, Figures 2-1, 2-2, 3-4.

LIST OF ILLUSTRATIONS

FIGURES

TABLES

INDEX

Note: This index covers the material in Chapters 1–9 of this book. The Glossary and other appendixes should also be consulted as necessary.